Adobe® Dreamweaver® CC
Digital Classroom®

Michael Arguin, Greg Heald, and the AGI Creative Team

Adobe® Dreamweaver® CC Digital Classroom®

Published by
John Wiley & Sons, Inc.
10475 Crosspoint Blvd.
Indianapolis, IN 46256

3 1984 00326 2654

Copyright © 2013 by John Wiley & Sons, Inc., Indianapolis, Indiana
Published simultaneously in Canada
ISBN: 978-1-118-64015-9
Manufactured in the United States of America
10 9 8 7 6 5 4 3 2 1

For general information on our other products and services or to obtain technical support, please contact our Customer Care Department within the U.S. at (877) 762-2974, outside the U.S. at (317) 572-3993 or fax (317) 572-4002.

Wiley publishes in a variety of print and electronic formats and by print-on-demand. Some material included with standard print versions of this book may not be included in e-books or in print-on-demand. If this book refers to media such as a CD or DVD that is not included in the version you purchased, you may download this material after registering your book at www.digitalclassroombooks.com/CC/Dreamweaver. For more information about Wiley products, visit www.wiley.com.

Please report any errors by sending a message to errata@agitraining.com

Library of Congress Control Number: 2013936333

Credits

President, American Graphics Institute and Digital Classroom Series Publisher
Christopher Smith

Executive Editor
Jody Lefevere

Technical Editors
Sean McKnight, Elaina Featherstone, Cathy Auclair

Editor
Karla E. Melendez

Editorial Director
Robyn Siesky

Business Manager
Amy Knies

Senior Marketing Manager
Sandy Smith

Vice President and Executive Group Publisher
Richard Swadley

Vice President and Executive Publisher
Barry Pruett

Senior Project Coordinator
Katherine Crocker

Project Manager
Cheri White

Graphics and Production Specialist
Jason Miranda, Spoke & Wheel

Media Development Project Supervisor
Chris Leavey

Proofreading
Karla E. Melendez

Indexing
Michael Ferreira

Stock Photography
iStockPhoto.com

About the Authors

Michael Arguin is a web applications specialist at American Graphics Institute and an expert on web and interactive technology. He has more than 20 years of experience in areas ranging from application development support, programming, curriculum development, project management, and technical training for desktop and web based technologies. He studied Computer Information Systems at the University of Massachusetts, Dartmouth and is a licensed instructor in the area of Programming and Web Development from the Massachusetts Department of Elementary and Secondary Education.

Greg Heald has 20 years of design and production experience in both web and print environments. He has served as a contributing author or editor on a number of books on Dreamweaver, Flash, InDesign, and Acrobat. Greg has contributed to the development of Adobe's certification exams, and as Training Manager for American Graphics Institute, he oversees the delivery of professional development training programs for individuals and organizations. Greg holds a degree in Advertising Design from the acclaimed College of Visual and Performing Arts at Syracuse University.

The **AGI Creative Team** is composed of Adobe Certified Experts and Instructors from AGI. The AGI Creative Team has authored more than 25 Digital Classroom books and has created many of Adobe's official training guides. The AGI Creative Team works with many of the world's most prominent companies, helping them use creative software to communicate more effectively and creatively. They work with design, creative, and marketing teams around the world, delivering private customized training programs, while also teaching regularly scheduled classes at AGI's locations. The AGI Creative Team is available for professional development sessions at companies, schools, and universities. Get more information at *agitraining.com*.

Acknowledgments

A special thanks to our many friends at Adobe Systems, Inc. who made this book possible and assisted with questions and feedback during the writing process. To the many clients of AGI who have helped us better understand how they use Dreamweaver and provided us with many of the tips and suggestions found in this book. And thanks to the instructional team at AGI for their input and assistance in the review process and for making this book such a team eff ort.

Thanks to Lesa and the team at iStockPhoto for the use of their exclusive *iStockPhoto.com* photographers' images.

Register your Digital Classroom book for exclusive benefits

Registered owners receive access to:

 The most current lesson files

 Technical resources and customer support

 Notifications of updates

 Online access to video tutorials

 Downloadable lesson files

 Samples from other Digital Classroom books

Register at *DigitalClassroomBooks.com/CC/Dreamweaver*

Contents

Starting up

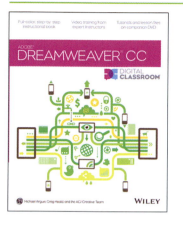

Lesson 1: Dreamweaver CC Jumpstart

Lesson 2: Setting Up a New Site

Lesson 3: Adding Text and Images

Lesson 4: Styling Your Pages with CSS

Lesson 5: Creating Page Layouts with CSS

Lesson 6: Advanced Page Layout

Lesson 7: CSS3 Transitions and Styles

Lesson 8: Using Web Fonts

Lesson 9: Working with Tables

Lesson 10: Fine-Tuning Your Workflow

Lesson 11: Adding Video, Audio and Interactivity

Lesson 12: Maximizing Site Design

Lesson 13: Working with Code-editing Features

Lesson 14: Building HTML5 Web Forms

Lesson 15: Adding Interactivity with the jQuery UI Library

Lesson 16: Responsive Design and Layout for Mobile Devices

Lesson 17: Managing your Website: Reports, Optimization, and Maintenance

Lesson 18: Dreamweaver CC New Features

Starting up

About Dreamweaver Digital Classroom

Adobe® Dreamweaver® lets you design, develop, and maintain web pages and websites. Designers and developers both use Dreamweaver, which lets you create and edit content using either a visual layout or a coding environment. Dreamweaver CC also provides tight integration with other Adobe products such as Photoshop® CC.

The *Adobe Dreamweaver CC Digital Classroom* helps you to understand these capabilities, and how to get the most out of your software, so that you can get up-and-running right away with the CC version of the software. You can work through all the lessons in this book, or complete only specific lessons. Each lesson includes detailed, step-by-step instructions, along with lesson files, useful background information, and video tutorials.

Adobe Dreamweaver CC Digital Classroom is like having your own expert instructor guiding you through each lesson while you work at your own pace. This book includes 17 self-paced lessons that let you discover essential skills, explore new features, and understand capabilities that will save you time. You'll be productive right away with real-world exercises and simple explanations. Each lesson includes step-by-step instructions and lesson files available on the included DVD. The *Adobe Dreamweaver CC Digital Classroom* lessons are developed by the same team of Adobe Certified Instructors and Dreamweaver experts who have created many official training titles for Adobe Systems.

Prerequisites

Before you start the *Adobe Dreamweaver CC Digital Classroom* lessons, you should have a working knowledge of your computer and its operating system. You should know how to use the directory system of your computer so that you can navigate through folders. You also need to understand how to locate, save, and open files, and you should also know how to use your mouse to access menus and commands.

Before starting the lesson files in the *Adobe Dreamweaver CC Digital Classroom*, make sure that you have installed Adobe Dreamweaver CC. The software is sold separately, and not included with this book. You might use the free 30-day trial version of Adobe Dreamweaver CC available at the *Adobe.com* website, subject to the terms of its license agreement.

System requirements

Before starting the lessons in the Adobe Dreamweaver CC Digital Classroom, make sure that your computer is equipped for running Adobe Dreamweaver CC. The minimum system requirements for your computer to effectively use the software are listed on the following page and you can find the most current system requirements at *http://www.adobe.com/products/dreamweaver/tech-specs.html*.

Windows

- Intel® Pentium® 4 or AMD Athlon® 64 processor
- Microsoft® Windows® 7 or Windows® 8
- 1 GB of RAM
- 1 GB of available hard-disk space for installation; additional free space required during installation (cannot install on removable flash-based storage devices)
- 1280×1024 display with 16-bit video card
- Java™ Runtime Environment 1.6 (included)
- Internet connection and registration are required for software activation, membership validation, and access to online services.

Mac OS

- Multicore Intel processor
- Mac OS X v10.7 or v10.8
- 1 GB of RAM
- 1 GB of available hard-disk space for installation; additional free space required during installation (cannot install on a volume that uses a case-sensitive file system or on removable flash-based storage devices)
- 1280×1024 display with 16-bit video card
- Java™ Runtime Environment 1.6
- QuickTime 7.6.6 software required for HTML5 media playback
- Internet connection and registration are required for software activation, membership validation, and access to online services.

Starting Adobe Dreamweaver

As with most software, Adobe Dreamweaver is launched by locating the application in your Programs folder (Windows) or Applications folder (Mac OS). If you are not familiar with starting the program, follow these steps to start the Adobe Dreamweaver CC application:

Windows

1   Choose Start > All Programs > Adobe Dreamweaver.
2   Close the Welcome Screen when it appears. You are now ready to use Adobe Dreamweaver CC.

Windows 8

1   Use your mouse to right-click an empty area of the Start screen and click All Apps.
2   Click the Adobe Dreamweaver tile to launch Dreamweaver.

3 Close the Welcome Screen when it appears. You are now ready to use Adobe Dreamweaver CC.

Mac OS

1 Open the Applications folder, and then open the Adobe Dreamweaver CC folder.

2 Double-click the Adobe Dreamweaver application icon.

3 Close the Welcome Screen when it appears. You are now ready to use Adobe Dreamweaver CC.

Menus and commands are identified throughout the book by using the greater-than symbol (>). For example, the command to print a document appears as File > Print.

Access lesson files & videos any time

Register your book at *www.digitalclassroombooks.com/CC/Dreamweaver* to download the lesson files onto any computer you own, or watch the videos on your Internet connected tablet, smartphone, or computer. You'll be able to watch the Digital Classroom videos anywhere you have an Internet connection. Registering your book also provides you access to lesson files and videos even if you misplace your DVD.

Checking for updated lesson files

Make sure you have the most up-to-date lesson files and learn about any updates to your *Dreamweaver CC Digital Classroom* book by registering your book at *www.digitalclassroombooks.com/CC/Dreamweaver.*

Resetting the Dreamweaver workspace

To make certain that your panels and working environment are consistent, you should reset your workspace at the start of each lesson. To reset your workspace, choose Window > Workspace Layout > Designer.

Loading lesson files

The *Dreamweaver CC Digital Classroom* DVD includes files that accompany the exercises for each of the lessons. You can copy the entire lessons folder from the supplied DVD to your hard drive, or copy only the lesson folders for the individual lessons you wish to complete.

For each lesson in the book, the files are referenced by the name of each file. The exact location of each file on your computer is not used, as you might have placed the files in a unique location on your hard drive. We suggest placing the lesson files in the My Documents folder (Windows) or at the top level of your hard drive (Mac OS).

Copying the lesson files to your hard drive:

1   Insert the *Dreamweaver CC Digital Classroom* DVD supplied with this book.

2   On your computer desktop, navigate to the DVD and locate the folder named dwlessons.

3   You can install all the files, or just specific lesson files. Do one of the following:

   • Install all lesson files by dragging the dwlessons folder to your hard drive.

   • Install only some of the files by creating a new folder on your hard drive named dwlessons. Open the dwlessons folder on the supplied DVD, select the lesson(s) you wish to complete, and drag the folder(s) to the dwlessons folder you created on your hard drive.

Unlocking Mac OS files

Mac users might need to unlock the files after they are copied from the accompanying disc. This applies only to Mac OS computers, and is because the Mac OS could view files that are copied from a DVD or CD as being locked for writing.

If you are a Mac OS user and have difficulty saving over the existing files in this book, you can use these instructions so that you can update the lesson files as you work on them, and also add new files to the lessons folder

Note that you only need to follow these instructions if you are unable to save over the existing lesson files, or if you are unable to save files into the lesson folder.

1   After copying the files to your computer, click once to select the dwlessons folder, then choose File > Get Info from within the Finder (not Dreamweaver).

2   In the dwlessons info window, click the triangle to the left of Sharing and Permissions to reveal the details of this section.

3   In the Sharing and Permissions section, click the lock icon, if necessary, in the lower-right corner so that you can make changes to the permissions.

4   Click to select a specific user or select everyone, then change the Privileges section to Read & Write.

5   Click the lock icon to prevent further changes, and then close the window.

Working with the video tutorials

Your *Dreamweaver CC Digital Classroom* DVD comes with video tutorials developed by the authors to help you understand the concepts explored in each lesson. Each tutorial is approximately five minutes long and demonstrates and explains the concepts and features covered in the lesson.

The videos are designed to supplement your understanding of the material in the lesson. We have selected exercises and examples that we feel will be most useful to you. You might want to view the entire video for each lesson before you begin that lesson. Additionally, at certain points in a lesson, you will encounter the DVD icon. The icon, with appropriate lesson number, indicates that an overview of the exercise being described can be found in the accompanying video.

DVD video icon.

Setting up for viewing the video tutorials

The DVD included with this book includes video tutorials for each lesson. Although you can view the lessons on your computer directly from the DVD, we recommend copying the folder labeled videos from the *Dreamweaver CC Digital Classroom* DVD to your hard drive for best performance.

Copying the video tutorials to your hard drive:

1   Insert the *Dreamweaver CC Digital Classroom* DVD supplied with this book.

2   On your computer desktop, navigate to the DVD and locate the folder named videos.

3   Drag the videos folder to a location onto your hard drive.

Viewing the video tutorials with the Adobe Flash Player

The videos on the *Dreamweaver CC Digital Classroom* DVD are saved in the Flash projector format. A Flash projector file wraps the Digital Classroom video player and the Adobe Flash Player in an executable file (.exe for Windows or .app for Mac OS). The file extension might not always be visible. Projector files allow the Flash content to be deployed on your system without the need for a browser or prior stand-alone player installation.

Playing the video tutorials:

1   On your computer, navigate to the videos folder you copied to your hard drive from the DVD. Playing the videos directly from the DVD might result in poor quality playback.

2   Open the videos folder and double-click the Flash file named PLAY_DWCCvideos to view the video tutorials.

3   After the Flash player launches, click the Play button to view the videos.

   The Flash Player has a simple user interface that allows you to control the viewing experience, including stopping, pausing, playing, and restarting the video. You can also rewind or fast-forward, and adjust the playback volume.

A. Go to beginning. B. Play/Pause. C. Fast-forward/rewind. D. Stop. E. Volume Off/On. F. Volume control.

Playback volume is also affected by the settings in your operating system. Be certain to adjust the sound volume for your computer, in addition to the sound controls in the Player window.

Hosting your websites

While you can work on everything in this book using only your computer, you will eventually want to create websites that you share with the world. To do this, you will need to put your website on a computer connected to the Internet that is always accessible. This is known as a web server. If you don't want to get involved in hosting a website, you can pay a company to provide space on their web servers for you. Subscribers to Adobe's Creative Cloud service can publish and host their sites using Adobe Business Catalyst and Adobe Dreamweaver. Another good place to look for a hosting provider is here: *http://www.microsoft.com/web/hosting/home/*. If you want to set up your own computer for hosting a web server and you are using any Windows computer, you can turn it into a web server at no cost by using the Web Platform Installer available at: *http://www.microsoft.com/web*. If you are a Mac OS user, you can get Mac OS X server from Apple to use a Mac OS computer as a web server.

If you are just getting started, you don't need to worry about web hosting just yet. But you'll find this information useful once you start creating sites, and you learn how to manage sites using Dreamweaver.

Additional resources

The Digital Classroom series goes beyond the training books. You can continue your learning online, with training videos, at seminars and conferences, and in-person training events.

On-demand video training from the authors

Comprehensive video training from the authors are available at *DigitalClassroom.com*. Find complete video training along with thousands of video tutorials covering Dreamweaver and related Creative Cloud apps along with digital versions of the Digital Classroom book series. Learn more at *DigitalClassroom.com*.

Training from the Authors

The authors are available for professional development training workshops for schools and companies. They also teach classes at American Graphics Institute, including training classes and online workshops. Visit *agitraining.com* for more information about Digital Classroom author-led training classes or workshops.

Additional Adobe Creative Cloud Books

Expand your knowledge of creative software applications with the Digital Classroom book series. Books are available for most creative software applications as well as web design and development tools and technologies. Learn more at *DigitalClassroomBooks.com*

Seminars and conferences

The authors of the Digital Classroom seminar series frequently conduct in-person seminars and speak at conferences, including the annual CRE8 Conference. Learn more at *agitraining.com* and *CRE8summit.com*.

Resources for educators

Visit *digitalclassroombooks.com* to access resources for educators, including instructors' guides for incorporating Digital Classroom into your curriculum.

What you'll learn in this lesson:

- An overview of Dreamweaver CC features

- How the Web works

- An introduction to HTML

Dreamweaver CC Jumpstart

Whether you are a novice web designer or an experienced developer, Dreamweaver is a comprehensive tool you can use for site design, layout, and management. In this lesson, you'll take a tour of Dreamweaver's key features and get a better understanding of how web pages work.

Starting up

Before starting, make sure that your tools and panels are consistent by resetting your workspace. See "Resetting the Dreamweaver workspace" in the Starting up section of this book.

Before you start, be sure to register your book at *www.digitalclassroombooks.com/CC/Dreamweaver* to learn about updates to any of the lesson files and gain access to the accompanying video tutorials on any Internet connected computer, tablet, or smartphone.

You will work with several files from the dw01lessons folder in this lesson. Make sure that you have loaded the dwlessons folder onto your hard drive from the supplied DVD. See "Loading lesson files" in the Starting up section of this book.

If you want to get started and create a page, jump ahead to "Tag structure and attributes" later on in this lesson. Otherwise, the next few pages provide you with an overview of key capabilities and features of Dreamweaver CC.

See Lesson 1 in action!

Use the accompanying video to gain a better understanding of how to use some of the features shown in this lesson. The video tutorial for this lesson can be found on the supplied DVD.

What is Dreamweaver?

Dreamweaver is an excellent web design and development tool for new and experienced users alike. Over the years it has become the preferred website creation and management program, providing a creative environment for both designers and developers. Whether you design websites, develop mobile phone content, or script complex server-side applications, Dreamweaver has something to offer.

Design and layout tools

Dreamweaver's many icon-driven menus and detailed panels make it easy to insert and format text, images, and media (such as HTML5 video files and Flash movies). This means that you can create attractive and functional web pages without knowing a single line of code—Dreamweaver takes care of building the code behind-the-scenes for you. Dreamweaver does not create graphics from scratch; instead, it is integrated with Adobe Photoshop CC so you can import and adjust graphics from within the application.

The Insert panel features objects in several categories that let you easily add images, web forms, and media to your page.

Site management and File Transfer Protocol

Dreamweaver has everything you need for complete site management, including built-in File Transfer Protocol (FTP) capabilities between a server and your local machine; reusable objects (such as page templates and library items); and site optimization tools (such as link checkers and site reports) so you can ensure that your site functions properly and looks good. If you're designing your pages with Cascading Style Sheets (CSS), then the W3C Validation, and the Browser Compatibility Check features will help you locate and troubleshoot any potential display issues that might occur across different web browsers.

Coding environment and text editor

Dreamweaver lets you work in a code-only view of your document that acts as a powerful text editor. Features such as color-coding, indentation, and visual aids make Dreamweaver an excellent text editing or coding environment for web designers of any level.

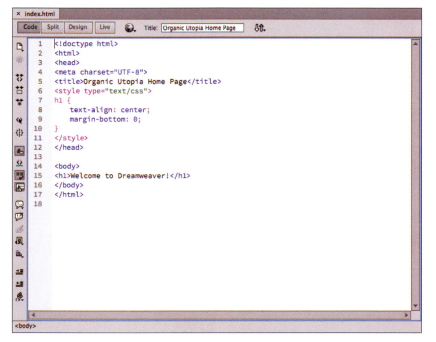

Code view is a full-featured text editor that color-codes, tags, and scripts for editing that's easier to decipher.

For more experienced developers, Dreamweaver supports popular coding and scripting languages, such as JavaScript, in addition to server-side languages like PHP. Specialized insert menus and code panels help you build pages and applications in the language of your choice.

Scripting languages, such as those used to build interactive web pages or e-commerce sites, fall into two categories: client-side and server-side. Client-side languages (such as JavaScript) run in your browser, while server-side languages (such as PHP) require that special software be installed on the server in order to run.

Mobile design and development features

The tools in Dreamweaver have evolved as the Web has evolved. The most recent versions of the application have numerous features designed to help make your website look good and function well in the rapidly growing arena of mobile phones and devices. The Fluid Grid Layout and Window Size viewports allow you to design your pages using a responsive grid with multiple screen sizes for smartphones and tablets.

Additionally, there is support for creating Media Queries, which are a CSS3 feature aimed at creating unique page layouts for different-sized screens. For more advanced users there is support for jQuery Mobile, which creates unique user interfaces for touchscreen devices. There is also support for creating native applications for iOS and Android operating systems with PhoneGap integration.

Multiple Window Size viewports allow you to view your pages in common screen sizes for mobile and other devices.

Who uses Dreamweaver?

Dreamweaver's popularity is a result of its flexibility. Its ability to build a site from conception to launch—and provide continued maintenance afterward—makes it a preferred tool among industry professionals, businesses, and educational institutions while remaining easy and accessible enough for novice designers to get up-and-running quickly. It's not unusual to see Dreamweaver utilized for personal projects or by small businesses and media professionals, such as photographers and painters, to maintain a web presence.

Dreamweaver's workspace features

This book is dedicated to exploring, learning, and putting to use all that Dreamweaver has to offer. This section looks at some of the application's key features.

Four different points of view: When you work with a document, Dreamweaver lets you see your work in one of four views: Code, Split, Design, or Live view. Dreamweaver's default Design view lets you add elements to your page in a visual fashion, either by dragging objects onto the page selecting them from the Insert panel, or by directly adding text, image or multimedia content. More experienced web designers and coders can use the Code view to edit a document's HTML code and scripts directly, enhanced with easy-to-read color-coding and visual aids.

For those who like something in between, the Split view provides a split-pane Design and Code view all at once. You can easily change views at any time with a single click in the Document toolbar. The Live view allows you to view your page as it would appear in a native web browser, eliminating the need to leave the program in order to preview your designs.

The Split view lets you edit your page visually while also seeing the code being created behind the scenes.

Built-in FTP: You can easily upload and download files to and from your web server using the Files panel's drag-and-drop interface. You can also use the Get/Put button at any time to post pages you're currently working on. In either case, there's no need for separate software. Dreamweaver also provides Check In/Check Out functionality and synchronization features; these allow multiple people to work more safely and efficiently on the same site.

Page and code object Insert panels: You can find intuitive icons for most common web page elements in a categorized Insert panel, from which you can add elements to your page with a single click. You can use additional panels to fine-tune any page element to ensure that you see exactly what you want. Included in the default Insert panel are tools for formatting text, building forms, and creating layouts. You can also customize a Favorites tab with your most-used icons.

Customizable workspace layouts: You can save combinations and positions of panels and toolbars for easy recall at any time. You can also save multiple workspace layouts for different users, or create different workspaces for specific tasks, such as coding or designing page layouts.

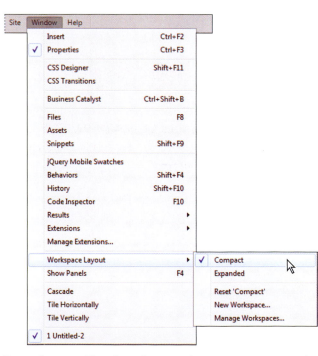

You can choose a specific workspace layout in order to create an arrangement of panels that suits you best.

Powerful visual aids: Take advantage of the precision you're accustomed to in other design programs through Dreamweaver's guides, rulers, measuring tools, and customizable positioning grid. Many of these features are found and can be activated within the View menu. Dreamweaver's Design-Time style sheets let you customize the look of your page exclusively for the editing process, making layout quicker and easier without permanently altering the page's appearance.

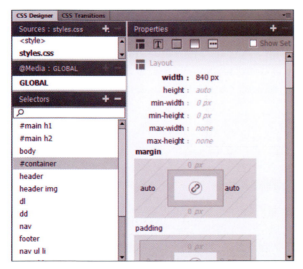

Rulers, a document grid, and guides help you size and position page items with precision.

CSS Designer: Take advantage of the vast design and formatting options that CSS provides through Dreamweaver's full-featured CSS Designer panel, which lets you visually create, edit, and manage styles on-the-fly from a single panel.

The CSS Designer Panel provides a visual interface for styling your pages.

Live View and Live Code

Experience tells you that visual web editors often display differently than the browsers they're emulating. As script-driven interactivity gains popularity, the need to accurately design the different states of your page (including menus, panels, and interface elements), has become increasingly important. The static nature of the Design view in Dreamweaver often times does not meet users' advanced needs.

Dreamweaver's Live View mode uses the WebKit rendering engine (which is also the basis for the Safari and Google Chrome web browsers), to give you a more accurate preview of your page in the same way that a browser would render it.

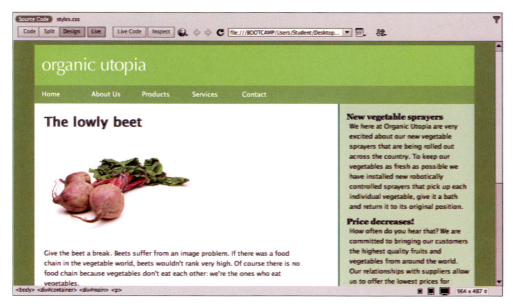

Live View enables you to preview your page as if it were in a web browser.

When you are in the Live View mode, the Live Code feature is enabled. Live Code allows you to see, in real time, how visually changing your page affects the code behind the scenes. If you have added interactive elements such as drop-down menus or accordion panels, then you can visually select an item on the page and see how the HTML code might be affected.

Also useful is the Freeze JavaScript button (or the F6 key). This feature freezes your page in a particular state (for example, with a menu locked open and a hover effect in place). You can then edit those interactive elements directly in Dreamweaver.

CSS Inspection and the Enable/Disable feature

Another feature that is enabled when in Live View is the Inspect Mode. This mode allows users to peek at the visual model and structure of a page by hovering over elements on the page. When hovering in Inspect Mode you can see the relationships between the

HTML elements on your page and the styles assigned to them. This is useful because it dramatically shortens the time it takes to locate any given style for any given object on the page. However, when paired with the Enable/Disable feature, the Inspect Mode becomes even more powerful.

The Enable/Disable feature allows you to temporarily turn off an applied style on your page. This can be very useful when dealing with unfamiliar or complex designs where half the battle is simply understanding what styles are being used. Disabling a style will remove its properties so that you can visually observe the results. Keep in mind that disabling is always temporary, and that it is just as easy to restore the style by clicking Enable.

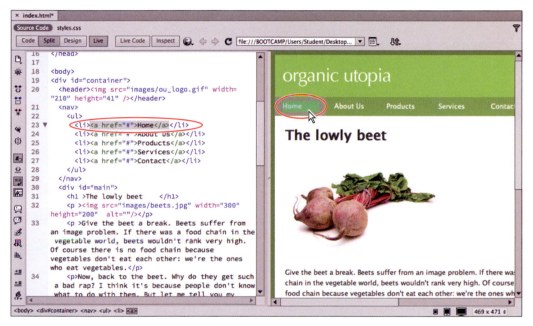

In the Inspect Mode, mousing over the elements in the Design view reveals the HTML and CSS code.

Related files

Web-based projects are becoming more complex than ever before, and you often find that even a single page is composed of a variety of assets. These assets can include Cascading Style Sheets (CSS), external JavaScript files, and more. Dreamweaver CC has a feature that will help you become much more effective at designing and managing sites and applications with multiple assets.

The Related Files bar runs across the top of your document window, just below the document tabs. The bar shows you all the various files that, when combined, create your finished page. You can switch between these files using the Related Files bar without losing the visual preview of their parent page. Design view (or Live View) always shows the parent file, but you can now edit any of the related files without losing their important visual context.

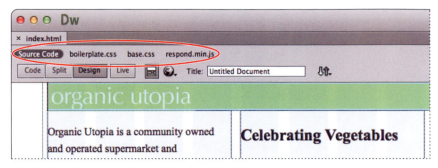

The Related Files bar shows you the various files that are part of your finished page.

Code Navigator

The Code Navigator (❈) is a feature enabled in the Design view that appears when you hover over an element on the page. Clicking the Navigator will let you see a quick summary of any CSS styles that have been applied, and if you choose to, you can click the style in order to view the code directly. The benefit is that it is no longer necessary to manually hunt through your style sheets to find a specific rule; it's just a click away in Dreamweaver.

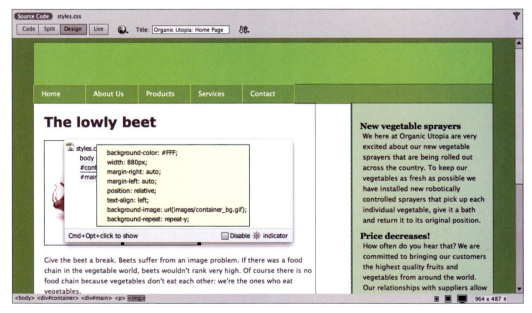

The Code Navigator allows you to easily view the location and properties of your CSS styles in the Design View.

Photoshop smart objects

Dreamweaver offers support for Photoshop smart objects, meaning you can drag a PSD file into a web page within Dreamweaver, optimize the image for the Web, and even resize it.

Inserting a native Photoshop file into Dreamweaver will trigger an automatic conversion into a suitable web graphic, such as JPG, PNG, or GIF.

Also, if you decide to update the original PSD file at a later time, a red arrow will appear on the image in Dreamweaver to indicate that the source file has changed. You can then click the Update from Original button in the Property Inspector and a new version of the image will be created.

Support for Content Management Systems

Enjoy authoring and testing support for content management systems like WordPress, Joomla! and Drupal. A CMS/blog software like WordPress provides users with an easy way to publish content online and has features such as automatic archiving and database integration. In the past, designers have been frustrated with creating the page designs for a CMS using Dreamweaver because these systems generally rely on a relatively complex combination of dynamic pages (often PHP) that could not be previewed in Dreamweaver. For designers or users who are not code-savvy, the complexity of these files can be daunting. Dreamweaver can now help you discover the related files needed to put together the pages in your CMS framework.

Access to these features in Dreamweaver CC requires installing the Database, Bindings, and Server Behavior extensions using the Adobe Extension Manager. Once installed and properly configured, you will be able to preview the files of a CMS framework in the Design view (as long as you have a testing server defined), using the built-in Live View option. With this feature, Dreamweaver CC also lets you interact directly with a database, which means you can test online forms, insert and modify database records, and more.

HTML5, CSS3, and PHP code hinting

For advanced users, there is now built in code-hinting support for HTML5 and CSS3 syntax. This means the "library" of HTML and CSS syntax that is now available within Dreamweaver is larger than ever, which is a good sign for those designers and developers who need to build modern web pages.

Additionally, advanced users who use the scripting language PHP will be happy to learn that Dreamweaver CC provides support for PHP syntax. This includes code hints, code completion and syntax checking, as well as full support for all core functions, constants, and classes. PHP code hints have also been improved substantially.

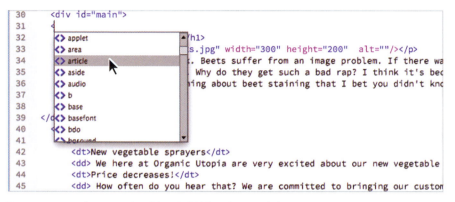

Dreamweaver provides support for HTML5, CSS3, and PHP code-hinting.

HTML and CSS Starter Pages

HTML and CSS Starter Pages have been around in Dreamweaver for a few versions now. These pages allow you to get a jumpstart on building page layouts by choosing from a variety of pre-built page layouts that you can subsequently modify. In Dreamweaver CC, the code for these starter pages is new and improved for modern web browsers and comes with plenty of code commenting behind the scenes to help you start modifying your pages quickly. You can view starter pages by choosing File > New. The Layout column features a number of page layouts. CSS starter pages can also be found by clicking the Page From Sample button.

Subversion

Dreamweaver features support for Subversion, a version control system similar to CVS and GitHub. Subversion is typically used by companies to maintain a team environment on larger projects that require changes to be logged and versions to be controlled. Without Subversion, if you wanted to maintain versions, you would have to do the work yourself by maintaining folders and copies of previous versions. With Subversion, all files are kept on the Subversion server. Changes are tracked so that you can restore your project to any previous state. Subversion is enabled by choosing Site > New Site (or Site > Manage Sites), choosing Version Control and then clicking the Access menu and choosing Subversion.

Business Catalyst integration

Adobe's Business Catalyst is offered as part of the Creative Cloud online subscription that provides a variety of features such as online store/shopping cart capabilities, e-mail marketing, web form functionality, analytics extension, and more. With the Business Catalyst extension in Dreamweaver, you can log-in to Business Catalyst and synchronize multiple sites at once. Dreamweaver can be used to access and edit the style module used on your Business Catalyst connected sites.

How websites work

Before embarking on the task of building web pages (and in turn, a website), it's a good idea to know the basics of how websites work, how your users view them, and what you need to know to make sure your website functions and looks its best.

A simple flow chart

What happens when you type in a website address? Most people don't even think about it—they just type in a URL (Uniform Resource Locator) and the website appears. They most likely don't realize how many things are going on behind the scenes to make sure that pages gets delivered to their computer so that they can do their shopping, check their e-mail, or research a project.

When you request a web page from your browser, the request is sent to a server that handles the request and sends the necessary files back to your browser to be displayed.

When you type a URL or IP address in the address bar of a web browser, you are connecting to a remote computer (called a server), and downloading the documents, images, and resources necessary to render the pages you will view while on the site. Web pages aren't delivered as a finished product; your web browser is responsible for reconstructing and formatting the pages based on the HTML code included within the pages. HTML (Hypertext Markup Language) is a simple, tag-based language that instructs your browser how and where to insert and format pictures, text, and media files. Web pages are written in HTML, and Dreamweaver builds the HTML as you construct your page in the Design view.

An Internet Service Provider (ISP) enables you to connect to the Internet. Some well-known ISPs include Verizon, Comcast, and Time Warner Cable. You view web pages over an Internet connection using a browser such as Internet Explorer, Firefox, Chrome, or Safari. A browser can decipher and display web pages and their content, including images, text, and video.

Domain names and IP addresses

When you type in a website address, you usually enter the website's domain name (such as *DigitalClassroom.com*). The website owner purchased this domain name and uses it to mask an IP address, which is a numerical address used to locate and dial up the pages and files associated with a specific website.

So how does the Web know what domains match up with what IP address, and in turn, with what websites? It uses a Domain Name Service (DNS) server, which makes connections between domain names and IP addresses.

Servers and web hosts

A DNS server is responsible for matching a domain name with its companion IP address. Think of the DNS server as the operator at a phone company who connects calls through a massive switchboard. DNS servers are typically maintained by either the web host or the registrar from which the domain was purchased. Once the match is made, the request from your user is routed to the appropriate server and folder where your website resides. When the request reaches the correct account, the server then directs it to the first page of the website, which is typically named index.html, default.html, or whatever the server is set up to recognize as a default starting page.

A server is a machine very much like your desktop computer, but it's capable of handling traffic from thousands of users (often at the same time!), and it maintains a constant connection to the Internet so that your website is available 24 hours a day. Servers are typically maintained by a web host. Web hosts are companies that charge a fee to host and serve your website to the public. A single server can sometimes host hundreds of websites. Web hosting services are available from a variety of providers, including well-known Internet service companies such as Yahoo!, and other large, dedicated hosting companies. It is also common for a large company to maintain its own servers and websites on its premises.

The role of web browsers

A web browser is an application that downloads and displays HTML pages. Every time you request a page by clicking a link or typing in a website address you are requesting an HTML page and any files that it includes. The browser's job is to reconstruct and display that page based on the instructions in the HTML code, which guides the layout and formatting of the text, images, and other assets used within the page. The HTML code works like a set of assembly instructions for the browser to use.

An introduction to HTML

HTML is what makes the Web work; web pages are built using HTML code, which in turn is read and used by your web browser to lay out and format text, images, and video on the page. As you design and lay out web pages in Design view, Dreamweaver writes the code behind the scenes that is necessary to display and format your page in a web browser.

Contrary to what you may think, HTML is not a programming language, but a simple text-based markup language. HTML is not proprietary to Dreamweaver—you can create and edit HTML in any text editor, even in simple applications such as Windows Notepad and Mac OS X's TextEdit. Dreamweaver's job is to give you a visual way to create web pages without having to code by hand. If you like to work with code, however, Dreamweaver's Code view is a fully featured text editor with color-coding and formatting tools that make it easier to write and read HTML and other languages.

Tag structure and attributes

This exercise is for users who are completely new to HTML and Dreamweaver, and it will cover basic concepts such as the role of tags in HTML documents. HTML uses *tags*, or bracketed keywords, that you can use to place or format content. Many tags require a closing tag, which is the keyword preceded by a forward slash (/).

1   Launch Dreamweaver. Choose File > Open. When the Open dialog box appears, navigate to the dw01lessons folder. Select **BasicHTML.html** and click Open.

2   Select the Split button in the Document toolbar to see the layout as well as the code that makes up the page.

Take a look at line 10 (indicated at the left edge of the Code panel). The text *My Bold Title* is inside a Strong tag, which is simply the word *strong* contained within angled brackets. Any words or characters inside these tags are formatted in bold, and appear as shown in the Design view.

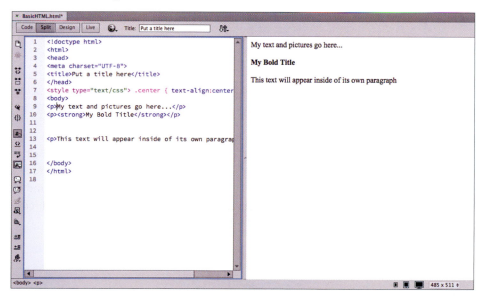

A look at the code reveals the tags used to format text in your page.

Tags can also accept CSS rules that specify additional information for how the tag should display the content. CSS rules might have one or more properties such as size, color, or alignment. Take a look at the line that reads: *This text will appear inside of its own paragraph*. This line is enclosed in a *p* (paragraph) tag, which separates it from the other text by a line above and below. You can add a CSS class rule to this to align the text.

3   Highlight the entire line that reads: *This text will appear inside of its own paragraph* at the bottom of the Design view.

4   Locate the Properties window, often referred to as the Property Inspector, at the bottom of the screen. Make sure the HTML button is selected so you can see the Class menu. Click the small down arrow and select *center* from the menu. This will format the selected paragraph using the center class by setting the CSS property text-align to center. You will learn how to create your own CSS rules using the CSS Designer later in this book.

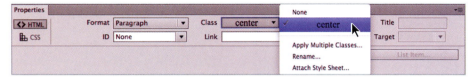

Select the center class from the Class menu in the Property Inspector to center your paragraph.

5   The text is now centered. Take a look at the Code view, and notice that the .center rule has been added to the opening <p> tag. This is not the only method of centering a paragraph using CSS, but it begins to introduce you to the practice of integrating HTML and CSS.

Align or format text in the Property Inspector, and then see the appropriate rules and attributes created in your code.

For more information on formatting text with CSS rules, see Lesson 3, "Adding Text and Images."

6   Choose File > Save to save your work, then choose File > Close.

The structure of an HTML document

In HTML a pair of tags is referred to as an *element*. For example, in the last exercise you created a style for one of the paragraph elements on the page. HTML elements define the structure of a page and examples include lists, images, tables, and even the HTML documents themselves. The HTML element is the most fundamental element you will use. It is used to specify the beginning and end of HTML in a document:

```
<html></html>
```

The HTML element consists of two tags that contain two key sections of your web page: the head and the body. The head element of your page contains items that are not visible to your user, but are important nonetheless. Search engine keywords, page descriptions, and links to outside scripts or style sheets are all found in the head element. You create the head of the document inside the HTML tags using the `<head>` tags:

```
<html>
<head></head>
</html>
```

The body of your page is where all the visible elements of your page are contained. This is where you insert text, images, and other media. You define the body of the page using the `<body>` element:

```
<html>
    <head></head>
        <body>

            My text and pictures go here...

        </body>
</html>
```

Whenever you create a new HTML document in Dreamweaver, this structure is created automatically before you add anything to the page. Any visual elements you add to the page are added using the appropriate HTML code inside the `<body>` element.

Placing images in HTML

You use some elements in HTML to place items, such as pictures or media files, inside a web page. The `<img>` element is the most common example; its job is to place and format an image on the page. To place an image and see the resulting code, follow these steps:

1   Choose File > Open. When the Open dialog box appears, navigate to the dw01lessons folder. Select the **Images.html** file and click Open to edit the file.

2   If necessary, click the Split button in the Document toolbar so that you're viewing both the layout and the code for your page. In the Design view portion of the Split view, place your cursor at the end of the line and press Enter (Windows) or Return (Mac OS) to insert a new line. This is where you'll place a new image.

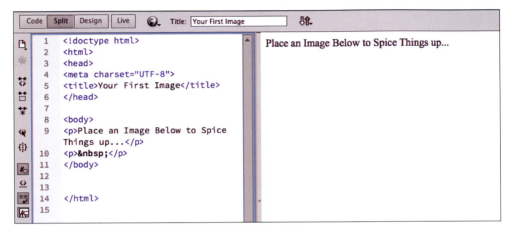

Enter the Split view before you insert the image onto your page.

3   From the Common category in the Insert panel on the right side of the screen, click the Image element and choose Image. When the Select Image Source dialog box appears, select the file named **gears.jpg**, located in the images folder within the dw01lessons folder and click OK (Windows) or Choose (Mac OS).

Choose Image from the Common tab in the Insert bar.

4   The code shows that the HTML <img> element has been used to place the image. Click once on the image in the document window to select it. The Property Inspector at the bottom of the page displays and sets the properties for the image.

5 Type the words **Gears Image** in the Alt Text field in the Property Inspector to add informative text to the `<img>` element .

When adding images, it is a recommended practice to provide additional information for users with special needs (such as the visually impaired). You should always provide each image with alternate text, located in the Properties Inspector at the bottom of the screen.

6 Choose File > Save to save your work, then choose File > Close.

Note that in HTML, images and media are not embedded, but linked. This means that the elements contain additional information known as attributes and values that point to the location of an image file and could even contain other information such as the width and height values.

Colors in HTML

In Dreamweaver's various panels and in your code, each color is referred to by a six-character code preceded by a pound sign. This code is called hexadecimal code, and it is the system that HTML pages use to identify and use colors. You can reproduce almost any color using a unique hexadecimal code. For example, you represent dark red in HTML as `#CC0000`.

The first, middle, and last two digits of the hexadecimal code correspond to values in the RGB spectrum. For instance, white, which is represented in RGB as R:255 G:255 B:255, is represented in HTML as `#FFFFFF` (255|255|255). Choosing colors is easy thanks to a handy Swatches panel, which you can find in many places throughout the work area.

The Swatches panel makes it easy to work with colors.

The color pickers in Adobe Photoshop and Illustrator also display and accept hexadecimal codes, making it easy to copy and paste colors between these applications and Dreamweaver.

Case sensitivity and whitespace rules

HTML is a flexible language that has very few rules regarding its own appearance. Based on how strictly you want to write it, HTML can be either very specific about whether tags are written in upper- or lowercase (called case sensitivity), or not specific at all. To see how HTML treats whitespace, follow these steps.

1   Choose File > Open. When the Open dialog box appears, navigate to the dw01lessons folder. Select the **Whitespace.html file**, and then click Open.

2   If your file is not in Split view, click the Split button in the Document toolbar at the top of the page, so that you can view both the layout and the code. The first three paragraphs have different amounts of space between them in the HTML but will be rendered on the page one after the other.

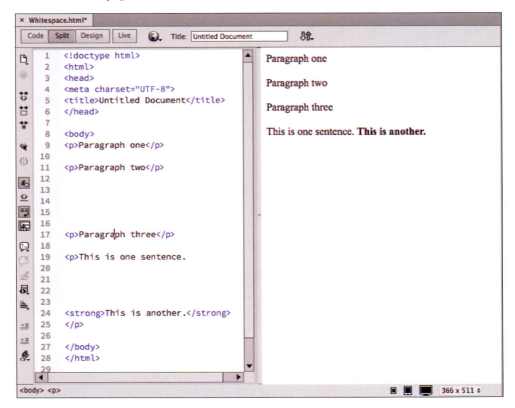

The browser ignores any white space between the paragraphs.

This tells you that whitespace and line returns are ignored by the browser. You have to begin making a distinction between code that is readable by humans versus the way a web browser interprets and renders code.

3   You will see there are a few different ways to format your text. In the Design view, click once after the sentence that reads: *This is one sentence*, and then press Shift+Enter (Windows) or Shift+Return (Mac OS) twice. This creates two line returns—you can see that each line return is created in your code by a `<br>` (break) tag. When rendered in the browser, the `<br>` tag adds blank lines between the sentences; however the sentences are technically within the same paragraph. This is sometimes referred to as a soft return. This method is actually not the ideal way to add new lines on your page, although it does occasionally come in handy.

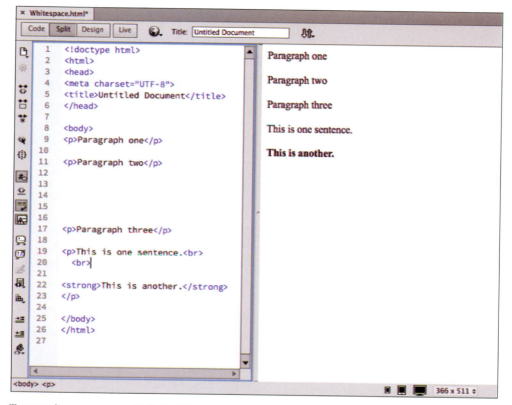

To create a line return, press and hold the Shift key while pressing the Enter or Return key.

4   To create a new paragraph, position your cursor before the phrase: *This is another*, and press Enter (Windows) or Return (Mac OS). The text is separated by a line above and below, and is wrapped inside a set of `<p>` (paragraph) tags. This is the preferred method of adding paragraphs.

Other than a standard single space (such as the space used between words), several consecutive spaces created by the spacebar are ignored and are displayed as only one space in Design view and in a browser.

5   Choose File > Save to save your work then choose File > Close.

Element hierarchy

HTML elements should have a well-formed hierarchy or nesting structure in order to make sure that everything displays as it should. The element at the top of the hierarchy is the <html> element, and every other element you create is contained within it. Elements such as the <body> end up nesting all the other elements on a page, such as the <p> (paragraph), <img> (image), and <strong> (bold) elements. In addition, structural elements (such as those that create divs, paragraphs, lists, and tables) hold more weight than formatting tags such as <strong> (bold) and <em> (italic). Take this line of code, for example:

```
<strong><p>Big bold paragraph</p></strong>
```

Although code such as this could work in certain browsers, it isn't structured well because the <strong> tag technically holds less weight than the <p> tag. The following code represents a better way to include the bold type:

```
<p><strong>Big bold paragraph</strong></p>
```

Dreamweaver generally does a great job of keeping tags properly nested or contained within each other. When you choose to manipulate the code by hand, you should always keep good coding techniques in mind.

HTML5

The language of HTML has continued to evolve over the years and there are a few different page types currently in use. Unless you specifically change it, the default page type that Dreamweaver creates is named HTML5. HTML5 the 'next' version of the HTML specification and while it is not formally ratified at the time of this writing, it is widely supported by all major browsers and is the language of choice for creating new web pages. HTML5 replaces HTML4 and XHTML (which were introduced around the year 2000). HTML5 is designed to make web pages more compatible with newer platforms, such as mobile phones and handheld devices, and to create rich interactive and animated experiences.

Explorations in code

Although this book occasionally refers to the code for examples, hand-coding is not a primary goal of these lessons. The best way to learn how code represents the layouts you are building visually is to switch to the Code view and explore what's happening behind the scenes.

It's important to remember that every button, panel, and menu in Dreamweaver represents some type of HTML tag, attribute, or value; very rarely will you learn something that is unrelated or proprietary to Dreamweaver alone. Think of the Dreamweaver workspace as a pretty face on the HTML language.

A look at the Welcome Screen

A common fixture in most Creative Cloud applications is the Welcome Screen, which is a launching pad for new and recent documents. In Dreamweaver, the Welcome Screen appears when the application launches or when no documents are open. From the Welcome Screen, you can create new pages, create a new site, open a recent document, or use one of Dreamweaver's many starter pages or layouts.

The Welcome Screen appears when you launch the application, or when no documents are open.

Here's what you'll find on the Welcome Screen:

Open a Recent Item: A list of the last few documents you worked on appears in the far left column, or you can browse to open a different file using the Open button at the bottom.

Create New: In addition to HTML pages, you can choose from a variety of new document formats, such as CSS, JavaScript, and XML. Dreamweaver is not just a web page-building tool, but also a superior text editor, making it ideal for creating many non-HTML files. You can also define a new Dreamweaver site using the link at the bottom, or choose the More folder for even more new file options.

Top Features (videos): On the far right side of the Welcome Screen, there is a column that contains links to videos of Top Features. These videos explore some of the new top features of Dreamweaver CC, including the Visual Styling with the CSS Designer, Enhanced Responsive Design, and Building Mobile Apps, among others. The videos are located on Adobe's website, *adobe.com*, and when you click one, Dreamweaver launches the site in your web browser to give you access to the video.

Creating, opening, and saving documents

The lessons throughout this book require that you create, save, and open existing files. You can accomplish most file-related tasks from the File menu at the top, or from the Welcome Screen that appears when you launch Dreamweaver.

Creating new documents

Dreamweaver creates text files most commonly in the form of HTML files (or web pages). It can also create files in a variety of text-based languages, including CSS, XML, and JavaScript.

You can create blank files that you build from the ground up, or you can get started with a variety of layout templates and themes. You can create new documents from the File menu or from the Welcome Screen. Here, you'll create a new page using the File menu.

The New Document dialog box gives you a choice of new files in a variety of formats and templates.

1   To create a new document, choose File > New. The New Document dialog box appears.

2   Select Blank Page and under the Page Type column, choose HTML. Under Layout, choose <none> to start a new blank document. Leave the DocType drop-down menu at its default. Click Create.

3   Choose File > Save or File > Save As to start the process of saving your document.

4   When prompted, choose a location for your file and assign it a name. Note that you must save HTML files with an .html extension, or they will not be interpreted properly in a browser. This rule applies for files of any type (such as .xml, .css, and .cfm).

Opening a recently opened document

To open a document you've worked on recently, Choose File > Open Recent or, from the Welcome Screen, select a document under the Open a Recent Item column.

Now that you've seen what Dreamweaver can do, it's time to put what you've learned into practice. In the next lesson, you will start building your first Dreamweaver site.

Self study

Explore the ready-to-use CSS layouts available in Dreamweaver by choosing File > New, then selecting HTML from the Page Type column. Browse the options listed in the Layout column and open a few layouts. Identify some that you'd like to use as a starting point for any future project.

Review

Questions

1 From what two locations in Dreamweaver can a new document be created?

2 In what three views does Dreamweaver allow you to view and edit documents?

3 True or False: When a web page is requested, it is delivered to a user's browser as a completed, flat file ready for viewing.

Answers

1 You can create a new document from the Welcome Screen or by choosing File > New.

2 Design, Split, and Code views allow you to view and edit documents.

3 False. Files are delivered individually; the browser uses HTML code to assemble the resources together to display a finished page.

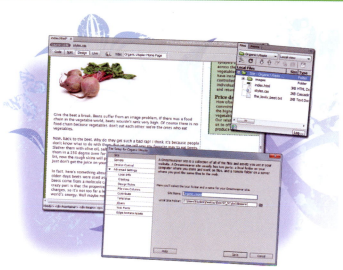

What you'll learn in this lesson:

- Defining site settings
- Establishing local and remote folders
- Selecting, viewing, and organizing files with the Files panel
- Defining Page Properties

Setting Up a New Site

Dreamweaver's strength lies in its powerful site creation and management tools. You can use the software to create everything from individual pages to complete websites. The pages you create within your site can share similar topics, a cohesive design, or a common purpose. And, once your Dreamweaver site is complete, you can efficiently manage and distribute it from within the program.

Starting up

Before starting, make sure that your tools and panels are consistent by resetting your workspace. See "Resetting the Dreamweaver workspace" in the Starting up section of this book.

You will work with several files from the dw02lessons folder in this lesson. Make sure that you have loaded the dwlessons folder onto your hard drive from the supplied DVD. See "Loading lesson files" in the Starting up section of this book.

See Lesson 2 in action!

Use the accompanying video to gain a better understanding of how to use some of the features shown in this lesson. The video tutorial for this lesson can be found on the included DVD.

Creating a new site

In Dreamweaver, the term *site* refers to the local and remote storage locations where the files that make up a website are stored. A site can also include a testing server location for processing dynamic pages. To take full advantage of Dreamweaver's features, you should always start by creating a site. Dreamweaver CC can also be used to setup and manage a Business Catalyst Site. Business Catalyst is a part of the Creative Cloud service that Adobe provides (for a fee) that allows you to connect your website with analytic software and other features. However, we do not cover setup of Business Catalyst sites in this book.

The easiest way to create a standard new site in Dreamweaver is to use the Site Setup dialog box. One way to access this dialog box is by choosing Site > New Site from the menu bar.

You can also use the Manage Sites dialog box to create a new site. This and other functions of the Manage Sites dialog box are discussed later in this book.

In this lesson, you begin by using the Site Setup dialog box to accomplish the following tasks:

• Define the site

• Name the site

• Define the local root folder

• Set up a remote folder

• Explore advanced settings

• Save the site

By default, the Site Setup dialog box opens with the Site Settings available. The options available here will help guide you through the essentials of defining your site. The Servers, Version Control, and Advanced Settings options allow you to set up local, remote, and testing servers directly.

1   Launch Dreamweaver CC, if it is not already open, then choose Site > New Site. First, you have to name the site. In the Site Name text field, type **Organic Utopia**.

Type the Site Name into the text field.

Next, you need to set up a local root folder, which is where Dreamweaver stores the files with which you're currently working. The Local Site Folder field allows you to enter information regarding where you'll be working with your files during development.

To ensure that the links you set up on your computer will work when you upload the site to a web server, it is essential that you store all the site's resources in one main folder on your hard drive, then identify it within Dreamweaver. This is because the links will only work properly if all the site's elements remain in the same relative location on the web server as your hard drive.

2   Click the Folder icon (📁) to the right of the Local Site Folder text field to navigate to any pre-existing files. In the next step you will locate the lesson files we have provided for this chapter.

If you did not click on the folder icon and just clicked Save, Dreamweaver would simply create a new folder on your system where you could begin to create new pages in your site. In this case, you will be pointing to a preexisting folder that already has files within it.

It is important to distinguish between adding a new site (which is what you are doing now) and creating a new site from scratch. In both cases, the important part is that Dreamweaver knows where this folder is on your system. This folder is known as the root folder and will always contain the content that will eventually be your website.

3 Navigate to your desktop and locate the dw02lessons folder you copied to your desktop earlier.

4 Select the dw02lessons folder. On the Windows platform, click Open to open this folder, then press Select (Windows). On the Mac OS platform, click Choose to choose this as your local root folder. The field now shows the path to your newly defined local root folder.

At this point, you have done the minimum amount of steps required to begin working on a site. Now you will take a look at some of the optional features within the Site Setup process.

5 Click the Servers tab. This section allows you to define the remote server where your website will end up being hosted. Take a moment to read the heading in the dialog box. Note that it says you do not need to fill in this information to begin creating a website. It is only necessary if you are connecting to the Web.

You are not connecting to the Web in this lesson, but you should take a look at the screen anyway to understand the information needed.

6 Click the + button and the Basic site settings window appears. Here there are fields for Server Name, Connect Using, FTP Address, Username and Password, along with other options. These settings allow you to choose both a destination and a method (FTP being the most common) for Dreamweaver to use to transfer files.

Set up access to your remote folder.

As noted earlier, this is an optional step, and you do not have to define your remote folder at this stage. Dreamweaver allows you to define your remote folder at a later time, such as when you're ready to upload.

7   Click the Advanced tab. Click the Server Model menu in the Testing Server section. Here there are choices for different scripting languages such as PHP and ASP pages. If you are an advanced user, this is where you would set up the connections to your testing server.

    Again, you won't be making any changes here, so click Cancel.

8   Click the Version Control option on the left to access Subversion settings. Subversion, a VCS (or version control system), keeps track of changes made to files, enabling users to track changes and return to previous versions of any file. For this exercise, make sure the Access pull-down in this window is set to None, as you won't be using Subversion.

    You've now completed the site setup process using basic settings. Don't close the Site Setup dialog box yet, though, as you'll now explore the options found under the Advanced Settings option.

Advanced site-creation options

Chances are if you are new to Dreamweaver or web design you won't need these advanced settings. If you are in this category, click Save and skip to the Adding Pages section. Other users might be curious as to what these settings are and should proceed.

1   Click the arrow next to Advanced Settings in the Site Setup dialog box.

2   From the categories listed below Advanced Settings, choose Local Info.

Choose Local Info from Advanced Settings.

The information you set in the Local Info window identifies your Default Images folder, what your links are relative to, and a web URL to be used if you don't have a remote server defined. One of the more important Local Info settings is case-sensitive link checking.

The case-sensitive links checking feature ensures that your links will work on a Unix server, where links are case-sensitive. If you're using a Windows or Mac OS server, this doesn't matter as much, but it is a good idea to follow the strict naming and linking conventions of a Unix system in case you ever move your site to a different server.

If you happen to have already defined a CSS3 site-wide Media Query file, this is where you could redefine or modify it.

(We cover the creation of site-wide Media Query files in Lesson 15, "Mobile Design and Layout".)

The remaining categories to the left of the Advanced tab of the Site Setup dialog box help to define your site's production, collaboration, and deployment capabilities. They include the following:

Cloaking allows you to specify file types or specific files that you do not want uploaded to the server.

Design Notes is a collaboration tool that keeps notes regarding the development of the page or site.

File View Columns is an organizational tool. If you want to share the custom columns with others, you must enable Design Notes as well.

Contribute is a separate application that enables users with basic word processing and web browser skills and little or no HTML knowledge to create and maintain web pages.

Templates can be automatically updated with rewritten document paths using this option.

jQuery is a JavaScript library for web designers. It allows designers to build pages that provide a richer experience for their users.

Web Fonts allows you to define where you are storing the web fonts you would like to use for this site.

Edge Animate Assets allows you to define where you are storing any assets created in Edge Animate that you would like to use for this site.

3 At this point you are finished defining your settings, so click Save. Dreamweaver creates a site with the settings you have defined.

You are now ready to work with pages for your defined website and take advantage of Dreamweaver's site features.

Adding pages

Dreamweaver contains many features to assist you in building pages for your site. For example, you can define properties for pages, including titles, background colors or images, as well as default text and link colors.

The first step for creating a new page correctly was taken when you defined the site in the last exercise. By defining the root folder, Dreamweaver will always create new pages in your site automatically. These pages are now visible in the Files panel in the lower right of your screen.

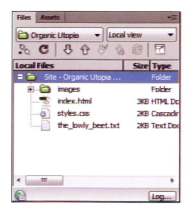

The Files panel.

If your Files panel does not look the same as it does here, choose Window > Workspace Layout > Reset 'Compact'.

1   Choose File > New. The New Document dialog box opens.

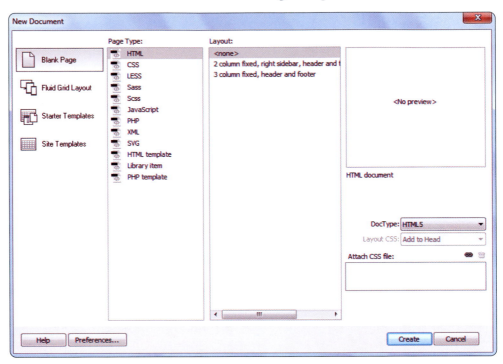

Use the New Document dialog box to add a page to your site.

2   You can create a new page using a predesigned layout, or start with a blank page and build a layout of your own. In this exercise, you'll start with a blank page while in later lessons you will get a chance to explore some of the other options. Click the Blank Page category on the left side of the New Document dialog box.

3   In the Page Type column, you can select the type of page you want to create (for example, HTML, PHP, and so on). Select HTML if it is not currently selected.

In the Layout column, you can choose to base your page on a prebuilt design. These predesigned layouts fall into one of three categories:

Fixed creates a layout with columns that do not resize based on the user's browser settings. They are measured in pixels.

Liquid creates a layout with columns that resize if the user resizes the browser window, but not if the user changes the text settings.

HTML5 creates a fixed layout that uses the new HTML5 elements such as <header>, <section> and <article> among others.

4   Click <none> in the Layout column to build the page without using a prebuilt layout.

5   Click the DocType menu in the lower-right corner. This DocType drop-down menu defines the document type for different versions of HTML including XHTML 1.0 Transitional and HTML5. HTML5 is the default setting and is suitable in most cases, so be sure to bring it back to this option.

Choose HTML5 as your DocType.

The Layout CSS and Attach CSS settings are irrelevant here, as you didn't choose a CSS-based layout for this page.

6 Click Create to create a new, blank HTML page. You will learn more about Workspaces a bit later, but to make sure you are working as we are, choose Window > Workspace Layout and choose Reset 'Compact'. Your screen should now look like ours. (Although if you are in Code View, you should switch to the Design view now.)

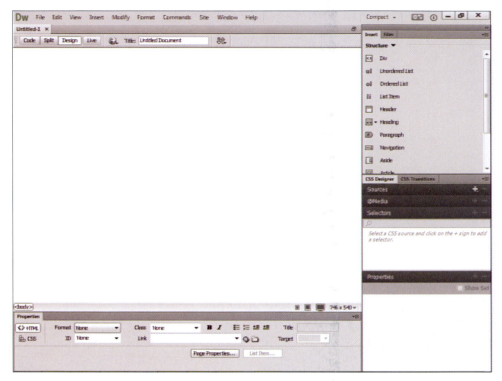

Your new, blank HTML page.

Saving a page to your site

You should get accustomed to saving pages to your local root folder early and often. It is very important that you store all your site's resources in one main folder on your hard drive so that the links you set on your computer will work when your site is uploaded to a server.

1 Choose File > Save.

2 In the Save As dialog box, Dreamweaver should have automatically opened your dw02lessons folder which was defined earlier in the Site Settings.

If this is not the case, navigate to your desktop and locate the dw02lessons folder.

3 In the Save As text field, name your file **about_us.html**.

Notice that even though the file is for the About Us page, you are naming it about_us.html. When naming your files and directories, avoid using spaces, periods, slashes, or any other unnecessary punctuation, as doing so will likely cause the server to misdirect your files.

4   Click Save to save the page in your local root folder. In the Files panel note that the file about_us.html has now been added. Again, site settings are very important in Dreamweaver because files are automatically saved and organized based on having a site definition.

Defining page properties

Now that you've created a page in Dreamweaver, you'll use the Page Properties dialog box to specify its layout and formatting properties. For example, you can set page titles, background colors and images, text and link colors, as well as other basic properties of every web page. You use this dialog box to define page properties for each new page you create, and to modify the settings for pages you've already created.

1   To access the Page Properties dialog box, choose Modify > Page Properties, or use the keyboard shortcut Ctrl+J (Windows) or Command+J (Mac OS). The Page Properties dialog box appears with the Appearance (CSS) category selected by default.

The Page Properties dialog box.

Settings found in the Appearance (CSS) category will automatically create a Cascading Style Sheet that defines the appearance of your page. Using a CSS file to define these page properties adds flexibility to your design, as styling can be changed more easily and more universally than if your defaults are defined using HTML code.

2   The Page Font and Size fields define the default appearance of text on your page. For now, leave these settings at their defaults. You'll be styling type with CSS in later lessons in this book.

3   The Text color option allows you to set a default color in which to render type. To set a text color, click the color swatch next to Text and the Swatches panel appears. You can choose your default text color by clicking the appropriate swatch from the Swatches panel. Try this by clicking any color swatch, then clicking Apply to apply your desired default text color.

You can also type the hexadecimal notation for your desired color into the text field. Type the hex code **#666666** in the text field to specify a dark gray as the default text color.

You'll see the effects of this change later in this lesson, when you add text to your page using the Files panel.

4   Use the Background color option to choose a background color for your page. Click the color swatch next to the Background text field and the Swatches panel appears. You can choose your background color by clicking the appropriate swatch from the Swatches panel. Try this by clicking any color swatch, then clicking Apply to see the results.

You can also choose the background color by typing the hexadecimal notation for your desired color into the Background text field. Type the hex code **739112** in the Background text field, then click Apply to specify a green as the background color.

Set a background color for your page.

5   The Background image field allows you to set a background image for your page. Dreamweaver mimics a browser's behavior by repeating, or tiling, the background image to fill the window. To choose a background image, click the Browse button next to the Background image text field. The Select Image Source dialog box appears.

6   Navigate to the folder titled images within the dw02lessons folder and select
bg_gradient.gif for your page background; then click Apply. You will see the
background image, which is a gradient, appear on the page. Background images are
tiled both horizontally and vertically by default, which is not appropriate for this
image, so you will fix this with the Repeat property.

7   From the Repeat drop-down menu, choose repeat-x. Click Apply to see the change.

Page Properties

Category   Appearance (CSS)

Appearance (CSS)
Appearance (HTML)   Page font: ⌨ Default Font
Links (CSS)
Headings (CSS)   Size: px
Title/Encoding
Tracing Image   Text color: ▮ #666666

                          Background color: ▮ #739112

                          Background image: images/bg_gradient.gif   Browse...

                                 Repeat: repeat-x

                               Left margin: px   Right margin: px

                                Top margin: px   Bottom margin: px

        Help   OK   Cancel   Apply

Choose a background image for your page (**bg_gradient.gif**).

You can also type the path to your background image into the Background image text field.

8   By default, Dreamweaver places your text and images in close proximity to the top
and left edges of the page. To build in some extra room between your page edges and
the content on them, use the Margin settings in the Page Properties dialog box. In the
Left margin text field, type **25** to place your content 25 pixels from the left edge of the
page. In the Top margin text field, type **25** to place your content 25 pixels from the
top edge of the page.

The Appearance (HTML) category in the Page Properties dialog box contains many
of the same settings you just defined. Setting default page attributes with HTML code,
however, is not recommended. Setting appearance with CSS is a better option.

The Links (CSS) category allows you to define the appearance of linked text within
your document. For more information on creating hyperlinks, see Lesson 3, "Adding
Text and Images."

9   Click the Links (CSS) category on the left side and leave the Link font and Size
settings at their defaults (same as Page font). This ensures that your hyperlinks will
display in the same typeface and size as the rest of the text on your page.

10 Set the colors for your different link types in the following fields:

Link Color: Type **#fc3** for the default link color applied to linked text on your web page.

Visited links: Type **#ccc** for the color applied to linked text after a user has clicked on it.

Rollover links: Type **#f03** for the color applied to linked text when a user rolls over it.

Active links: Type **#ff6** for the color applied when the user clicks on linked text.

Hexadecimal codes can be written in shorthand using only three alphanumeric characters when the two digits that make up each RGB component are the same value. For instance, #fc3 is the same as writing #ffcc33.

11 Because you're using CSS formatting, you can choose whether or not (and/or when) you want your links to be underlined. This is not possible with HTML formatting. Choose the default setting of Always underline in the Underline style drop-down menu.

Choose default colors for links, visited links, and active links.

The Headings (CSS) category allows you to define the font, style, size, and color of heading text within your document.

12 Click the Headings (CSS) category and leave the settings at their defaults for now. You'll be using CSS to style your heading text later in this book.

13 Click the Title/Encoding category to the left of the Page Properties dialog box to expose more settings. Most of these settings are better left alone unless you know what they do and why you need to change them, with the major exception of the first one: Title.

14 Type **Organic Utopia: About Us** in the Title text field. This sets the title that appears in the title bar of most browser windows. It's also the default title used when a user bookmarks your page.

Leave the Document Type (DTD) set to HTML5. This makes the HTML document HTML5 compliant.

Unicode (UTF-8) will likely be set as the default option. This specifies the encoding used for characters in your page, letting the browser know which character set to use.

The Unicode Normalization Form is likely set to C (Canonical Decomposition). This setting is rarely changed unless you have a specific reason for changing it. Unicode Normalization Forms have to do with the way special characters such as glyphs are rendered on the screen.

The Title/Encoding category allows you to title your page or specify the encoding used.

15 Click the Tracing Image category in the left part of the Page Properties dialog box. A tracing image is a JPEG, GIF, or PNG image that you create in a separate graphics application, such as Adobe Photoshop or Fireworks. It is placed in the background of your page for you to use as a guide to recreate a desired page design.

16 Click the Browse button next to the Tracing image text field. You can also type the path to your image directly into this text field.

17 In the Select Image Source dialog box, navigate to your dw02lessons folder, select the file named **tracing.gif** from the images folder, then click OK (Windows) or Choose (Mac OS).

18 Set the transparency of the tracing image to 50 percent by sliding the Transparency slider to the left.

Place a tracing image in the background of your page.

19 Click Apply to see the results. Tracing Images can be useful tools for building layout. Oftentimes, you can import a page mockup created originally in Photoshop or another application and use it as a visual guideline.

20 When activated, the tracing image replaces any background image you've added to your page, but only in Dreamweaver. Tracing images are never visible when you view your page in a browser. Now that you have a sense of how the tracing feature works, you'll remove it. Select the path within the Tracing Image field and click Delete to remove it.

21 Click OK to close the Page Properties dialog box.

22 Choose File > Save. Now that you've finished setting up your page properties, you'll examine your page in Dreamweaver's three different work view modes.

Work views

In this book's lessons, you'll do most of your work in the Design View, as you're taking advantage of Dreamweaver's visual page layout features. You can, however, easily access the HTML code being written as you work in the Design View and use it to edit your pages through Dreamweaver's other work views. You'll switch views, using the Document toolbar.

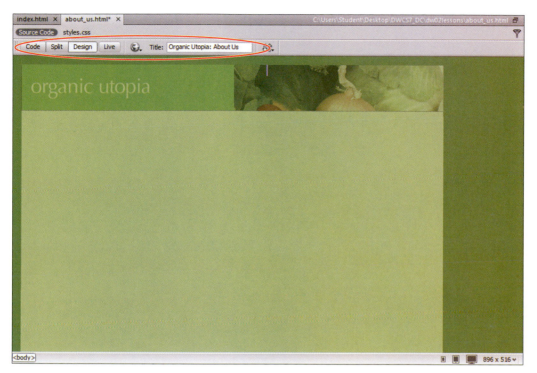

The Document toolbar.

1 In the Document toolbar, click the Design view button if it is not currently selected. Design view is a fully editable, visual representation of your page, similar to what the viewer would see in a browser.

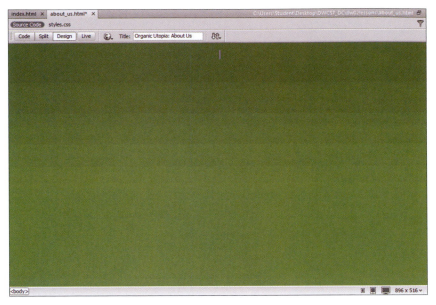

With Design view, you see your page as the viewer will see it.

2 Click the Code view button to switch to the Code view. Your page is now displayed in a hand-coding environment used for writing and editing HTML and other types of code, including JavaScript, PHP, and ColdFusion.

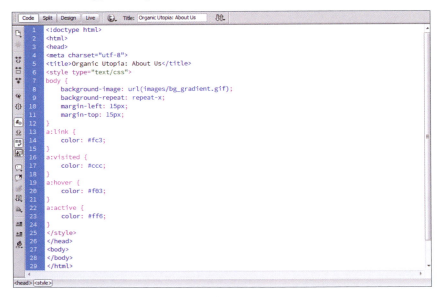

Code view shows the HTML code generated to display your page.

3 Click the Split view button to split the document window between the Code and Design views. This view is a great learning tool, as it displays and highlights the HTML code generated when you make a change visually in Design mode, and vice versa.

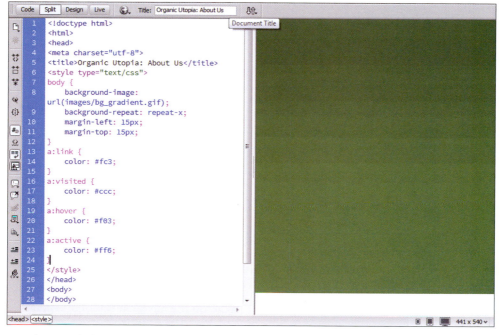

Use Split view to display your page in both modes at once.

4 Switch back to the Design view to continue this lesson.

A deeper look into the Files panel

You have already seen how Dreamweaver populates the Files panel when you define a new site. However, the Files panel is more than just a window into your root folder; it also allows you to manage files locally and transfer them to and from a remote server. The Files panel maintains a parallel structure between local and remote sites, copying and removing files when needed to ensure synchronicity between the two.

The default workspace in Dreamweaver displays the Files panel in the panel grouping to the right of the document window.

When you chose to use the dw02lessons folder as your local root folder earlier in this lesson, Dreamweaver set up a connection to those local files through the Files panel.

Viewing local files

You can view local files and folders on the right side of your screen within the Files panel, whether they're associated with a Dreamweaver site or not.

1   Click the drop-down menu in the upper-left part of the Files panel, and choose Desktop (Windows) or Computer > Desktop folder (Mac OS) to view the current contents of your Desktop folder.

2   Choose Local Disk (C:) (Windows) or Mac HD (Mac OS) from this menu to access the contents of your hard drive.

3   Choose CD Drive (D:) (Windows) from this menu to view the contents of an inserted CD. On a Mac, the CD icon and the name of the CD appear in the menu.

4   Choose Organic_Utopia to return to your local root folder view.

Selecting and editing files

You can select, open, and drag HTML pages, graphics, text, and other files listed in the Files panel to the document window for placement.

1   Double-click the index.html file located in the Files panel. The page opens for editing. Click beneath the heading *The lowly beet*.

2   Click the plus sign (Windows) or arrow (Mac OS) to the left of the images folder to expand it and then click and drag the beets.jpg image file from the Files panel to the index.html document window.

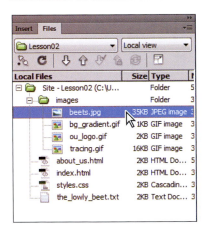

Click and drag the **beets.jpg** *file to* **index.html***.*

If you have an image editor such as Photoshop or Fireworks installed on your computer, you can double-click on the beets.jpg image file to open for editing and optimizing.

3   Double-click on **the_lowly_beet.txt** in the Files panel to open it directly in Dreamweaver.

4 Choose Edit > Select All to select all the text in this file. You could also use the keyboard shortcuts, Ctrl+A (Windows) or Command+A (Mac OS).

5 Choose Edit > Copy to copy the text to the clipboard. You could also use the keyboard shortcuts, Ctrl+C (Windows) or Command+C (Mac OS).

6 Click the index.html tab of the document window to return to the index page. Click your page to the right of the beet image to place an insertion cursor, and press Return once to start a new paragraph.

7 Choose Edit > Paste. You could also use the keyboard shortcuts, Ctrl+V (Windows) or Command+V (Mac OS). The text has now been added to the open page, beneath the image, in the default text color you chose earlier.

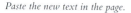

Paste the new text in the page.

8 Choose File > Save and then close this file.

In the next lesson, you will get a chance to work far more with text and images.

Self study

Using your new knowledge of site creation techniques in Dreamweaver, try some of the following tasks to build on your experience:

1 Choose Site > New Site to invoke the Site Setup dialog box, and use it to create a new local site called Practice Site on your desktop. Make sure you understand the difference between creating an empty site from scratch (as you are doing here) and adding a pre-existing site (as you did in the opening exercise of this lesson).

2 Use the File > New command to create a new, blank HTML page and save it to your Practice_Site. Then choose Modify > Page Properties to access the Page Properties dialog box, and experiment with the background, links, margin, and title options available. Finally, switch to the Code and Design view in the document window to view the code generated by your experiment.

Review

Questions

1 What characters should you avoid using when naming files and folders on your site and why?

2 How is the local root folder essential to the creation of your site?

3 Where can you view, select, open, and copy files to and from your local root folder, and to and from remote and/or testing servers?

Answers

1 Avoid using spaces (use underscores instead), periods, slashes, or any other unnecessary punctuation in your site name, as doing so will likely cause the server to misdirect your files.

2 It's essential that you store all your site's resources in your local root folder to ensure that the links you set on your computer will work when your site is uploaded to a server. In order for your links to work properly, all the elements of your site must remain in the same relative location on the web server as on your hard drive.

3 Dreamweaver provides the Files panel to help you both manage files locally and transfer them to and from a remote server. You can view, select, open, and copy files to and from your local root folder, and to and from remote and/or testing servers in this panel.

What you'll learn in this lesson:

- Previewing pages
- Adding text
- Understanding styles
- Creating hyperlinks
- Creating Lists
- Inserting and editing images

Adding Text and Images

Text and images are the building blocks of most websites. In this lesson, you'll learn how to add text and images to web pages to create an immersive and interactive experience for your visitors.

Starting up

Before starting, make sure that your tools and panels are consistent by resetting your workspace. See "Resetting the Dreamweaver workspace" in the Starting up section of this book.

You will work with several files from the dw03lessons folder in this lesson. Make sure that you have loaded the dwlessons folder onto your hard drive from the supplied DVD. See "Loading lesson files" in the Starting up section of this book.

Before you begin, you need to create site settings that point to the dw03lessons folder from the included DVD that contains resources you need for this lesson. Go to Site > New Site, and name the site **dw03lessons**, or, for details on creating a site, refer to Lesson 2, "Setting Up a New Site."

See Lesson 3 in action!

Use the accompanying video to gain a better understanding of how to use some of the features shown in this lesson. The video tutorial for this lesson can be found on the included DVD.

Typography and images on the Web

Dreamweaver CC offers some convenient features for placing images and formatting text. In this lesson, you'll be working with a few pages within a site and adding some photos and text to a simple page for a fictional store.

Adding text

You should already have created a new site, using the dw03lessons folder as your root. In this section, you'll be adding a headline and formatting the text on the events.html page.

1 If it's not already open, launch Dreamweaver CC.

2 Make sure your dw03lessons site is open in the Files panel. If not, open it now.

3 Double-click the **events.html** file in your Files panel to open it in the Design view. Without any formatting, the text seems random and lacks purpose. First, you'll add a headline to give the first paragraph some context.

4 Click to place your cursor in front of the word *There's* in the first paragraph. Type **OrganicUtopia Events** and press Enter (Windows) or Return (Mac OS) to create a line break.

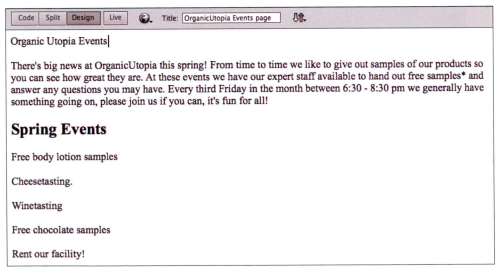

*Type the words **OrganicUtopia Events** and then put them on their own line.*

5   Click and drag to highlight the phrase you just typed. You will now format your text using the Property Inspector. Located at the bottom of the screen, the Property Inspector allows you to format your text using HTML. HTML stands for Hypertext Markup Language. You will learn much more about the use of HTML in the next lesson; however, you will need to have a basic understanding of this language in order to use the Property Inspector to format your text.

6   Locate the Property Inspector at the bottom of your screen. When you are in Design View and working with text, you will see your HTML formatting options. Choose Heading 1 from the Format drop-down menu. The text increases in size and becomes bold. By default, the style of any HTML text formatted as Heading 1 is generic: the color is black and the font-family is Times New Roman.

Use the Format drop-down menu in the Property Inspector to make the selected text a level-1 heading.

Although you are working in Dreamweaver's Design view, you have actually changed the HTML code for this page. Page content such as text is wrapped in opening and closing tags, and everything between these two tags is formatted according to the rules of these tags. The text OrganicUtopia Events originally had an opening and closing tag defining it as a paragraph. The code looked like this:

```
<p>OrganicUtopia Events</p>
```

The first `<p>` is the opening tag for a paragraph, and the second `</p>` is the closing tag for a paragraph. A pair of opening and closing tags in HTML is called an element. So in the previous step, you changed the formatting of the text from a paragraph element to a Heading 1 element, and the HTML code changed to this:

```
<h1>OrganicUtopia Events</h1>
```

Headings are important structural elements in HTML. The largest heading is H1, and the subsequent headings become smaller with H2, H3, and so on. For the next step, you will format this text in order to change the font style of this heading to Helvetica; however, you will not be using HTML to accomplish this, but rather CSS.

7 Click anywhere inside the heading OrganicUtopia Events; you do not need to have it selected. You will find the CSS Designer panel on the bottom-right side of your screen. You will use this panel to create CSS styles to change the appearance of your h1 heading.

The CSS Designer panel, located in the top-right corner of the workspace, is where you will create and edit all of your CSS styles.

8 Click the Add CSS Source button in the Sources menu bar and select Define in Page from the menu. This will allow you to create a new rule for this page.

The Sources menu of the CSS Designer will allow you to create or attach an external style sheet or create an embedded one.

9 Click the Add Selector button in the Selectors menu to create a new CSS style for our h1 heading element. This will create a new text box in the Selectors list where you can add a new selector.

The Selectors menu of the CSS Designer allows you to define new selectors such as tags, classes or IDs.

10 Type **h1** to create a selector for Heading 1 headers and press Enter (Windows) or Return (Mac OS).

The Properties menu of the CSS Designer panel allows you to specify individual CSS properties for your selectors.

11 Click the Add CSS Property button in the Properties pane to create a new CSS property to apply to our h1 heading. This will allow us to add properties to our h1 selector.

12 If necessary, clear the Show Set check box on the Navigation Bar in the Properties pane of the CSS Designer to show all the available CSS properties. Click the Text button in the Properties menu to only show the text-related properties.

13   Locate the font-family property and click default font to the right of font-family to view the font selection menu. Choose Gotham, Helvetica Neue, Helvetica, Arial, sans-serif from the list. Your heading is now styled in Helvetica.

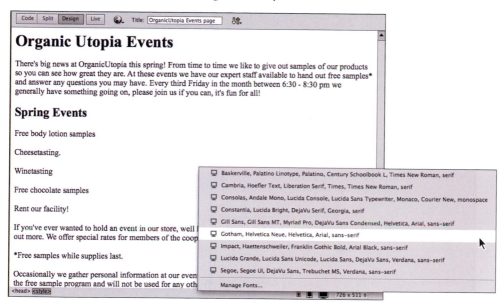

The font-family property allows you to choose a font list from the font selection menu.

14   Click OK. Your heading is now styled in Helvetica.

Dreamweaver allows you to format text in a way that is similar to desktop publishing and word processing applications, but there are important differences to keep in mind. When you chose the styling, Gotham, Helvetica Neue, Helvetica, Arial, sans-serif, they were listed together as one option in the Font drop-down menu. When a web page is rendered in a browser, it typically uses the fonts installed on the user's computer. However Dreamweaver CC uses free web fonts made available through Creative Cloud and powered by TypeKit.

Using web fonts means that anyone viewing your web page will see the page using the fonts you intended. Dreamweaver still provides a font list in the event the user's computer cannot access the web fonts. Assigning multiple fonts allows you to control which font is used if the person viewing your page doesn't have a specific font installed. In this case, if the user doesn't have Helvetica, Arial displays instead. Sans-serif is included as the last option in case the user doesn't have either Helvetica or Arial. A generic font family (either sans-serif or serif) is listed at the end of all the options in the Font drop-down menu.

You will now change the text color using the CSS Designer Panel.

15   Locate the color property in the Properties pane of the CSS Designer panel and click the Set Color button to the right of the label color. When the Swatches panel appears, hover over the color swatches. At the top of the Swatches panel, a different hexadecimal color value appears for each color. When you locate the value labeled #9C3 (an olive green), click once to apply the color.

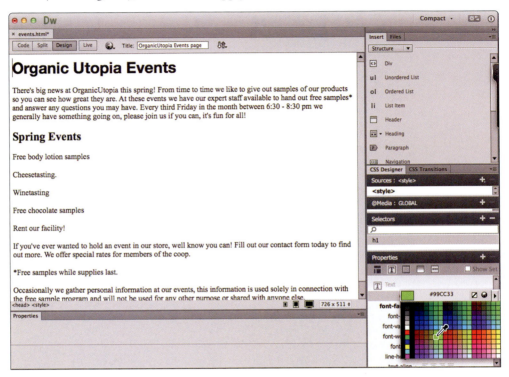

Click the Text Color swatch and choose the #9C3 color from the swatches.

16   Choose File > Save. Keep this file open for the next part of this lesson.

An introduction to styles

You have styled the first element on your page by first formatting the text as a Heading 1 in HTML, and then you changed the font and color using CSS. It's important to realize that every change you make in the Design view creates or modifies the code. In the next exercise, you'll begin to explore the HTML and CSS code behind the Design view. To help put this exercise in context, a little background on HTML and CSS is in order.

The HTML language has been around since the dawn of the Web. It's easiest to think of HTML as the structure behind the pages that are rendered in your web browser. An HTML page at its most basic is a collection of text, images, and sometimes multimedia such as Flash or video files. The different sections of a web page, such as a paragraph, a heading, or a list, are all elements.

CSS is also a language, but it has not been around as long as HTML. In many ways, CSS was created in order to allow HTML to do what it does best: create the structure of a page, but not style. CSS is a simple language that works in combination with HTML to apply style to the content in web pages, such as text, images, tables, and form elements. CSS uses rules, or style instructions, that the HTML elements on your page follow. The most important thing to remember is that HTML and CSS are two separate languages, but they are very closely aligned and work together very well.

In the last exercise, you were introduced to this interplay between HTML and CSS. There was an HTML element for the Heading 1 formatting. In the code it looks like this:

```
<h1>OrganicUtopia Events</h1>
```

That was the HTML element. The CSS rule that defines the appearance of the *<h1>* element looks like this:

```
h1 {
    Gotham, "Helvetica Neue", Helvetica, Arial, sans-serif;
    color: #9C3;
}
```

CSS has a different syntax than HTML. In HTML, tags are defined by angled brackets, and you have opening tags, <h1>, and closing tags, </h1>. In CSS code, you are not working with tags at all, instead you use selectors. In the CSS code above, the h1 is referred to as the selector because it is selecting the HTML element and then declaring some rules for its appearance. Because you've established that HTML and CSS are two separate languages and have different syntax, it's important that you see where this code lives in your web page. You will do this by changing Dreamweaver's workspace.

This exercise is intended to help you understand the relationship between HTML and CSS code that is created in Dreamweaver, and is not necessarily the way you will always work in the program. Many people will work in the Design view most of the time, but the Split view you are about to use is very helpful for learning the languages of HTML and CSS.

1   Click the Split button in the Document toolbar at the top of your page to open up the Split view. The Split view allows you to see your code and the design of your page simultaneously.

2 Click quickly three times in the paragraph beneath OrganicUtopia Events in the Design view. In the Code view the text is highlighted between the opening and closing paragraph tags. As noted above, this is referred to as the paragraph element.

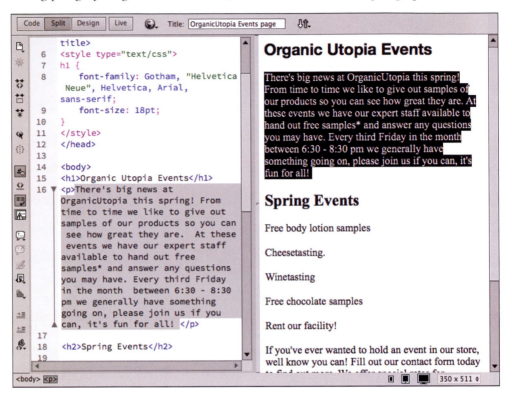

A paragraph highlighted in the Split view.

You will now change the font size of your paragraphs.

3 Click <style> in the Sources menu to alert Dreamweaver that you want to add another embedded style. Click the Add Selector button in the Selectors menu to create a new CSS style for our p element.

4 In this case, Dreamweaver has recognized that you have selected text in a paragraph within the body tag of your page so it prefills the text box with body p. Select the body and delete it leaving the letter p to create a selector for our paragraph. Then press Enter (Windows) or Return (Mac OS).

5 If necessary, clear the Show Set check box on the Navigation Bar in the Properties pane of the CSS Designer panel to show all the available CSS properties. Click the Text button In the Properties menu to limit the choices and only show the text-related properties.

In this case, the font size is set to 18 pixels. Now let's look at the CSS code that is defining this font size.

6   Locate the font-size property in the Properties pane of the CSS Designer and click medium to the right of the property label. Select px from the menu and enter the number **18** in the text box that appears. Press Enter (Windows) or Return (Mac OS) to apply the change.

7   Within the Code view of the split screen is all the HTML and CSS code that defines the appearance of this page. On the right side of the Code view, scroll up by clicking the up arrow or by clicking the scroll bar and dragging upward. Toward the top of the page, you are looking for a few lines of code that look like this:

```
<style type="text/css">
h1 {
    font-family: Gotham, "Helvetica Neue", Helvetica, Arial, sans-serif;
    color: #9C3;
}
p {
    font-size:18px;
}
</style>
```

Between the two `<style>` tags are all the CSS rules you have created up to this point. Previously, you learned that CSS has a different syntax than HTML: because all the CSS rules are actually contained within an opening `<style>` tag and a closing `</style>` tag, they are allowed to have a different syntax. Additionally, the style tag itself is nested inside an opening and closing `<head>` tag. In the world of HTML, nothing contained within head tags is rendered on a web browser's screen. You will explore this further in the next lesson, but this is referred to as an internal style sheet.

You will now see that changes made in Dreamweaver's Code view apply to the Design view as well.

8   In the Code view, locate the line `font-size:18px` in the rule for p, and select the value 18 by clicking and dragging over it. Type **14** to change the value. Although you made a change in the Code view, it has not yet been automatically updated in your Design view. You need to refresh your page in order to see the changes occur in the Design view.

9 In the Property Inspector, click the Refresh button to apply the changes; your paragraph text becomes smaller.

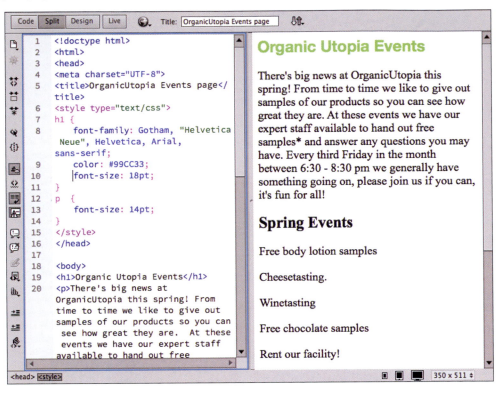

Changes made in the Code view are reflected in the Design view after clicking the Refresh button.

You can also click once inside the Design view for the page to refresh automatically.

On the Web, font sizes are specified differently than they are in print. The numerical choices in the Size drop-down menu refer to pixels instead of points. Also, the xx-small through larger options could seem oddly generic if you are accustomed to the precision of print layout. Because web pages are displayed on a variety of monitors and browsers, relative measurements can be a useful way for designers to plan ahead for inevitable discrepancies in the rendering of pages.

10 Click inside the first paragraph in the Design view. You will now change the color of the paragraph slightly to a dark gray rather than the default pure black. Click the p selector in the Selectors pane of the CSS Designer panel so that we can modify the properties for our paragraph element.

11 If necessary, clear the Show Set check box on the Navigation Bar in the Properties pane of the CSS Designer panel to show all the available CSS properties. Click the Text button in the Properties menu to only show the text-related properties.

12 Locate the color property in the Properties pane of the CSS Designer and click the Set Color button to the right of the label color. When the Swatches panel appears, locate the dark gray swatch in the top-left corner of the palette, which is hexadecimal color #666. Click the swatch to apply the color. Notice that not only does the appearance in the Design view change, but in your Code view a new line of CSS has also been created (color: #666666).

Working in the Split view can be a great way to learn about hand-coding without diving in completely. Even if you're not quite comfortable editing code, keeping an eye on the code that Dreamweaver writes for you can give you a better understanding of how things like CSS affect your web pages.

13 Click the Design view button to return to Design view.

14 Choose File > Save. Keep this file open for the next part of this lesson.

For more information about Cascading Style Sheets, see the Web Design with HTML and CSS Digital Classroom *book available in electronic and print formats.*

Previewing pages in a web browser

Viewing your pages in the Design view is helpful, but visitors to your site will be using a web browser to access your site. In Lesson 1, "Dreamweaver CC Jumpstart," you learned how browsers use HTML code to render a page. Unfortunately, not every browser renders HTML code in exactly the same way, so it's important to test-drive your pages in a number of different browsers to check for inconsistencies and basic functionality.

Next, you'll use Dreamweaver's Preview in Browser feature to see how the OrganicUtopia site looks in a web browser.

1   With **events.html** open in Dreamweaver, choose File > Preview in Browser and select a browser from the available options. This list varies, depending on the browsers you have installed on your hard drive.

Preview in Browser allows you to see how a selected browser would render your page.

The options found under File > Preview in Browser can be customized by choosing File > Preview in Browser > Edit Browser List.

2   When **events.html** opens in the browser of your choice, look for differences between the Design view preview and the version rendered by your browser. At this stage, there shouldn't be anything too surprising, but there could be subtle differences in spacing and font style. Close your web browser.

There is another method to preview your pages: the Live View feature. Live View allows you to preview your page without having to leave the Dreamweaver workspace. You can think of Live View as a browser within Dreamweaver (in fact, it is the same WebKit rendering engine found in browsers such as Apple's Safari and Google's Chrome, among others).

3   Click the Live button located in the Document toolbar at the top of your page. You will not see a dramatic difference, but your text could shift slightly. Select the first heading in the window and try to delete it; you will be unable to, because Live View is a non-editable workspace. However, Live View does allow you to edit your page when you are in Split view. You are allowed to edit in the Code view and changes will be reflected in real time. An additional advantage is that your document does not have to be saved in order to see the changes.

When Live View is enabled, Dreamweaver simulates a web browser.

4   Click the Live button again to deactivate this view. While Live View is a useful addition to Dreamweaver, it does not replace the need to preview your page in a browser. Web pages might be rendered differently depending on your visitor's browser, and so it is a good habit to check your page occasionally as you make changes to your design.

Understanding hyperlinks

When people visit a website, they usually expect to see more than one page. Imagine trying to shop for a new book by your favorite author on a site that consisted of nothing more than a single order form with every book offered by a retailer like *Amazon.com*. This might seem absurd, but without hyperlinks you wouldn't have much choice.

Hyperlinks make the Web a truly interactive environment. They allow the user to freely navigate throughout a website, or jump from one site to another. There are a number of ways to create links in Dreamweaver, but before you get started, you should be aware of some fundamental facts.

Links rely on directory paths to locate files. A directory path is simply a description of a file's location that can be understood by a computer. A classic, real-world example is an address. If you wanted to send a letter to your friend Sally in Florida, you would have to specify the state, city, street, and house number where Sally can be found. If Sally lived at 123 Palm Street in Orlando, the path would be:

Florida/Orlando/123 Palm Street/Sally

This simply means that inside Florida, inside Orlando, in the house numbered 123 on a street named Palm Street, you can find a person named Sally. Hyperlinks follow the same logic:

www.somewebsitesomewhere.com/photos/mydog.jpg

This URL address is a link to a JPEG image named mydog.jpg, which is inside a folder named photos on a website named *somewebsitesomewhere.com*.

Creating hyperlinks

Later in this lesson, you'll be creating a gallery page to showcase some of the sample products mentioned in the main paragraph. Before you work on that page, you'll link it to the home page by creating a hyperlink. If you are not already in Design view, select Design view now.

1 In the Property Inspector, click the HTML button to access the HTML properties.

2 In the first paragraph, highlight the word *products* in the second sentence.

3 In the Property Inspector, type **products.html** in the Link text field. Press Enter (Windows) or Return (Mac OS). The highlighted word automatically becomes underlined. It is important to note that we have created this page for you and it is currently inside your site folder, you are simply linking to it.

Type **products.html** *into the Link text field in the Property Inspector.*

4 Choose File > Save and then File > Preview in Browser.

5   Click the new products link. The products page appears in your browser window. This is because a previously existing page named products.html was located in this folder.

Now visitors can easily navigate to the products page, but what happens when they want to go back to the events page? It looks like you'll need another link.

6   Return to Dreamweaver and double-click products.html in the Files panel. Click to the right of the word Produce and press Enter (Windows) or Return (Mac OS) to create a new line. Choose Insert > Hyperlink to open the Hyperlink dialog box.

The Hyperlink dialog box is one of the many ways to create a link in Dreamweaver. It offers all the options found in the Property Inspector, with a few additions.

7   Type **Events** in the Text field.

The Hyperlink dialog box is one of the many ways to create links in Dreamweaver.

8   Click the Browse button to the right of the Link text field to open the Select File dialog box. The dw03lessons folder you defined as the root for this site should be selected for you by default. If not, click the Site Root button. Select **events.html** and click OK (Windows) or Open (Mac OS).

9   Click inside the Title field and type **Organic Utopia events page**. Titles are strictly optional for hyperlinks, but they improve accessibility for users with assistive technologies, such as Screen Readers. Additionally, adding titles to your hyperlinks can also improve your site's search engine rankings. Click OK to commit the changes; notice that a link to events.html has been created for you using the text entered into the Text field in the Hyperlink dialog box.

10   Choose File > Save and keep this file open for the next part of this lesson.

Relative versus absolute hyperlinks

After reading about the fundamentals of hyperlinks and directory paths a few pages ago, you might be surprised by the simplicity of linking **events.html** and **products.html**. Instead of entering a long directory path in the Link text fields, you merely typed the name of the file. This kind of link is called a relative link. Let's go back to the address example to see how this works.

Remember Sally from Orlando? Imagine you were already standing on Palm Street, where she lives. If you called her for directions to her house, she probably wouldn't begin by telling you how to get to Florida. At this point, all you need is a house number. Relative links work the same way. Because events.html and products.html both reside in the dw03lessons folder, you don't need to tell the browser where to find this folder.

Now you'll create an absolute link that will allow visitors to access the Adobe website to learn more about Dreamweaver CC.

1   Click the **events.html** tab above the Document toolbar to bring the page forward. Scroll down to the bottom of the page if necessary. Using the Design view window, create a new line at the bottom of the page after the text that reads "Occasionally we gather...", and type **This page was created with Adobe Dreamweaver**.

2   Highlight the words Adobe Dreamweaver and in the Common section of the Insert panel on the right side of the screen, click the Hyperlink icon to open the Hyperlink dialog box.

The Hyperlink icon in the Insert panel is another convenient way to create links.

3 The Hyperlink dialog box opens. Notice that Adobe Dreamweaver has been entered into the Text field for you. In the Link text field, type **http://www.adobe.com/ products/dreamweaver.html**. Make sure to include the colon and the appropriate number of forward slashes.

The absolute link *http://www.adobe.com/products/dreamweaver.html* instructs the browser to find a website named *adobe.com* on the World Wide Web. Then the browser looks for a file named dreamweaver.html located inside a folder named products.

You do not have to type the absolute hyperlinks if you have the website open in your browser. In your web browser, select the address in the address bar, copy it, and then paste it into the Link field in Dreamweaver.

4 Choose _blank from the Target drop-down menu. Choosing the _blank option will cause the hyperlink to the Adobe website to open in a new, blank browser window or tab (depending on the browser).

Set the target window for the hyperlink to open in a blank browser window or tab.

5 Click OK to close the Hyperlink dialog box. Choose File > Save, then File > Preview in Browser, or click the Preview/Debug in Browser button (●) in the Document toolbar.

6 Click the Adobe Dreamweaver text. Unlike the Events and Products links you created earlier, this link causes your browser to open a new tab or window, and it is pointing to an external web page on the Internet.

7 Close your browser and keep this file open; you will be adding to it in the next exercise.

Linking to an e-mail address

Absolute and relative links can be used to access web pages, but it's also possible to link to an e-mail address. Instead of opening a new web page, an e-mail link opens up the default mail program on a visitor's computer and populates the address field with the address you specify when creating the link. As you can imagine, this kind of link can work differently depending on how your visitors have configured their computers.

In the previous part of this lesson, you gave the visitor a link to some information on Dreamweaver. Now you'll link them to an e-mail address where they can get some information on learning Dreamweaver from the folks who wrote this book.

1   Place your cursor at the end of the last line, then press and hold your Shift key and press Enter (Windows) or Return (Mac OS). Instead of creating a new paragraph, this creates a line break, or a soft return, and the text begins immediately below the previous line. Type **Contact info@agitraining.com for information on Dreamweaver classes**.

2   Highlight the text *info@agitraining.com* and click the Email Link button in the Insert panel.

3   The Email Link dialog box opens with both fields automatically populated. Click OK. You can preview this page in your browser. Remember that if you click the link, your e-mail client will begin to launch.

The Email Link dialog box allows you to link to an e-mail address.

Creating lists

Bulleted lists might be familiar to you if you have worked with word processing or desktop publishing applications. Lists are a helpful way to present information to a reader without the formal constraints of a paragraph. They are especially important on the Web. Studies indicate that people typically skim web pages instead of reading them from beginning to end. Creating lists will make it easier for your visitors to get the most from your website without sifting through several paragraphs of text.

1   On the **events.html** page, click and drag to highlight the four lines below Spring Events.

2   Make sure you have the HTML button selected in the Property Inspector at the bottom of your page, and click the Unordered List button. The highlighted text becomes indented, and a bullet point is placed at the beginning of each line.

Spring Events

- Free body lotion samples
- Cheesetasting
- Winetasting
- Free chocolate samples

Use the Unordered List button in the Property Inspector to create a bulleted list.

3   Click the Ordered List button to the right of the Unordered List button. The bullets change to sequential numbers.

4   Choose Format > List > Properties to open the List Properties dialog box. Choose Bulleted List from the List type drop-down menu to return to your first style of list. The Numbered List and Bulleted List options in the List type drop-down menu also allow you to switch between ordered and unordered lists.

5   From the Style drop-down menu, choose Square. This changes the default circular bullets to square bullets. Click OK to exit the List Properties dialog box.

Change the bullet style to square in the List Properties dialog box.

You might have noticed that the four lines of text in your list have lost their style. They are slightly larger than your paragraphs and they are black, not dark gray. This is because a style has been defined for paragraphs, but not an unordered list. You will now create a new CSS rule for the appearance of all unordered lists in the document. After you define the properties, all text formatted as an unordered list will appear the same.

6   With all four lines still highlighted, click `<style>` in the Sources menu of the CSS Designer panel.

7   Click the Add Selector button in the Selectors menu to create a new CSS style for the ul element.

8   In this case, Dreamweaver has recognized that you have selected text in an unordered list within the body tag of your page so it prefills the text box with body ul li; ul is the tag for unordered list. Replace this text by typing **ul** to create a selector for our unordered list. Then press Enter (Windows) or Return (Mac OS).

9   Locate the font-size property in the Properties pane of the CSS Designer panel and click medium to the right of the property label. Select px from the menu and enter the number **14** in the text box that appears. Press Enter (Windows) or Return (Mac OS) to apply the change.

   Now you need to change the color of the unordered list to match the color of your paragraph.

10 Locate the color property in the Properties pane of the CSS Designer panel and click the Set Color button to the right of the label color. When the Swatches panel appears, locate the same dark gray swatch, hexadecimal color #666. Click the swatch to apply the color.

11 Choose File > Save. Leave this file open for the next part of this lesson.

Using the Text Insert panel

There are a number of ways to format text in Dreamweaver. One method you haven't explored yet is the Text Insert panel. Because most of the options available in the Text Insert panel are also available in the Property Inspector, you might find it more convenient to use the Property Inspector for common tasks. However, you should be aware of the Characters menu located in the Text Insert panel. One of the most common items in the Characters menu used on the Web is the copyright symbol, ©. You will now insert a copyright notification at the bottom of your Events page.

1   Click to the left of the sentence *This page was created with Adobe Dreamweaver* and type **2013** and then add a space.

2   Click before the text 2013 to insert your cursor.

3 Click the menu at the top of the Insert panel on the right side of your page and choose Common. Scroll all the way to the bottom of the resulting list and choose Copyright from the Character menu to insert the Copyright symbol to the beginning of the line.

The copyright symbol can be inserted from the Insert menu.

4 Highlight the last two lines on your page, beginning with the newly inserted copyright symbol and ending with Dreamweaver classes. You are going to set these two lines apart from the rest of the page by italicizing them. Layout considerations such as headers and footers will be discussed throughout the following lessons in this book, but for now you can use the Property Inspector to italicize these two lines.

5 Click the Italic button in the Property Inspector to apply an inline italic style to your text.

Additionally, you could have selected the text and chosen Insert > HTML > Text Objects to accomplish the same thing.

6 Choose File > Save.

Inserting images

Images are an essential part of most web pages. Just as lists make content friendlier and more accessible, images help to give your visitors the rich, visual experience that they've come to expect on the Web. However, before you learn to insert images, you will briefly learn about web graphics.

Image resolution

While it is possible to resize images with Dreamweaver, it's generally not a good idea. Specifying the width and height of an image in the Property Inspector changes the display size of the image, but it does not resample the image the way a graphic processing application like Photoshop does. For example, a JPEG image that is 150 pixels by 150 pixels might have a file size of 30k. You could resize this image in Dreamweaver by 50% and the result would be a thumbnail image displayed at 75 pixels by 75 pixels. However, even though the image is visually smaller, the file size remains the same. A visitor to your website still must download the 30k file which translates to slower loading time for the image (and possibly the page) and a potentially poor user experience, especially if they have low bandwidth.

Image formats

The three most common image formats on the Web are JPEG, GIF, and PNG. While an exhaustive description of how each of these formats compresses data is beyond the scope of this book, a general overview can help you avoid some common pitfalls.

The JPEG format was created by a committee named the Joint Photographic Experts Group. Its sole purpose is to compress photographic images. Specifically, it uses lossy compression, which means that it selectively discards information, to reduce the size of a file. When you save a JPEG, you decide how much information you are willing to sacrifice by selecting a quality level. A high-quality image preserves more information and results in a larger file size. A low-quality image discards more information, but produces a smaller file size. The goal is to reduce file size as much as possible without creating distortion and artifacts.

Because JPEGs were designed to handle photographic images, they can significantly reduce the size of images containing gradients and soft edges, without producing noticeable degradation. However, reproducing sharp edges and solid areas of color often requires a higher quality setting.

The GIF format was created by CompuServe. GIF is an acronym for Graphics Interchange Format. Unlike the JPEG format, GIFs do not use lossy compression. Instead, GIFs rely on a maximum of 256 colors to reduce the size of images. This means that images with a limited number of colors can be reproduced without degradation. Logos, illustrations, and line drawings are well-suited to this format. Unlike JPEGs, GIFs excel at reproducing sharp edges and solid areas of color. However, because photographic elements such as gradients and soft edges require a large number of colors to appear convincing, GIF images containing these elements look choppy and posterized.

The PNG format has become increasingly popular on the Web in recent years because it incorporates many of the best features of JPEGs and GIFs. The PNG format is closer to GIFs in that it offers lossless compression and comes in two categories: 8 bit and 24 bit. This means it can be used quite effectively for simple graphics as well as continuous tone photographic images. A PNG also offers better transparency features than a GIF, most significantly the support of alpha channels. For many years the adoption of PNGs (especially the use of the transparency) was held back because Internet Explorer 6 ignored the transparency. As the number of people using this browser continues to decline, the PNG format is being used more frequently. For more information on web graphics see the *Web Design with HTML and CSS Digital Classroom* book, which is available in both print and electronic formats.

Creating a simple gallery page

Now that you have a better understanding of the types of images that are appropriate for use on your website, it's time to build the products.html page that you linked to earlier in this lesson.

1   Double-click **products.html** in the Files panel or click the tab, as it's still open. Place your cursor after the word Produce and press Enter (Windows) or Return (Mac OS) to create a new line.

2   Choose Insert > Image > Image. The Select Image Source dialog box appears. If your site folder does not open automatically, click the Site Root button, and then double-click the images folder. Select **beets.jpg** and click OK (Windows) or Open (Mac OS).

3   In the Property Inspector, locate the Alt field and type **Beets** in the text box. Press Enter (Windows) or Return (Mac OS).

In previous versions of Dreamweaver, the Image Tag Accessibility Attributes dialog box would open upon inserting an image. Dreamweaver CC instead inserts an empty value for the Alt attribute of the <img> tag. Including a description of the inserted image recommended by the Web Content Accessibility Guidelines (WCAG) published by the W3C. For more information on the WCAG, visit http://www.w3.org/TR/WCAG10/. It provides information about the images to visually impaired visitors using screen readers. Also, Alt text is displayed in place of images on some handheld devices, and browsers where images are disabled.

4 Click the Split button in the Document toolbar to view the code that was written by Dreamweaver when you inserted beets.jpg. An `<img>` tag was created, with four attributes. The src attribute is a relative link to the .jpg file in your images folder. The alt attribute is the alternate text string created in the last step. The width and height attributes are simply the width and height of the image, which have automatically been added by Dreamweaver. Click the Design button to return to this view.

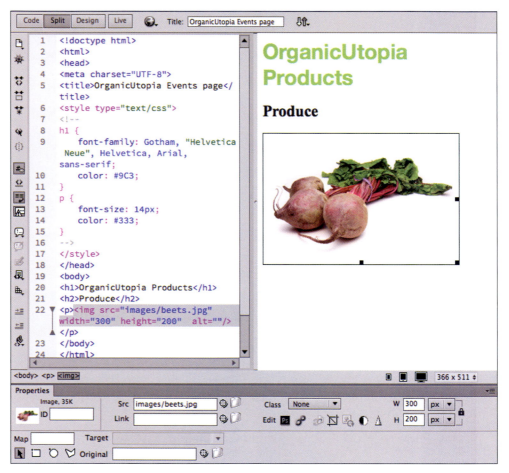

Dreamweaver creates an `<img>` tag with a number of attributes when you insert an image.

5   Double-click the images folder in the Files panel to reveal its contents. In the document window, click to the right of the beets image and press Enter (Windows) or Return (Mac OS) to create a new line. Click and drag **cucumbers.jpg** from your Files panel directly below the beets image in the Design view.

6   In the Properties panel, locate the Alt field and type **Cucumbers** in the text box. Press Enter (Windows) or Return (Mac OS).

7   Click to the right of the cucumber image to place your cursor, and press Enter (Windows) or Return (Mac OS) to create a new line. To add the last image, you'll use the Insert panel on the right side of your page. Click the menu at the top of the Insert panel and choose Common from the list. Click the Images:Image option, and the Select Image Source dialog box appears.

Choose Image from the Images drop-down menu in the Common section of the Insert panel.

8   Navigate to the images folder if necessary, select the **eggplants.jpg** image, and click OK (Windows) or Open (Mac OS).

9   Type **Eggplants** in the Alt field of the Properties panel. Press Enter (Windows) or Return (Mac OS).

10 Choose File > Save and leave products.html open for the next part of this lesson.

Linking images

Often, gallery pages on the Web contain small thumbnail images that are linked to larger, high-resolution images. Like many web conventions, there are practical reasons for this format. Because all the images on a gallery page must be downloaded by visitors in order to view the page, small images are necessary to keep the page from taking too long to load. Additionally, a user's screen isn't large enough to accommodate multiple large pictures at one time. Giving your visitor a way to preview which pictures they would like to see on a larger scale makes the page more user friendly and interactive.

1   In products.html, click the image of the beets to select it. In the Property Inspector, type **images/beets_large.jpg** into the Link text field. Press Enter (Windows) or Return (Mac OS).

Manually typing in the link is one way to link to the image, but can introduce errors. Here is a second method using Dreamweaver's Point to File feature.

2   Click the image of the cucumbers to select it. In the Property Inspector, locate the Point to File icon (⊕) next to the Link text field. Click and drag this icon into the Files panel. An arrow with a target at the end follows your cursor. As you hover over items in the Files panel, they become highlighted. Release the mouse while hovering over the **cucumbers_large.jpg** file.

With the Point to File feature, you can click and drag to create a link.

3   Select the image of the eggplants and use the Point to File icon to link it to **eggplants_large.jpg**.

4   Choose File > Save, and then File > Preview in Browser. Click the thumbnails to see the large versions of each image. You'll have to use your browser's back button to get back to the products page.

Editing images

Although it's best to make adjustments to your images using a professional graphics-editing program like Adobe Photoshop, sometimes that's not an option. Dreamweaver offers a number of editing options, including an Edit link that allows you to quickly open a selected image in the graphics editor of your choice.

The Edit button can be customized in the File Types/Editors section of the Preferences dialog box, found under the Dreamweaver drop-down menu. You can use this section to add or subtract programs from the list of available editors, and set programs as the primary choice for handling specific file extensions.

Adjusting brightness and contrast

Now you'll use Dreamweaver's Brightness and Contrast button to lighten up the eggplants image on your products page.

1   Click the **eggplants.jpg** image in products.html to select it, then click the Brightness and Contrast button in the Property Inspector.

Select the Brightness and Contrast button in the Property Inspector.

A warning dialog box appears, indicating that you are about to make permanent changes to the selected image. Click OK.

2   When the Brightness/Contrast dialog box appears, drag the Brightness slider to 20 or type **20** in the text field to the right of the slider.

3   Drag the Contrast slider to 10 or type **10** in the text field to the right of the slider.

4   Click the *Preview* check box in the lower-right corner to see the original photo. Click the Preview check box again to see the changes. Click OK.

While changing the brightness and contrast is very convenient in Dreamweaver, you should be sure you are not performing the corrections on the original, as these changes are destructive.

Optimizing images

In most cases, if you need to have fine control over the appearance of your graphics, you should open an image editor designed for that purpose. Both Dreamweaver and Photoshop are made by Adobe, and you'll see some of the integration between the two in this exercise. However, sometimes you will just want to make a quick-and-easy change to a graphic. In this scenario, you can use the Edit Image Settings option in the Property Inspector.

You'll use this feature to change the optimization of the belgianchocolate.jpg image, but before you make any permanent changes, you'll duplicate this image in the Files panel. It's good practice to save copies of your image files before making permanent changes. Later, you'll use this backup copy to undo your changes.

1   In the Files panel, click the **belgianchocolate.jpg** file to select it. Drag it to your document window to place it beneath the other images inside your web page.

2   Go back to the Files panel and click the belgianchocolate.jpg file to select it again. From the Files panel menu ( ), select Edit > Duplicate. A new file named **belgianchocolate – Copy.jpg** appears in the list of files inside the images folder.

3   Click on the **belgianchocolate.jpg** image in the document window to make sure it is selected, then click the Edit Image Settings button ( ) in the Property Inspector at the bottom of your page. The Image Optimization window appears. This window allows you to either choose from a number of compression presets, or to create your own. Currently, the format is set to JPEG because Dreamweaver recognizes the type of file you have selected. Notice in the bottom-left corner that the file size is listed; in this case, 31k. Pay attention to this number as it plays a role in the rest of this exercise.

The Image Optimization window appears when you click the Edit Image Settings button.

4   Click the preset menu and choose GIF for Background Images. The optimization settings appear. Click the Color menu and choose 4. The image of the chocolate changes to a preview of these settings, and the image has become flat with most of the detail removed. Notice that the file size has changed to 3K.

This tells you that you would achieve a tremendous reduction in file size, but it would occur at the expense of image quality. In fact, the GIF file format is not generally suited for photographic images. You will now try a custom setting.

5 Click the Format menu and choose JPEG from the list. You now have a slider for quality, the default value is 80 and you can see the file size has changed to 9K. Drag the slider to the left to a quality of 10 and notice that the image quality changes instantly. Again, this is too drastic a trade-off. Drag the quality slider to 90. The image looks slightly better than it did at a quality of 80, and you have a file size of around 14K (which is approximately 50% of the original image).

Click OK to commit the change. Note that this method of optimization is risky if you do not have a backup. (Recall the backup created in step 1.)

6 You can also choose to do your optimization in Photoshop. Click the cucumbers image, and then in the Property Inspector, click the Photoshop icon if available. Note that you must have Photoshop installed for this icon to be visible. As noted earlier, you can always change the photo editor that Dreamweaver uses by opening Edit > Preferences > File Types/Editors (PC) or Dreamweaver > Preferences > File Types/ Editors (Mac), and then changing the application associated with images.

Click the Photoshop icon to launch Photoshop.

7 The image will open in Photoshop, and then you can make any changes you want, as well as use the more in-depth controls of the Save for Web feature. We will not walk through that process now, so you can close this image and return to Dreamweaver.

Updating images

Assuming you have a backup copy of an image, it is possible to swap one image for another. To swap out the image, you'll simply change the Src attribute using the Property Inspector. But first, it's a good idea to rename the duplicate image.

1 Right-click (Windows) or Ctrl+click (Mac OS) the file named **belgianchocolate – Copy.jpg** in the Files panel and choose File > Rename. Type **belgianchocolate_original.jpg** and press Enter (Windows) or Return (Mac OS).

2 Click the chocolate image in the Design view to select it. In the Property Inspector at the bottom of your page, highlight the text that reads *images/belgianchocolate.jpg* in the Src text field.

3 Click and drag the Point to File icon to the **belgianchocolate_original.jpg** image you just renamed. The compressed image is replaced with the copy you made earlier.

4 Choose File > Save.

Self study

To practice styling text with the CSS Designer Panel, create styles for the text in events.html. If you're feeling bold, try copying the CSS styles from the Code view.

To make the thumbnail links in **products.html** open in a new window, set their target attributes to _blank in the Property Inspector.

Try adding your own photos to the products page. Remember to be careful when resizing them!

Review

Questions

1   Of the two most common image formats used on the Web, which is better suited for saving a logo?

2   If an inserted image is too small, can you make it larger by increasing its size in the Property Inspector?

3   How do you insert a copyright symbol (©) in Dreamweaver?

Answers

1   Because logos usually contain a lot of hard edges and solid areas of color, the GIF format is the most appropriate choice.

2   Yes, it is possible to increase the display size of an image; however, doing so reduces image quality.

3   Use the Characters drop-down menu in the Text tab of the Insert bar to insert a copyright symbol.

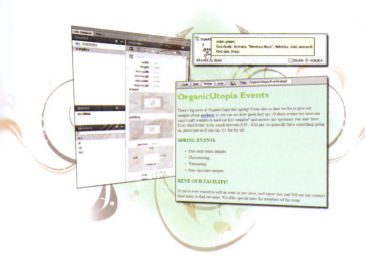

What you'll learn in this lesson:

- An introduction to Cascading Style Sheets (CSS)

- Using the CSS Designer panel

- Creating tag and class styles

- Styling text and hyperlinks

- Creating external style sheets

Styling Your Pages with CSS

Many years ago, creating a beautiful web page required a lot of work, using the limited capabilities of HTML tags. The introduction of Cascading Style Sheets changes the way pages are created, giving designers an extraordinary amount of control over text and page formatting, as well as the ability to freely position content anywhere on a page. In this lesson, you'll focus on the fundamentals of working with CSS in Dreamweaver.

Starting up

Before starting, make sure that your tools and panels are consistent by resetting your workspace. See "Resetting the Dreamweaver workspace" in the Starting up section of this book.

You will work with several files from the dw04lessons folder in this lesson. Make sure that you have loaded the dwlessons folder onto your hard drive from the supplied DVD. See "Loading lesson files" in the Starting up section of this book.

Before you begin, you need to create site settings that point to the dw04lessons folder from the included DVD that contains resources you need for these lessons. Go to Site > New Site, or, for details on creating a site, refer to Lesson 2, "Setting Up a New Site."

See Lesson 4 in action!

Use the accompanying video to gain a better understanding of how to use some of the features shown in this lesson. The video tutorial for this lesson can be found on the included DVD.

What are Cascading Style Sheets?

In the last lesson you had a brief introduction to Cascading Style Sheets (CSS); now you will dive in a bit deeper. CSS is a simple language that works alongside HTML to apply formatting to content in web pages, such as text, images, tables, and form elements. Developed by the World Wide Web Consortium (W3C), CSS creates rules, or style instructions, that elements on your page follow. There are three locations for CSS: (1) An internal style sheet where the styles are located directly within the `<head>` section of an HTML document, (2) inline styles (the CSS is located side by side with your HTML tags), or (3) An external style sheet where styles are located in an external file that can be linked to any number of HTML pages. If you completed Lesson 3, "Adding Text and Images," you have had experience with the first option.

A style sheet is a collection of CSS rules; typically, rules that belong to a specific project, theme, or section are grouped together, but you can group rules in any way you want. You can place styles directly within your page using the `<style>` tag or in an external .css file that is linked to your document with the `<link>` tag. A single page or set of pages can use several style sheets at once.

You can apply CSS rules selectively to any number of elements on a page, or use them to modify the appearance of an existing HTML tag. Each CSS rule is composed of one or more declarations. A declaration contains both a property and a value. Examples of properties include color, width, and font size. Examples of values for these properties are green, 450px, and 12px, respectively. Dreamweaver's CSS Styles panel lets you easily view and modify any of these properties and values and change the appearance of your page in real time.

This sample rule is composed of three declarations that control the color, typeface, and size of any text to which it's applied. In the simplest example, the CSS rules define the appearance of an H1 or heading element:

```
h1 {
    color: red;
    font-family: Gotham, "Helvetica Neue", Helvetica, Arial, sans-serif;
    font-size: 28px;
}
```

Here is the result of the preceding code snippet applied to text:

CSS-styled text shown in the Design view.

CSS rules can affect properties as simple as typeface, size, and color, or as complex as positioning and visibility. Dreamweaver uses CSS as the primary method of styling page text and elements, and its detailed CSS Styles panel makes it possible to create and manage styles at any point during a project.

CSS replaces inefficient HTML styling

Before CSS came along, you styled text on a page using the `<font>` tag in HTML; you could wrap this tag around any paragraph, phrase, or tidbit of text to apply color, or to set the font size and typeface. Although it was reliable, it was also very inefficient. Imagine a page with 10 paragraphs. Using the `<font>` tag, you would have to add the `<font>` tag 10 times, even if the color, size, and typeface values were exactly the same. Although the `<font>` tag is not in use as much anymore, you should still understand how it works. You will now open an HTML document in which the list is styled using the `<font>` tag.

1   In your Files panel located in the lower-right corner of your screen, locate and double-click the HTML file named **FontTagList.html** to open it in the document window.

2   Click the Code view button in the Document toolbar at the top of the document window. Notice that the `<font>` tag is used to style the items in the bulleted list.

Here, a `<font>` tag is used to format each bullet point. If you add more bullet points, you'll need to use more `<font>` tags to keep the style of those bullets consistent with the others.

As you can see, there's a lot of repetition in this code.

3   Click the Design view button on the Document toolbar. Position your cursor at the end of the last bulleted item, press Enter (Windows) or Return (Mac OS) to add a new bullet point, and type **Peppers**. You see that the text reverts to the default typeface, size, and color. You would have to add a new <font> tag with the same attributes as the others to get it to match. If you wanted to change an attribute such as the color for all the bullet points, you would have to adjust each tag separately. In early versions of Dreamweaver, there were actually ways to perform global changes using HTML; however, these were sometimes tricky to control, and CSS offers a better solution in any case.

You could lose the formatting between bullet points when using <font> tags.

4   Choose File > Save to save your work, then choose File > Close.

The benefits of CSS styling

CSS introduces a new level of control and flexibility far beyond the <font> tags in HTML. A significant benefit of CSS is the ability to apply consistent formatting of elements across one or all pages in a website. In the following exercises you will learn a few different ways to create CSS rules that affect the style of your text. The first method you will explore involves creating tag- or element-based style rules. If you completed Lesson 3, "Adding Text and Images," you saw this method used to format text. This type of rule alters the appearance of an existing HTML tag, so the tag and any content that appears within it always appears formatted in a specific way. Instead of having to add a <font> tag around the contents of each new bullet point in a list, it would be easier for you to set a rule that states that items in a list should always be blue, for example.

1   Locate and double-click the file named **CSSList.html** from the Files panel to open it.

2   Click the Design view button in the Document toolbar if necessary. The list that appears onscreen, unlike the one you saw in the previous example, is formatted without the use of <font> tags, and uses only CSS.

3   Position your cursor after the last bulleted item and press the Enter (Windows) or Return (Mac OS) key to create a new bullet point. Type **Peppers**. The new text matches the bullet points above it.

4   Press Enter/Return again to add a fifth bullet point, and type **Okra**.

No matter how many bullet points you add, the formatting is applied automatically every time.

5 Select Split view at the top of the document window so that you can see both code and design:

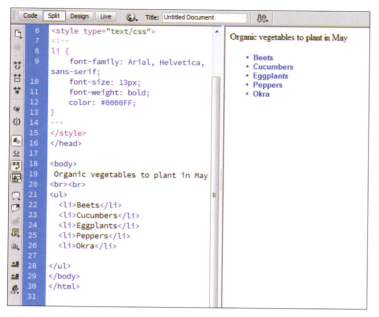

CSS allows you to define a style rule for a list item. All list items on this page will be blue.

What you'll notice is the absence of any formatting tags like the `<font>` tags you saw in the last exercise. In this example, you have several list items; however, all the styling information, such as the font-family, size, font style, and color, is being defined in one place: the CSS rule for the `<li>` tag.

6 If necessary, scroll to the top of the page and you'll see the code that makes this possible:

```
<style type="text/css">
<!--
li {
    font-family: Gotham, "Helvetica Neue", Helvetica, Arial, sans-serif;
    font-size: 13px;
    font-weight: bold;
    color: #0000FF;
}
-->
</style>
```

In the code above, a CSS selector (seen here as `li`) is being used to define the style of all list items. It's almost like a dress code for all `<li>` tags; they know that when they are used on the page, they must look a certain way. Best of all, if you need to modify their appearance, you make your changes to that single style rule at the top of the page. You will get a chance to do this shortly; however, let's take a step back and look at how CSS is controlled in Dreamweaver.

7 Choose File > Save to save your work, then choose File > Close.

How do you create CSS rules in Dreamweaver?

In this exercise, you will take a tour of Dreamweaver's CSS controls. If you haven't worked with CSS before, this is a chance to learn a bit more about how it works. If you have worked with CSS previously, this section will help you understand the Dreamweaver interface and how it applies to familiar concepts. Regardless of your comfort level with CSS, you won't be making any changes, merely getting familiar with features that you will be using in later exercises.

You work with CSS rules in a few ways in Dreamweaver:

Using the CSS Designer panel

Dreamweaver CC introduces CSS Designer panel, a new interface to create rules and/or style sheets that you can place directly within one or more pages in your site. You can easily modify rules directly from the CSS Designer panel. Furthermore, you can selectively apply rules from several places, including the Style or Class menu on the Property Inspector, or the tag selector at the bottom of the document window.

You can switch from the new CSS Designer panel to the Classic CSS Styles panel at any point by clicking the Panel Menu in the CSS Designer and choosing > Switch to Classic CSS Styles panel from the drop-down.

The CSS Designer panel contains four panes labeled Sources, Media, Selectors and Properties. You'll get a chance to explore these shortly. In the following figure, the panel with the Selectors and Properties panes is expanded.

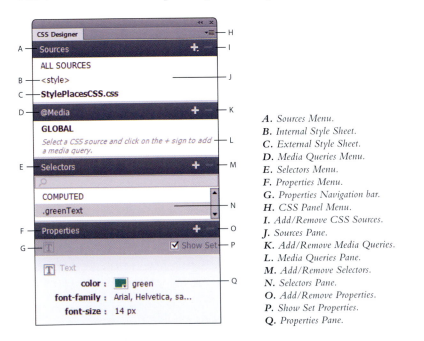

A. Sources Menu.
B. Internal Style Sheet.
C. External Style Sheet.
D. Media Queries Menu.
E. Selectors Menu.
F. Properties Menu.
G. Properties Navigation bar.
H. CSS Panel Menu.
I. Add/Remove CSS Sources.
J. Sources Pane.
K. Add/Remove Media Queries.
L. Media Queries Pane.
M. Add/Remove Selectors.
N. Selectors Pane.
O. Add/Remove Properties.
P. Show Set Properties.
Q. Properties Pane.

To ensure that you are seeing the same panels we are, you'll reset your workspace. Choose Window > Workspace Layout > Designer. Then choose Workspace Layout > Reset 'Designer' to make sure the panels are reset.

After resetting your workspace, the CSS Designer panel should be expanded. Click the File panel tab at the bottom of the screen to expand it.

1 Double-click the **StylePlaces.html** document in your Files panel to open it, and click the Design View button, if necessary.

2 Click in the first line, *Hi there! I'm styled with an INLINE style!* and then choose `<inline style>` : p from the Selectors Pane of the CSS Designer Panel.

3 Locate and click the Show Set check box in the Properties Navigation bar at the top of the Properties pane. Selecting this option enables you to see the CSS properties for the current selection. Depending on your monitor resolution, you might not have enough room to see all the information in this panel. You can adjust the different panel groups by hand.

4 Place your cursor at the top of the Properties pane in the CSS Designer panel. A black double-arrow cursor will appear. You can now click and drag downward to lengthen this pane.

You can expand a panel by clicking and dragging the edges.

Take a few moments to read through this panel and absorb the summary. Don't worry too much about each detail; you'll have plenty of time to familiarize yourself with this panel. It hopefully makes sense that the properties of the first paragraph are the color blue, the font-family Arial, and the font size of 14 pixels.

5   Click in the second paragraph and notice that the color property changes to red. Click in the third paragraph and notice that the color property changes to green. The current selection always lists the properties of the selected text.

6   Click the `.greenText` Selector in the Selectors Pane of the CSS Designer Panel, then click the Show Set check box in the Properties Navigation bar to clear the check box Again, this will allow you to see all of the available CSS properties. You will toggle between these two views often. Checking Show Set allows you to see the specific CSS properties and values of a selected object while clearing the check box allows you to see all of the possible styles you can set in your document.

In the Code view

CSS rules can also be created and modified directly in the Code view. Editing CSS in Dreamweaver's Code view offers a great degree of control and is often called *hand-coding*. Many coders and designers prefer hand-coding because of this control, but it's not for everyone. For example, when you work in the Code view misspellings or an incomplete knowledge of CSS syntax can easily break a page.

1   Click in the second paragraph if you are not currently inside it. Click the Code View button to view your page in Code view. If you haven't worked with code previously, see if you can locate the second paragraph of HTML. (It has the class named *red*.)

2   On the left side of the screen, notice that the line numbers are running from top to bottom; when working with code, each line has its own number, making it easy to refer to and locate objects.

On line 10, select the value *red* in the color property and then delete it. Now type **#CE1A30**. As soon as you start typing, Dreamweaver's code-hinting appears, giving you a color picker. Code-hinting is a form of assistance from Dreamweaver that can make the task of typing code by hand a little easier. However, you can also ignore it, and you should for this exercise.

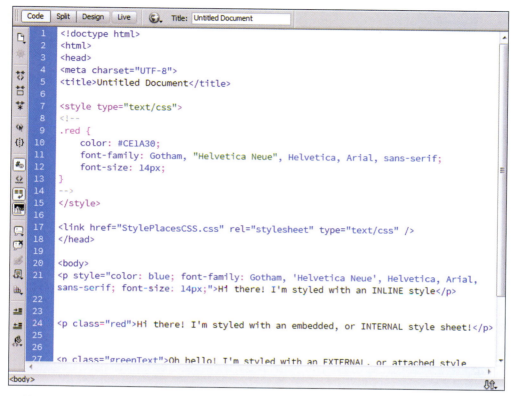

Modifying the CSS color property in Code View.

3   Click the Design view button. The text is still red; however it is using a hexadecimal color instead of a keyword. The danger of adding CSS properties manually is that if you mistype the value, you might get a different color or no color at all.

Working with the Code Navigator

The Code Navigator allows you to view the CSS properties directly in the Design view through a small pop-up window. Additionally, it allows you to click a property and edit it directly in the Split view.

1   Press Alt (Windows) or Command+Option (Mac OS) and click the third paragraph. A small window appears, listing the properties of the CSS rule applying to this paragraph. The window lists the name of the style sheet, as well as the rule `.greenText`.

2   Place your cursor over the `.greenText` class, and the properties appear in a yellow pop-up window. This feature allows you to quickly view the properties without needing to move to the CSS Styles panel or go into Code view.

The Code Navigator displays the CSS rules applied to a paragraph.

Understanding Style Sheets

The term Cascading in Cascading Style Sheets alludes to the fact that styles can live in three different places, each of which has its strengths and weaknesses. You've actually been working with all three types of styles in the last exercise. The first paragraph is being defined with an inline style, the second with an internal style sheet, and the third with an external style sheet.

Inline styles

An inline style is a set of CSS properties defined directly in an HTML tag using the style attribute. These are slightly less common because you can't reuse them easily, and reusability is one of the major benefits of CSS. Nevertheless, inline styles are a part of the CSS language, and you should know what they are.

1   In the file **StylePlaces.html**, click three times rapidly to select the first paragraph.

2   Click the Split view button, and notice that your selected text is nested inside a paragraph or <p> element; however, the CSS style rules for color, font-family, and font-size are contained directly inside the opening paragraph tag. This is called an inline style because the CSS rules are not separated from the HTML.

Although inline styles are part of CSS, they are used infrequently. They present many of the same problems as the older <font> tags in HTML. They only apply to one tag at a time and are not easily reusable. Inline styles are useful when an internal or external style sheet might not be available; a good example of this is HTML-based e-mail. They are also used in certain situations to override other styles, but you will learn more about this later.

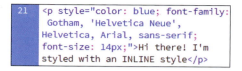

```
21   <p style="color: blue; font-family:
      Gotham, 'Helvetica Neue',
      Helvetica, Arial, sans-serif;
      font-size: 14px;">Hi there! I'm
      styled with an INLINE style</p>
```

An inline style places rules within a HTML opening tag.

Internal versus external style sheets

Internal style sheets are CSS rules that are contained directly within a document, using the `<style>` tag. The entire style sheet is contained within the opening and closing `<style>` tags. External style sheets are style rules saved in a separate document with the extension *css*. One of the fundamental differences between internal and external style sheets is that with internal style sheets, the CSS rules apply only to the HTML in a single document.

For example, if you had a ten-page website and could only use internal style sheets, you would essentially have ten style sheets: one per page. If you made a change on one page and then needed to make the other pages look the same, you would have to either copy or redefine internal styles from page to page—not an enjoyable prospect.

External style sheets, by contrast, have CSS rules located in one single document. You can attach .css files, or external style sheets, to an unlimited number of HTML pages. This method is extremely flexible: if a style rule such as the font-color for a paragraph is changed in the external style sheet, all paragraphs in the site are instantly modified, whether it be two pages, ten pages or 100 pages.

In Dreamweaver, when you create a new style, the default behavior is to use an internal style sheet. In many ways, a web browser doesn't care which type of style sheet you use; it renders the page exactly the same. There are certain situations when an internal style sheet makes more sense than an external style sheet and vice-versa. You will explore this in more detail in later exercises, but first you need to know how to determine whether a style is internal or external.

1   Open **StylePlaces.html** if you do not already have it open and click the Design View button to enter the Design view. In the CSS Designer panel, click the Sources panel heading. In this panel you will see a listing for `<style>` and one for `StylePlacesCSS.css`. The first line is the internal style sheet, and the second is for the external style sheet. The internal style sheet also is visible in the Related Files portion of the document toobar.

2   Click the `<style>` tag in the Sources pane. The rule for properties set in the class .red will be displayed in the Properties pane below. Next, click `StylePlacesCSS.css` in the Sources pane to show the properties for the class `.greenText`. You might have noticed that the listing for the inline style is not here; only rules for internal and external style sheets are visible in the Sources pane.

In the last exercise, you used the Code Navigator to view the CSS rules applied to a paragraph. You can also use the Code Navigator to quickly determine where the CSS rules are located.

3   Back in Design view, Alt+click (Windows) or Command+Option+click (Mac OS) inside the second paragraph to open the Code Navigator. The window reads StylePlaces.html and the class `.red` is indented below it. If a style is located inside an HTML document, as it is in this case, it must be an internal style.

The Code Navigator has located the origin of this CSS rule to be in StylePlaces.html.

4   Place your cursor over the `.red` class, once again, all the properties appear.

5   Click the `.red` rule, and Dreamweaver's Split view opens, sending you directly to the internal style. An experienced hand-coder might use this to directly edit the rule as you did earlier, although you will not be making any changes at this point. Now you will look at the external style sheet again using the Code Navigator.

6   Alt+click (Windows) or Command+Option+click (Mac OS) in the third paragraph to open the Code Navigator.

7   This time, the Code Navigator window lists StylePlacesCSS.css first. If a style is located inside a .css document, as it is in this case, it is an external style. Place your cursor over the `.greenText` class, and all the properties appear.

8 Click the `.greenText` class, and in the Split view, the external style sheet StylePlacesCSS.css appears. Doing this actually opens the external style sheet, which is a separate document.

An External Style Sheet is a separate document with the extension .css and is accessible through the Related Files bar.

To return to the original HTML document, click the Source Code button immediately to the left of the button labeled StylePlacesCSS.css.

9 Choose File > Save All. Close this document for now. Choosing *Save All* saves not just the HTML document, but the external stylesheet at the same time.

Understanding why they're called Cascading

You have learned how CSS integrates with HTML, and that there are three categories of styles: inline, internal, and external. Additionally, you have seen that an HTML document, such as the one from the last exercise, can contain all three types. Now you'll begin to explore when you might use one type over the other. A good way to look at this is to ask the question: Which one of the three style types is most dominant?

To help you picture this, consider the following situation: you have a paragraph, or more accurately, a <p> tag in your document, and you have the three style types (inline, internal, and external). Each one targets the <p> tag with the same property (color, for example) but they all have different values. So which one wins? The answer is the inline style, which is the most dominant because it is closest to the HTML source. The strength of competing styles is largely related to where the style is in relation to the HTML source. For internal and external styles, if they have competing rules, whichever style comes last within the HTML is the strongest. So in the following scenario, imagine that there is a paragraph style in the external style sheet (styles.css) declaring paragraphs to be blue. Because it comes *after* the internal style sheet's rule for red paragraphs, the external style sheet wins and the paragraph is blue.

```
<style type="text/css">
p {
    color: red;
}
</style>
<link href=" styles.css" rel="stylesheet" type="text/css" />
```

However it is equally possible that the author of the HTML has arranged the styles in a different order:

```
<link href=" styles.css" rel="stylesheet" type="text/css" />
<style type="text/css">
p {
    color: red;
}
</style>
```

Here, the paragraphs will be red because the internal style sheet comes last in the HTML code. There is no default order of styles in the documents that Dreamweaver creates, so you do need to be aware of this rule.

We have simplified the relationship for now. The strength of internal styles versus external styles can actually change depending on where the references to these styles are in the HTML. If the reference to the internal style sheet appears last in the HTML, these rules would be strongest. If the reference to the external style appears last in the HTML, then these would be the strongest.

Creating and modifying styles

You will now get a chance to begin working more deeply with CSS. In this exercise, you'll be picking up where you left off in the last lesson with the events page for the OrganicUtopia website. In that lesson, you covered the creation of new CSS rules; however, you essentially worked with just one category of CSS rules, the element or tag-based rules. In all instances from the last lesson, you defined the properties for a tag, such as <h1>, <p>, and <ul> (unordered lists). You will now explore how to create classes and IDs. First, a brief review of the styles you used in the last lesson for tag styles.

A tag style assigns rules directly to a specific HTML tag to alter its appearance. You can attach tag styles to any tag from the <body> tag down; as a matter of fact, when you modify page properties (Modify > Page Properties) to change default text formatting and background color, you are using a tag style assigned to the <body> tag.

The most basic tag styles are very straightforward. For instance, when you create a rule definition for the <p> (paragraph) tag, all paragraphs appear the same. The limitations begin when you want to customize one specific paragraph to appear different from the others. You will explore some solutions to this dilemma; for now, keep in mind that tag styles are a great way to ensure consistency across multiple elements and pages where specific tags are used, such as lists, tables, and paragraphs.

1   Double-click the **events.html** file in the Files panel to open it. This page has already had its Heading 1, paragraph, and list styled. You will now style the Heading 2.

2   In the Design view, click inside the heading *Spring Events*. This is already formatted as a Heading 2 for you.

3   Click the <style> item under Sources pane in the CSS Designer panel. This will activate the Selectors pane and allow us to create a new style rule for the Heading.

4   Click the Add Selector button in the Selectors menu to create a new CSS style for our h2 heading element. Notice that Dreamweaver recognized that your cursor was within an h2 element within the body so it added body h2 to the text box in the Selector pane. In this case you will simply use h2 as our selector.

5   Select body h2 and type **h2** to create a selector for Heading 2 headers then press Enter (Windows) or Return (Mac OS).

6   Make sure the Show set checkbox is unchecked to allow you to view all of the available styles.

7   Click the Text button in the Properties menu to limit the choices to only show the text-related properties.

8   Locate the font-size property and choose pt from the list of items.

9   Dreamweaver will place your cursor within a text box to the left of pt. Type **18** and then press Enter (Windows) or Return (Mac OS).

10 Locate the color property from the selection list. Click the color swatch to choose a color for your text from the Swatches panel that appears. Select a green color. The color #339900, located in the top row, is used in this example.

Your heading now changes to green. You have just styled the font-size and color of the <h2> tag. At this point, all text formatted as h2 appears this way. You will now format the last heading in the page in order to see this.

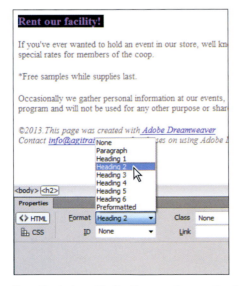

The CSS Designer panel shows the current, or computed, values of the actively selected element.

11 Click inside the text, *Rent our facility.*

12 In the Property Inspector, make sure that you are viewing the HTML mode by clicking the HTML button and note that the Format for this text is currently set to None. From the Format drop-down menu, choose Heading 2 to see your text change.

Formatting text as a Heading 2 assumes the properties of the CSS rule.

What you have seen in this exercise is an example of HTML and CSS working together with a tag style. In this case, all text tagged in the HTML as a Heading 2 or <h2> is defined by the CSS rule as green and 18 pixels. At this point, you might want to create more complex layouts; if you understand the fundamentals of styling tags, it will pay off as you move to the next level of CSS.

13 Choose File > Save but keep this file open. You will be working on it in the next exercise.

Creating a class style with the CSS Designer panel

In the last exercise, you created a new CSS rule by defining the properties of the <h2> tag. Now you will create another CSS rule, this time using a class. In CSS, class styles have unique names and are not associated with any specific HTML tag. A CSS class can have a specific style that can be applied to one or more elements in your website. So you might create a class called holidayText, for example, and the properties of this class might be a single rule defining the font-color. Once the class is created, this text could then be applied to a table, paragraph, heading, or form element simultaneously. So on Halloween, if you change the property of the font-color to orange, all text that is defined by the holidayText class is orange, and on Valentine's Day, if you change the property of the font-color to red, it all changes to red.

In this exercise, you will create a class for the copyright text at the bottom of the page in order to distinguish it from the rest of the page.

1 Locate the paragraph at the bottom of your page, click immediately before the copyright symbol, and then drag across until the two lines are selected.

2 Look at the Properties pane in the CSS Designer panel and note that this text has a size of 14 pixels and a dark grey color. This is because these are paragraphs and the CSS rules for paragraphs in this document currently have these properties. You will now format all this text with a different size and font, and then add a background color.

The CSS Designer panel displays the computed or current value of the selected text.

Because CSS is so flexible, you often have many options for styling. You could update the paragraph rule that already exists or you could create a new rule using a specific class or id. For now, we will create our rule using a class which we will only apply to the copyright paragraph.

3 Click the `<style>` item under Sources pane in the CSS Designer panel. This will activate the Selectors pane and allow us to create a new style rule for our paragraph within the current document.

4 Click the Add Selector button in the Selectors pane to create a new CSS style for our class. This will create a new text box in the Selectors list where you can add a new class name. Because you have selected a paragraph within the body, Dreamweaver has pre-filled the text box with `body p em`. Select and delete this text so that you can create a class selector in the next step.

5 Class selectors begin with a period (.) and include a descriptive name to describe how the class will be applied. Type **.copyright** in the text box in the Selectors list then press Enter (Windows) or Return (Mac OS).

6 Click the Text button in the Properties menu to limit the choices to only show the text-related properties.

7   Locate the font-size property and choose px from the list of units. Dreamweaver will place your cursor in the text box to the left of the unit to allow you to enter the value.

8   Type **10** and then press Enter (Windows) or Return (Mac OS).

9   Now that you have created the rule for the .copyright class, you still have to apply it to our text selection. Make sure the text is selected or your cursor is within the paragraph and click the drop-down arrow for Class in the Property Inspector.

10 Choose copyright from the menu to apply our new class to this paragraph. You may want to click once within the paragraph to deselect the text. You should now see that the last paragraph of text is formatted using the 10pt font size specified in the copyright class CSS rule.

The Property Inspector Class field and Tag Selector show that the copyright class has been applied to the selected paragraph.

11 Click once in the first line of the copyright text. Click the CSS button in the Property Inspector to see the CSS styles and properties. Notice in the Property Inspector, in the Targeted Rule section, the menu is now set for .copyright. This is important, as it confirms that you are modifying the class, not creating a new rule or modifying the paragraph tag style. In the Property Inspector, choose "Gill Sans", "Gill Sans MT", "Myriad Pro", "DejaVu Sans Condensed", Helvetica, Arial, sans-serif from the Font menu to add this property to the copyright class. Now you'll add a new line of text and apply the copyright class to it.

12 Place your cursor at the end of the last line of the paragraph and press Enter (Windows) or Return (Mac OS) to add a new line. Type the following text: **All images on this website are the copyright of Glenn "The Hodge" Hodgkinson.** Notice that the text is still using the copyright style. If you wanted to remove this class for any reason, you could click the Targeted Rule drop-down menu and choose Remove Class.

Creating and modifying styles

To take advantage of the full power of CSS, you will begin to dive further into the new CSS Designer panel. In this exercise, you'll explore some of the powerful options that CSS has at its disposal. The first thing you'll do is change the background color of your page by adding a new style to the body tag.

Before you get started, click the Workspace button and select Expanded from the menu. This will show the CSS Designer panel in an expanded mode with the Sources, Media and Selectors panes on the left side and the Properties pane on the right. This Expanded view will make it easier for you to select and modify the style rules in the following exercises. If you want to go back to the narrower version of the CSS Designer panel, you can choose Window > Workspace Layout > Compact from the menu.

The expanded mode of the CSS Designer panel makes it easier to select and modify style rules.

1   Place your cursor at the end of the last line of text in your document window.

2   Click the <style> item under Sources pane in the CSS Designer panel. This will activate the Selectors pane and allow us to create a new style rule to change the background color of the page.

3   Click the Add Selector button in the Selectors menu to create a new CSS style for our body tag. This will create a new text box in the Selectors list. Dreamweaver will prepopulate this field based on where you clicked in your document.

4   If Dreamweaver prepopulated this field with text, delete this text and type **body** in this field instead. Press Enter (Windows) or Return (Mac OS) to create the selector for our body element.

5   Click the Background button in the Navigation Bar of the Properties menu to limit the choices to background-related properties.

6   Locate the background-color property and click the set color field to the right of the color swatch to enter a color for your background,

7   Type in the following hexadecimal number: **#E0F0E4** and press Enter (Windows) or Return (Mac OS) to apply the color change. You will now change the background color for the copyright class at the bottom of the page.

8   In the list of Selectors in the CSS Designer panel, click the .copyright class to enable editing of these properties. You might have to click <style> in the Sources menu to see the copyright class selector.

9 Click the Background button in the Properties menu to display the background properties.

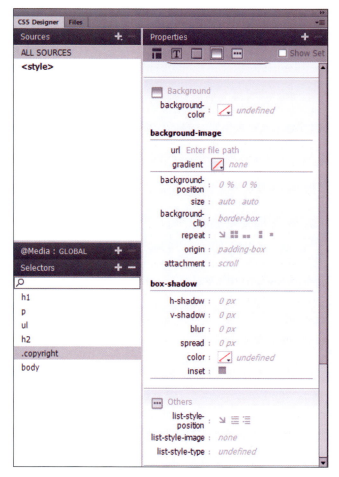

The CSS Designer panel displays the background properties for the copyright class rule.

10 Click the Background Category, click the Background-color swatch, and choose white (#FFF) from the list. The two copyright paragraphs at the bottom of the page are styled with white backgrounds. The gap between the two paragraphs reveals the background color because these are separate paragraphs, and are both block elements. The gap is somewhat visually unappealing and is something you will be fixing a bit later in the lesson.

Advanced text formatting with CSS

Text on the Web is necessarily limited due to the fact that designers cannot assume that fonts they choose in Dreamweaver will be available to the user. There is a small set of fonts that designers can use that are essentially guaranteed to be on all users' systems. Given this limitation, you can use some of the properties in CSS to give your text a distinctive look. In this exercise, you will work with the line spacing of your paragraphs and lists, and the letter spacing of your headings.

The limitations on web fonts are slowly changing, and in Dreamweaver CC, there is now a new feature that makes it easier to use web fonts and allows you access to a wider range of font choices. For now, it is still important to learn the basics. We cover the new web fonts feature in Lesson 8, "Using Web Fonts."

1   Click p in the Selectors list so you can edit the paragraph properties. You might have to click the `<style>` item under the Sources pane in the CSS Designer panel first.

You will now override the default line-height for your paragraphs. If you have a print background, you might be familiar with leading, which is the amount of space between the lines in a paragraph. Line-height is the same thing as leading.

2   Click the Text button in the Navigation Bar of the Properties menu to limit the choices to only show the text-related properties.

3   Locate the line-height property and click the text *normal* in the Set line-height field to bring up the units menu. Select px from the menu for pixels then type **20** and press Enter (Windows) or Return (Mac OS) and you will see the space between your paragraph lines increase. Extra line-height can often make your text more readable, so it is great that you have this option in CSS. However, a problem might arise if you change the font-size. For example, setting the fixed value of 20 pixels looks good with 14-pixel type, but what if you were to later change the font-size of your paragraph? The 20-pixel line-height would look strange. A more flexible way to assign line-height is to use a percentage.

4   Click the px value to the right of line-height and choose percent (%). Change the value from 20 to **120**, and press Enter (Windows) or Return (Mac OS). You won't actually see a dramatic difference because the end result is similar, but by assigning the line-height to 120 percent, your initial font-size isn't as important. There will always be the height of the line plus 20 percent extra, no matter what the font-size is. Click OK.

Changing the line-height value of a paragraph to a percentage is more flexible than using pixels.

Notice that the list under Spring Events did not change. This is because the line-height property applies solely to paragraphs, not lists. If you want to make this list appear the same, you could always apply the same value of line-height. However, you will be adding extra space between the lines to make the list stand out from the rest of the page.

5   Click the ul selector in the Selectors pane. You might have to click `<style>` in the Sources pane to show all the selectors.

6   You will notice the ul element's line-height is set to 120%. In the field for line-height, click the value 120% and change it by typing **150**, then press Enter (Windows) or Return (Mac OS). You now have extra space between your list items. Next, you'll style your Heading 2 element.

7   Click the h2 selector in the Selectors list and locate text-transform in the list of text properties. You might have to click the Text button on the Properties menu. Click the Uppercase icon to set the text for your h2 headings to display in Uppercase and you will see your two headings *Spring Events* and *Rent Our Facility!* transform to uppercase. This helps your headings stand out and is faster than retyping these headings by hand. Now you'll add some space between all the letters.

Transforming your text to uppercase is just a style; in the HTML, your original text still has the standard formatting. One of the few times this might be an issue is if your web page is being viewed without a style sheet; older cell phones and PDAs with web browsers do not fully support style sheets (or use them at all), and so your text would appear lowercase as it is in the HTML.

8   Locate the letter-spacing property just below the text-transform property. In the text field to the right of letter-spacing, click the word *normal* and choose px from the drop-down menu. In the text box to the left type **5**, press Enter (Windows) or Return (Mac OS), and the two headings are extended. Each letter pair now has 5 pixels of space between them. When used correctly, letter-spacing can make your headings more readable and unique.

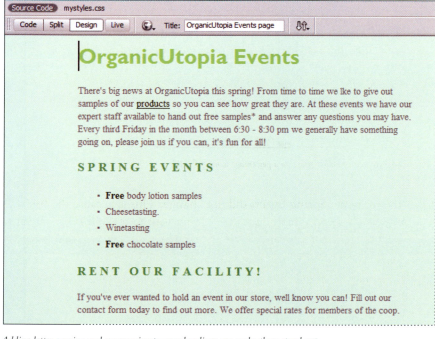

Adding letter-spacing and uppercasing to your headings can make them stand out.

Fine-tuning page appearance with contextual and pseudo-class selectors

CSS allows you to create styles that are targeted at specific HTML elements on your page. Understanding these techniques is crucial if you want to gain control over the appearance of your page. Look at the Spring Events list on your page: lines 1 and 4 both begin with the word Free. Let's say you wanted to emphasize this word to attract your user's attention. You could simply bold the word, but what if you not only wanted to bold it, but change the color as well? It would be possible to create a class to do this, but there is another option that has some useful benefits called *contextual selectors*.

Dreamweaver actually refers to contextual selectors, which is the official CSS term for them, as *compound selectors*. Despite the terminology, they are very powerful and important to understand.

Contextual selectors apply formatting to tags and classes when they appear in a specific combination. For instance, you often have separate rules for the <p> (paragraph) and <strong> (bold) tag, but what if you want a rule for <strong> tags that are used inside <p> tags? Contextual selectors can handle this; for instance, you can designate that any text inside a <strong> tag must be red, unless it is used within a <p> tag, in which case it should be blue. This breathes new life into your tag styles by multiplying the number of times you can use them in conjunction with each other.

1   In the first line of the Spring Events list, select the word *Free*. Click the HTML button in the Property Inspector, then click the Bold button. (This actually creates a <strong> tag in the HTML.) Using the example from above, let's say that simply bolding this wasn't enough and you wanted to add some color.

2   Click <style> in the Sources pane of the CSS Designer panel and then click the Add Selector button in the Selectors menu to create a new CSS style for our selection. Dreamweaver will recognize that you have selected a list item within an unordered list in the body of your page and will pre-fill the selector field with body ul li strong. Select and delete the word *body* from the field leaving ul li strong and press Enter (Windows) or Return (Mac OS).

3 Click the Text button in the Properties Navigation Bar to show the text-related properties.

This might look strange at first, but it's logical if you read it from left to right. The body tag is the ancestor, or parent, of the ul tag, which is the parent of the li tag, which is the parent of the strong tag. In other words, your style will only apply to strong tags, which are nested in a list item (which is nested in the unordered list, and so on).

Selectors	+ −
⌕	
h1	
p	
ul	
h2	
.copyright	
body	
ul li strong	

The CSS Designer panel can be used to create contextual selectors, such as ul li strong.

4 Click the color swatch to the right of the color property and choose the dark green swatch in the top row, #003300. The text will immediately change color.

5 Select the word *Free* in the fourth line and click the Bold button in the Property Inspector. The word takes on the same appearance. Bolding anything in the list causes it to have the same appearance, while bolding anything outside of a list has the default effect.

Styling hyperlinks

You're slowly beginning to pull together a page with a color theme to it, even if there is no layout *per se*. A frequently asked question when people are learning to create web pages is how to style the hyperlinks on a page. This can be accomplished with CSS, although there are some precautions. Since the early days of CSS, the default style for unvisited hyperlinks has been a bright blue with an underline and a purple color with an underline for visited hyperlinks. An argument can be made that users might be confused by hyperlinks that do not fit this mold. On the other hand, many designers like being able to color their hyperlinks to match the rest of their page. Regardless of the debate, it's important to understand how to do this.

Technically speaking, hyperlinks live in a category called a *pseudo-class*. A pseudo-class selector affects a part or state of a selected tag or class. A state often refers to an item's appearance in response to something happening, such as the mouse pointer rolling over it. One of the most common pseudo-class selectors is applied to the <a> tag, which is used to create hyperlinks. You'll now create a pseudo-class selector to affect the appearance of hyperlinks on the events.html page in different states.

1   Click the products link in the first paragraph, and then click the Add Selector button in the Selectors pane to create a new CSS style for our selection. You might have to click <style> in the Sources pane of the CSS Designer panel to enable the Add Selector button.

        Again, Dreamweaver will recognize that you have selected a hyperlink or anchor in the body of your page and pre-fill the text box in the Selectors list with body p a but you will change this.

2   Type **a:** in the text box and notice that Dreamweaver presents you with a list of pseudo-class selectors including link, visited, hover, active and more. Press Enter (Windows) or Return (Mac OS) to select the first option, :link. The a:link psuedo-class selector will affect the appearance of a hyperlink that hasn't been visited.

3   Click the Text button in the Properties Navigation Bar to show the text-related properties.

Selectors   **+ −**
◌
h1
p
ul
h2
.copyright
body
ul li strong
a:link

Using a psuedo-class selector can alter the appearance of an element in a given state.

4   Click the color swatch to the right of the color label and choose the green shade you used in the previous exercise. The product link in the first paragraph, as well as the two links at the bottom of the page are now green instead of blue. Now you'll set the style for hover links, or a:hover.

5   Make sure that the products link in the first paragraph is selected and choose <style> from the Sources pane in the CSS Designer panel. Click the Add Selector button in the Selectors pane and Dreamweaver will create a new text box in this pane. You will add the next pseudo-class selector for the a:hover state of the products link. The a:hover state defines the color of a hyperlink when a user places their cursor over it.

6   Once again remove any text Dreamweaver added, then type **a:** in the text box and notice that Dreamweaver presents you with the list of pseudo-class selectors. This time select :hover and then click the Text button of the Properties Menu Bar to display the text-related properties.

7   Click the color palette to the right of the color property and select the bright orange swatch near the center of the Swatches panel (#CC6600).

8 Locate the text-decoration property and click the icon for none (an empty box with a line through it). This removes the underline from the hyperlink for the hover state only.

Set properties for a:hover, or the appearance of hyperlinks when the mouse pointer rolls over them.

You can preview the appearance of the hyperlinks by clicking the Live View button in the Application bar or opening your page in a browser.

9 Choose File > Save; then choose File > Preview in Browser and choose a browser from the list to launch it. Place your cursor over the products link, but don't click it. This is the hover link. Click the products link to bring you to the products page, and then click back to the events page by clicking the Events link at the bottom of the page. The products link is now purple because the browser understands you have visited it.

You will leave off styling the `a:active` link for now. Setting the `a:active` property defines the way a link appears when it is being clicked on by a user.

10 Close the web browser. Return to Dreamweaver and select Window > Workspace Layout > Compact to collapse the CSS Designer panel.

Div tags and CSS IDs

Your page is coming along nicely on the style front, as you have used quite a bit of CSS, but looking at your page, it's fair to say that it is still lacking a cohesive style. All your various headings and paragraphs, as well as your list, are floating about on the page, and with the exception of the copyright text at the bottom of the page, it's difficult at a single glance to get a sense of where one section ends and another begins. It's time to add more structure to your page through the use of the `<div>` tag and more control of your CSS with ID selectors.

Let's look at the structure first. It would be nice to gather the text on the bottom of your page, starting with the line, *Occasionally we gather…*, and then the two paragraphs below, and put it all into a single section. You could then take this new section and style it separately from the rest of the page. This is possible with the `<div>` tag. In this exercise, you will begin by creating a footer ID.

1   Click and drag to select all the text from the line, *Occasionally we gather…*, down to the bottom of the page. You will be grouping these three paragraphs together.

2   Just above the CSS Designer Panel, alongside the Files Panel, is the Insert tab. Click this once to open the Insert panel. If the drop-down menu is not set to Common, select Common from the menu now. In the Common section, click Div and the Insert Div dialog box opens. In the Insert section, the default choice is *Wrap around selection*; this is exactly what you want to do, so leave this option as is.

The Insert Div window allows you to create a section within your page.

A `<div>` tag by itself doesn't do anything until some CSS properties are attached to it. In other words, unlike other HTML tags, which often have a default visual effect in the browser (think of headings), the `<div>` tag has no effect on your rendered page unless you specifically instruct it to. You will now get to do this.

3   In the field labeled ID, type **footer**. Just like classes, IDs should have good, descriptive names to help identify them. You'll now apply a background color of white to the entire block of text you selected. Notice that there is a field for class as well. Classes and IDs are very similar. The difference between them is that classes can be used multiple times on different elements on a page, whereas an ID can only be used once. In this case, an ID is appropriate because there is only one footer on this page.

4   Click OK and Dreamweaver will insert `<div>` tags around your selection which will be represented in the design view as a box surrounded by a dotted border. This representation will not be displayed in the browser or Live View and is only used to assist you in identifying divs within your page.

5   Click the CSS Designer tab to the left of the Insert tab to bring the CSS Designer panel to the front then select `<style>` in the Sources pane to tell Dreamweaver you want to create a new embedded style.

6 Click the Add Selector button in the Selectors pane to create a new CSS style for our selection. This will create a new text box in the Selectors list which will be populated with the value `#footer`.

You don't need to change anything here; just confirm that you are creating an ID with the name footer. The footer name is preceded by the pound sign (#). This is the main difference between ID names and class names. If this were a class named footer, it would be named `.footer`. Press Enter (Windows) or Return (Mac OS) to create the new selector.

7 Select the Background icon from the Navigation Bar in the Properties pane, then click the swatch next to background-color and choose the pure white swatch (#FFFFFF). In Dreamweaver's Design view, the box around the text now has a white background unifying the footer text.

Set the Background-color to #FFFFFF in the Properties pane of the CSS Designer panel.

If you haven't guessed by now, these are the first steps toward page layout with CSS. A footer is a common element on most pages, and there are a few other obvious ones as well: headers, sidebars, and navigation bars to name a few. You'll begin working with these page structures more deeply in upcoming lessons, but first you'll need to have some more control of the CSS rules that you've been working with this lesson.

Internal versus external style sheets

Now that you've seen how to modify a few items in a single page at once, you can imagine how powerful a style sheet shared by every page in your website can be. As noted earlier, when you create new CSS rules, you have the opportunity to define them in the current document or in a new CSS file. A collection of rules stored in a separate .css file is referred to as an *external style sheet*. You can attach external style sheets to any number of pages in a site so that they all share the same style rules.

So far, you've created internal, or embedded, styles. This means you wrote the style rules directly into the page using the `<style>` tag. Although you can format a page with an internal style sheet, this method is not very portable. To apply the same rules in another page, you have to copy and paste the internal style sheet from one page to another. This can create inconsistency among pages if the same rule is updated in one page and not the other.

To utilize the true power of style sheets, you need to create an external style sheet that any or all pages on your site can share. When you change an external style, pages linked to that style sheet are updated. This is especially handy when working with sites containing many pages and sections.

You can create external style sheets in the following ways:

- Move rules from an internal style sheet into a new CSS file.
- Define styles in a page in a new document using the Sources pane of the CSS Designer panel.
- Create a new CSS document from the Start page or File menu.

Now you will export internal styles from your **events.html** page into a separate CSS file so that other pages can share them.

1   First, you need to create a new CSS file. Click the plus icon in the Sources pane and choose Create a New CSS File.

2   The Create a New CSS File dialog box appears. Click the Browse button and navigate to your dw04lessons folder. Type **mystyles.css** in the File/URL field and click Save. You can leave the Add as value set to Link to link your new CSS file to the current document and click OK.

3   The new CSS file is now listed beneath the `<style>` source for the internal style sheet in the Sources pane. You are now ready to move your rules.

4   With the **events.html** document open, expand the Selectors pane shown in the CSS Designer panel so that you can see all the rules you have created. If you have limited screenspace, double-click the Insert panel to collapse it. Also remember you can expand a pane by clicking the bottom edge and dragging down.

5 Choose `<style>` from the Sources pane in the CSS Designer panel, then click the first rule at the top of the panel and scroll down if necessary to locate the last rule. Shift+click the last rule in the panel so that all the rules in the list are selected. Click and drag the selected rules to mystyles.css in the Sources pane. Release your mouse button as your cursor hovers over the file name.

Select all rules in your style sheet and then click and drag them to mystyles.css in the Sources pane.

6 Look inside your Selectors pane and note that the styles you had selected are no longer listed. Click mystyles.css in the Sources pane and you will see that the new style sheet now includes all of your rules. The internal style sheet (shown as `<style>`) is still in your docum, but it contains no rules.

Attaching an external style sheet to your page

Dreamweaver automatically made the new external style sheet available to the current page by attaching it. However, you will have to link this style sheet to other pages in your site to use it. You can accomplish this with the Attach Existing CSS File command in the Sources pane of the CSS Designer panel.

1 Double-click the **products.html** file from the Files panel. This page is a version of the products page you created in Lesson 3, "Adding Text and Images." You will now link your new style sheet to this page.

2 Click the Add CSS Source in the Sources pane and choose Attach Existing CSS File from the menu. The Attach Existing CSS File dialog box appears.

3 Next to File/URL, click the Browse button to locate a style sheet to attach. In the dw04lessons folder, select the **mystyles.css** file from the Select Style Sheet dialog box and click OK (Windows) or Open (Mac OS). Click OK to close the Attach Existing CSS File dialog box.

Adding an external style sheet.

The page refreshes with the styles defined in the external style sheet. You can also see that the CSS Design panel shows that mystyles.css and all its rules are now available for use and editing.

Modifying attached style sheets

Because an attached style sheet appears in your CSS Designer panel, you can modify any of its rules and the changes will apply across other pages that share that style sheet. You'll be another step closer to layout now by modifying the body property in order to add some margins to your page.

1 Click mystyles.css in the Sources pane of the CSS Designer panel to display the selectors and properties set in the external file.

2 Click the body selector in the Selectors pane to display the properties for the body tag. You might need to click the Show Set check box in the Properties Navigation bar to clear the checkmark and show all of the available properties.

3　Click the Layout icon in the Properties Navigation Bar and scroll down to the margin control. The margin control provides a new visual interface for setting the margin properties. The link button in the center of the margin control is used to set the four margin settings to the same values. You can set the individual margins by clicking the areas representing the top, bottom, left and right margins.

The margin control allows you to set margins using a visual interface.

Because CSS is based on a box model, it treats every element as a container. Because the `<body>` tag is the largest container, if you modify its margins, it affects all the content on the page. You'll specifically be changing the left and right margins to create a more centered layout.

4　Click the unit px in right side of the margin control to set the right margin. Select % from the units menu, then type **15** in the value text box and press Enter (Windows) or Return (Mac OS) to set the margin.

5 Click the unit px in the left side of the margin control to set the left margin. Select % from the units menu, then type **15** in the value text box and press Enter (Windows) or Return (Mac OS) to set the margin.

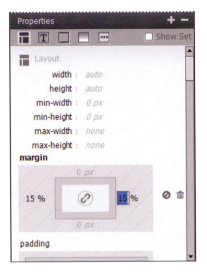

Change the left and right margin for body to 15 percent.

After both margins are set, your content should now sit in the middle of the page.

6 Choose File > Save All, and then preview your page in the browser. You are able to navigate between the products page and the events page using the hyperlinks in each document. Shorten the width of your browser, and notice that the content adjusts accordingly. There will always be 15 percent space to the left of content in the browser window and 15 percent to the right, thereby centering your content. Open the events.html file in your web browser to see how this page's appearance is now being controlled by the external style sheet. When done, close the browser.

Creating a new .css file (external style sheet)

Although it's easy to move styles to a new .css file, you can also create styles in a new .css file from the beginning. The CSS Designer panel gives you this option by clicking the Add CSS Source button in the Sources pane. By creating styles in an external .css file, you can avoid the extra step of exporting them later and make the style sheet available to other pages immediately.

1 In the Files panel, double-click the **event1.html** file.

2 From the CSS Designer panel menu, choose Create a New CSS File and the Create a New CSS File dialog box appears. Browse to your dw04lessons folder and name the new file **morestyles.css**. Keep the Add as: option set to Link and click OK to create the file.

3 Click the `<body>` tag in the lower-left corner of the document status bar, then click the Add Selector button in the Selectors menu. You might have to click `morestyles.css` in the Sources pane after selecting the `<body>` tag to make the Add Selector button active.

When you click the Add Selector button, Dreamweaver prefills the selector name box with `body p`. Delete the letter `p` leaving only the word `body` as the name, and then press Enter (Windows) or Return (Mac OS) to create the selector.

4 Click the Background button in the Properties Navigation bar to show the background properties.

5 Click the swatch to the right of the background-color property and set the background color to light yellow, **#FFFFCC**.

Your page's background color should be yellow, and the CSS Designer panel reflects that the style was created in a new external style sheet. Now you can attach this style sheet to any other page in your site.

6 Choose File > Save All.

More details on CSS

Inheritance

When you nest one rule inside another, the nested rule inherits properties from the rule in which it's contained. For instance, if you define a font-size and font-family for all `<p>` tags, then it carries over to a class style used within the paragraph. This paragraph might not specify values for either property. It automatically inherits the font-size and font-family from the `<p>` tag selector.

CSS rule weight

What happens if two classes of the same name exist in the same page? It is possible to have two identically named styles, either in the same style sheet or between internal and external style sheets used by the same page. Along the same lines, it is possible to have two rules that both apply to the same tag. If either of these cases exists, how do you know which rule is followed?

You know which rule is followed based on two factors: weight and placement. If two selectors are the same weight (for instance, two tag selectors for the body tag), then the last defined rule takes precedence.

If a rule of the same name is defined in both an internal and external style sheet in your document, the rule from the last defined style sheet takes precedence. For instance, if an external style sheet is attached to the page anywhere after the internal style sheet, the rule in the attached style sheet wins.

Self study

Create a new document and add some unique content to it, such as text or images. Afterwards, use the Designer panel to define at least one tag style, two class styles, and one contextual selector (advanced) in a new, external .css file. Create a second document and attach your new external style sheet to it, using the Attach Existing CSS File command from the Sources pane of the CSS Designer panel. Add content to this page, and style it using the style rules already available from your external style sheet. If desired, make changes to the rules from either document, and watch how both documents are affected by any modifications made to the external style sheet.

Review

Questions

1   What are the four types of selectors that can be chosen when creating a new CSS rule?

2   In what three places can styles be defined?

3   True or false: A style sheet is composed of several CSS rules and their properties.

Answers

1   Tag, Class, ID and Compound (which includes contextual and pseudo–class selectors).

2   Inline (written directly into a tag), internal (embedded inside a specific page using the `<style>` tag), or external (inside a separate .css file).

3   True. A style sheet can contain many CSS rules and their properties.

- Understanding the CSS Box model
- Creating Divs and AP Divs
- Stacking and overlapping elements
- Styling box contents
- Using visual aids to fine-tune positioning

Creating Page Layouts with CSS

Now that you've used Cascading Style Sheets, you've seen how powerful they can be for styling a page. CSS is equally powerful as a layout tool, allowing you to freely position page content in ways not possible with HTML alone.

Starting up

Before starting, make sure that your tools and panels are consistent by resetting your workspace. See "Resetting the Dreamweaver workspace" in the Starting up section of this book.

You will work with several files from the dw05lessons folder in this lesson. Make sure that you have loaded the dwlessons folder onto your hard drive from the supplied DVD. See "Loading lesson files" in the Starting up section of this book.

Before you begin, you need to create site settings that point to the dw05lessons folder. Go to Site > New Site, or, for details on creating a site, refer to Lesson 2, "Setting Up a New Site."

See Lesson 5 in action!

Use the accompanying video to gain a better understanding of how to use some of the features shown in this lesson. The video tutorial for this lesson can be found on the included DVD.

The CSS Box model

CSS positions elements within a page using the Box model, which refers to the fact that all HTML elements have default boxes that you can choose to style. You can think of a box as a container for text, images, media, tables, and other content. In most cases, the width and height of a box is determined by the amount of content; however, you can also assign an explicit width and height to any box. Additionally, each box can have its own optional padding, margin, and border settings (described in detail shortly).

Toward the end of Lesson 4, "Styling Your Pages with CSS," you began to explore page structure through the use of the HTML <div> element. The Box model in CSS applies to all elements in HTML but is often paired with <div> tags. The <div> element, in conjunction with CSS rules, can be freely positioned, formatted, and even told how to interact with other boxes adjacent to it. You can also stack and overlap <div> containers, opening the door to flexible and creative layouts that are not possible with HTML alone.

This lesson dives deeper into the many uses of the <div> element. If you have jumped directly to this lesson, it is highly recommended that you understand the basic concepts in Lesson 4, "Styling Your Pages with CSS," before starting this one.

If you've worked with layout applications such as InDesign, the idea of creating and positioning containers for page content should be very familiar to you. Boxes created with the <div> tag can be thought of as analogous to the text and image frames you create in InDesign.

The basics of CSS margins, padding, and borders

The Box model allows each element on a page to have unique margin, padding, and border settings.

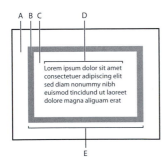

Lorem ipsum dolor sit amet consectetuer adipiscing elit sed diam nonummy nibh euismod tincidund ut laoreet dolore magna aliquam erat

A. Margin. B. Border. C. Padding.
D. Content width. E. Visible width.

Margins refer to the transparent area surrounding the box, which you set using the margin group of CSS properties. Margins can play an essential role in creating distance between a box and the content surrounding it (such as other boxes), or the boundaries of the page itself. You can set margins for all sides at once or uniquely for each side.

Padding is the distance between the inside edge of the box and its contents. By setting padding, you create space between the box and any text, images, or other content that it contains. You set padding using the padding group of CSS properties, and, like margins, you can set padding for all four sides of a box at once or for each side individually.

The **border** of a box is transparent by default, but you can add width, color, and a border style for decoration or definition around boxes. Borders sit directly between margins and padding, and define the actual boundaries of the box. You set borders using the border group of CSS properties and, like margins and padding, you can define borders for all four sides at once or for each side individually.

You can incorporate each property into any style rule and attach it to a box, similar to the way you've attached classes to paragraphs and tables in previous lessons.

Reviewing the `<div>` element

As mentioned earlier, when exploring and creating page layouts with CSS, you will frequently encounter and use the `<div>` element. The `<div>` element creates areas or divisions within an HTML document; you can place page content such as text and images directly within sets of `<div>` tags. Dreamweaver enables you to create CSS-driven page layouts using the Insert > Div menu item and Insert Div button in the Insert panel; both of these features use `<div>` tags to create areas of layout in similar ways.

Reviewing the ID selector

In Lesson 4, "Styling Your Pages with CSS," you learned about the different selector types in CSS: classes, tags, pseudo-class selectors, and IDs. In this lesson, IDs take center stage and become an essential part of working with CSS boxes and positioning. An ID is a special selector type created for a unique element using the same name within a page, and it's meant for one-time use only. ID rules appear within a style sheet and are preceded by a pound sign (#), in contrast to classes, which are preceded by a period character (.).

Because IDs can be used only once per page, they are ideal for setting properties that need to be specific to a single element, such as positioning information. In other words, page elements such as headers or columns occupy a specific position on the page, such as top, right, left, and so on. When creating layouts using the `<div>` element, you need to create or assign an ID for each box created.

Because the `<div>` element has no display attributes, it is given its properties by either an ID or a class, or both. Think of an ID as a set of instructions that give a `<div>` its unique appearance and behavior (as DNA does to a human being). An ID rule is matched to a `<div>` using the tag's ID attribute.

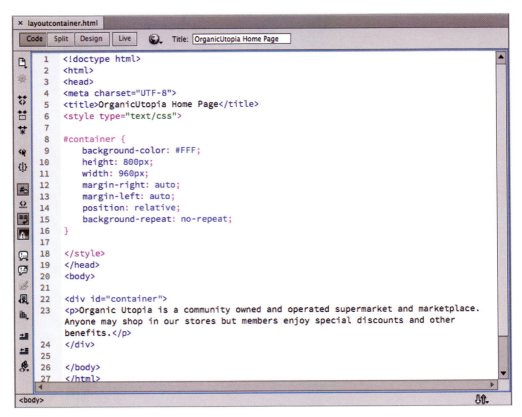

```
× layoutcontainer.html

Code   Split   Design   Live    🌐,  Title: OrganicUtopia Home Page

 1   <!doctype html>
 2   <html>
 3   <head>
 4   <meta charset="UTF-8">
 5   <title>OrganicUtopia Home Page</title>
 6   <style type="text/css">
 7
 8   #container {
 9       background-color: #FFF;
10       height: 800px;
11       width: 960px;
12       margin-right: auto;
13       margin-left: auto;
14       position: relative;
15       background-repeat: no-repeat;
16   }
17
18   </style>
19   </head>
20   <body>
21
22   <div id="container">
23   <p>Organic Utopia is a community owned and operated supermarket and marketplace.
     Anyone may shop in our stores but members enjoy special discounts and other
     benefits.</p>
24   </div>
25
26   </body>
27   </html>

<body>                                                              ⇕⇑,
```

The Code view shows the style sheet and `<div>` tag that create the container.

Creating a centered container for your page

The goal of this lesson is to create the home page for the Organic Utopia site. This page will look like the thumbnail below.

The completed layout you will be creating in this lesson.

The home page will be a different design and layout than the rest of the site (this layout is covered in more detail in Lesson 6, "Advanced Page Layout."), and you will start by creating a container that will end up nesting the other sections of your page such as the header, sidebar and other elements. This container will have a fixed width of 840 pixels and also be centered within the browser window.

This container will use a combination of relative positioning and automatic margins to achieve the centering effect. Relative positioning allows you to position this box relative to the body of the page, and the automatic margins will force the fixed-width container to stay centered regardless of the browser window's width.

1   In the Files panel, navigate to the dw05lessons folder and double-click the **layout.html** file to open it. This document has been partially prepared for you, with a background color and a page title added. Additionally, the default font, font color, and font size have been defined as Lucida Sans, grey, and small, respectively. Your first step will be to add a box, which will become your main column of text.

2   If it's not already visible, open the Insert panel by choosing Window > Insert. The Insert panel features a list of objects that can be added to your pages easily.

3   In the bottom–left corner of your document window, click the `<body>` tag. Remember, the `<body>` tag encloses all the other tags within a page. You will now create a new `<div>` element that will function as a container for the other layout elements. In the Insert panel, click the drop-down menu and choose Structure, then click the Div button. The Structure category lists items you will use to define your page structure, in this case a new div element.

The CSS Designer Panel displays the properties of the div and allows you to set its background color.

4   The Insert Div Tag dialog box appears. Click in the ID text field and type **container**, and then click OK.

5 Click the CSS Designer tab to bring up the CSS Designer panel and click `<style>` in the Sources panel. Click the Add Selector button in the Selectors menu to create a new Selector for the container. Dreamweaver will populate the selector field with `#container`; press Enter (Windows) or Return (Mac OS) to accept this value.

6 Click the Layout button in the Properties Navigation Bar to show the layout properties. Click *auto* to the right of the width label and choose px for the units and type **840**. Press Enter (Windows) or Return (Mac OS) to accept the value.

7 Click to set the value for `height`; select px then type **800** for the value and press Enter (Windows) or Return (Mac OS) to accept the new height value.

8 Scroll down to the margin control and click the px for `margin-left` and then choose auto from the menu. Click the px value for `margin-right` and again choose auto from the menu.

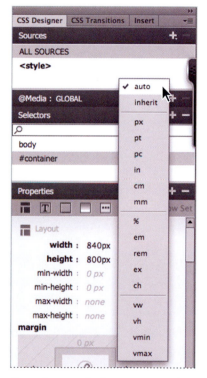

Choose the settings for the `#container` *element.*

You'll explore using margins in more depth, but by setting a margin value of auto to the left and right side of the container, you are instructing the browser to put equal amounts of space on the right and left sides. The end result will be a box that is centered within the browser window.

9   With the layout options still in view, scroll down to the `position` property. Click *static* to the right of the `position` label and choose relative from the menu. This is key to the success of your next steps. By setting the position of the container to relative you will be able to position the page elements using the container as a frame of reference.

10   Click the Background button from the Properties Navigation menu, then click the color swatch to the right of `background-color` and choose the white (#FFFFFF) swatch. This adds a background color of white to your entire container, separating it from the background.

11   Choose File > Save, then choose File > Preview in Browser. Your container will be centered in the middle of your browser window and Dreamweaver's default placeholder text is aligned in the top left of your container. (Occasionally, Dreamweaver does not add this placeholder text; if this is the case for you, return to Dreamweaver, click within the container, and then type **Content for id "container" Goes Here.**)

Content for id "container" Goes Here.

With position set to relative and auto margins, the container element will always be centered.

Resize the browser width; the container stays centered until the window is narrower than 840 pixels, at which point the box is cropped. Close your browser.

Absolute versus relative positioning

Absolute positioning: An element that is set to absolute strictly follows the positioning values given to it, relative only to its containing element. The containing element can be another div or the page itself. Absolutely positioned elements are pulled out of the normal flow of HTML content, and regardless of what surrounds them (for example, text content or neighboring divs), they always appear at the exact coordinates assigned to them.

Here is an example of a div absolutely positioned within another div. The larger div (Box #1) is the containing element, and so any positioning values assigned to Box #2 are relative to the element boundaries of Box #1.

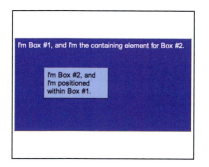

Box #2 is contained, or nested, within Box #1.

Adding additional content to the containing box (#1) has no effect on the nested div. It remains positioned outside the flow of HTML.

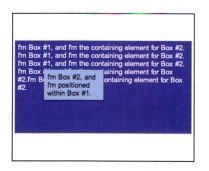

Box #2 remains in position even with added content in Box #1.

Relative positioning: A relatively positioned element accepts values for position properties such as top and left, but it also takes the normal flow of neighboring HTML content into account. Here are boxes and values shown in the preceding two figures; the only difference here is that the position property for Box #2 has been set to relative instead of absolute.

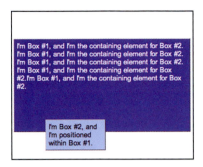

Box #2 is still offset, just as before, but it's being displaced by the content before it.

Although it appears that the top and left values have changed, they haven't. Unlike absolutely positioned elements, relatively positioned elements stay within the normal flow of HTML content, which means that they can be displaced by the elements (in this case, the text) surrounding them. In this example, Box #2 is still 50 pixels from the top and 50 pixels from the left, but its point of reference is the end of the preceding text content, not Box #1.

Positioning items relatively is useful when you want an item to flow with the items surrounding it. The following image shows five divs nested inside a larger div to create a menu.

All menu items are positioned relative to one another, and so they fall into place based on each other's position.

The same example is shown in the figure below, with the position set to absolute for all menu items. The result is a collapse of the menu—all the menu items are trying to occupy the same place at the same time, without regard for their neighbors.

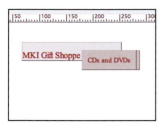

When set to absolute, the menu items stack on top of one another, because they all must be at the same place, regardless of the elements that surround them.

The files used for these examples are located in the dw05lessons folder, and are named **absolute_relative.html** *and* **relative_menu.html**. *Open them in Dreamweaver and explore the code to further your knowledge.*

Any element, or, in this case, any box, can have the position property applied, and one of five possible values can be set: absolute, fixed, relative, static, or inherit. The two most commonly used are absolute and relative, and although both can accept positioning properties such as top and left; they are rendered differently, even with identical positioning values.

Creating a header using a relative positioned div

We now have a container that is centered within your page. Next we'll add the other layout elements, starting with the header. We will use the Insert panel to insert a div as you previously did with the container div. Once a div is added, you can set the location and style it with CSS (change the width and height, add background color and more). You can also add content such as text or images.

1 Select the placeholder text *Content for id "container" Goes Here* and delete it.

2   In the Insert panel, click the Div button. When the Insert Div dialog box appears, choose After start of tag from the Insert drop down and select `<div id="container">` in the second drop down menu. Click in the ID text field and type **header** and click OK.

Insert Div		
Insert: After start of tag ▼	<div id="contai... ▼	OK
Class: ▼		Cancel
		Help
ID: header ▼		
New CSS Rule		

Create a new header div within the container div.

3   In the Sources panel of the CSS Designer panel, click `<style>`. In the Selectors menu choose the Add Selector button to create a new selector for the header. Dreamweaver will populate the selector field with `#container #header`. Change the text so the selector name is simply **#header** and press Enter (Windows) or Return (Mac OS) to accept this value.

4   Click the Layout button in the Properties Navigation Bar to show the layout properties width and height. Set the `width` to **840px** and the `height` to **80px**.

5   Scroll down to the `Position` property and click *static* to the right of the property text label and choose relative from the menu.

6   Click 0px to set the top position of the div to zero pixels and press Enter (Windows) or Return (Mac OS). The top of the box is now positioned vertically at 0 pixels.

7   Click 0px for the left property and press Enter (Windows) or Return (Mac OS) to accept the new left value. The left side of the box is now positioned horizontally at 0 pixels.

8   Click the Background button in the Properties Navigation bar to display the background-related properties. This time, instead of clicking the color palette to choose a color, click *undefined* and type **#9FCC41**, then press Enter (Windows) or Return (Mac OS). The yellow-green color is now applied.

9   Select the placeholder text *Content for id "header" Goes Here* and delete it. In its place, type **Organic Utopia**. You'll be replacing this with the logo a bit later, but for now this will serve as a placeholder.

10 Choose File > Save to save your work, and then preview your page by choosing File > Preview in Browser or by clicking the Preview/Debug in browser button (◉) at the top of the document window. Close the browser when finished.

You now have a header section within your page that is positioned relative to the container created earlier. The header will always appear at the top and aligned to the left side of the container because of the position values specified in your CSS rules.

Positioning content with absolute-positioned divs

Now that you have a header at the top of the page, you'll need to add boxes to hold content within the container. To accomplish this you will use absolute-positioned divs. An absolute-positioned div is placed exactly where you want it using the top, left, bottom and right properties.

For this exercise, you'll want your divs to be positioned using the container as their point of reference.

Adding an introduction section to your page

Now you can add additional sections to your page. The first section you'll add is a box below the header where you'll format an introductory paragraph to state the mission of the site, and grab the user's attention.

1   In the Insert panel, click the Div button. When the Insert Div dialog box appears, choose After tag in the Insert menu and select `<div id="header">`. Click in the ID text field and type **intro**, then click OK.

2   Choose `<style>` in the Sources panel. Click the Add Selector button in the Selectors menu to create a new selector for the introduction. Dreamweaver will populate the selector field with `#container #intro`; change this so the selector name is **#intro** and then press Enter (Windows) or Return (Mac OS).

3   Click the Layout button in the Properties Navigation Bar to show the layout properties and scroll down to the `position` property.

4   Click `static` to the right of the property text label, then choose absolute from the menu. Set the `top` value in the position control to **100px** to move the div down below the header div. Notice that the div now has a box around it with a handle in the top left corner.

The newly created absolute positioned div has a handle in its top-left corner.

5   Click the selection handle in the top-left corner of the new div and click and drag the box around the screen to see how you can position the box manually. Notice in the Property Inspector that the properties for your box are displaying and dynamically changing as you move it; currently just the Left and Top position (L and T) will change. Your settings will likely be different than those in the figure.

6   Click the resize handle in the bottom-right corner of the intro div and resize it so that it is roughly half the width of the header div and twice the height. Don't worry about the exact size of the box for now.

7   Click inside the intro box and type the following text: **Organic Utopia is a community owned and operated supermarket and marketplace. Anyone may shop in our stores but members enjoy special discounts and other benefits.**

The #intro *div with added text.*

Now you'll format the text in this box using techniques from the last lesson.

8   In the Property Inspector, click the HTML button if necessary. Select and highlight the text you entered and choose Paragraph from the Format drop-down menu.

9   Select <style> in the Sources panel of the CSS Designer panel. Click the Add Selector button in the Selectors menu to create a new selector for the intro div paragraph. Dreamweaver will populate the selector field with #container #intro p; change this text so the selector name is simply **#intro p** and press Enter (Windows) or Return (Mac OS).

10 Click the Text button (T) in the Properties Navigation Bar and then click default font to the right the font-family property. Click the font listing with Cambria, Hoefler Text, Liberation Serif, Times, Times New Roman, serif from the menu to change the font.

11 Locate the `font-size` property, click *medium* to the right of the label and choose large.

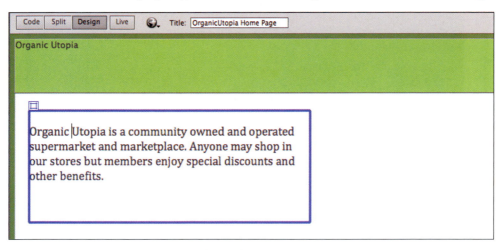

Set the paragraph text inside the intro box to Cambria and large.

Depending on how large you made your intro box, you will likely need to adjust the width and height of the box.

12 Click the edge of the intro box to activate it and then click any of the anchor points on the box to adjust the width and height. We used a width of **720px** and a height of **130px**. Click anywhere on the background of the page to deselect the intro div.

Another way to set the height and width values is by using the Layout properties in the Properties pane of the CSS Designer panel.

Adding images to your layout

Before you add the remaining sections of your page, you'll add images to both the header and container sections of the page. First, you'll add a background image of vegetables to the right side of your header.

1 In the CSS Designer panel choose `<style>` in the Sources pane and click the `#header` selector in the Selectors pane. Click the Background button in the Properties Navigation pane to bring up background-related properties. In addition to the background color, you can also add CSS background images.

2 In the `background-image` section, click the label *Enter file path* to the right of url, then click the Browse button (▢). In the select Image Source dialog box, navigate to the images folder within the dw05lessons folder and select **veggies.jpg**. Click OK (Windows) or Open (Mac OS) and you will see the image tiled across the header. (If you see a Missing Profile message click OK.)

By default, background images in CSS have this tiled effect, so you will need to add additional properties in order to remove the tiling and position the image to the right.

3 From the `background-repeat` property click the no-repeat button (■). From the `background-position` property click the first percent symbol % in the set background position control and choose right from the menu. The image is now aligned to the right side of the header.

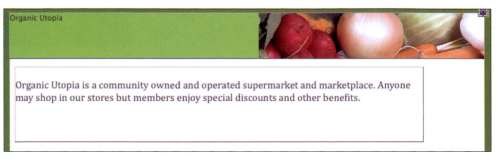

Background images can be added and positioned within a `<div>` element.

A background image is controlled by CSS, and you can only have one background image per element. In order to have two images inside the header, we'll add the Organic Utopia logo as an inline element. This means the logo is being added to the HTML code, not the CSS.

4 Select the Organic Utopia placeholder text in the `#header` div and delete it. Then choose Insert > Image > Image. In the Select Image Source dialog box, navigate to the images folder in the dw05lessons folder and select **ou_logo.gif**. Click OK (Windows) or Open (Mac OS).

5 Type **OrganicUtopia Logo** into the alt text field in the Property Inspector and press Enter (Windows) or Return (Mac OS). The image appears in the top-left corner of the header.

You will position this image away from the sides of the header box later in the lesson. (If you receive a Missing Profile message, click OK.)

When working with images, follow this rule of thumb: HTML inline images should be used for content; CSS background images should be used for decoration. One way to test this rule is to imagine the impact on the page if the image were not displayed. In the example above, the image of the vegetables is not essential, so the website would not be adversely affected if the image is not displayed; however, the logo is important, so it should be considered content, not decoration.

Photoshop integration

Often the images used in your web page need to be modified in Photoshop before they integrate well with your design. Photoshop and Dreamweaver are integrated in a few ways. In this exercise, you will see how Dreamweaver can optimize .psd files when you insert them into your page.

1 In the CSS Designer panel, then click the `#container` selector in the Selectors pane. Click the background button in the Properties Navigation Menu and click to the right of the URL label for the `background-image` property. Click the Browse button and navigate your dw05lessons folder, open the artwork folder. Choose the **veggie_background.psd** file and click OK (Windows) or Open (Mac OS) The Image Optimization dialog box appears.

This dialog box appears because you have chosen a .psd file to import and this is not a valid file format for the Web. Dreamweaver triggers the Image Optimization dialog box, which allows you to optimize the graphic and save it in a more appropriate format.

Importing a .psd file into Dreamweaver will trigger the Image Preview, allowing you to save as a web graphic.

2 Click the Preset menu and choose JPEG high for Maximum Compatibility if it is not already selected. Slide the Quality slider to 1 and notice that the preview of the image on your page becomes pixelated. Reducing the quality results in a smaller file size, but going too low results in unacceptable loss of detail.

3 Drag the Quality slider to 70, and notice that the quality improves dramatically. As with most compression, the goal is to find a good balance between small file size and image quality.

4 Click OK, and when the Save Web Image dialog box opens navigate to the images folder in the dw05lessons folder and double-click it. In the URL section, notice the path **images/veggie_background.jpg**. It's important to understand that you are saving a copy of the original PSD file as a JPEG in this step. Click Save and you now have a link to the new background image.

5 Scroll down to the background-repeat property and click the no-repeat button (■).

Adding Main and Sidebar content areas

Now you'll add two more sections to your page: a main column, which will feature the latest news from our fictional company Organic Utopia and a sidebar column, which features incentives for visitors to become members.

1 In the Insert panel, click the Div button. When the Insert Div dialog box appears, click in the ID text field and type **main**. Choose After tag from the Insert drop-down menu, then select <div id="intro"> and click OK.

2 Click the CSS Designer tab to bring up the CSS Designer panel and in the Sources pane click <style>. Click the Add Selector button in the Selectors menu to create a new selector for our main content section. Dreamweaver will populate the selector field with `#container #main`; change this so the name is simply **#name** and press Enter (Windows) or Return (Mac OS).

3 Click the Layout button in the Properties Navigation Bar to show the layout properties and scroll down to the Position property.

4 Click *static* to the right of the property text label, then choose absolute from the menu. The box appears with a blue border around it and a handle in the top left corner.

The width and height of an absolute position div can be change by clicking and dragging the resize handles.

Click the border and drag the div just below the intro div. Next, click and drag the handles to make the div roughly 450px wide by 200px high. Don't try to get the exact dimensions, as it is very difficult to be precise when resizing. You can always fine-tune the width and height in the Property Inspector.

5 Click the #main selector in the Selectors pane and click the Background button in the Properties Navigation Bar. Click the background-color swatch and choose white from the color palette.

6 We can also insert a div using the menu: Select Insert > Div to bring up the Insert Div dialog box. Choose After Tag and <div id="main"> from the drop-down menus then type **sidebar** in the ID field and click OK.

7 Click <style> in the Sources pane of the CSS Designer panel, then click the Add Selector button in the Selectors menu. Dreamweaver will populate the selector field with #container #sidebar; change this to **#sidebar** and press Enter (Windows) or Return (Mac OS).

8 Click the Layout button in the Properties Navigation bar and set the width to **240px** and the height to **200px**. Scroll down to position and choose absolute from the menu. Set the left value to **515px** and the top to **260px**.

9 Click the Background button in the Properties Navigation Bar and choose white for the background-color of this div as well.

You'll now make sure the top edges of the two boxes are lined up.

10 Click the handle on the top-left of the main div and reposition it to the following left and top values: L (Left) should be **35** and T (Top) should be **260**.

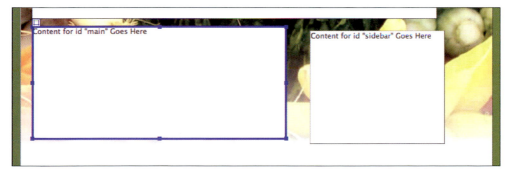

Setting the Left and Top values of an absolute positioned div.

With the top values the same for both boxes, the top edges line up. Once the boxes are lined up, you can always move them as a unit by selecting and dragging or nudging them.

11 Click the edge of the main div to select it and then Shift+click the sidebar. With both boxes selected, press your up arrow keys to move both boxes upward. There is no right value here, use your judgment and push the two boxes closer to the intro text.

Adding additional content and styles

Up to this point, you've been working with the base structure of your layout. Now it's time to add additional content in the form of text so that you can see how your layout works with real content, and make any necessary changes.

1   Select and delete the placeholder text *Content for id "main" Goes here*. Double-click the **main_content.html** file in the Files panel to open it. This is text that has already been formatted; all that is necessary is to copy and paste it into your layout.

2   Choose Edit > Select All and then choose Edit > Copy. Close the **main_content.html** document. In the **layout.html** document, click inside the main div and choose Edit > Paste. The content appears styled as Lucida Grande because there is a rule in the body defining the font-family; however, there are no CSS rules yet for headings or paragraphs.

*The results of copying and pasting the **main_content.html** page into your main div element.*

You pasted more content than can fit inside this box, which is why the text is flowing outside the boundaries of the container. In fact, what you are seeing is one of the disadvantages of using AP Divs. Defining the width and height of a box in pixels creates an inflexible container. One solution to this is simply to expand the size of the box.

3   Click the bottom of the blue border for the div and then click the resize handle in the middle of the border. While still pressing and holding the mouse button, drag the handle down slightly. The box will automatically expand to fit the existing content.

Now you'll add the content to the member benefit section.

4 Select and delete the placeholder text Content for id "sidebar" goes here. Double-click the **memberbenefits_content.html** file in the Files panel. Choose Edit > Select All and then choose Edit > Copy. Close the memberbenefits_content.html document. In the **layout.html** document, click inside the sidebar and choose Edit > Paste.

5 Click the bottom of the #sidebar div and then click the resize handle in the middle of the border. While still pressing and holding the mouse button, drag the handle down slightly to expand the box to fit the content.

Setting margins and borders

As you learned earlier, CSS uses the Box model for elements, and as such, each element can be given unique margins, padding, and borders, either for decorative or practical purposes.

Now that you have content inside your columns, it is clear that you need to do some fine-tuning. Your text and logo are crowded against their respective div elements and you should make them more pleasing and readable. Technically, you can start anywhere, but in this exercise, you'll start at the top of your page and work down.

1 Select the Organic Utopia logo in the header. In the CSS Designer panel, click <style> in the Sources pane then click the Add Selector button (**+**). Dreamweaver will add a new selector with the name #container #header img. Since the rule gets more specific from left to right, ultimately you are targeting the <img> tag located inside the header div, which is inside the container div; change this to **#header img** and press Enter (Windows) or Return (Mac OS).

2 Click the Layout button in the Properties Navigation Menu and scroll down to the margin control. In the Top text field, type **20** and press Enter (Windows) or Return (Mac OS). The logo is pushed down 20 pixels from the top of the header div, because there is now a 20-pixel margin applied to the top of the image.

3 In the Left margin text field, type **15** and press Enter (Windows) or Return (Mac OS). Adding a 15-pixel left margin pushes the logo to the right. Now you'll add similar margins in the main column.

4 Click anywhere inside the heading Celebrating Vegetables in the main div. In the CSS Designer panel click <style> in the Sources pane and click the Add Selector button in the Selectors menu. Make sure the selector name reads #main h2. Press Enter (Windows) or Return (Mac OS).

5   In the Properties Navigation Bar click the Layout button and scroll down to the margin control. In the Left text field, type **15** and press Enter (Windows) or Return (Mac OS).

Applying a left margin of 15 to the main heading.

6   Click inside the paragraph below the Celebrating Vegetables heading. In the CSS Designer panel click `<style>` in the Sources pane and click the Add Selector. Make sure that `#main p` is the selector name. Press Enter (Windows) or Return (Mac OS).

7   In the Properties Navigation bar, click the Layout button and scroll down to the margin control. In the `margin-left` field, type **15** and press Enter (Windows) or Return (Mac OS). In the `margin-right` field, type **15** and press Enter(Windows) or Return (Mac OS). You need to add both left and right padding because the text fills the main container from left to right.

Overriding default margins in CSS

If you are new to Dreamweaver and/or CSS, an important concept is that of default margins. Web browsers will apply default margins to most block elements unless there is a value overriding them. So paragraphs and headings, for example, will have space between them even if you haven't set a value. You can see this space by using Dreamweaver's Inspect feature.

1   In your document window, click the Live button to cause the Live Code and Inspect buttons to appear. Click the Inspect button and then click Split to display a split window with Code view on the left and Design view on the right. Now you can hover over elements on your page and see the normally invisible margins.

2 Place your cursor over the Celebrating Vegetables heading. The yellow highlight shows the margins being applied to this element.

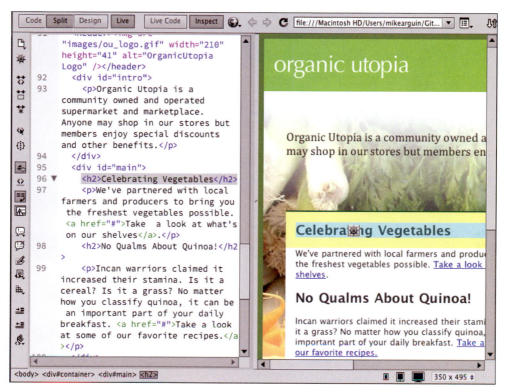

The Inspect feature in Dreamweaver CC highlights the margins of an element in yellow.

Hover over the paragraph below the heading and note there are margins being applied here as well. In order to reduce the space, you will need to reduce the bottom margin of the heading and the top margin of the paragraph.

3 In the CSS Designer panel, click `<style>` in the Sources pane, and then locate and click the `#main h2` style. Select the Layout button in the Properties pane and scroll down to the margin control. Set the bottom margin value to **0px** and press Enter (Windows) or Return (Mac OS).

4 Place your cursor over the heading. Note that the bottom margin is gone (in other words, there is no yellow border). You now need to set the top margin of the paragraph to 0 as well.

5 In the CSS Designer panel, click the `#main p` style and select the Layout button from the Properties pane. Scroll down to the margin control and set the top margin value to **0px** and press Enter (Windows) or Return (Mac OS). Now all the paragraphs in the main column shift upward.

6 Click the Live button to de-activate this mode, and then click the Design button to return to your default mode.

Because margins and padding are invisible, many designers resort to applying either background colors or borders to elements at the beginning of the layout process. This helps to understand the relationship between various sections on the page. The Inspect button in Dreamweaver partially removes the need to do this, but you could still find the original technique useful.

Adding borders to elements

The ability to add borders to elements is a great feature in CSS. Because of the CSS Box model, almost anything can be styled with borders: div elements, headings, lists and more. Additionally, the style, width and color of these borders can be set globally or for any given side.

1 In the CSS Designer panel, click `<style>` in the Sources pane and click the `#main` selector in the Selectors pane. Next, click the Border button in the Properties Navigation Bar to begin setting these properties.

2 Scroll down to `border-top-style`, select none in the Set top border style control and choose solid from the menu. Scroll down to the `border-bottom-style` property, click none in the Set `border-bottom-style` control and choose solid from the menu.

   In the Style menu, note the other options available. Styles such as dotted and dashed are the most reliable styles. For various reasons the other options such as groove, ridge, etc. are not particularly well-supported in older browsers and you should use them sparingly.

3 Locate the `border-top-width` property, click the Set top border width control and choose px from the menu. Note that you can also choose keywords here for thin, medium or thick. Select the 0 in the width value field and type **2**. Press Enter (Windows) or Return (Mac OS) to apply the changes. Locate the `border-bottom-width` property and set it to **2px** in the same manner.

4 In the `border-top-color` field, click *undefined* and type **#063**. Press Enter (Windows) or Return (Mac OS) to apply the dark green border color. Repeat this step to set the border-bottom-color to the same color.

   The borders will be hard to see since the div is still selected.

5 Choose File > Save All and preview the results by choosing File > Preview in Browser.

   Take a moment to admire your layout. You're almost done; however the last step is to future proof your page layout.

6 Close the browser and return to Dreamweaver.

Future proofing your layout

Absolutely positioning the elements of your page layout is very stable and reliable, but it also has some fundamental limitations. You have already seen what happens when there is more content than can fit inside a box: the box overflows resulting in unattractive content. You have also seen one solution, which is simply to expand the size of the box. Even this is not an ideal solution. Content on the Web changes constantly; text is added and removed, images are inserted and so on. The designer of the page might have little or no control over this, especially if they are handing a website off to a client who will eventually be updating and modifying the site.

To help strengthen your layout for future modification, you can use a CSS property called overflow. This will help you prevent the worst-case scenario of text that breaks your layout as it overflows its container. For this exercise, you'll apply overflow to the Members Benefits sidebar.

1   Click the bottom edge of the sidebar and then drag the bottom of the box upward until half of the list items are overflowing out of the box.

Text that is overflowing over the sidebar.

2   Click <style> in the Sources pane of the CSS Designer panel and then click the #sidebar selector in the Selectors pane. Click the Add CSS Property button in the Properties menu and type **overflow** in the text field that opens in the Properties pane. Press Enter (Windows) or Return (Mac OS) to create the overflow property.

3   Dreamweaver will place your cursor in the text box to the right of the newly created overflow property. Type **auto** and press Enter (Window) or Return (Mac OS) to set the `overflow` value to `auto`. This automatically adds scrollbars to any `<div>` element that has more text than can fit inside. You will see in Dreamweaver's design view that the box has snapped to fit the original height.

4   Choose File > Save, then File > Preview in Browser. Your `#sidebar` div now has a scrollbar. While it might not be an ideal solution if you do not like scrollbars, at least it doesn't break the layout. Close the browser and return to Dreamweaver.

The pros and cons of Absolutely Positioned CSS layouts

You will now take a look at the limitations and weaknesses of the layout you have just created. Absolutely positioned layouts in Dreamweaver are the quickest and easiest way to get a web page up and working, however, as noted earlier they are not the most flexible.

In this exercise, we hope to point out some of the limitations of Absolutely Positioned layouts so that you can judge for yourself whether they fit all your needs or whether you need to be looking at the next step of creating pages using more advanced layout techniques, which are covered in Lesson 6, "Advanced Page Layout."

To illustrate this, you will take a look at your existing layout with the premise that someone has asked you to make the entire container larger and also switch the position of the two columns on your page.

1   In the CSS Designer panel, click `<style>` in the Sources pane and choose the `#container` selector from the Selectors pane. Click the Show Set check box in the Properties Navigation bar to set the check box and show only those properties which have been set. Change the `Width` from 840 to **960**. The container width expands but when adding this extra 120 pixels of space, your header and the other sections are no longer well-aligned.

Your background image is now also too narrow. This cannot be easily resolved in Dreamweaver. You would have to go back to Photoshop, resize the image, and export it again. For now, you'll simply turn it off temporarily.

2 In the CSS Designer panel, click the `#container` selector, and click the Show Set button if necessary. Now scroll to the `background-image` property. Click the Disable/Enable CSS Property button (▦) to the right of the panel to turn off this image for now.

Clicking the Disable/Enable CSS Property button removes the style for the background image.

With the background image temporarily removed, it is easier to see the structure of your layout.

3 Click the `#header` selector in the Selectors pane. If necessary, click `<style>` in the Sources pane to show all selectors. Set the width in the Properties pane to **1024px** and notice it is easy to break your layout. This is because absolutely positioned elements don't interact with the other elements on the page; you need to manually adjust them.

4 Change the `width` of the header to **960px** so that it matches the width of the container exactly. You'll also notice that the background image of the vegetables remains flush right.

5 Click the edge of the intro box and using your arrow keys, nudge it to the right until it is centered within the page.

Now you need to switch the position of the main and sidebar divs.

6 Click the edge of the `main` div and use your arrow keys to nudge it to the right. Notice that it overlaps your sidebar. This is due to the behavior of absolutely positioned elements allowing them to occupy the same space on the page.

The property that controls which element is highest in the stacking order is called the z-index. Dreamweaver sets this property automatically when you create AP Divs. Elements with the higher z-index value will always win and be visible over elements with a lower z-index. You can also modify z-index values if you choose to adjust this.

7   Click the edge of the `sidebar` div and using your arrow keys nudge to the left until it reaches the original position of the `main` div.

You might need to nudge the position of the two boxes until you are satisfied with their position. Additionally, feel free to adjust the width of the boxes if needed.

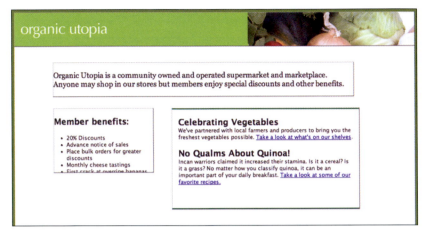

Switching the position of the two boxes requires you to move them manually.

Adjusting the width of the layout and the columns is not significantly difficult but it's also not very efficient. Wouldn't it be nice if expanding the width of the container automatically readjusted the columns within the new space? In fact, there are techniques you can use to accomplish this. They are called float-based layouts and you will learn these techniques in the next lesson. For now, save and close the files.

Self study

Get some practice with layout by creating a new div named footer in layout.html. Bring in the content from the footer.html file provided in your assets folder. Style the footer using the techniques learned in this lesson.

Open the style for the sidebar and apply similar margins and borders to those that you applied for the main div.

Experiment with your layout by expanding the width of the container div, changing the background color and adding borders. You will be surprised at how small changes to these properties can have dramatic effects on the appearance of your page.

Review

Questions

1   In what two ways can `<div>` elements be automatically positioned for the purpose of layout in Dreamweaver?

2   Why is it beneficial to name each div on your page? What two ways can you use to name your divs?

3   What is the `overflow` property and why would you use it?

Answers

1   Divs can be positioned relative to the rest of the content on the page or in an absolute location. Relative positioned divs maintain their flow within the document and are positioned with respect to the surrounding content. Absolute divs are removed from the flow of the document and remain where positioned regardless of the surrounding content.

2   It is beneficial to name your divs so that you can create style rules to apply to each named div. You can name your divs using IDs or classes. A div named using an ID can only appear once in the document while divs named using classes can occur in a document more than once.

3   The `overflow` property allows you to change the way a box appears if there is too much content. For example, an `overflow` set to auto creates a scroll bar if there is more content than can fit in the box.

What you'll learn in this lesson:

- Working with the CSS `float` property

- Creating columns with floated elements

- Working with the CSS `clear` property

- Creating a list-based CSS navigation bar

Advanced Page Layout

The best web layouts account for variable content on a page. As text and images are added and/or removed, your layout can adapt. In this lesson, you will create from scratch a two-column CSS layout using the float and clear properties in order to create an adaptable page layout.

Starting up

Before starting, make sure that your tools and panels are consistent by resetting your workspace. See "Resetting the Dreamweaver workspace" in the Starting up section of this book.

You will work with several files from the dw06lessons folder in this lesson. Make sure that you have loaded the dwlessons folder onto your hard drive from the supplied DVD. See "Loading lesson files" in the Starting up section of this book.

Before you begin, you need to create site settings that point to the dw06lessons folder from the included DVD that contains resources you need for these lessons. Go to Site > New Site, or, for details on creating a site, refer to Lesson 2, "Setting Up a New Site."

See Lesson 6 in action!

Use the accompanying video to gain a better understanding of how to use some of the features shown in this lesson. The video tutorial for this lesson can be found on the included DVD.

Layout with absolute-position divs versus layout with floats

In this lesson, you'll learn an advanced method of layout in Dreamweaver using CSS boxes that are floated as columns. Unlike the inflexible nature of absolute-position divs, floated layouts can accommodate additional content more easily, and once you learn how to use them, they will allow you to use more creative layout options.

There are two methods of layout in Dreamweaver, and you will learn about both of them. To understand this, it helps to keep in mind that historically Dreamweaver has been designed for use in the Design view (in other words, not working in code). As you will soon see, the CSS float property that you will be using to create columns was not truly designed to be a tool for layout, and requires a good understanding of CSS to be useful.

Floated layouts are trickier to control and understand than absolute-position divs. Additionally, older web browsers such as Internet Explorer 6 have well-documented bugs and quirks that can prevent floated layouts from rendering correctly. To address these problems, coding techniques known as *browser hacks* have been developed over the years. The browser hacks involve adding additional code targeted toward one browser in order to make the pages look the same.

As users of Dreamweaver seek to duplicate some of the sophisticated sites they see online, they really have no choice but to work with floats. As you walk through this lesson, it is important to keep in mind that you do not necessarily have to choose between absolutely positioned layouts and floated layouts. Layouts that combine both absolute-position divs and floated layouts are commonplace and combine the strengths of both.

In addition to the two layouts described above, Dreamweaver CC also has a third category of layouts: *fluid layouts*. The fluid layout feature represents the latest development in web design and development: creating web pages designed to adapt to screens of different sizes. You will have the opportunity to work with this feature at the end of the lesson; however, you should note that this form of layout is not for everyone, so understanding the fundamentals of float-based layouts is still the recommended path for most Dreamweaver users.

To start creating more sophisticated and flexible layouts, you will first need to have a good understanding of the float property.

Creating a floated image

One of the reasons the float property in CSS was created was to allow for the appearance of text to wrap around an image. This concept was borrowed from print design, where the effect is standard practice and often called text wrap or runaround. In CSS, this effect is achieved by allowing elements following a floated element in the HTML markup to surround the element, effectively changing position. This behavior also makes it possible to create columns on a page, although this might not have been the original intent of the rule.

In this exercise, you will learn the basics of using the float property by applying it to an image in order to wrap text.

1   From the dw06lessons site, open the **floatimage.html** page. You will see a page with a large paragraph block of text. Click in the middle of the paragraph, immediately before the sentence, *We also have added recyclable shopping bags.*

2   Now choose Insert > Image > Image and in the Select Image Source dialog box, choose the image **recycle_bag.gif** from the images folder, and choose OK. While the image is still selected, locate the Alt field in the Properties panel and type **shopping bag** in the text box, then click anywhere in the Design view to apply the change. The image has width and height dimensions of 81 × 101 pixels and is inserted as a block inside the paragraph.

An image with default styling placed inside a paragraph.

The amount of space between the two sentences is determined by the height of the graphic. This is the default flow of HTML when an inline image is inserted into a paragraph.

You'll now wrap the text around the image by applying the float property to the shopping bag graphic.

3   Click the `<style>` item under Sources pane in the CSS Designer panel. This will activate the Selectors panel and allow you to create a new style rule for the heading image.

4   Click the Add Selector button (⊞) in the Selectors menu to create a new CSS selector and type **.floatimage** in the selector name text box, replacing any text Dreamweaver might have added. Press Enter (Windows) or Return (Mac OS) to create the selector.

5   Click the Layout button (▥) in the Properties Navigation bar, locate the `float` property and click the Right button (▤) from the float settings.

6   Make sure the shopping bag graphic is still selected; if it is not, do so now. Look at the Property Inspector, there is a Class drop-down menu, which by default is set to None.

The default Class is set to None.

From the Class drop-down menu, choose floatimage. With the class applied, the image will now be removed from the flow of the text and pushed far right, to the edge of the container.

Change the Class to floatimage.

7   Choose `<style>` from the Sources pane and then click the `.floatimage` selector in the Selectors pane.

8   Click the Layout button (▥) in the Properties Navigation bar of the Properties pane and change the `float` property to left by clicking the Left button (▤) from the float options.

The image now floats to the left and the text wraps around it. This wrapping behavior is extremely important to keep in mind as you work with floated elements. You can float elements to the left or right only.

9 Locate the margin control. Click the `margin-top` value and type **10**, then click the value for `margin-right` and again, type **10**. Press Enter (Windows) or Return (Mac OS). The image now is set off from the text, adding needed space.

Set the Margin for the image.

10 Choose File > Save, and then File > Preview in Browser and choose a browser the your list to see the results in your browser. This technique is a simple and useful application of the `float` property. The next step is to apply this same concept to other elements, not just images. In the next exercise, you will float elements to create columns. Close your browser and then close the **floatimage.html** document.

Creating columns with HTML and CSS

One of the most important aspects of working with floated elements is understanding how they interact with their surrounding elements. This relationship is easy to understand when you have an object with a fixed width and height such as the shopping bag graphic from the last exercise. When floated elements are objects that are not fixed in size, such as a column which is defined by the amount of text inside, things can get interesting.

Using HTML5 Semantic elements

HTML5 introduces new semantic elements allowing you to add more detail and information to the structure of your documents. These semantic elements replace the multitude of divs that were previously used to divide your page into sections. Like divs, there is no set style or presentation defined and how they are displayed is determined by the CSS style rules you create.

The new semantic elements used in this lesson include:

header: The header element is used to indicate an area of your page as a heading, usually a page or section header

nav: The nav element is used to indicate an area of your page that will serve as navigation or a menu area

section: The section element is used to indicate an area of your page that contains content

aside: The aside element is used to indicate content that is related to but not included in the main content flow, typically used for sidebars and callouts

footer: The footer element is used to indicate a section of content as a footer, usually a page or section footer.

Creating the structure with divs and HTML5 semantic elements

To begin, you'll start with a page similar to the Organic Utopia layout from Lesson 5, "Creating Page Layouts with CSS." Specifically, the container div is 960 pixels wide and styled to be centered within the browser. The header element has one inline image (the Organic Utopia logo). You will first define the structure of the page by adding elements for the various sections.

1   In the Files panel, double-click the **layout.html** page. Your first step will be to add the navigation section. You will do so using the HTML5 nav semantic element.

2   In the Insert panel, choose the Structure category, then click the Navigation button (⬛) from the list of elements. The Insert Navigation dialog box opens. Here you can choose where you would like the new nav element to be inserted. You need the navigation element to follow the header element.

3   In the Insert Navigation dialog box, click the Insert drop-down menu. Select
the After tag option, then in the drop-down menu to the right, choose
`<header id="header">` Type **navigation** in the ID text field, and then click OK.

Insert Navigation

Insert: After tag   `<header id="header">`   OK

Class: Cancel

ID: navigation   Help

New CSS Rule

Set the properties in the Insert Navigation dialog box.

4   Click the CSS Designer tab to bring the CSS Designer panel to the front then select
`<style>` from the Sources pane. Click the Add Selector button in the Selectors pane
and Dreamweaver will add a new selector to the list as `#container #navigation`.
Select and delete the text `#container` so that the selector is simply `#navigation`,
place your cursor after `#navigation` and press Enter (Windows) or Return (Mac OS).

5   Click the Background button ( ) in the Properties Navigation bar. Locate the
`background-color` property and type **#88b036** into the Set `background-color` text
field and press Enter (Windows) or Return (Mac OS) to add a green background color.

6   Click the Layout button ( ) in the Properties Navigation bar and locate the `width`
property, then click the Set Width field to display the units popup menu. Choose
% from the menu and type **100** in the Set width text field. Click in the Set height
text field and choose px from the menu, then type **36** and press Enter (Windows)
or Return (Mac OS). Your navigation section now spans across the width of the
container.

You'll now add three elements for the main and sidebar columns, as well as the footer.
These next three steps are essentially variations on step 3: you are adding structural
elements to your page and giving the elements good names to begin styling them.

7   In the Insert Panel, scroll down and click the Section button ( ). Click the Insert
drop-down menu and choose the After Tag option, and then in the drop-down menu
to the right choose `<nav id="navigation">`. Type **main** in the ID text field and
then click OK.

8   Click the Aside button ( ) in the Insert panel. Click the Insert drop-down menu
and choose the After Tag option, then in the drop-down menu to the right, choose
`<section id="main">`. Type **sidebar** in the ID text field and then click OK.

The last section you will add will be for the footer at the bottom of the page.

9   Click the Footer button (⬛) in the Insert panel. Click the Insert drop-down menu. Select the After Tag option, then in the drop-down menu to the right choose `<aside id="sidebar">`. Type **footer** in the ID text field and then click OK.

10   You will now style these new elements using the CSS Designer panel. Select `<style>` from the Sources pane, then click the Add Selector button in the Selectors pane and Dreamweaver will add a new selector to the list as `#container #footer`. Select and delete the text `#container` so that the selector is simply `#footer`, place your cursor after `#footer` and press Enter (Windows) or Return (Mac OS).

You will be adding a `background-color` style now so you can more easily see how the footer interacts with the two columns.

11   Click the Add CSS Property button in the Properties pane, and then click the Background properties button in the Properties Navigation bar. Locate the `background-color` property and type **#CCC** into the Set `background-color` text field and press Enter (Windows) or Return (Mac OS) to add a light gray background color.

You now have the main sections of your page, and you will have to start setting the widths of the columns.

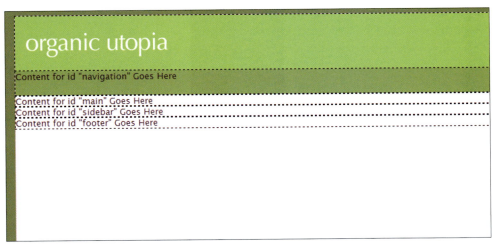

The main sections of your web page are now created.

Setting the width and floating the columns

With the basic structure of your page set up in HTML, you will now set the width of the main and sidebar columns and float them using CSS. You will return to the navigation bar in a later exercise.

1   Click to place your cursor within the main section of your document window then click <style> in the Sources pane of the CSS Designer panel. Click the Add Selector button in the Selectors pane and type **#main** in the new selector field, then press Enter (Windows) or Return (Mac OS).

2   Choose the Layout button from the Properties Navigation menu. Double-click to the right of the width property, type **600px** inside the Set-width text field and press Enter (Windows) or Return (Mac OS). Scroll down to the float property; choose right and you will see the main column move to the right and the sidebar column move up to fill in the remaining space. Now you'll add some content to see how it fits into the column.

3   In the Files panel, double-click the **main_content.html** page. Select all the text on this page, then press Ctrl+C (Windows) or Command+C (Mac OS) to copy it. Close the file, then select the placeholder text in the main element and press Ctrl+V (Windows) or Command+V (Mac OS) to paste. The column expands to accommodate all the content. Notice that the footer appears to be behind the main column. This is a result of the floated properties you just added. You'll take a look at this shortly, but first you will style the sidebar.

4   Click inside the sidebar, then in the CSS Designer panel, click <style> in the Sources pane and click the Add Selector button in the Selectors pane. Change the text so that the selector name reads #sidebar and press Enter (Windows) or Return (Mac OS). Choose the Layout button (▥). Double-click the Set width text field, type **360px** and press Enter (Windows) or Return (Mac OS). Scroll down to the float property and choose Left. Visually, very little will change, but the two columns now have explicit widths and both are floating.

5 In the Files panel, double-click the **sidebar_content.html** page. Select all the text on this page and copy it. Close the file, and then click inside the sidebar and paste, replacing the placeholder text. The sidebar expands to fit this content, which is a definition list.

The sidebar section is floated to the left and has a width of 360. The main section is floated to the right and has a width of 600.

We have cheated a bit in this exercise and created pre-existing styles for the sidebar content. Many of the techniques for modifying the margins of elements have been covered in earlier lessons. You can look at the styles for the <dl> and <dd> elements within the styles panel or the code view to see the details.

The behavior and appearance of the footer element could be somewhat confusing. As noted earlier, it appears to be behind your two columns. The reason for this has to do with the nature of floated elements. Floated elements are removed from the default flow of HTML and since both columns are floated, the footer ignores them and moves up directly below the navigation section. This is also why the height of the footer has expanded. From the perspective of the footer, there are no columns to interact with so it assumes its default behavior.

In order to push the footer below the columns, you need to add another CSS property to the footer called clear.

Using the `clear` property

When you apply the `clear` property to an object, you are essentially adding a rule that says *No floated elements are allowed on either side of me*. In fact, you can specify whether the left, right or both sides can have floated elements. You'll try two different options in order to understand the `clear` property better.

1   Choose `<style>` from the Sources pane of the CSS Designer panel. In the Selector pane, click the `#footer` selector, then click the Layout button (▦) in the Properties Navigation bar. Scroll down to the `clear` property and click the Right button (▤). This puts the footer element on the bottom of the page. You might need to scroll down to see it.

   Although this seems to do the trick, there is a potential pitfall. You set the clear value to Right, but what would happen if the content in the main column were shorter than the content in the sidebar? Understanding the answer to this question will go a long way toward your understanding of floats and clears, so you'll do a short experiment.

2   In the main `section` select the last three paragraphs and headings and then delete them. With less content in this column now, the footer still behaves the same and stops at the bottom of the main column, but the sidebar is longer now so the footer overlaps it.

Select and delete the last three paragraphs and headings in the Main div.

Of course, you could fix this by switching the value of the `clear` property from Right to Left. This would prevent the footer from being next to the sidebar, but the problem is that you might never know which column will have the most content, so the safest solution is to apply the `clear` property to both sides.

3   Choose Edit > Undo Delete to bring the content back into the main `section`.

4   Choose `<style>` in the Sources pane of the CSS Designer panel. Click the footer element and click the `#footer` selector in the Selectors pane, then click Show set check box (Show Set) in the Properties Navigation bar. Locate the `clear` property and click the Both button. The footer element will now always be at the bottom because no floated elements are allowed to the left or the right.

Creating a list-based CSS navigation bar

Floats can not only be used for simple image wrapping and creating columns, but also to create navigation. Here you'll start creating a list-based navigation that uses CSS. This is a great way to create easily editable navigation bars that are also search engine-friendly because they use text instead of images. Additionally, you can think of navigation as simply a list of links to other pages, so it makes sense to use the list element. The first step is to add the content and then style the list items and the navigation element.

1   Select the placeholder text in the navigation element and if necessary click the HTML button in the Property Inspector. Click the Unordered List button and the text will become the first bullet in an unordered list.

2   Replace the placeholder text by typing **Home**, and then press Enter (Windows) or Return (MacOS).

This adds a new list item. Add the following navigation sections pressing Enter/Return after each one: **About Us**, **Products**, **Services**, **Contact**. Your layout will appear to break as the list items are added. Don't worry; you will be using float properties to turn this list into a horizontal navigation bar.

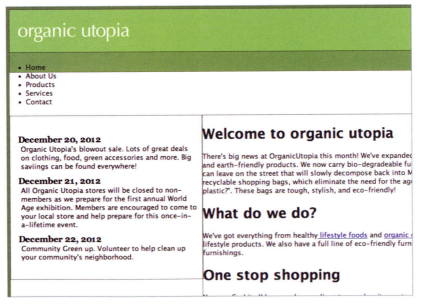

Add the list items that will serve as your navigation.

You will now link the 5 items. The pages in this case have not been created so you will use a placeholder link for each item.

3 Select the Home list item, click inside the Link text field in the Property Inspector and type **#** and then press Enter (Windows) or Return (Mac OS). This symbol creates a placeholder hyperlink. Repeat this step for each list item until all five are hyperlinked.

Now you'll apply the `float` property and turn this vertical list into a horizontal one.

4 Click the `<li>` element in the tag selector.

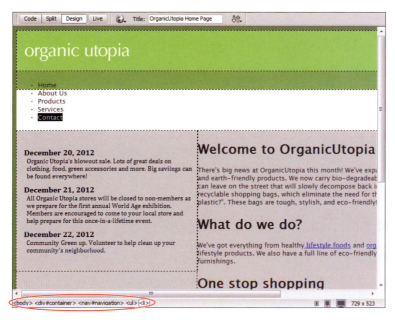

Select the `<li>` element in the tag selector.

Click `<style>` in the Sources pane. Click the Add Selector button in the Selectors Pane and change the text supplied by Dreamweaver so the compound selector reads `#navigation ul li`. Press Enter (Windows) or Return (Mac OS).

5 Uncheck the Show Set button and then click Layout button from the Properties Navigation bar. Scroll down to the `float` property and choose Left. You will see that your list items are now stacked horizontally rather than vertically. By applying the `float` property, you have overridden the list items' default behavior. However, there is still more work that you need to do.

6 Click the Other button (⬛) in the Properties Navigation bar then choose none from the Set list-style-type drop-down menu. This removes the bullet points from each list item.

You still need to do more work; specifically, you need to create styles for the `<a>` element that is for hyperlinks. You'll style the appearance and position of these links now.

7   Click inside any link in the navigation and click <style> in the Sources pane. Next, click the Add Selector button from the Selectors pane. The selector type is compound, but unnecessarily complex; edit the text so the selector name is set to #navigation ul li a, place your cursor at the end of the line, and then press Enter (Windows) or Return (Mac OS).

Create a new CSS rule for the navigation hyperlinks.

8   Click the Text button (T) from the Properties Navigation menu. Locate the text-decoration property and click the button labeled none. This will remove the default underline below your hyperlinks. Locate the color property, click the color swatch, and choose white. Finally, locate the white-space property and chose nowrap from the menu of options. This will make sure your navigation links do no wrap to a second line and disrupt the content below.

9   Click the Layout button (▥) from the CSS Navigation menu and scroll down to the padding control. Type **8 px** for the top value and press Enter (Windows) or Return (Mac OS). Repeat the steps setting the bottom to **8px** the left and right values to **15 px**.

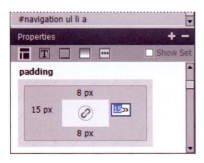

Apply padding to the hyperlink styles to create more space between your navigation.

10   Scroll down to the display property and choose block from the pop-up menu. This property and value changes the appearance of the list item: it expands and also allows the entire block to be clickable, not just the text.

You're almost finished; however, your navigation links are currently overlapping the boundaries of the green navigation bar. This is because of some default margins—a topic you have run into before. In this case, the default margins of the unordered list are the culprit.

11 Click anywhere inside the navigation, if necessary, and then click the `<ul>` tag in the Tag Selector. Click `<style>` in the Sources pane of the CSS Designer panel and click the Add Selector button. Edit the text making sure the selector reads `#navigation ul`, and then press Enter (Windows) or Return (Mac OS).

12 Click the Layout button in the Properties Navigation bar. Scroll down to the margin control and click the link button in the middle of the control. This will link all of the margins together using the same value. Click the `margin-top` property and type **0**, then press Enter (Windows) or Return (Mac OS). Repeat these steps using the padding control and the hyperlinks will be centered within the navigation element.

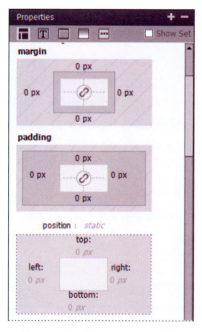

Set the margins for the navigation to give it a more defined look.

The last piece to add is a little interactivity. Say that when the user mouses over any one of the navigation links, you would like it to change color. This improves usability by letting the user know the links are active. You can do this with the `hover` property for hyperlinks.

13 Click within any link and then click `<style>` in the Sources pane of the CSS Designer panel. Click the Add Selector button and type **#navigation a:hover** in the selector name field.

Create a selector for #navigation a:hover.

Adding `#navigation` in front of the `a:hover` property creates a compound selector ensuring the styles only apply to links within the navigation menu. Press Enter (Windows) or Return (Mac OS).

14 Click the Background button in the Properties Navigation bar. Click the Set background-color text field and type **#9fcc41** and press Enter (Windows) or Return (Mac OS). This is the same green as the header.

15 Save your document and choose File > Preview in Browser to see your list-based CSS menu. Be sure to mouse over the links to see the hover effect. Close the browser window and return to Dreamweaver.

Creating a style for the `a:hover` property produces a color rollover effect when the user's cursor is on a link.

Changing column layout and size

Another benefit of using floated containers for layout is that they are very easy to modify. For example, perhaps you would like to experiment with your sidebar being on the right rather than the left, or perhaps you would like to experiment with changing the width of the entire layout. This can all be accomplished with a few easy modifications of the styles.

1   In the CSS Designer panel, choose `<style>` from the Sources pane and click the `#main` style in the Selectors pane. Click the Show set check box to limit the list to only the properties that have been set and change the float property from right to left. This pushes the main box over to the left of the container and the sidebar slips to the right.

2   In the Selector pane, click the `#sidebar` selector; change the `float` property from left to right. There will be no visual change in this case, but it does ensure that the sidebar is flush against the container. That's it! Two simple style changes create a completely different layout.

Change the Float value of the `#sidebar` style from left to right.

If you'd like to change the overall width of your page layout, you can do this by modifying the `#container` div.

3   Click `<style>` in the Sources pane of the CSS Designer panel, then click the `#container` selector in the Selectors pane and change the width from 960 to **1100** and press Enter (Windows) or Return (Mac OS). This expands your container, and because your columns are floating, they will both remain aligned to their respective sides. For the purpose of this exercise, the original value of 960 is better, so type this value back again. For now, the important part is to understand the concept.

4   While you are here, select the `height` property and delete it, removing it from the list. Having a fixed height is useful at the beginning of the layout progress, but it should be removed at some point in order to accommodate more content.

Fine-tune your page: currently, the main column is aligned flush left against the container and the text is too close to the edge of the container. This is a common layout problem; you will now look at some techniques designed to help you create your own custom layouts and to better understand the behavior of floated elements.

5   Click the `#main` selector in the Selectors pane of the CSS Designer panel, and then clear the Show set check box in the Properties Navigation bar. Click the Layout button and scroll down to the margin control. Type **20** inside the Set left margin text field, and then press Enter (Windows) or Return (Mac OS).

Adding 20 pixels of left margin to the `#main` column pushes it below `#sidebar`.

Notice that this change had the desired effect of adding space between the main column and the surrounding container. However, there is another effect: the `#main` column has now slipped down below. This effect is to be expected because you are trying to squeeze two boxes into a fixed width space. Remember that the container is 960 pixels wide. The main column is 600 pixels wide, and you just added 20 pixels to it, thus making the true width 620 pixels. The sidebar is 360 pixels wide; adding the combined widths results in 980 pixels.The `#main` column slips below `#sidebar` because we added `#sidebar` before `#main` so it appears first in the HTML code.

This is a common dilemma with fixed width layouts, but as long as you understand the relationships, it is easy to fix. In this case, you'll try reducing the width of the main column.

6   Click the Show set check box to show the current properties and change the `width` from 600 to **580**, then press Enter (Windows) or Return (Mac OS). The width is reduced and the sidebar slips back up.

However, you can take this a bit further: the columns are actually very close to each other. You can add more space by reducing the width of the main section even further.

7   Type **550** as the width, and then click OK. You now have an additional gap of space between the main section and the sidebar.

Keep in mind that you could have decreased the width of the #sidebar *style if you preferred to keep the width of the* #main *column intact. There are no set rules for how to do this correctly. Layout in CSS becomes interplay between width, margins, padding, and content; every page has slightly different requirements. Just be sure to keep track of all these relationships in your own designs, since it can get confusing as you add more elements.*

Creating the appearance of equal height columns

There is now another part of your layout that you need to pay attention to: the column height. Currently, the main column is longer than the sidebar; visually this isn't really a problem because neither column has a background color, so the whole page appears white. But what happens if your design requires that explicit columns be defined by color? In this exercise, you'll look at one solution for this issue.

1   Choose <style> from the Sources pane of the CSS Designer panel, then click the #sidebar selector in the Selectors pane. You might have to click <style> to enable all of the selectors to display. Make sure the Show set check box is unchecked, and then click the Background button (▭) in the Properties Navigation bar. Finally, in the Set background-color text field, type **#C8D9BC** and press Enter (Windows) or Return (Mac OS).

2   Click the Border button (▭) in the Properties Navigation bar and locate the border-left-style property. Choose solid in the Set left column style drop-down menu. Locate the border-left-width property, double-click the Set left border width field, and type **2px**. Press Enter (Windows) or Return (Mac OS). Finally, scroll to the border-left-color property and type **#060** in the Set left border color text field. Press Enter (Windows) or Return (Mac OS).

Set the border for the #sidebar *element.*

The problem with the column is an aesthetic one. A column sometimes looks better when it spans to the bottom of the page rather than cutting off abruptly. Additionally, if you are using this layout throughout your site, every page will likely have different amounts of content. As a user moves from page to page, this would create irregular page appearance, as the column height jumps up and down based on the amount of content. To solve this, you'll add a background image to the container div, which simulates the appearance of the column from top to bottom.

3 In the Selectors pane of the CSS Designer panel, click the `#container` selector. You might have to click `<style>` in the Sources pane to display all of the selectors. Click the Background button ( ) in the Properties Navigation bar, and click the Enter file text box for the `background-image` property. Click the Browse button ( ) and locate the **container_bg.gif** file in the images folder. Click OK (Windows) or Open (Mac OS).

This graphic is 960 pixels wide (which matches the width of your container), but it is only 2 pixels high. Essentially, it is a thin horizontal slice of the page and includes the sidebar color and green border.

4 From the `repeat` property, click the button for repeat-y ( ). This ensures the graphic will only be tiled from top to bottom and you will now see your columns filled in.

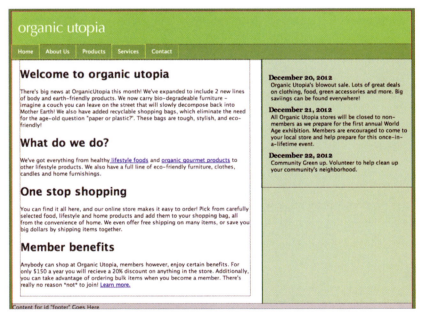

A fake column background image creates the effect of a column extending the height of the page.

Now, the length of the column is irrelevant. The image background will always reach the bottom of the page and maintain a consistent appearance.

Although this technique is useful, it relies on your layout being finalized. If the width of your container or the position of any of your columns changes, you must then change the background image. Additionally, other changes, such as the color of a column or any padding adjustments, could require you to modify your background image. For this reason, you should wait until the small changes and adjustments to your layout are complete before making a column background.

How to create a fake column background in Photoshop

The easiest way to make the fake column background is if you happen to have a mockup of your website as an image file or as a Photoshop file with layers. However, if you don't have a mockup, you need to be more creative. Here's how we created our page background.

1 Preview your web page in the browser. Look to make sure you have a clear cross-section of your columns from left to right. If there are any text or images in the column, you might need to go back to Dreamweaver and remove them temporarily.

2 Use your system's screen capture program capture your screen. In the Mac OS, this can be done with the keyboard shortcut, Command+Shift+3. In Windows, use the Print Screen button to capture.

In the case of the Mac OS, this will create a png file that will be saved to your desktop. In the case of Windows, this will copy the screen image to your clipboard.

3 In Photoshop, either open the screen capture image directly (Mac OS) or if in Windows, choose File > New, then click OK and press Ctrl+V.

4 Click the Rectangular Marquee tool, then in the Options panel, change the style from Normal to Fixed Size. Type in a width of **960 px** and a height of **2 px**. If your original layout has a different width, you will need to change this width value to match.

5 Click anywhere in the image with the Marquee tool to add a floating selection. Using your arrow keys, you must line up the selection exactly with the edges of the container. If the selection is even 1 pixel off, it will result in a mismatch between the image and the real HTML columns.

6 Choose Image > Crop, then choose Save for Web and Devices to save it as a gif, jpg or png. Try to optimize the image in order to make it as small as possible. For example, in our case, we saved it as a gif using only 4 colors.

Applying finishing touches

You'll now tidy up some loose ends with your layout. Specifically, you'll add a background image to your header, and then move the rules in your current style sheet to an external style sheet so you can use these styles for other pages in your site.

1   Choose `<style>` in the Sources pane of the CSS Designer panel, then click the `#header` selector in the Selectors pane. Click the Background button (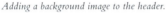) in the Properties Navigation bar and locate the `url` property in the background-image section. Click the Enter the file path field, and then click the Browse button. Navigate to your images folder, choose **veggies.jpg**, and then click OK.

2   Click the no-repeat button (▪) from the `background-repeat` property. Click the first percent sign in the `background-position` property and choose Right. Notice that the veggies image has been applied to the right side of your header.

Adding a background image to the header.

Now you will move all the style rules to an external style sheet so you can use these styles on new pages.

3   Click the Add CSS Source button (▪) in the Sources pane of the CSS Designer panel and choose Create A New CSS File. The Create a New CSS File dialog box will appear. Click the Browse button and navigate to your site root directory. Type **styles.css** in the File name field, and then click Save. When you return to the Create New CSS File dialog box, click OK. You now have an external style sheet that we can use to save your rules.

4   Choose `<style>` from the Sources pane of the CSS Designer panel, then click the first selector in the list `body`. Scroll down, and then Shift+click the last style. This will select all the styles for the page. Click the selected items and drag them to the styles.css file in the Sources pane and release your mouse. The rules should disappear from the internal `<style>` source and be moved to the external styles.css file. Click **styles.css** in the Sources pane to verify that your rules have been moved.

You now have an external style sheet that can be attached to new or existing pages in your site. (If you receive a message saying that duplicate names are being copied, confirm the save, don't cancel.)

5   Choose File > Save All, which will save both the HTML and CSS files. Then choose File > Close to close this page.

Creating more sophisticated layouts

The two-column layout you created represents a good foundation for a website. You would refer to this as a Two-column fixed-width layout with a header and footer. However, you might be looking for more options. For example, what about a three-column layout, or a liquid layout in which the content adjusts to the width of the browser (also referred to as a flexible or fluid layout)? It is beyond the scope of this book to walk through all these options. However, Dreamweaver does offer a way to create different layouts on the fly. You can choose from a gallery of new layouts whenever you create a new page.

1   Choose File > New and make sure HTML is selected as the Page Type. In the Layout column, the None option is the default, but you can also choose from a number of pre-made options.

2   Choose the 2 column fixed, right sidebar, header and footer option. Notice that a small thumbnail with a description of the layout appears. Click Create.

The thumbnail preview of the two column layout.

3   Choose File > Preview in Browser and when prompted, save this file as **2col_fixed.html**. Adjust the width of the browser and you will see that the width of the container page remains fixed, as well as the content within.

Take a moment to read the text in this page. It mentions that the code for this page has been commented. You'll take a look at this code now, in order to better understand the pros and cons of using these pre-generated pages.

Close the browser and return to Dreamweaver.

4   Click the Code View button and scroll to the top if necessary. The code in light gray represents comments that describe virtually every line of the CSS. So why is there a need to comment this file so heavily? To make a long story short, the code in this file is very robust and is optimized for cross-browser display. This means there are styles that address various bugs across different browsers, as well as other relatively advanced CSS code.

This presents a dilemma: You will benefit most from these templates only as long as you know how to modify them. In order to modify them effectively, however, you need to understand the rules of HTML and CSS relatively well. There is a limit to how far a WYSIWYG (What You See Is What You Get) application can take you in learning these rules.

This should not stop you in exploring these page layouts. They are extremely useful, and can be incredible time-savers. Just be aware that reverse-engineering how a page works can also be time-consuming, and that the answers might lie in the rules of HTML and CSS, and not in the Dreamweaver application.

5   Choose File > Close All and save any files if prompted.

Dreamweaver Fluid Grid Layout

A feature introduced in Dreamweaver CS6 was the addition of Fluid Grid Layouts. This is a system for creating websites that are alternatively known as adaptive or responsive, meaning that the layout of your pages changes depending on the size of the user's screen. The model for this form of layout is in many ways radically different than the techniques presented in this lesson. Fluid Grid Layout uses a combination of HTML5, CSS3, and JavaScript to create layouts that are optimized for mobile devices and monitor screens of different sizes.

The techniques covered in this lesson are very well-tested and reliable in the current crop of web browsers; the techniques used for Fluid Grid layout introduce new complexities that are best covered in a separate lesson. This is why we cover them in Lesson 16, "Responsive Design and Layout for Mobile Devices."

Self study

Experiment with the float property by opening the floatimage.html used in the first exercise. Add five or six instances of the shopping bag graphic in a row and apply the floatimage class to all of them. How could you create a thumbnail photo gallery using this technique?

Review

Questions

1   The float property allows you to float an element to the left, right and center. True or False?

2   What are the three possible values for the clear property? Name a situation where you might use this property.

3   How would you apply padding to a floated column?

Answers

1   False. The float property only has three values: left, right and none. You cannot float an element to center.

2   You can apply the clear property to an element with one of the following values: left, right or both. Elements with a clear property do not allow a floated element to the side specified. A common situation where you might use this would be when you need the footer element on your page to appear below any floated columns.

3   Select the selector for the column in the Selectors pane of the CSS Designer panel that you want to apply padding to by clicking it. Click the Layout button in the Properties Navigation bar. Then set a value for padding using the padding control.

What you'll learn in this lesson:

- The role of CSS3 in Dreamweaver CC
- Creating a CSS Transition
- Creating a CSS Gradient
- Creating rounded borders

CSS3 Transitions and Styles

Dreamweaver CC supports a number of CSS3 styles including CSS3 Transitions, Gradients and rounded borders for upgrading the style and appearance of your site. CSS3 Transitions add a way to create basic animations using CSS properties such as background-color and size to add interactivity to your website.

Starting up

Before you begin, reset your workspace to ensure your tools and panels are consistent. For more information, see "Resetting the Dreamweaver workspace" in the Starting up section of this book.

In this lesson, you will work with several files from the dw07lessons folder. Make sure that you have loaded the dwlessons folder onto your hard-drive from the supplied DVD. For more information, see "Loading lesson files" in the Starting up section of this book.

Before you can proceed with the exercises in this section, you need to create site settings that point to the dw07lessons folder. Go to Site > New Site, or for details on creating a site, refer to Lesson 2, "Setting Up a New Site."

See Lesson 7 in action!

Use the accompanying video to gain a better understanding of how to use some of the features shown in this lesson. The video tutorial for this lesson can be found on the included DVD.

Understanding the role of CSS3

Cascading Style Sheets is a separate language from HTML; however, both languages are constantly evolving. The original CSS1 specification was released in 1996 and included many of the basic CSS properties used today, such as background–color, font-family and so on. Over the years, new versions of CSS have emerged with revisions and additions to the original specification. CSS3 is the latest version of the language and offers a number of new CSS properties that give designers new tools for adding style to their pages.

The details of the evolution of CSS are not as important as understanding the key issue: browser support. Although CSS3 offers a number of exciting and useful features, designers and developers need to know which features the different web browsers can reliably support. There are a tremendous number of new features in CSS3, and these features have different levels of browser support. Most features you can use today very reliably, others might not yet be fully supported in all browsers. The architects of CSS3 have broken up the language into categories called modules; examples include Backgrounds, Borders and Animation, among others. In this lesson, you'll learn how to use CSS Transitions from the Animation module, Gradients from the Backgrounds module and Border radius from the Borders module.

Adding a CSS Transition

CSS Transitions in Dreamweaver CC offer a way to create simple animations on your page using only CSS. This is in contrast to the traditional method of creating effects, such as image rollovers, using JavaScript or Flash.

The basic concept of CSS Transitions is this: an object is animated by changing a property (or properties) over time. For example, in the following exercise you will start with a box that has its height property set to 350 pixels. You will then animate the height property down to 50 pixels over a period of two seconds. The result will be a slow collapsing effect when the user places their cursor over the box.

You'll start with a simple example file, and then in a later exercise, you will apply CSS transitions to the Organic Utopia layout.

1   Open the **07_csstransitions.html** document. Currently, this page has a single style rule for the ID #box. You should take a look at these styles before proceeding.

2   In the Design view, click the edge of the box to select it. To be sure that you have the actual box selected, check for the blue outline that will appear around the box, which confirms that it is selected. In the CSS Designer panel, choose <style> from the Sources pane if necessary, and then click the #box selector. This will expose the properties currently used. (If your Properties panel does not look like our screenshot, click the Show set check box in the Properties Navigation bar).

The CSS properties associated with the CSS ID #box.

The properties used here are background-color, border, height, width, font-family, and text-align. All these properties (and many more within CSS) can be animated using transitions.

Pay particular attention to the height property and the value, currently set to 300 pixels. You will now create a single transition that will animate the height of the box from the original 300 pixels to a more narrow height.

3   Choose Window > CSS Transitions to open the CSS Transitions window. This window lists all the existing transitions used in a document, and also allows you to Create, Remove, and Edit transitions.

4   Click the + sign in the upper-left of the CSS Transitions window; the New Transition window appears.

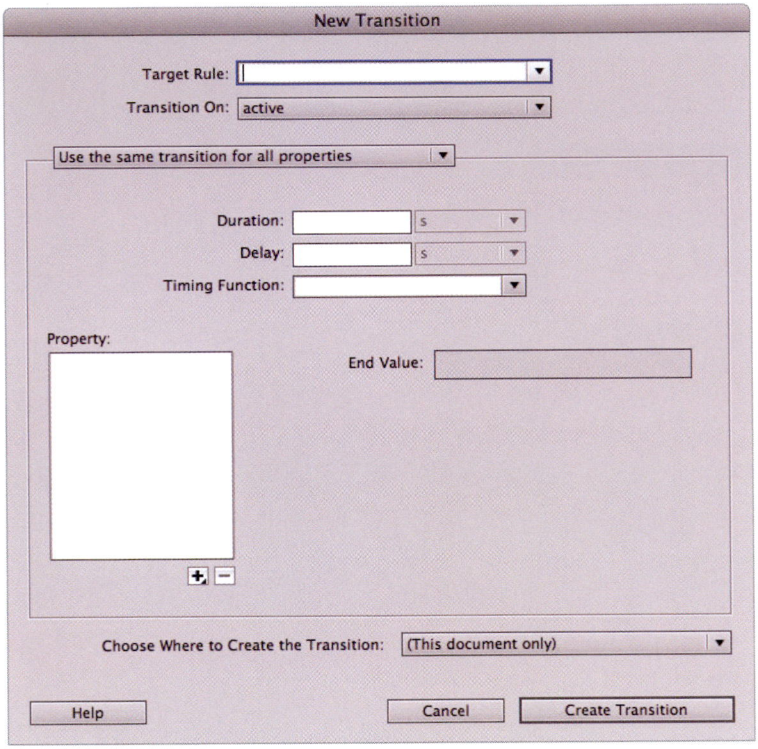

New Transition

Target Rule: |

Transition On: active

Use the same transition for all properties

Duration: ___ s

Delay: ___ s

Timing Function: ___

Property:

End Value: ___

Choose Where to Create the Transition: (This document only)

Help   Cancel   Create Transition

The New Transition window offers a number of options for you to create transition effects.

5   Click the Target Rule menu. The only choice available is for #box, the rule you examined in Step 2. In more complex documents, you would see all the rules used and could choose any of them. Choose #box from this drop-down menu.

6   Click the Transition On menu to see all the options available. A transition starts in one state and then moves to another, but something must trigger the transition. This menu lists the various options: active, checked, disabled, enabled, focus, hover, indeterminate, and target. You'll learn more about these options shortly.

The options available within the Transition on menu.

7   Choose the Hover option.

8   Click inside the Duration field and type **2**.

CSS Transitions provide a way to control the speed of animation changes for one or more CSS properties. In this instance, you are stating that you want this transition to last 2 seconds. You will return to the two other options—Delay and Timing Function—in the next exercise, but first you need to define which property you want to animate.

9 Click the + sign at the bottom of the Property section. A menu appears with the entire list of CSS properties you can control. Select the height property.

New Transition

Target Rule: #box

Transition On: hover

Use the same transition for all properties

Duration: 2   s

Delay:

Tim

Property:

background–color
background–image
background–position
border–bottom–color
border–bottom–width
border–color
border–left–color
border–left–width
border–right–color
border–right–width
border–spacing
border–top–color
border–top–width
border–width
bottom
color
crop
font–size
font–weight
height
left
letter–spacing
line–height
margin–bottom
margin–left
margin–right

Choose Whe   document only)

Help   ncel   Create Transition

Choose the height property from the available list of CSS properties.

As this list shows, you cannot animate every single CSS property. For the official list of available properties visit:
http://www.w3.org/TR/css3-transitions/#animatable-properties-

10   Click inside the field labeled End Value, type **50**, and make sure the menu to the right remains on pixels (px). The starting height of the box is 300 pixels; using this transition, you will change it to 50 pixels over a period of two seconds when the user hovers over the box.

Click the Create Transition button to add it.

11   Choose File > Save As, type **07_csstransitions_work** in the File name and click Save to save this file in the dw07lessons folder. Choose File > Preview in Browser.

Place your cursor inside the top of the box; you will see the box animate from the original height of 300 down to 50 pixels. As you move your cursor off the box, it begins to animate back to its original height.

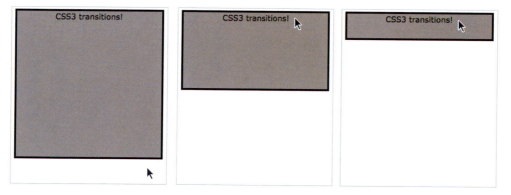

When the user hovers over the box, it animates from a starting height of 300 pixels to an ending height of 50.

This is a very basic example of a single CSS transition. In the next exercise, you will add more transitions and learn how to edit your existing one.

12   Close both the browser window and the original **07_csstransitions.html** page. Return to Dreamweaver. Keep the **07_csstransitions_work.html** file open, since you'll be working with it in the next exercise.

What if you can't see the transition?

You might not be able to see the transition effect in the last exercise if your web browser does not support the transition property. The support for CSS3 Transitions is relatively new and not all properties are equally supported across all browsers, specifically the most popular versions of Internet Explorer 6, 7, 8, and 9.

At the time of this writing, Microsoft has released Internet Explorer 10 with support for CSS Transitions. The following online resource provides a useful table to help you see the level of support for CSS Transitions for past, present, and future (planned) browsers.

http://caniuse.com/#feat=css-transitions

Modifying a CSS Transition

Now that you have seen how a CSS Transition works, you'll now see how to modify the existing transition speed, add a delay, and adjust the timing of the animation using a feature called Easing.

Before you get started with the modifications, you'll take a quick look at the CSS code that Dreamweaver creates in the background.

1   Click the Code View in your document and locate the `<style>` section at the top; specifically, the `#box` rule. Notice that there are five lines of code that were created by adding the transition, starting with `-webkit-transition: all 2s;` and ending with `transition: all 2s;`

```
 8    #box {
 9        background-color: #999;
10        height: 300px;
11        width: 300px;
12        font-family:Verdana, Geneva, sans-serif;
13        border:#000 4px solid;
14        text-align: center;
15        -webkit-transition: all 2s;
16        -moz-transition: all 2s;
17        -ms-transition: all 2s;
18        -o-transition: all 2s;
19        transition: all 2s;
20    }
21
22    #box:hover {
23        height: 50px;
24    }
```

The generated transition CSS that was created by Dreamweaver.

Five lines of code might seem like a lot; however, each line is exactly the same code, and each targets a specific web browser. The code `-webkit-transition: all 2s;` begins with a vendor-specific prefix to target Webkit browsers such as Apple Safari and Google Chrome. The code `-moz-transition: all 2s;` targets Mozilla browsers (Firefox). The next two lines, `-ms-transition: all 2s;` and `-o-transition: all 2s;` target Microsoft and Opera browsers.

The last line, `transition: all 2s;` is the "official" CSS3 property name for transitions. The reason for having five lines of almost-identical code is that each browser has its own timeline for supporting a new CSS3 property. For example, Google Chrome might have required the prefix `-webkit` in version 8.0. When it becomes evident that transitions are working reliably and are well-liked by designers, Google Chrome might choose to drop the requirement for the prefix in version 10.0. The goal is for all browsers to eventually support the "official" property transition; the only reason to use the vendor-specific ones would be to provide support for older browsers.

2   Look below the code for the #box style; you will see the style #box:hover. This code represents the trigger you set for the transition in the last exercise.

3   Click the Design view to toggle back to your page. Most likely, you will not need to modify the CSS transition code by hand, but you should understand where you can find it within the CSS, and understand some of the underlying concepts.

4   In your CSS Transitions window, click hover and then click the Pencil icon to edit the transition.

Select hover and then click the Pencil icon to edit a transition.

The Edit Transition window opens, allowing you to modify the values you created in the last exercise.

You can also double-click hover *or* div#box *to open this window.*

5   Select the value 2 inside the Duration field and type **0.5**. This will change the duration from two seconds to half a second.

6   Click inside the Delay field, type **1**, and make sure the menu to the right is set to s (for second). Delaying a transition simply means the transition will not begin until one second after the user hovers over the box.

7 Notice that there is a value in the Timing Function field set to ease. This is the default setting, so while you didn't set this in the last exercise, Dreamweaver fills it in as though you had.

What is easing?

Easing is a term well known in computer animation that you might have seen before, particularly if you have used Adobe Flash. Easing allows you to vary the speed of a transition over time. For example, you might want an animation to start off slow and then speed up, or perhaps the reverse: start off quickly and then slow down.

Dreamweaver CC has six options for easing:

Linear

Maintains a constant speed for the duration of the transition.

Ease

The animation starts slowly, accelerates, and then slows down when approaching the end of the transition.

Ease-in

The animation begins slowly, and then progressively accelerates until the end of the transition.

Ease-out

The animation starts quickly, and then progressively slows down until the end of the transition.

Ease-in-out

The animation starts slowly at the beginning, maintains a steady rate in the middle, and then slows down toward the end of the transition.

Cubic-bezier(x1,y1,x2,y2)

Allows you to create a custom animation using the cubic bezier model. A sample value might be `cubic-bezier(0.4,0.2,0.8,0.7)`. This particular example would result in an animation that starts off slowly and speeds up toward the end of the transition.

8   Click the Timing Function menu and choose `ease-out`. The ease-out timing will cause the animation to start off quickly and then slow down. (Note that this effect will be difficult to see with the new half second duration.)

Choose ease-out from the menu of Timing Functions.

9   Click the + sign at the bottom of the Property section. You will now animate a second property to go with the height transition.

10 Choose background-color from the list, and then click the End-Value swatch; the color picker appears. Choose a dark pink color, such as #C36.

Choose a dark pink color for the background-color *property.*

Notice that the values for Duration, Delay, and Timing Function are the same. If you want to create separate values for the background-color animation, you would need to click the menu at the top of the Edit Transition window and change it to Use a different transition for each property.

11 Click Save Transition, and then choose File > Save. Preview the page in your browser and place your cursor at the top of the box. Remember that there is a one-second delay that you added in Step 5; after this delay, the box will change height rapidly and simultaneously fade from gray to pink.

CSS3 Transitions are supported in all major browsers, including Internet Explorer. The current release of Internet Explorer is version 10 (as of this writing), however most users are using version 9 or earlier without support for CSS3 Transitions. For a detailed look at browser support visit: http://caniuse.com/#feat=css-transitions.

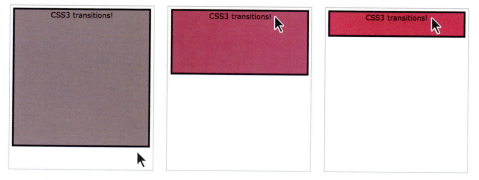

After a delay of one second, the box quickly reduces its height and animates its background color.

12 Close the browser as well as the **07_csstransitions_work.html** file.

In these two exercises, you learned the fundamentals of CSS Transitions on a sample file. Now you'll apply what you've learned to a more realistic layout.

Adding CSS Transitions to a navigation menu

User interface elements such as navigation bars, menus, or buttons are great to use with CSS Transitions. Subtle animation can add an extra bit of sophistication and style to your pages.

1   Open the **07_nav_transition.html** document by double-clicking it in the Files panel.

2   Choose File > Preview in Browser to view this page in a browser. Hover over the navigation to see the default styles. The effect you are seeing is a traditional CSS2 hover effect; the background color of a list item changes to a lighter green when the cursor hovers over it. However, the change is instant in CSS2 syntax; you have no control over how long it takes for the background color to go from the darker green to the lighter green. In CSS3 syntax you have control using transitions. We will add a transition to make the hover effect more interesting.

The current hover effect is either on or off.

Close the browser and return to Dreamweaver.

3   If your CSS Transitions window is not currently open, do so now by choosing Window > CSS Transitions.

4   Click the + sign to open the New Transition window, and then click the Target Rule. Choose the `#navigation ul li a` style. (This is currently the style for list items that are also hyperlinks inside the navigation div.)

Choose the `#navigation ul li a` *style from the menu.*

5   Click the Transition On menu and choose hover.

6   Click the + sign in the Property section and choose `background-color` from the list. For Duration, type **400**; click the menu to the right and change it from s to ms (milliseconds). Leave the delay set to 0. For the Timing Function, choose ease-in-out and for the End Value, type **#9FCC41**. (This color matches the one currently used.)

You'll now combine another effect by changing the foreground color of the text inside the navigation.

7   Click the + sign in the Property section and choose `color` from the list. By default, this second property is inheriting all the values added for the first value. You want more control, so you'll have to define separate rules for this `color` property.

8 At the top of your New Transition window, click the menu and change it to Use a different transition for each property.

You must specify whether you want to set different transitions for each property.

9 Make sure the color property is selected. In the Duration field, type **500**; click the menu to the right and choose ms if it is not already selected. In the Delay field, type **100**; click the menu to the right and choose ms. Leave the Timing Function set to ease-in-out. Lastly, click the End Value swatch and choose the dark green value #060.

Click Create Transition. Notice that your CSS Transitions panel now reads [5 instances] for hover. This automatically reflects the number of list items in your navigation.

10 Choose File > Save All, and then preview your page in the browser. Hover over the navigation and you will see the navigation background color fade up and down slightly. The text also fades, but because you added the 100ms delay in the last step, it creates a subtle fading effect every time the user moves to another navigation.

Adding two separate transitions for the navigation: one for the background color, the other for the color of the text.

11 Close your browser. Choose File > Close All. Close the CSS Transitions window. You are done with this lesson file.

Adding a CSS Gradient

CSS Gradients in Dreamweaver CC offer a way to apply gradient backgrounds to your layout using only CSS. This is in contrast to the traditional method of creating tiled or repeating gradient background images. Using CSS instead of background images will make your sites quicker and more efficient by eliminating the need for extra images, and saving both bandwidth and download time for users; both of which are at a premium on mobile devices. An additional benefit of CSS Gradients is that they allow you to more easily change colors and apply different gradient effects without having to modify image files.

In this exercise, you will apply a CSS3 gradient to the sample document. Later, you will apply the same effect to the Organic Utopia layout.

1 Open the **07_cssgradients.html** document. The box background has been added using a traditional CSS2 single-pixel width gradient image set to repeat horizontally using repeat-y. A background color matching the bottom of the gradient has been added to allow the box to be resized vertically to maintain the gradient effect.

The properties used to achieve the gradient are `background-url`, `background-repeat`, and `background-color`. It is helpful to take a look at these styles before proceeding.

2   In the Design view, click the edge of the box to select it. In the CSS Designer panel, click the `#box` selector in the Selectors pane. This will expose the properties currently used. (If your Properties panel does not look like the screenshot, you might have to first click <style> in the Sources pane and then click the Show set check box in the Properties Navigation bar.)

The CSS properties associated with the CSS ID #box.

The problem with using this method to add a gradient background is that you would have to create a new image if the color scheme of the site were to change. You will now replace these properties with a CSS3 Gradient, allowing you to apply and modify the gradient effect without an image.

3   In the Properties pane, locate the `background-color` property and click the Remove CSS Property icon to the right of the value #00000. This will remove the background color. Repeat this step to remove the `background-image` and `background-repeat` properties.

4   Clear the Show set check box to display all of the available properties. Next, click the Background button in the Properties Navigation pane to display the background properties. Locate the `gradient` property in the `background-image` category. This will bring up the Gradient control. Choose Hex from the tabs at the bottom of the control to add a color using the hexadecimal color code.

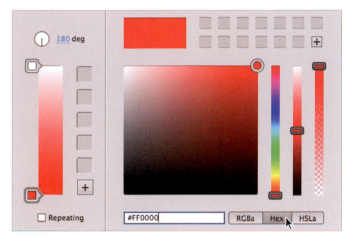

The Gradient control allows you to set the color stops to create gradients using RGB, Hex or HSLa values.

5   Click the top color stop in the left pane of the Gradient control and type **#993399** in the text box to set the top color stop value. Click the bottom color stop and type **#000000** to set the bottom value. Press Enter (Windows) or Return (Mac OS) to apply the gradient color. This will recreate the same effect of the gradient image used previously.

CSS3 Gradients are supported in all major browsers though each implementation may need browser-specific prefixes to enable the effect. Dreamweaver CC will insert these vendor-specific syntaxes. You can choose the vendors in Preferences > CSS Styles > Use Vendor Prefix For. For a detailed look at browser support visit:

   http://caniuse.com/#feat=css-gradients.

6   Choose File > Save As, type **07_cssgradients_work** in the File name and click Save
to save this file in the dw07lessons folder. Choose File > Preview in Browser.

The box background is now created in the browser using CSS3 rather than using an
image. This technique can be used to create complex gradient backgrounds that scale
with the page elements in a responsive layout.

*The gradient background is created using the CSS3 gradient
property.*

7   Close both the browser window and the original **07_cssgradients.html** page.
Return to the **07_csstransitions_work.html** file in Dreamweaver.

8   Click the #box selector in the Selectors pane and change the height to **600px**. Click
the Live view button in the document toolbar and notice how the gradient now
stretches the entire length of the box.

9   Turn off Live view, then Choose Edit > Undo to return the box to the original height
of 300px. Save your file again by pressing Control+S (Windows) or Command+S
(Mac OS) and leave it open for the next exercise.

Applying a CSS Gradient to the page background

Now that you have seen how a CSS Gradient works, you'll add a gradient to the body of the Organic Utopia home page.

1   Open the **07_page_gradient.html** document by double-clicking it in the Files panel.

2   Choose File > Preview in Browser to view this page in the browser. Notice that the background of the page uses a solid color, in this case #739112. You will modify the styles of the body element so that the background displays using a CSS3 gradient. Close the browser window and return to Dreamweaver.

The body of the Organic Utopia home page uses a solid green background color.

3   In the CSS Designer panel, click the `body` selector in the Selectors pane. This will expose the properties currently used.

The CSS Designer panel displays the style properties for the body element.

If your Properties panel does not look like our screenshot, you might have to first click `<style>` in the Sources pane then click body in the Selectors pane, and set the Show set check box in the Properties Navigation bar.

4   In the Properties pane, locate the `background-color` property and click the Remove CSS Property icon (🗑) to the right of the value #739912. This will remove the background color.

5   Clear the Show set check box to display all of the available properties then click the Background button in the Properties Navigation pane to display the background properties. Locate the `gradient` property in the `background-image` category. This will bring up the Gradient control. Choose Hex from the tabs at the bottom of the control to add a color using the hexadecimal color code.

6 Type **#739112** in the text box to set the top color stop value, then click the bottom color stop and type **#739112** to set the bottom value to the same color. Next, click in the middle of the color stops control to create a new color stop and type **#EEEEEE** to set the value of this color stop. Press Enter (Windows) or Return (Mac OS) to apply the gradient color. This will create a gradient that gradually shifts from the original background color to a light grey and back to the original background color.

Using the Gradient control to create a gradient from #739112 to #EEEEE and back to #739112.

7 Choose File > Save As, type **07_page_gradient_work** in the File name and click Save to save this file in the dw07lessons folder. Choose File > Preview in Browser.

The page background is now displayed as a gradient rather than a solid background image. This technique can be used to create multi-color gradient backgrounds that scale with the page elements in a responsive layout.

The body of the Organic Utopia home page using our newly created CSS3 Gradient.

Creating rounded borders

Dreamweaver CC adds support for the CSS3 `border-radius` property to add rounded corners to HTML elements. Previously, creating rounded corners required visual trickery including using images of rounded corners to create the desired effect. The advent of the CSS3 border-radius property renders these techniques obsolete and simplifies the process.

1   Open the **07_rounded_borders.html** document by double-clicking it in the Files panel.

2   Choose File > Preview in Browser to view this page in the browser. There are two boxes on the page identified as `#box1` and `#box2`. Currently, there is a border visible on the box on the left and a background-color applied to the box on the right. You will modify the styles of these two elements by applying the `border-radius` property to round off the corners of the boxes. Close the browser window and return to Dreamweaver.

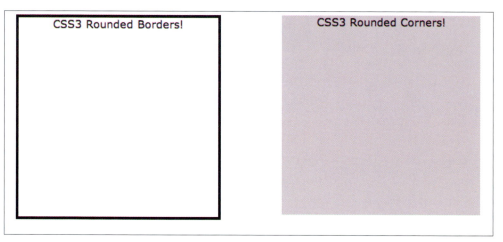

Before CSS3, there was no easy way to create softer, rounder edges for page elements.

3   You will first apply rounded corners to the borders of `#box1`. In the CSS Designer panel, choose `<style>` from the Sources pane if necessary, and then click the `#box1` selector. This will expose the properties currently used. (If your Properties panel does not look like our screenshot, click the Show set check box in the Properties Navigation bar).

4   Click the Border button in the Properties Navigation bar to display the border properties and scroll down to the border-radius control. Click the chain link icon in the center of the border-radius control to link the four radius values together allowing you to apply one value to all four settings. Click the 0 in one of the four corners of the border-radius control and type **15** to set the radius to 15 pixels. Press Enter (Windows) or Return (Mac OS) to apply the settings.

The border-radius control allows you to set the radius of one or more corners of an element.

5 Choose File > Save As, type **07_rounded_borders_work** in the File name and click Save to save this file in the dw07lessons folder. Choose File > Preview in Browser.

The corners of the borders of #box1 are now curved producing a rounded–rectangle effect. You can also round the corners of elements without a border style applied to them and you will do this next.

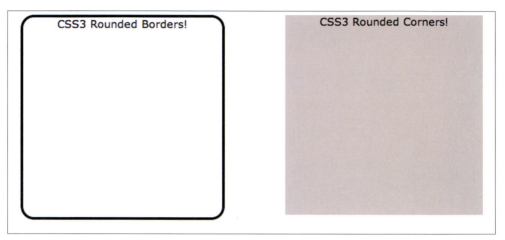

The box1 div rendered using rounded borders with the CSS3 border-radius style.

6 Close both the browser window and the original **07_rounded_borders.html** page. Return to the **07_rounded_borders_work.html** file in Dreamweaver.

7 In the CSS Designer panel, choose <style> from the Sources pane if necessary, then click the #box2 selector and click the Border button in the Properties Navigation bar. Scroll down to the border–radius control.

8   Click the chain link icon in the center of the border-radius control to link the four radius values. Click the 0 in one of the four corners of the border-radius control and type **15** to set the radius to 15 pixels. Press Enter (Windows) or Return (Mac OS) to apply the settings.

Setting the border-radius *property of all four corners to 15px using the border radius control.*

9   Save your file again by pressing Control+S (Windows) or Command+S (Mac OS) then choose File > Preview in Browser.

The corners of #box2 are now rounded producing a rounded-rectangle effect even though there is no actual border style applied.

Both #box1 *and* #box2 *rendered using border-radius with and without border styles.*

Self study

Using your new knowledge of creating CSS3 Transitions and Styles in Dreamweaver, try some of the following tasks to build your experience.

To practice CSS transitions, build a web button labeled *Subscribe Now!* and give it transition effects such as background color and border effects. You can make a copy of the **07_csstransitions.html** document and base your button upon the original #box style. You will have to set the starting width and height to a number more appropriate for a button, such as 25 pixels high and 100 pixels wide.

The transition effects that you created for the **07_nav_transition.html** exercise were designed for educational purposes to show you how the effects work; however, they might be too slow for real-world use. Try experimenting with the Duration and Delay values; specifically, try lowering the values. Also try experimenting with different Timing Functions, such as Ease, Linear, Ease-in, and Ease-out.

To practice CSS Gradients, open **07_page_gradient_work.html** and apply a background gradient to the #sidebar div. Experiment with setting multiple color stops and angles in the Gradient tool.

To practice using the CSS3 border-radius property, modify the **07_rounded_borders.html** file by using different values for each corner and applying various border styles to #box1 and #box2.

Review

Questions

1   How would you add a CSS Transition to a document in Dreamweaver CC?

2   Where can you find the available list of properties that can be animated using CSS properties?

3   What are the benefits of using a CSS3 Gradient over using a gradient image file?

4   What CSS property is used to create a rounded corner effect on an element?

Answers

1   CSS Transitions can be added by going to the menu bar and choosing Window > CSS Transitions.

2   You can find the list of CSS properties that can be animated by clicking the + sign located below the Property section in the CSS Transitions window.

3   The benefits of using CSS Gradients over using a gradient image file are that they can make your sites quicker and more efficient by eliminating the need for extra images, saving both bandwidth and download time for users (both of which are at a premium on mobile devices) and they allow you to more easily change colors and apply different gradient effects without having to modify image files.

4   The CSS property used to create rounded corners is the border-radius property.

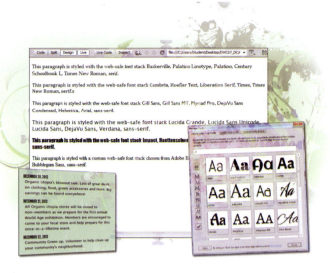

What you'll learn in this lesson:

- Web fonts in Dreamweaver CC
- Using Adobe Edge Web Fonts
- Creating custom font stacks
- Using local web fonts

Using Web Fonts

Dreamweaver CC offers improved support for web fonts, including the addition of the free Adobe Edge Web Fonts service. Web fonts offer a way to enhance your page by embedding custom fonts, even if visitors to your site do not have the font on their system.

Starting up

Before you begin, reset your workspace to ensure your tools and panels are consistent. For more information, see "Resetting the Dreamweaver workspace" in the Starting up section of this book.

In this lesson, you will work with several files from the dw08lessons folder. Make sure that you have loaded the dwlessons folder onto your hard-drive from the supplied DVD. For more information, see "Loading lesson files" in the Starting up section of this book.

Before you can proceed with the exercises in this section, you need to create site settings that point to the dw08lessons folder. Go to Site > New Site, or for details on creating a site, refer to Lesson 2, "Setting Up a New Site."

See Lesson 8 in action!

Use the accompanying video to gain a better understanding of how to use some of the features shown in this lesson. The video tutorial for this lesson can be found on the included DVD.

The basics of web fonts

The limited choice of fonts for the Web has been a problem for many years. (The way fonts work on the Web was outlined in Lesson 3, "Adding Text and Images.") The core issue is that if you define a specific font in your CSS and a visitor to your site does not have that font, a substitute font is used. Unfortunately, the list of fonts that are guaranteed to be installed on all users' computers is very small. Over the years designers have looked for alternatives and workarounds to this limitation. These workarounds ranged from using decorative fonts saved in images to font-replacement technologies such as Cufon, sIFR, FLIR and `@font-face`.

Of these technologies, web fonts have emerged as the accepted technique using the `@font-face` property in CSS3. The use of web fonts has gained industry support from designers and developers, and more importantly, from companies that make and license fonts. Simply put, web fonts allow you to embed any font within a page by declaring the font you want to display and placing this font on your web server. When a user visits your site, their browser renders the page using this font wherever specified. Adding web fonts is a straight-forward process in Dreamweaver; however, there are some details (technical and legal) that you need to be aware of.

Web Fonts in Dreamweaver CC

Previously, Dreamweaver only supported `@font-face` allowing you to embed local web fonts in your web pages. This method had a few drawbacks for web designers. First, you had to make sure the fonts you used were properly licensed for web use (see the Font Licensing sidebar in the `@font-face` exercise later in this lesson). Second, the varied support for `@font-face` across browsers meant that web designers needed to provide multiple files for font formats, font weights and styles (see the Browser Font Support sidebar in the `@font-face` exercise later in this lesson). Finally, the fonts were downloaded from the site, increasing bandwidth use and potentially download speeds.

Dreamweaver CC improves upon web font support by including the free Adobe Edge Web Font service giving you access to a vast web font library through the Creative Cloud (*http://html.adobe.com/edge/webfonts/*). Powered by TypeKit, this free service is made possible by contributions from Adobe, Google and designers around the world. It provides web fonts functionality as an integrated workflow directly within Dreamweaver. You will explore both methods of using web fonts throughout the following exercises.

Using Adobe Edge Web Fonts

In this exercise, you will explore the new Web Font Manager and the Adobe Edge Web Fonts workflow available within Dreamweaver CC.

1   Open the **08_edgefonts.html** file by double-clicking it in the Files panel. This file includes several paragraphs that are styled with a different set of fonts, called a font stack.

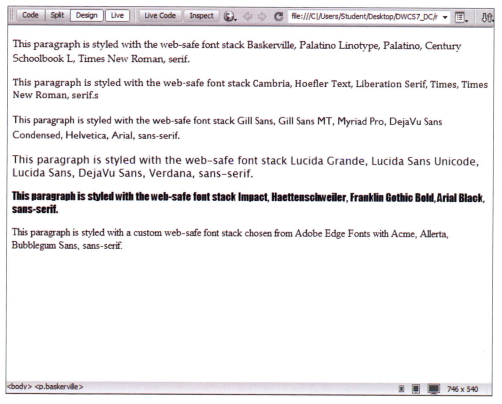

Each paragraph is styled with a different font stack.

2   In the Design view, click anywhere in the first line of text. If you look at the tag selector you will notice this paragraph is styled using a class called .baskerville. Click the CSS Designer tab to access the CSS Designer panel and choose <style> from the Sources pane.

3   Click .baskerville in the Selectors pane and view the font-face property in the Properties pane. It might be helpful to check Show set in the Properties Navigation bar to limit the list to properties that are set for the current selector. The only property set is font-family: Baskerville, Palatino Linotype, Palatino, Century Schoolbook L, Times New Roman, serif.

This font-stack is comprised of web-safe fonts, which are fonts that are generally available on most users' computers. Dreamweaver CC includes an entirely new font stack selection to take advantage of more web-safe fonts than ever before.

The first paragraph is styled using the web-safe font stack including Baskerville, Palatino, Century Schoolbook L, Times New Roman, and serif.

4   You will now add a web font from the Adobe Edge Web Font collection and use it to style the last paragraph in the document. Choose Modify > Manage Fonts to bring up the new Manage Fonts dialog box. This window is comprised of three tabs to manage Adobe Edge Web Fonts, Local Web Fonts and Custom Font Stacks.

The Manage Fonts dialog box provides a new interface to simplify using web fonts.

The Adobe Edge Web Fonts tab of the font manager allows you to search for and view the many web fonts available from the service. You can search for fonts by name or use the buttons to the left to filter fonts appropriate for headings, paragraphs, typeface properties or a combination of settings.

5   Choose the Acme font from the list; Dreamweaver will display a checkmark on the font indicating it is selected, then click Done. The font will now be available for use on any website you create through Dreamweaver.

6   Select the last line of text in the document, click <style> in the Sources pane of the CSS Designer, and then click the Add Selector button in the Selectors pane. Dreamweaver will add a new selector in the Selectors pane. Select the text Dreamweaver added and type **.custom** in the selector name text box. Press Enter (Windows) or Return (Mac OS).

7   Click the Text button in the Properties Navigation bar to display the available text properties. You might need to clear the Show set check box to display the Properties Navigation bar. Locate the font-family property and click the text 'default font' in the Set font-family text box. The Acme font now shows up in the popup menu as a valid font choice. Click Acme to select this font for our property.

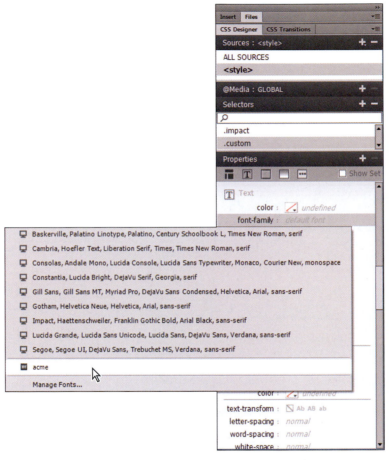

The Acme web font is available in the font list for any website you create with Dreamweaver.

8   Make sure the last paragraph of the document is still selected. Using the Property Inspector, select .custom from the Class drop-down menu to apply this class to the last paragraph. You will not notice the change immediately because some web fonts do not display in Design view. Click Live from the document toolbar to go into Live view to see the new web font applied.

When Dreamweaver adds a web font to your page it also adds a script tag to instruct the browser to download the font from another location. We will now take a look at the added script to better understand it. We will not need to make any changes as Dreamweaver handles inserting and managing this code for you.

9   Click the Live button to exit Live view. Next, click the Code button to view the source code of your page. Scroll down to the HTML comment that begins '`<!--The following script tag...`' you will see a line of JavaScript that points to the Adobe Edge Web Fonts server requesting the Acme font added earlier.

10   Click File > Save as and type **08_edgefonts_work.html** to save your progress.

Creating a custom font stack using web fonts

1   Choose Modify > Manage Fonts to bring up the Manage Fonts dialog box. You will now add two additional Adobe Edge Web Fonts and create a new font stack to apply to the last paragraph in **08_edgefonts_work.html**. Choose Acme, Allerta, and Bubblegum Sans from the list of available fonts.

2   Click the Custom Font Stacks tab to bring up the font stack manager. This window displays the current font stacks and allows you to create custom stacks from both locally installed and remotely served web fonts.

Create your own custom font stacks to ensure viewers see the page the way you intended it to display.

3 Scroll down to the bottom of the list of Available Fonts where you will find the three Adobe Edge Web Fonts you added; Acme, Allerta and Bubblegum Sans. Click Acme in the list and click the << button to move this font to the Chosen fonts list. Repeat this step with Allerta, Bubblegum Sans and sans-serif. Finally, click Done to create the new font stack.

4 You will now modify the .custom class to use this new font stack to style the last paragraph. Click <style> in the Sources pane of the CSS Designer, and then click .custom in the Selectors pane.

5 Click the Show set button in the Properties pane to display the font-family property you set earlier and click Acme to display the font selection pop-up menu. You will now see a new font stack entry listed in the web fonts area. Click the newly created font stack to apply it to the .custom font-family.

Select the new font stack from the font lists.

6 Click the Live view button to see the changes. Since you are using web fonts directly from the Adobe Edge Web Fonts server, the font displayed will still be Acme but you have provided a font stack that will enable the browser to default to other fonts including sans-serif in case the font cannot be loaded.

7 Press Ctrl+S (Windows) or Command+S (Mac OS) to save your work. Next, you will apply a web font to the Organic Utopia project.

Styling your content with Adobe Edge Web Fonts

In this exercise you will apply an Adobe Edge Web Font to your Organic Utopia home page.

1 Open the **08_edgeutopia.html** document by double-clicking it in the Files panel.

2 Choose Modify > Manage Fonts and click the first button in the top left of the Manage Fonts dialog box; List of fonts recommended for headings. Choose League Gothic from the list of heading fonts displayed and click Done.

3 Place your cursor within the first heading in the sidebar, *December 20, 2012* and then click styles.css in the Sources pane of the CSS Designer panel.

4 Click the Add Selector button in the Selectors pane and change the selector name so it reads **#sidebar dl dt**. Press Enter (Windows) or Return (Mac OS).

5 Click the Text button in the Properties Navigation pane to display the text properties. Click the text *default font* in the Set font family field and choose league-gothic from the list of fonts.

6 Locate the `text-transform` property and click the Uppercase button to transform the definition term items to uppercase.

7 Choose File > Save As and save the file as **08_edgeutopia_work.html**. Click File > Preview in Browser to view the changes. You have now applied an Adobe Edge Web Font to your page layout.

The Organic Utopia sidebar formatted with League Gothic Adobe Edge Web Font.

8 Close the browser and return to Dreamweaver for the next exercise.

Adding local web fonts with `@font-face`

In this exercise, you will add the web font *Droid Sans Bold* (which is licensed for web use) to your website, embed that font so that it is available for use on a page, and then style a heading with the new web font.

1   Open the **08_fontface.html** document by double-clicking it in the Files panel.

There are a few steps you should take before adding a web font. In this example, you will style the first heading, "Welcome to organic utopia." You should first understand where the current style comes from.

2   In the Design view, click anywhere inside the heading, "Welcome to organic utopia." You can easily determine this is a Heading 1 element in two ways: 1) The tag selector indicates this is an <h1>; and 2) In the HTML section of the Property Inspector at the bottom of your page, you can see that Heading 1 is the value of the Format.

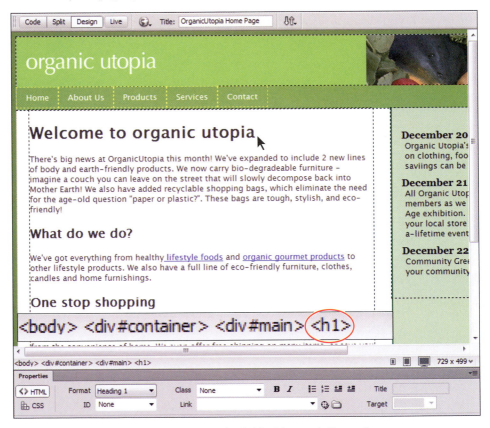

You can identify this element as a Heading 1 using either the Tag Selector or the Property Inspector.

You should also determine the style that is currently used for the heading.

3   Click the <h1> tag in the tag selector to highlight the tag. In the CSS Designer panel, adjust the height of the Rules and Properties panes as needed to show the COMPUTED style.

You are looking for the rules or selectors used to style this heading, and there are three: body, #container, and #main. You can see that there is no CSS style for an h1 on this page. Click the body rule.

CSS Designer	CSS Transitions

Sources : styles.css

ALL SOURCES

styles.css

@Media : GLOBAL

Selectors

COMPUTED

#main

#container

body

Properties

☑ Show Set

T Text

color : ▣ #333

font-family : Lucida Sans Unico...

font-size : small

text-align : ≡ ≣ ≡ ≡

Identifying the styles applied to the h1.

The body rule indicates that the following properties are used: a color of *#333*; the font-family "*Lucida Grande,*" "*Lucida Sans Unicode,*" "*Lucida Sans,*" "*DejaVu Sans,*" *Verdana, sans-serif*; and the font-size *small*. Remember that the word cascading is part of Cascading Style Sheets, and you are seeing that effect here. The font Lucida Sans Unicode is defined in the body, and because there are no other styles for h1, the cascade is in effect, so it inherits the color and font-family styles.

Lucida Sans Unicode is a font that is extremely common on most users' computer systems; you'll now add a web font that is not so common.

4 Choose Modify > Manage Fonts; the Manage Fonts dialog box opens. This dialog box will allow you to embed fonts that are located in your system.

5   Click the Local Web Fonts tab to display the fields to add a local web font.

The Local Web Fonts tab of the Manage Fonts dialog box allows you to point to web fonts on your system.

6   Click inside the Font Name text field and type **Droid Sans Bold**. This typeface was created specifically as an open-source font for screen use and we have provided it for you in your lesson folder.

7   Click the Browse button immediately to the right of the field labeled EOT Font; the Open window appears. Navigate within your dw08lessons folder to the webfonts folder and locate the file **DroidSans-Bold-webfont.eot**. The only files you are allowed to select are .eot files.

8   Choose **DroidSans-Bold-webfont.eot** and click Open; the EOT font is selected as well as the other three options: WOFF, TTF, and SVG. All four of these fonts should be used to ensure maximum compatibility across all web browsers.

Browser font support

The use of web fonts has been complicated because you cannot use a single font format and have it supported across all browsers. The following table lists the level of browser support for the different font types. Essentially, it comes down to the need to include them all if you want your font styles to be consistent.

The following table lists the various levels of support for the different font-types:

- **OpenType (OTF)**: A widespread font format that is heavily supported by the industry. Initially developed as a collaboration between Adobe and Microsoft, one of the primary advantages of OpenType is cross-platform support. However, there are additional typesetting features, including glyph support, that make OpenType fonts the primary font of choice for professional font foundries.

- **TrueType (TTF)**: Originally developed by Apple and later adopted by Microsoft, TrueType fonts are still widely in use today as they are largely cross-platform compatible and also offer sophisticated typesetting controls, such as hinting, which is a technique that improves the quality of the font in low resolution screens.

- **SVG**: A vector-based format that is notable because it is currently the only font type supported by Apple's iOS for iPod and iPad devices. SVG fonts are text documents that define the font outlines as vector objects within the SVG (Scalable Vector Graphic) language.

- **Web Open Font Format (WOFF)**: The latest addition to the world of web fonts, WOFF has the potential to become a standard for web fonts, since it is in the final stages of being recommended as a standard by the World Wide Web Consortium (W3C). One of the key benefits of WOFF is the ability to heavily compress the font files and optimize them for distribution over an Internet connection.

- **Embedded OpenType (EOT)**: A variation on OpenType created by Microsoft and largely supported only by Internet Explorer. EOT has a variety of copy-protection features built-in, designed to prevent copying of fonts.

9   Click the check box labeled, I have properly licensed the above font(s) for website use. This is a required step and will be explained in more detail at the end of this lesson.

10   Click the Add button. You will now see Droid Sans Bold listed in your Available Web Fonts.

Click the Done button in the Manage Fonts dialog box.

```
Manage Fonts                                                 [x]
  Adobe Edge Web Fonts    Local Web Fonts   Custom Font Stacks

  Add fonts from your computer. The added fonts will be available in all Font lists in Dreamweaver.

       Font Name: [                        ]
        EOT Font: [                        ]  [ Browse... ]
       WOFF Font: [                        ]  [ Browse... ]
        TTF Font: [                        ]  [ Browse... ]
        SVG Font: [                        ]  [ Browse... ]

              [ ] I have properly licensed the above font(s)
                  for website use.
                  What's this?
                                              [  Add  ]
  ─────────────────────────────────────────────────────────
  Current list of    ( ) Doid Sans Bold
  Local Web Fonts:   ┌──────────────────────────────┐
                     │                              │
                     │                              │
                     │                              │
                     └──────────────────────────────┘
                                        [ Remove ]



  [ Help ]                                      [ Done ]
```

The Manage Web Fonts dialog lists the available fonts for your current site.

At this point, your new web font, Droid Sans Bold, has been made available to all existing pages and any new pages in the current site. Additionally, this web font will be available to any document in Dreamweaver, even if it is part of another site.

Font licensing

Understanding the rules of font licensing is an important part of using web fonts. You can technically add a font to a page, but this does not mean you are always *allowed* to. The fonts on your system could have specific licenses that only let you use them in print or for other specific uses. Even if you have paid for a font, this still does not necessarily mean you have paid for the web license of this font. You will need to ensure that you are allowed to use the fonts you add with the Web Font Manager.

For more information on web font licensing issues, visit the Web Font Licensing FAQ from the Adobe Type Team:

http://blogs.adobe.com/typblography/web-font-licensing-faq

Styling your heading with a local web font

In addition to the legal licensing limitations involved with web fonts, there is also an aesthetic consideration. Not all fonts are designed to be rendered on the screen. The creators of a typical font are often more concerned with how the font renders in print or how the font looks at small sizes versus large sizes (or vice-versa). The web font you are using, Droid Sans Bold, was specifically designed to render well on small and large screens alike. Many designers felt the majority of web fonts worked best as headings rather than as large blocks of body text in paragraphs. This opinion has changed as many more fonts have been released for web use.

In this exercise, you will style your main heading with your new web font option.

1   Make sure you have clicked inside the Heading 1 labeled, *Welcome to organic utopia*. In the tag selector, make sure you click the <h1> tag.

This highlights your Heading 1 and makes it easier for Dreamweaver to understand that you want to target this style.

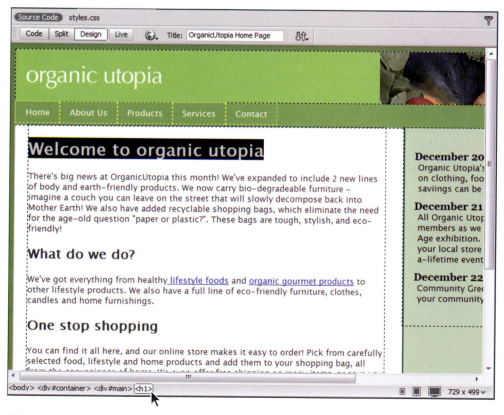

Click the <h1> tag in the Tag Selector to select the top heading.

2   Click style.css in the Sources pane of the CSS Designer panel, then click the Add Selector button in the Selectors pane. Type **h1** in the Selector Name text box and press Enter (Windows) or Return (Mac OS).

3   Click the Text button in the Properties Navigation bar. Click the shaded text *default font* in the Set font family text box to display the font list and choose Droid Sans Bold.

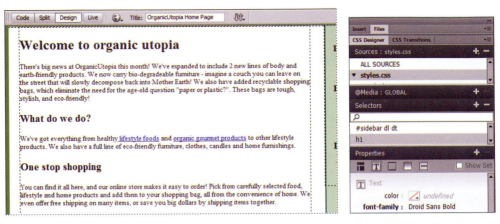

Although you have applied the web font style, it might not be reflected in the Design view.

You have just applied the font style to your heading, but you might not see this change in your Design view. This is a limitation for some web fonts; you will only see an accurate view in the browser or in Dreamweaver's Live View.

5   Click Dreamweaver's Live View; you will see your heading set in Droid Sans Bold. You might not notice the difference immediately because Droid Sans and Lucida Sans are fairly similar; however, if you compare the letter "g" in the word organic to the letter "g" in the heading further down the page (One stop shopping), you will see the difference.

You can still use certain CSS formatting to make the web font-styled heading more distinctive. You'll now add a style to make the heading uppercase.

6   In the CSS Designer panel, choose **stylesheet.css** from the Sources pane, and then click `@font-face` in the Selectors pane. Click the Show set check box in the Properties Navigation bar to see the properties that have been set to enable the Droid Sans Bold web font. You will likely never modify this style—it is simply worth pointing out that Dreamweaver created this file and the `@font-face` style when you applied the web font to your `h1` heading.

7   Choose **styles.css** from the Sources panel, and then click the h1 selector in the Selectors pane. Next, clear the Show set check box in the Properties Navigation bar and click the Text button to display the available text properties. Locate the text-transform property and click the uppercase button. Click the Live button to show your new heading in Live view.

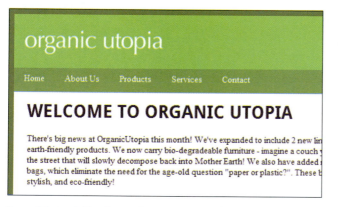

Your web font-styled heading now has an uppercase style.

8   Exit Live View by clicking the Live button. Choose File > Save All, and then preview your page in the browser. If your browser supports web fonts, you should see your style.

Self study

To practice working with web fonts, add the other set of fonts we provided in the lesson folder for the Droid-Sans font. Try applying this font to your paragraph styles and headings to see the effect.

To practice working with Adobe Edge Web Fonts, add another font from the Edge Fonts collection. Apply this font to the text in the sidebar to see the effect.

Review

Questions

1   Name at least one benefit and one drawback of web fonts in Dreamweaver CC.

2   What is the easiest way to avoid the drawbacks of using web fonts in Dreamweaver CC?

3   What is the purpose of creating a font-stack when formatting text on your web page?

Answers

1   Some benefits of web fonts in Dreamweaver include the variety of choices available for use in your designs, the ease of adding multiple fonts using the Web Manager, and the fact that web fonts will work in virtually all modern browsers. Drawbacks to web fonts include the need to use fonts with a specific web license (which means your favorite font might not be available for web use), the fact that Dreamweaver does not display them reliably in the Design view, and the fact that even if a font is licensed for web use, it might not be optimized for the computer screen.

2   These drawbacks of using web fonts are eliminated when using the free Adobe Edge Web Fonts service on Creative Cloud, powered by TypeKit. An added benefit of using this font service is that you no longer have to manage your own web fonts or have them downloaded from your server.

3   A font-stack ensures that the text on your page will display appropriately. The browser will try to apply the fonts in successive order from left to right, from the closest match you specified in the stack to the least specific default font at the end of the stack.

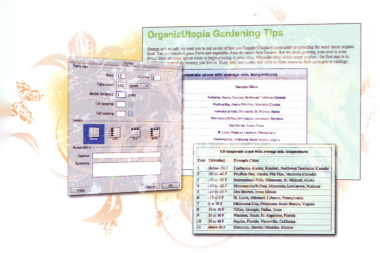

What you'll learn in this lesson:

- Creating and modifying tables
- Styling tables in CSS vs. HTML
- Importing table data
- Sorting table data

Working with Tables

Tables have a long and storied history in web design. In this lesson, you will learn how to structure and style tabular data using tables. Additionally you will understand the basics of using tables for layout and be able to compare and contrast them with Cascading Style Sheets (CSS) for layout.

Starting up

Before starting, make sure that your tools and panels are consistent by resetting your workspace. See "Resetting the Dreamweaver workspace" in the Starting up section of this book.

You will work with several files from the dw09lessons folder in this lesson. Make sure that you have loaded the dwlessons folder onto your hard drive from the supplied DVD. See "Loading lesson files" in the Starting up section of this book.

Before you begin, you need to create site settings that point to the dw09lessons folder from the included DVD that contains resources you need for these lessons. Go to Site > New Site, or, for details on creating a site, refer to Lesson 2, "Setting Up a New Site."

See Lesson 9 in action!

Use the accompanying video to gain a better understanding of how to use some of the features shown in this lesson. The video tutorial for this lesson can be found on the included DVD.

Using tables in web design

Tables are ideally suited for displaying tabular data. As discussed in Lesson 5, "Creating Page Layouts with CSS," in the beginning days of the Web, tables were the best tools available for designers when it came to layout. Over the years, Dreamweaver has steadily introduced a number of tools and visual aids to help people work with tables. Dreamweaver has mirrored the Web in that it has begun to shift its focus to CSS layout rather than table layout. Slowly, the table is reclaiming its original purpose: displaying tabular data.

In this lesson, you will learn how to automatically import and format existing data into a table. You will also explore how to modify rows and columns, style tables with CSS, and create new tables from scratch.

Importing table data

You'll get a chance right away to see tabular data in action by importing a .csv file into Dreamweaver. A majority of tabular data is exported from spreadsheet programs in the .csv (comma-separated values) and .txt (text) file formats. These are called comma, tab, or other delimited files. Essentially this means that a spreadsheet application converts the data within its rows and columns to an intermediate format that Dreamweaver can read.

Although Dreamweaver can open these files, it does not format them directly. With a comma-delimited file, for example, each column value is separated by a comma and each line break starts a new row. For example, here is how Dreamweaver displays the raw .csv file that you are going to be working with:

```
× temperate_zones.csv

Code   Split   Design   Live        Title:

Zone,Fahrenheit,Example Cities
1,Below -50 F,"Fairbanks, Alaska; Resolute, Northwest Territories (Canada)"
2,-50 to -40 F,"Prudhoe Bay, Alaska; Flin Flon, Manitoba (Canada)"
3,-40 to -30 F,"International Falls, Minnesota; St. Michael, Alaska"
4,-30 to -20 F,"Minneapolis/St.Paul, Minnesota; Lewistown, Montana"
5,-20 to -10 F,"Des Moines, Iowa; Illinois"
6,-10 to 0 F,"St. Louis, Missouri; Lebanon, Pennsylvania"
7,0 to 10 F,"Oklahoma City, Oklahoma; South Boston, Virginia"
8,10 to 20 F,"Tifton, Georgia; Dallas, Texas"
9,20 to 30 F,"Houston, Texas; St. Augustine, Florida"
10,30 to 40 F,"Naples, Florida; Victorville, California"
11,above 40 F,"Honolulu, Hawaii; Mazatlan, Mexico"
```

The text editor's view of a comma-delimited file.

When imported into Dreamweaver, this file will be translated accordingly into the rows and columns of a new table.

1   In the Files panel, double-click the tips.html file to open it. This is a styled page for the tips section of the OrganicUtopia site. You will be inserting a .csv file with data on the vegetable-growing zones of North America.

2   Click after the last sentence in the main paragraph and press Enter (Windows) or Return (Mac OS) to make sure your cursor is below the text. Choose File > Import > Tabular Data. The Import Tabular Data dialog box opens.

3   In the Import Tabular Data dialog box, click the Browse button and locate the **temperate_zones.csv** file in your dw09lessons folder. Click Open.

4   Click the Delimiter menu to see the various options that are available. In your case, you will be choosing Comma. In the Table width section, leave the Fit to data option selected.

The settings in the Import Tabular Data dialog box affect the way a table is created.

You can either set a specific width for the generated table or let Dreamweaver construct the table automatically, based on the line-length of the incoming data.

5   Click OK and your table is imported into your document below the text. Your table is imported with 3 columns and 12 rows. A quick way to confirm this is to look in the Property Inspector, where there is a field for columns and rows as well as other useful ways to work with tables.

zones on their packages or catalogs.

Zone	Fahrenheit	Example Cities
1	Below -50 F	Fairbanks, Alaska; Resolute, Northwest Territories (Canada)
2	-50 to -40 F	Prudhoe Bay, Alaska; Flin Flon, Manitoba (Canada)
3	-40 to -30 F	International Falls, Minnesota; St. Michael, Alaska
4	-30 to -20 F	Minneapolis/St.Paul, Minnesota; Lewistown, Montana
5	-20 to -10 F	Des Moines, Iowa; Illinois
6	-10 to 0 F	St. Louis, Missouri; Lebanon, Pennsylvania
7	0 to 10 F	Oklahoma City, Oklahoma; South Boston, Virginia
8	10 to 20 F	Tifton, Georgia; Dallas, Texas
9	20 to 30 F	Houston, Texas; St. Augustine, Florida
10	30 to 40 F	Naples, Florida; Victorville, California
11	above 40 F	Honolulu, Hawaii; Mazatlan, Mexico

A three-column and 12-row table generated by Dreamweaver from a comma-delimited file.

6   Click Dreamweaver's Code view button to see the code that makes up this table. It's safe to say that this is something you would not want to code by hand.

The table is now ready to be formatted according to your specifications. As you can see, you can save yourself a lot of time if your source data is properly formatted. Dreamweaver creates a table for you with all the data properly placed, eliminating the need for you to build a table, and type, or copy and paste, content into each cell.

Selecting table elements

It's worth taking a few moments to learn how to select the various elements of your table. Selecting a specific part of a table can be little tricky until you learn how. In this exercise, you'll look at ways to select a table's rows and columns both by hand and using controls in the Property Inspector. The components of a table include rows, columns, and cells, and other elements such as table headers and footers. The table you created needs some modification. It's rare that a table is created exactly right, and making small tweaks to the column widths and the row heights is the norm.

1 Click the Design view button in the Document toolbar and click anywhere on the background of the page. In this case you do not want the table to be selected. Without clicking, place your cursor over the edges of the table; you see the different sections of the table light up with a red border. Also notice that your cursor switches to a black arrow. The red border is Dreamweaver's visual cue for which part of the table you will be selecting, and the black arrow points in the direction of the row or column to be selected.

2 Place your cursor high in the upper-left corner until the entire table is outlined in red. Click once, and the table is selected.

Zone	Fahrenheit	Example Cities
1	Below -50 F	Fairbanks, Alaska; Resolute, Northwest Territories (Canada)
2	-50 to -40 F	Prudhoe Bay, Alaska; Flin Flon, Manitoba (Canada)
3	-40 to -30 F	International Falls, Minnesota; St. Michael, Alaska
4	-30 to -20 F	Minneapolis/St.Paul, Minnesota; Lewistown, Montana
5	-20 to -10 F	Des Moines, Iowa; Illinois
6	-10 to 0 F	St. Louis, Missouri; Lebanon, Pennsylvania
7	0 to 10 F	Oklahoma City, Oklahoma; South Boston, Virginia
8	10 to 20 F	Tifton, Georgia; Dallas, Texas
9	20 to 30 F	Houston, Texas; St. Augustine, Florida
10	30 to 40 F	Naples, Florida; Victorville, California
11	above 40 F	Honolulu, Hawaii; Mazatlan, Mexico

A red border designates which section of the table you are selecting—in this case, the entire table.

3 Place your cursor to the left of the word Zone until you see the top row outlined; click once to select the row.

4 Move your cursor to the top of the word Zone until you see the numbered column outlined in red; click once to select the column.

Selecting a single cell is a little trickier, as the red outlines only appear when your cursor is on the edge of a table, not inside of one.

5 Click inside the cell with the word Zone. In order to select the cell, use the tag selector at the bottom left of your document window. These tags are an alternative way to select parts of the table.

6   Click the `<table>` tag first; this selects the table just as you did in step 2. Click the `<tr>` tag next; this selects the table row. The `<tr>` tag appropriately stands for table row. Lastly, click the `<td>` tag, and the cell itself is selected; `<td>` is defined as a table cell in HTML. Note that in each of these cases the selected element is outlined in black.

Clicking the appropriate table tag in the tag selector selects that part of the table.

Some people prefer this method of selecting elements of their tables because it removes the chance that clicking the table will move or modify it.

7   Click inside any cell in the table again, and choose Modify > Table > Select Table. This is yet another way to select tables. The Modify > Table command is one you'll be returning to. You can also select the table by right-clicking (Windows) or Ctrl+clicking (Mac OS) the table and choosing Table > Select Table from the context menu.

Modifying table size

Although importing tabular data from a text file is quick and easy, the data is seldom formatted perfectly. When you first imported the data, there was a choice to *Fit Table Width To Data*. The width of the table, when you choose this option, isn't always predictable due to the way Dreamweaver does its calculations. Although it is possible to set the width of the table during the import stage, this isn't always convenient if you don't know what the data looks like. Luckily, it's easy to change the size of tables in Dreamweaver. The first thing you'll do is set a fixed width for the table.

1   If your table is not currently selected, select it now by clicking the `<table>` tag in the tag inspector. In the Property Inspector, type **550** in the W text field and make sure the drop-down menu to the right is set to pixels, then press Enter (Windows) or Return (Mac OS). This expands the table to a width of 550 pixels.

If necessary, re-select the table and look closely at the top of it; there is a visual guide outlined in green that displays the width of your table as well as the width of each column. This guide will come in handy when you are trying to create precisely measured tables, although it can also be turned off.

You can turn off this guide by choosing View > Visual Aids > Table Widths.

2   Choose File > Save, then File > Preview in Browser and open this page in your browser. Resize the browser window a few times. Because the table has a fixed width of 550 pixels, its width stays constant. Close the browser and return to Dreamweaver.

3   In the Property Inspector, your table should still be selected. In the W (Width) text field, type **75** and choose % from the drop-down menu to the right; notice a change in your table width in the Design view.

You can set the table width to a percentage of the browser window by using the Property Inspector.

Choose File > Save, then preview the page in your browser again and resize the browser window. The table width now resizes because you set it to be a percentage rather than a fixed width. Close the browser and return to Dreamweaver.

4 Reset your table to the original width by typing **550** in the W text field and choosing pixels from the drop-down menu.

You also have the ability to resize the columns and rows in the Design view. You can do this manually using the Property Inspector.

5 Place your cursor inside the table and then over the dividing line between the first column and the second column. Your cursor changes to a double-arrow. Click and drag slowly to the right to expand the width of the first column. This has the effect of reducing the second column's width, although it leaves the third column's width alone. After changing the column widths, notice at the top of the two columns there are blue numbers that update showing the column widths. If these numbers do not appear, move your cursor over the top of the columns to display.

6 Expand the first column to at least 45 pixels; the content in the second column breaks to the next line. Place your cursor on the dividing line between the second and third column, and click and drag slowly to narrow the width of the third column (thereby expanding the width of the second column). This example uses values of 395 pixels for the third column and 88 pixels for the second.

If you are mathematically inclined, you may have noticed that the three column values don't add up to 550. This is because there are additional factors of cell padding, cell spacing, and borders to consider.

Oftentimes, approximate column widths are not sufficient; Dreamweaver allows you to apply exact column widths in the Property Inspector.

7 Place your cursor above the first column until the red outline appears and click once to select the column. The bottom half of the Property Inspector now allows you to adjust the properties of only this column. Type **40** into the W text field. The width does not appear to change dramatically, but it is now 40 pixels.

Selecting a column and entering a specific width in the Property Inspector sets the column to that width.

8 Click above the second column to select it. Type **100** into the W text field. Click above the third column and type **400** in the W text field. (This will have little effect on the appearance of the table.)

You also have the ability to create a fixed height for rows.

9 Click the left edge of the top row to select the whole row. In the Property Inspector, type **35** in the H text field, and press Enter (Windows) or Return (Mac OS) to apply the change.

Modifying table structure

In addition to modifying the width of columns and rows, the structure of a table often needs to be modified (for example, adding and deleting rows and columns, as well as merging cells in the column). First, you'll add a new row to the top of your table and then convert it to a header row. There are a few ways to add rows and columns in Dreamweaver, you'll begin with the Modify > Table command.

1 Click inside any of the cells within the first row. Dreamweaver needs to have some frame of reference when adding a row.

2 Choose Modify > Table > Insert Rows or Columns. The Insert Rows or Columns dialog box opens.

3 The Insert Rows radio button should be selected. For Number of rows, leave the default value of 1. In the Where section, select *Above the Selection*. Click OK to add the new row to the top of the table.

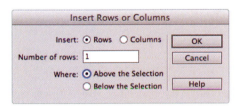

Use the Insert Rows and Columns dialog box to add new rows or columns to an existing table.

4 Place your cursor on the left side of the new row until the red outline appears. Click once to select it. In the Property Inspector, locate the Header check box and check it to designate this row as a Header row. Behind the scenes, Dreamweaver uses the HTML <th> tag to define this as a table header and the text will appear bold and centered. This will help you style your table later on.

Now you'll merge the three cells in this top row in order to add the header text that will span across your columns.

5 With the top row still selected, right-click (Windows) or Ctrl+click (Mac OS) to open a context menu. Choose Table > Merge Cells, and the three cells merge into one. This is referred to as columnspan.

6   Click inside this merged cell and type **US temperate zones with average min. temperatures**.

US temperate zones with average min. temperatures		
Zone	Fahrenheit	Example Cities
1	Below -50 F	Fairbanks, Alaska; Resolute, Northwest Territories (Canada)
2	-50 to -40 F	Prudhoe Bay, Alaska; Flin Flon, Manitoba (Canada)
3	-40 to -30 F	International Falls, Minnesota; St. Michael, Alaska
4	-30 to -20 F	Minneapolis/St.Paul, Minnesota; Lewistown, Montana
5	-20 to -10 F	Des Moines, Iowa; Illinois
6	-10 to 0 F	St. Louis, Missouri; Lebanon, Pennsylvania
7	0 to 10 F	Oklahoma City, Oklahoma; South Boston, Virginia
8	10 to 20 F	Tifton, Georgia; Dallas, Texas
9	20 to 30 F	Houston, Texas; St. Augustine, Florida
10	30 to 40 F	Naples, Florida; Victorville, California
11	above 40 F	Honolulu, Hawaii; Mazatlan, Mexico

Merging cells creates a columnspan, allowing you to add header text.

7   Choose File > Save to save your work.

Creating a table

In addition to creating a table from tabular data, you can also create a table from the ground up using Dreamweaver's Insert Table command.

1   Click to the right of your existing table, and then press Enter (Windows) or Return (Mac OS) two times. You will be placing a second table two lines below the first.

2   Choose Insert > Table, and the Table dialog box opens. Type **12** in the Rows text field, and **2** in the Columns text field. Type **550** in the Table width text field to match the width of your first table and make sure the drop-down menu is set to pixels. Set the Border thickness value to 1 if it is not already.

The Cell padding and Cell spacing values should have no value; you'll return to these properties shortly.

The Insert > Table command creates a new table.

3 In the Header section, select the third option, Top, in order to designate the top row as the header.

4 In the Caption field, type **Best months to plant vegetables (Zones 4–7)**. Table captions are a bit more specific than table headers. A table caption is a short description of the table contents and has its own `<caption>` element; by default, they are displayed centered and at the top of the table.

Table captions are not required, but they are useful, especially from an accessibility perspective, as they supply useful information to screen readers and other devices. Click OK to insert the table.

5 Below the caption, in the first cell of the first column, type **Month**. In the first cell of the second column, type **Vegetables to Plant**. Your columns could shift; in order to adjust them, click the divider between the two columns, and click and drag it as necessary to visually divide the two columns evenly.

6 In the second row of the *Month* column, type **April**, then five rows below, type **May**.

7 Below the *Vegetables to Plant* column, type **Broccoli**. Press the down arrow on your keyboard to move to the next row. Using this technique, first type **Cabbage** and then type each vegetable name in its own row—first **Carrots** and then **Spinach**. Skip one row and, making sure you are beginning in the same row as May, type **Corn**, **Tomatoes**, **Peppers**, **Cucumbers**.

Best months to plant vegetables (Zones 4-7)	
Month	**Vegetables to Plant**
April	Broccoli
	Cabbage
	Carrots
	Spinach
May	Corn
	Tomatoes
	Peppers
	Cucumbers

Press keyboard arrows to quickly move from one cell to another when typing text.

8 To delete the two extra rows at the bottom of the table, click in the first cell of row 11, and then drag down and to the right. The four cells are selected. Press Delete to remove the rows.

9 Choose File > Save, and keep this file open for the next exercise.

Formatting and styling tables in HTML

There are two different paths to take when it comes to styling a table. The first method is to use HTML tag properties to modify attributes such as the cell padding, border, and background color in a table. However, these same attributes can also be controlled with the second method, CSS. It's fair to say that there are more options for styling a table with CSS; however, styling a table with HTML tags is faster for most people. Which method you choose often depends on the project specifications. You'll be learning both methods here so that you have the option to choose. You'll also get a chance to consider the pros and cons of both methods. First, you'll start off with the *traditional* method of styling tables with HTML tags and properties.

1 In the second table you created (Best months to plant vegetables), click the edge of the header row to select it. In the Property Inspector, click the HTML category, if necessary, and then click the Bg (Background) color swatch. In the left column of swatches, choose the light gray (#CCCCCC). The background color of the header row changes to gray.

Select a row and click the Bg color swatch to apply a background color.

2 Click inside the April cell, then drag down and to the right until you reach the cell containing the text Spinach; this selects all the cells in these four rows and two columns.

3 Click the Bg swatch and choose **#FFFCCC**, a light yellow swatch in the lower-right corner. All four rows now have the same background color.

4 Select the empty row between *April* and *May*. Click the Bg color swatch and choose white for this background color. Then click in the May cell and drag down and to the right to the last cell containing the text *Cucumbers*. Click the Bg color swatch and choose the light pink color swatch, #FFCCFF, in the bottom-right corner.

Now, you will center the text in your columns.

5 Click at the top of the first column to select it. In the Property Inspector, from Horz (Horizontal) drop-down menu, select Center. Select the second column and repeat this step to center this text.

Select a column and click the Center option in the Horizontal menu of the Property Inspector.

6   Choose File > Save, then File > Preview in Browser. Your text is visually categorized by background color now, but it would be a stretch to say that this is a visually pleasing table. There are a few other properties that you can adjust to make this table look a bit better. Close the browser and return to Dreamweaver.

You'll now examine the properties of cell padding.

7   Click in one of the corners of the table until the entire table is outlined in red. Then click the table to select it. In the Property Inspector, locate the text field for CellPad and type **10**. Press Enter (Windows) or Return (Mac OS) to apply the change. There are now 10 pixels of space added to the inside of all cells. This has the effect of giving your text a bit more breathing room from the borders around it.

Cellpadding is a property that determines the amount of space, measured in pixels, between the sides of a cell and its contents.

8   With your table still selected, locate the text field for CellSpace in the Property Inspector. Type **10** in the CellSpace text field, then press Enter (Windows) or Return (Mac OS) to commit the change. The table changes appearance again. This time, the width between the cells is increased.

Cellspacing is the property that determines the amount of space between your cells.

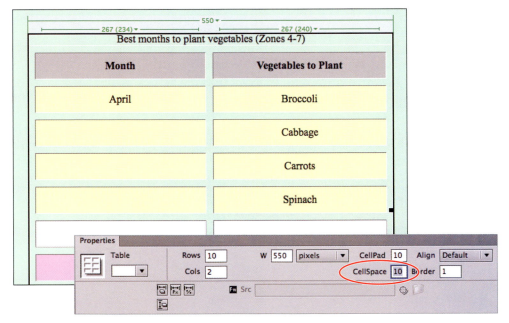

A table with cellpadding of 10 pixels and cellspacing of 10 pixels.

The space between the cells (the cellspacing) is taking on the properties of the background color. Unfortunately, you cannot control the color of the cellspacing, and so you will actually remove it completely.

9   In the Property Inspector, type **0** in the CellSpace text field and press Enter (Windows) or Return (Mac OS). This removes cellspacing completely. At this point, you only have properties for cellpadding.

10   With the table still selected, locate the text field for Border; it is currently set for 1 pixel, which is the default setting used when a table is created. Replace this value with 0 and press Enter (Windows) or Return (Mac OS). This removes the border completely.

This trick of removing borders completely is used quite a bit with pure HTML tables. This is because there are no good ways to control the appearance of borders using pure HTML. Increasing the border size creates a thick, beveled look that can detract from the rest of your page. Better control for borders exists in CSS.

11   Place your cursor on the small black square on the lower-right of the table until you see the double-arrow. Click and drag the table to the left to reduce its width. You can use the value at the top of the table if you choose, or just change the width until you're satisfied. This example uses a new width of 350 pixels.

350	
267 (146) ▾	267 (164) ▾
Best months to plant vegetables (Zones 4-7)	
Month	Vegetables to Plant
April	Broccoli
	Cabbage
	Carrots
	Spinach
May	Corn
	Tomatoes
	Peppers
	·Cucumbers

Click and drag the edge of a table to reduce the width.

12 With the table still selected, click the Split view button in order to see the code generated for this table. In the first line of the table, you see the settings for the width, height, border, and cell padding. In all the `<td>` or cells, you see the properties for alignment and background color repeated for every row. This extra code is part of the tradeoff for the easy application of the color and alignment. Part of the dilemma with this table now is that the alignment and background color settings, as well as the cellspacing, cellpadding, and border settings, are not linked to your CSS in any way.

The visual styling of the table elements is combined with the structure.

One problem of creating pure HTML tables is the inability to quickly copy the style of one table and apply it to another. Because the content of the table and the style are intertwined, it's hard to separate one from the other. The larger problem is that pure HTML tables have none of the benefits associated with CSS. If your tables are not linked to any CSS, what happens when you redesign your website? As you saw in the last lesson, a simple change in CSS code can change the background color of your entire site. If the design of your tables clashes with your page, you have a lot of work to do as you locate each table and tweak it to fit.

Formatting and styling tables with CSS

In this exercise, you'll style your initial table using many of the same concepts covered in the previous exercise, such as padding and borders, but this time you'll do it with CSS. There is a little bit more work involved initially, but the result will be a table that not only is more visually appealing than an HTML-based table but also has a reusable style that can be applied to new tables. It's possible to create tag-based styles for all your tables—in other words, to create CSS rules for the various HTML table elements (<td>, <tr>, and so on). In fact, this is not a bad idea when creating a *default* style for tables in a website. In this example, however, you will be creating a class style that can readily be applied to different tables. It's not unusual to have three or four different styles of tables in a large website, each with their own CSS class definitions.

First you'll start by creating general rules for the background color, border, and font appearance of the table; then you'll create more specific rules as you drill down into the table.

1   Click the Design View button to return to this view. Select the first table you created (US Temperate Zones…) by clicking one of the corners when you see the red outline. If necessary, choose Window > CSS Designer to open the CSS Designer panel.

2   In the CSS Designer panel, select the **mystyles.css** external style sheet in the Sources pane. This is an important step because you would like to add these styles to your external style sheet rather than writing them to the tips.html page only.

3   Click the Add Selector button (⊞) in the bar at the top of the Selectors pane to create a new rule for the table. Dreamweaver will populate the selector field with body table. Click this name and change it to **.styledtable**. Press Enter (Windows) or Return (Mac OS).

4   Select the Background button (▭) in the Properties Navigation bar to show the background properties. Then click the background-color swatch, and choose the color white (#FFFFF).

Creating a new class for the style of the table and defining it in the external style sheet.

You see no changes onscreen because you need to apply the .styledtable class to the table. You'll do that now, and then return to adding more styles.

5   Your table should still be selected; if it isn't, then select it now. In the Property Inspector, the table properties should be active. (If you are seeing the HTML and CSS properties, you have not selected the table.) On the right side of the Property Inspector, choose styledtable from the Class drop-down menu to apply the class. The background of your table changes to white.

Apply a class to a table by choosing the class name in the Property Inspector.

6   Now you'll return to the styledtable class style and add additional properties. You could have created all your rules first and then applied the styledtable class; however, doing it this way allows you to preview your styling in real-time. Now you'll add some borders and change the font-styling for the entire table.

7   Click once on `.styledtable` in the Selectors pane of the CSS Designer panel to reselect the class.

Then select the Text button (**T**) in the Properties Navigation bar to show the text properties.

8   In the text properties, click to the right of the font-family property to activate the drop-down menu, and choose the Gotham, Helvetica Neue, Helvetica, Arial, sans-serif font set.

9   If necessary, scroll down to the font-size text field, choose px for the units, and type **10** for the value. Press Enter (Windows) or Return (Mac OS).

10 Scroll back up to the color property, and click in the text field to the right of the color swatch. Type **#006** (a dark blue), and press Enter (Windows) or Return (Mac OS) to see your changes to the table. Now you'll add a thin border around the entire table.

11 Select the Border button (⬛) in the Properties Navigation bar, and scroll down to the border-style property. Click to activate the drop-down menu and choose solid. From the border-width drop-down, choose px, and type **1** in the text field to its left. In the border-color text field, type **#006**, which is the same dark blue you used for the font-color. Press Enter (Windows) or Return (Mac OS) to see the results.

Your styled table with background-color, font styling, and a border.

The last property you'll add to the .styledtable class is one that is not as common as the previous ones you've set. It's important to realize that the language of CSS is quite large to begin with, and will continue to expand in the future. There are CSS properties that might not be used every day but nonetheless can be very useful. You'll add one such property now called border-collapse. This property removes the space between table cells.

12 If it's not already selected, select the Border button (⬛) in the Properties Navigation bar, and scroll up to the border-collapse property. Click the collapse button (⊞) immediately to the right. You will not see an obvious change on screen; this property and value will help older browsers render the table correctly.

13 Choose File > Save All. Preview your page in your browser to see your styling. Close the browser and return to Dreamweaver.

Advanced CSS styling of tables

You have created a basic style for this table. You will now sharpen up the appearance of this table by adding a background image to the header, setting the text alignment and padding, and finally, creating subtle borders between each of the data cells.

1   Click anywhere inside the header, and in the lower-left corner of your document window, click the `<th>` tag to select the header. You defined this top row as a table header earlier in the lesson.

2   In the Sources pane of the CSS Designer panel, click **mystyles.css** to select your external style sheet file. This is an important step because you would like to add these styles to your external style sheet rather than writing them to the tips.html page only.

3   Click the Add Selector button (⊞) in the bar at the top of the Selectors pane to create a new rule for the header. The Selector Name text field has been automatically populated as `.styledtable tr th`. Press Enter (Windows) or Return (Mac OS) to accept this value.

This compound rule is what you want because you are creating a specific rule for `<th>` tags, but only those found inside the `.styledtable` class. Remember that compound rules are read from left to right. So, within the `.styledtable` class, you are targeting table rows `<tr>` and specifically, table headers `<th>` within table rows.

Create a compound rule to style all header rows within the `.styledtable` *class.*

4   With the compound rule selected, select the Background button (▭) in the Properties Navigation bar, and scroll down to the background-image property. Click in the url text field, and press the Browse button to the right. In the Select Image Source dialog box, locate the **bg_header.jpg** image and press OK (Windows) or Open (Mac OS).

5   Scroll down to the background-repeat property, and click the repeat-x button (■■) to the right. The source image is a gradient that is designed to tile horizontally, and you'll see a preview of this effect on your table. You'll add a few other touches to this header row.

Choose a background image and tile it horizontally in the header row with repeat-x.

6   Select the Border button (▭) in the Properties Navigation bar, and scroll down to the border-bottom-width property. Click to choose px from the pull-down menu to the right, and type **2** in the text field to its left. Then scroll up to the border-bottom-color property. Type **#006** in the text field to the right of the color swatch; this is the same dark blue color that you've been using for other styling in this table. Press Enter (Windows) or Return (Mac OS)to see the results.

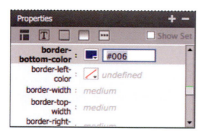

Applying a two-pixel-wide, solid, blue border to the bottom of the header row.

7 Select the Text button (T) in the Properties Navigation bar, and scroll down to the font-size property. Click to choose px from the drop-down menu to the right, and type **14** into the text field to its left to make the text slightly larger. Scroll down to the text-transform property, and click the Capitalize button (Ab). This property adds a capital letter to the beginning of each word.

US Temperate Zones With Average Min. Temperatures.		
Zone	Fahrenheit	Example Cities
1	Below -50 F	Fairbanks, Alaska; Resolute, Northwest Territories (Canada)
2	-50 to -40 F	Prudhoe Bay, Alaska; Flin Flon, Manitoba (Canada)
3	-40 to -30 F	International Falls, Minnesota; St. Michael, Alaska
4	-30 to -20 F	Minneapolis/St.Paul, Minnesota; Lewistown, Montana
5	-20 to -10 F	Des Moines, Iowa; Illinois
6	-10 to 0 F	St. Louis, Missouri; Lebanon, Pennsylvania
7	0 to 10 F	Oklahoma City, Oklahoma; South Boston, Virginia
8	10 to 20 F	Tifton, Georgia; Dallas, Texas
9	20 to 30 F	Houston, Texas; St. Augustine, Florida
10	30 to 40 F	Naples, Florida; Victorville, California
11	above 40 F	Honolulu, Hawaii; Mazatlan, Mexico

Your header row is now styled.

8 Choose File > Save All. Keep this file open as you will continue working on it in the next exercise.

Controlling cell alignment, padding, and borders with CSS

You'll now make the content within your table a bit more readable by aligning your text and padding your cells, as well as creating borders around each cell. Controlling borders and padding is much more flexible in CSS than in HTML; for example, the cellpadding values in HTML are uniform—there is no control over left, right, top, and bottom, as there is in CSS. The same applies to borders. However, before you begin styling padding with CSS, it's a good idea to remove these values from the HTML so that there are no surprises.

1 Click any corner of the table in order to select it. In the Property Inspector, notice the values for CellPad and CellSpace; they are empty, but this stands for default, not zero. You must specifically instruct Dreamweaver to use a value of zero.

2 For all three properties of CellPad, CellSpace, and Border, type **0**. Press Enter (Windows) or Return (Mac OS) when you have added the last value.

*Type **0** for CellPad, CellSpace, and Border to make sure they are removed.*

3 Click inside any cell of your table, and in the bottom-left corner of your document window, click the `<td>` tag to select a cell. You could also Ctrl+click (Windows) or Command+click (Mac OS) a cell to select it.

4 In the Sources pane of the CSS Designer panel, click **mystyles.css**. Then click the Add Selector button (■) in the bar at the top of the Selectors tab to create a new rule. As in the last exercise, you are creating a Compound rule that applies only to cells within the `.styledtable` class. Your selector name reads `.styledtable tr td`. Press Enter (Windows) or Return (Mac OS) to confirm this setting.

5 Select the Text button in the Properties Navigation bar, and scroll down to the text-align property. Click the center button to the right to see all text in the table center.

Applying a text-align of center to the `<td>` element centers all text in your cells.

6 Select the Layout button in the Properties Navigation bar, and scroll down to the padding property. Click the top value and type **5** in the text field. Do the same for the bottom value. Then click the left value and type **2** in the text field.

One of the main differences between HTML cellpadding and CSS cellpadding is the ability in CSS to control all four sides of a cell's padding individually.

7 Select the Border button in the Properties Navigation bar, and scroll down to the border-top-style. Click in the field to the right to choose dashed from the drop-down menu.

8 Scroll up in the Border properties, and in the border-color text field, type **#9AA8BD**, the hexadecimal number for a light blue-gray. Press Enter (Windows) or Return (Mac OS) to apply the style.

9   Select the row below the header row, and, if necessary, click the HTML button in the Property Inspector, then click the Bold button to bold the text for Zone, Fahrenheit, and Example Cities.

10 Choose File > Save All. Then preview your page in your browser to see your table.

OrganicUtopia Gardening Tips

Strange as it sounds, we want you to put us out of business! OrganicUtopia is committed to spreading the word about organic food. Yes, we feature organic fruits and vegetables from the area's best farmers, but we think growing your own is even better! Here are some tips on when to begin planting in your area. When deciding which crops to plant, the first step is to decide what zone of the country you live in. Many seed companies will refer to these zones on their packages or catalogs.

US Temperate Zones With Average Min. Temperatures.		
Zone	**Fahrenheit**	**Example Cities**
1	Below -50 F	Fairbanks, Alaska; Resolute, Northwest Territories (Canada)
2	-50 to -40 F	Prudhoe Bay, Alaska; Flin Flon, Manitoba (Canada)
3	-40 to -30 F	International Falls, Minnesota; St. Michael, Alaska
4	-30 to -20 F	Minneapolis/St.Paul, Minnesota; Lewistown, Montana
5	-20 to -10 F	Des Moines, Iowa; Illinois
6	-10 to 0 F	St. Louis, Missouri; Lebanon, Pennsylvania
7	0 to 10 F	Oklahoma City, Oklahoma; South Boston, Virginia
8	10 to 20 F	Tifton, Georgia; Dallas, Texas
9	20 to 30 F	Houston, Texas; St. Augustine, Florida
10	30 to 40 F	Naples, Florida; Victorville, California
11	above 40 F	Honolulu, Hawaii; Mazatlan, Mexico

The table as rendered in a web browser.

You're nearly finished. Now you'll add some final touches to your table to give it a little extra polish and readability. Close your web browser.

Creating alternate row styling with CSS

A common feature found in many tables is to alternate colors for every other row. When done correctly, this increases the contrast between the rows and allows the user to visually separate the content of the table. This is easily done in CSS by creating a new class solely for background color.

Unlike the last few exercises, you will not be using a compound selection. Instead, you will be creating a new class. The reason for this is that you only want to style every other row. There is no automatic way to do this in CSS; after you create the class, it will have to be applied manually.

1 Click the edge of the row labeled 1 to select it. In the Sources pane of the CSS Designer panel, click **mystyles.css**. Then click the Add Selector button (+) in the bar at the top of the Selectors tab to create a new rule. Dreamweaver will populate the selector name field. Click the suggested name and change it to **.oddrow**.

2 Select the Background button (▭) in the Properties Navigation Bar to show the background properties. Then click in the field to the right of the background-color swatch, and type **#EAF1F4**, the hexadecimal color for a light blue. Press Enter (Windows) or Return (Mac OS) to set the color.

Create a new class named oddrow *to style individual rows.*

Now you will apply the oddrow class to every other row.

3 The row labeled 1 should still be selected; if not, do so now. In the Property Inspector, click the HTML button. From the Class drop-down menu, choose oddrow. The light-blue background color is applied.

4 Starting with the row labeled 3, apply the oddrow class to all the odd-numbered rows.

Styling alternating rows with a background color can improve readability.

5 Choose File > Save All. Preview your page in the browser, then close the browser when you are finished.

Reusing CSS for other tables

As you have seen, CSS styling for tables is very powerful and capable of spicing up the appearance of tables without sacrificing their structure. Like CSS for text and layout, the real power is obvious when you apply and link the style to another table.

1   In the Files panel, double-click the file **veggie_names.html**. This page is currently linked to the same external style sheet as the tips.html page, and includes an unstyled table. All that needs to be done is to apply the styledtable class you created to this table.

2   Click anywhere in the table, and then click the `<table>` tag in the lower-left corner of the document window to select the table.

3   In the Property Inspector, choose styledtable from the Class drop-down menu on the far right. The style is applied, and the appearance of this table matches the other. The style is flexible enough that, even though the top row has three cells, it has the header style applied.

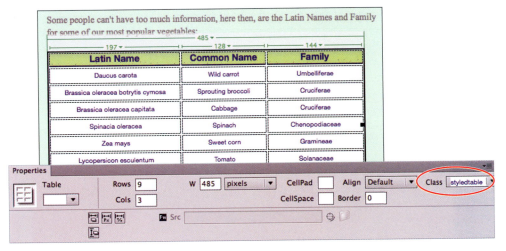

Applying the styledtable *class to a previously unstyled table.*

That's it! The hard work of creating the original style pays off when it comes time to creating new tables with identical style. Better yet, if you need to make a global change such as changing the background-color or font color, changing a property in the external sheet will ripple through to all tables.

4   To add the alternating rows of color, click the third row. In the Property Inspector, click the HTML button, and from the Class drop-down menu, choose oddrow. Repeat this step with every other row to add the style.

The added benefit of having this class handy is that some tables benefit from this style more than others, and so it is your decision whether or not to use it.

5   Choose File > Save All. Keep this file open for the next exercise.

Data sorting tables

There are a few other features related to managing tables that you might find useful. The structure of tables can be both a blessing and a curse. For example, take a look at the table from the previous exercise. What if you wanted to swap the order of the first two columns? There is no easy way to do this with a static HTML table. Another limitation of tables, especially tables created from tabular data where you might not have control over the order, is the difficulty of sorting the data. Dreamweaver has a feature that allows you to sort your data alphabetically by the column of your choice.

In the first part of the exercise, you will do some copy-and-pasting in order to switch the first two columns.

1   Click a corner of the table to select it. Choose Edit > Copy to copy the table.

2   Click to the right of the table, press Enter (Windows) or Return (Mac OS) twice, and choose Edit > Paste. You can copy and paste tables in Dreamweaver within a page, or from one page to another.

3   In the first table, click at the top of the second column (Common Name) to select the entire column. Choose Edit > Copy to copy the contents of the column. Now click at the top of the first column (Latin Name) to select it. Choose Edit > Paste to replace the content of the first column. You now have duplicate columns momentarily, but the next step is to copy content from the second table.

4   In the second table, click the top of the first column (Latin Name) to select it. Choose Edit > Copy to copy this column's contents. Return to the first table and click the top of the second column; then choose Edit > Paste.

5   Select the second table and delete it now, as you no longer need it.

Now you'll sort the first column alphabetically using Dreamweaver's little-known Sort Table feature.

6 Select the first table and choose Commands > Sort Table to open the Sort Table dialog box. You do not have to make any changes here because the default settings are fine, but take a quick look at the options. The Sort By menu allows you to choose which menu Dreamweaver will use to sort. The Order menu allows you to choose how the table should be sorted, either alphabetically or numerically. Alphabetically is correct for now.

Choose Commands > Sort Table to sort a table alphabetically.

7 Click OK, and the table is sorted, with the first column now in alphabetical order.

8 Choose File > Save All.

Self study

Using your new knowledge of creating tables to display data in Dreamweaver, try some of the following tasks to build on your experience:

Use the Import Tabular Data command to import a tab-delimited .txt file, setting the table's fixed width on import. Select the table using the Tag Selector, and change its width to 50 percent of the page size using the Property Inspector. Preview the table in a browser, noting the way the table changes as the browser window is resized.

Build another table using the Insert Table command, and add a caption to it. Type text into the cells, center the text, and drag the row and column dividers to make them consistent in size. Add a background color and a border to the table using the Property Inspector, and switch to Code View to note the changes to your HTML code.

Create and use an internal CSS rule to change the font used, add padding to the cells, and alternate the colors of your first table's rows. Experiment with applying the class rule to your second table, and note how its appearance changes. Finally, use the Sort Table command to organize both your tables' data alphabetically.

Review

Questions

1   What's the difference between a percentage-based table and a fixed-width table?

2   What is tabular data and how does it relate to tables in Dreamweaver?

3   Name an advantage and a disadvantage of using CSS to style your tables.

Answers

1   A percentage-based table stretches to fit the size of the browser window. A fixed-width table does not resize because it is pixel-based.

2   Tabular data is text often exported from a database or spreadsheet in a delimited format. Dreamweaver creates tables from these files through the Import Tabular Data command found in the File menu. Rows and columns are automatically created in Dreamweaver based on the structure of the text file.

3   One advantage of using CSS to style tables is the ability to link a single style to multiple tables using an external style sheet. A disadvantage might be that the process requires more time in the beginning, and a good understanding of HTML table tags and CSS selectors.

Fine-Tuning Your Workflow

Once you become familiar with building web pages in Dreamweaver CC, you'll find yourself using some features more often than others. In this lesson, you'll learn how to save time by customizing the Dreamweaver environment to streamline your workflow.

Starting up

Before starting, make sure that your tools and panels are consistent by resetting your workspace. See "Resetting the Dreamweaver workspace" in the Starting up section of this book.

You will work with several files from the dw10lessons folder in this lesson. Make sure that you have loaded the dwlessons folder onto your hard drive from the supplied DVD. See "Loading lesson files" in the Starting up section of this book.

Before you begin, you need to create site settings that point to the dw10lessons folder from the included DVD that contains resources you need for these lessons. Go to Site > New Site, or, for details on creating a site, refer to Lesson 2, "Setting Up a New Site."

See Lesson 10 in action!

Use the accompanying video to gain a better understanding of how to use some of the features shown in this lesson. The video tutorial for this lesson can be found on the included DVD.

Customizing panels and panel groups

Panels can be moved, grouped, and docked to help keep everything you regularly use at your fingertips. In the next part of this lesson, you'll create a custom workspace for CSS layouts. You'll start by removing certain panels and repositioning the remaining panels.

1 Make sure your dw10lessons folder has been defined as a site as described in the Starting Up section. This first exercise does not require any of the lesson files as you will be focusing on the workspace.

To ensure you are starting from the same workspace as we are, choose Window > Workspace Layout > Compact. Then choose 'Reset Compact'. You will now customize your panels.

2 Locate the CSS Designer tab, click the panel menu in the top right, and then choose Close Tab Group.

3 Double-click the Insert tab to close that panel. Click once on the Insert tab to show it again.

4 From the Window menu, choose CSS Designer to reopen that tab group.

5 Click once on the Files tab to expand that panel.

Click the Files tab to show the Files panel.

There are two panels within the CSS Designer panel group: CSS Designer and CSS Transitions. The CSS Transitions panel is currently hidden. In order to see both panels simultaneously, you'll drag the CSS Transitions panel out of the tab group.

6 Click and hold the CSS Transitions tab. Drag this tab into your workspace to remove it from the CSS panel group. This now becomes a floating window, which you can keep floating if you want. Many users prefer to have all their panels within a single column, so you'll add it back in now.

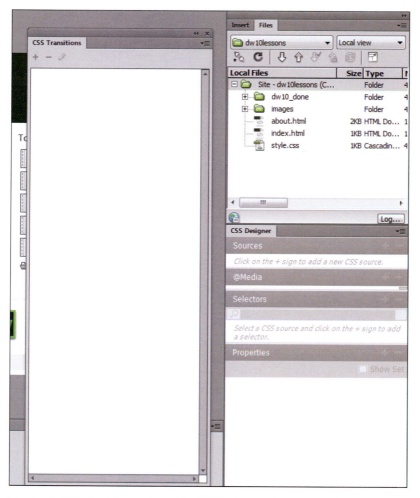

Dragging the CSS Transitions panel out of the CSS Designer panel group turns it into a floating window.

7 To keep the CSS Transitions panel from interfering with your workspace, you can dock it with the other panels. Place your cursor over the CSS Transitions tab at the top of the panel, and click and hold.

8 Drag the CSS Transitions panel immediately above the title bar of the CSS Designer panel group. Be careful here: if the entire CSS Designer panel is highlighted blue, you will be *adding* to the group. You are looking for a thin blue line above the CSS Designer tab; this indicates that you are creating a new group. When a solid line appears above the CSS Designer panel group, release the CSS Transitions panel to snap it into place.

9   If necessary, adjust the width and height of the panels by placing your cursor on the edges of any panel group. When the black double-arrow appears, you can click and drag to adjust as needed. When you're finished, the panels should look similar to the example shown here. This configuration gives you quick access to the panels you'll use the most when creating a CSS-based layout.

The customized panels.

10 Dreamweaver CC also has the same Icon view as the other applications in the Creative Suite. Click the double-arrows on the top-right corner of the entire column of panels; they will collapse to the icon view.

11 Click the Files icon; that group will expand so you can work with it. This group will temporarily stay open until you start working on the document or click another icon.

You can decide whether you prefer to work in the expanded panel view or the icon view. For now, you'll return to the panel view.

12 Click the double-arrows to return to the expanded panel view.

13 To save this workspace, choose Window > Workspace Layout > New Workspace. When the New Workspace Layout dialog box appears, type **CSS Layout** into the Name text field and click OK.

14 Choose Window > Workspace Layout > Compact to switch to the default workspace; then choose Window > Workspace Layout > CSS Layout to switch back to the custom workspace you just created.

Using the Favorites tab on the Insert bar

To help organize the many options available in the Insert bar, Dreamweaver groups similar items into categories. You might already be using some items more often than others. The Favorites category is a great way to group commonly used items into one place for quick access.

1 Double-click the **index.html** file in the Files panel. In this exercise, you'll be inserting a number of images and AP Divs to create two pages in the Sounds of Nature website. These options are currently hidden within the insert panel, so you'll need to expand it.

2 Expand the Insert panel by clicking the Insert tab at the top of the panel. If necessary, adjust the heights of your available panels by dragging the borders between them.

The Insert panel has a large number of options available within numerous categories. If you find yourself inserting the same objects over and over, you might want to group them. You can do this with the Favorites category of the Insert panel.

3 Select the Favorites category from the Insert panel's drop-down menu. Right-click (Windows) or Ctrl+click (Mac OS) in the empty gray area beneath the Favorite category, and choose Customize Favorites from the resulting context menu. The Customize Favorite Objects dialog box appears.

Right-click (Windows) or Ctrl+click (Mac OS) in the empty gray area beneath the Insert panel's Favorite category and choose Customize Favorites.

4   On the left side of the Customize Favorite Objects dialog box, the list of available objects is organized by the tabs, which indicate where each object can be found in the Insert bar. Select Image, then click the Add button (>>) in the middle of the dialog box.

Select Image and click the Add button.

5   Locate Div from the list of available objects; then click the Add button. Click OK. The Favorites category now features the Image and Div elements.

Resizing the document window

If you're familiar with any page layout or graphics programs, adjusting the size of the window in which you're working is probably something that you do regularly. However, when you're working on web pages in Dreamweaver, it's a good idea to think carefully about the size of your document. Because a number of different hardware and software configurations might be used to view your content, it can be tricky to make sure your website looks acceptable on every user's computer. In the next part of this lesson, you'll resize the document window to make sure the Sounds of Nature website is being designed with the target audience in mind.

1   **Index.html** should still be open in your document window. If not, open it now. Also, make sure you're in the Design view. If necessary, click the Design button in the Document toolbar.

2   Look at the very bottom of your document window; there are several controls relating to the Window Size on your screen.

*A. Mobile Size (480 × 800). **B.** Tablet Size (768 × 1024). **C.** Desktop Size (1000 × 620). **D.** Window Size.*

Pay particular attention to the numbers 1000 × 484 in our figure; this is the Window Size. It is quite likely your numbers will be different. This number represents the full width Dreamweaver is capable of displaying given the user's screen size. Because we are using a monitor set to 1024 × 768, this is as wide as Dreamweaver can display the page on *our* screen.

3 Click the Window Size numbers to access a menu. The default setting is actually set to the Full Size option. Dreamweaver calculates these numbers instantly.

You will also that see there are other monitor size options in this menu. From the menu, choose the option that reads *1260 × 875*. What happens on your screen depends on the size of your monitor. On our 1024 × 768 monitor, a scroll bar appears that allows us to scroll over to the right of the document. Generally speaking, you can leave this setting to Full Size unless you have a specific need to preview your page in different size screens.

The second value seen in this step, 1280 × 1024 Maximized, refers to the true size of the page as if the user were maximizing their browser window to the fullest. The 1260 × 875 number is a more realistic estimate of the available space a web browser would occupy on the screen (accounting for browser features, such as scroll bars).

There are three monitor icons that will allow you to change the window size to three different presets.

4 Click the first icon to the left of the Window Size numbers. This is the Mobile Size (480 × 800) preset.

The Mobile Size preset changes the dimensions of the screen to 480 pixels wide by 800 high.

This will set the window size to 480 pixels wide by 800 high and have the effect of cropping your current page. The goal here is to show you the window size as if you were viewing the site with a mobile device. Although this can be a useful feature, it's a bit deceptive. Dreamweaver is not trying to reproduce the behavior of a web browser on a smartphone; it's simply limiting the width and height of your current window.

A more sophisticated method of designing your pages for mobile devices is covered in Lesson 16, "Responsive Design and Layout for Mobile Devices."

5   Click the next icon to the right, which is the Tablet size. Note the change in the screen. Click the last icon, which is the Desktop view and is set to 1000w, indicating the width of the screen is 1000px and the height is unspecified.. All these settings can be useful if you want to see how your designs appear in these different size screens. Just remember that there is no substitute for seeing your design in a web browser.

6   Click the Window Size menu, and then click the *Full Size* option to set the screen back to the maximum amount of space on your monitor.

Using guides

In Lesson 5, "Creating Page Layouts with CSS," you learned how absolute-position divs can be added to a page for precise layout. Guides can be a useful tool for absolute-position divs, as well as the other types of layout techniques, because they allow you to line up and measure different elements on your page. In this exercise, you'll add an absolute-position div to **index.html**, and then place an image inside the div. First, you'll draw some guides to help you size and position the div.

1   If your rulers are hidden, choose View > Rulers > Show to turn them on.

Rulers can use inches, centimeters, or pixels in Dreamweaver. Because pixels are the most common unit of measurement on the Web, they are the default. If you prefer inches or centimeters, right-click (Windows) or Ctrl+click (Mac OS) on the rulers to access a context menu where you can choose your preferred unit. In this lesson, you'll be using pixels, so it's a good idea to stick with them for now.

2   Click inside the vertical ruler on the left side of your document window, and then drag a guide into the center of the page. Notice, as you drag, that a yellow box appears with the pixel number of your horizontal ruler. When you let go and move your cursor off the ruler, it will disappear.

Dragging a guide manually is useful, but you can also set a guide's position precisely.

3   Double-click this guide to open the Move Guide dialog box. From this dialog box, you can set an exact location for guides. This feature can be especially helpful when building a web page based on sketches or mockups.

4   Type **38** in the Location text field and click OK. The guide is repositioned 38 pixels from the left side of the document.

5 Create another vertical guide and set its position to 494 pixels, either by dragging it to this position or setting its value precisely.

What if you wanted to determine the exact width between these two guides you just added? Instead of using a calculator, you can allow Dreamweaver to do it for you.

6 Press and hold the Ctrl (Windows) or Command (Mac OS) key and move your cursor across the three sections of your page as defined by the guides. A blue line with arrows on either end indicates the distance between each of your guides, as well as the distance between guides and the edge of the document window. Between the two guides, you can now see that the width is exactly 456 pixels.

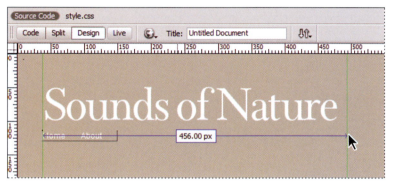

Press and hold Ctrl (Windows) or Command (Mac OS) and hover over the vertical areas defined by guides.

7 Drag two horizontal guides down from the ruler at the top of the document window. Double-click each of them, and then use the Move Guide dialog box to position one of them 152 pixels from the top of the document, and the other 380 pixels from the top of the document.

8 Next, you'll create an absolute-position div and start adding some content; but first make sure that Snap to Guides is turned on, by choosing View > Guides > Edit Guides. The Guides dialog box appears, with a number of options for customizing your guides.

If you happen to be using a color in your web page that makes the guides hard to see, you can change their color here. Also, the Lock Guides option can be a helpful way to avoid accidentally repositioning guides. For now, make sure Snap to Guides is checked and click OK.

The Guides dialog box allows you to change the color of guides and turn snapping on and off.

9 Now that your guides are set up, you're ready to add some content. With the Favorites category selected in the Insert panel, click the Div object.

10 In the Insert Div dialog box that appears, you can leave Insert set to At Insertion Point and type **photo** for the ID. Then click OK to create the div.

Next, you will use the CSS Designer panel to style this div as a absolute positioned div, which will allow you to resize and reposition it on the page.

11 With the newly created #photo div selected, click styles.css in the Sources pane, then click the Add Selector button in the Selectors pane. Dreamweaver will suggest the Selector name .body_style #photo. Change this to simply read **#photo** and press Enter (Windows) or Return (Mac OS).

12 Click the Layout button in the Properties Navigation bar and scroll down to the position property. Click the word *static* and select absolute from the menu.

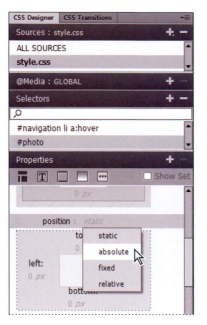

Set the position *property of the* #photo *div to absolute.*

13 The `#photo` div will now be displayed with a blue border, resize handles, and a tab in the top left corner. If the div does not appear this way at first, click the Design view button to refresh the layout. Click the tab in the top left corner and drag the div to align with the top left corner of the guides you created earlier.

Drag your newly-created div into position using the guides you added earlier.

14 Position your cursor over the handle on the lower-right corner of your newly-positioned div, then drag downward to expand it to fill the rectangular area created by the four guides.

15 Select the placeholder text and press Delete to remove it from the div. With your cursor positioned inside the div, select the Image object in the Favorites category of the Insert panel.

16 In the Select Image Source dialog box, select **hp_photo.jpg** from the Images folder inside the dw10lessons folder, and click OK (Windows) or Open (Mac OS). The **hp_photo.jpg** image fits nicely inside the div you created.

The hp_photo.jpg image placed inside of the absolute-position div.

17 Choose File > Save and leave **index.html** open.

Using grids

Much like guides, grids are a great way to help keep your layout precise and uniform. In the next part of this lesson, you'll be adding absolute-position divs and images to the About page of the Sounds of Nature website. Creating a custom grid will help you align and evenly distribute these new elements on the page.

1   Double-click the **about.html** file in your Files panel to open the About page. You might notice that this page has a white background and uses a default typeface. Later on, you'll use the tag selector to change this.

2   Choose View > Grid > Grid Settings to open the Grid Settings dialog box. Much like the Guides dialog box, the Grid Settings dialog box can be used to specify the grid color and turn on snapping. Type **#CCCCCC** in the Color text field and check Show Grid and Snap to Grid to turn the grid on and enable snapping.

3   For this layout, type **38** in the Spacing text field and make sure pixels are selected as the unit of measurement. Choosing a spacing of 38 pixels creates a series of squares that are 38 pixels high by 38 pixels wide. Click Apply to preview the grid settings, then click OK.

The Grid Settings dialog box.

4 With the grid established, add the absolute-position divs that will house your images. Using the techniques described in steps 9–13 above, create a square, absolute-position div that is 3 grid units wide and 3 grid units high. When prompted, name the new div ID **box_1** and name the new Selector **#box_1**.

Create a square, absolute-position div.

5 Using the same techniques as in step 4, create a second absolute-position div one grid unit below the first. When prompted, name the new div ID **box_2** and name the new Selector **#box_2**.

Draw a second absolute-position div one grid unit below the first.

6 Click inside the first div to place the cursor, and then click the Image element in the Favorites category of the Insert panel.

7 In the Select Image Source dialog box, select **tree.jpg** from the images folder inside the dw10lessons folder, and click OK (Windows) or Open (Mac OS). The tree image is positioned inside the div on your page.

8 Repeat steps 6 and 7 to add **forest.jpg** to the second div.

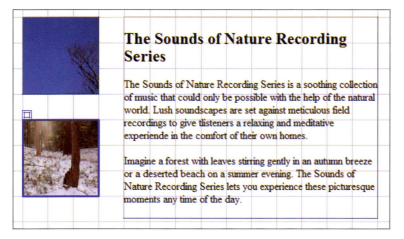

The about.html page after inserting the tree and forest images.

9 Choose File > Save and leave **about.html** open for the next part of this lesson.

The tag selector

In HTML, the organization of elements takes the form of a family tree. In the previous two exercises, you created absolute-position divs and then inserted images into them. In HTML terms, all these images are children of the divs within which they reside. The tag selector is a feature of Dreamweaver that allows you to select HTML elements based on their relationship to one another. The tag selector has been used in previous sections of this book, but in this exercise you'll use it to apply a single style that will affect the entire **about.html** page.

1   With the About page open, click once on the forest image that you inserted at the end of the last exercise. At the bottom-left corner of the document window are a number of HTML tags. This is the tag selector. The `<img>` tag at the end of this line is highlighted to indicate that the forest.jpg image is selected. In addition, the Property Inspector displays information and options related to this image.

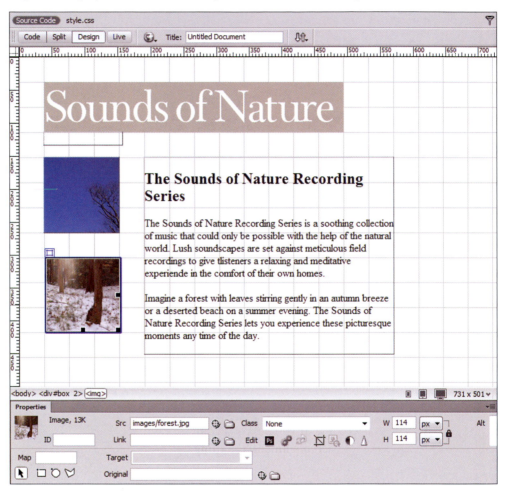

With the forest image selected, the `<img>` tag in the tag selector is highlighted and the Property Inspector displays information and options related to this image.

2   In the tag selector, click the `<div#box _ 2>` tag to the left of the `<img>` tag. Notice that the options in the Property Inspector change to reflect the selected div. In this case, you've selected the parent of the forest image.

3   To further illustrate this relationship, choose Edit > Select Child from the main menu. The `<img>` tag becomes highlighted in the tag selector, and the Property Inspector changes to reflect the selected element.

4 Now, select <body> on the far-left side of the tag selector. The Property Inspector displays options and information related to the <body> tag. Click the CSS button in the Property Inspector if necessary and then, from the Targeted Rule drop-down menu, choose body_style.

With the <body> tag selected in the tag selector, choose body_style from the Targeted Rule drop-down menu.

Because many CSS properties are inherited throughout the document, it is possible to write generalized rules that will be applied to all the elements on a page. In this case, body_style changes the font and text color for the entire document because every element is a descendant of the body.

5 Choose File > Save and leave **about.html** open for the next part of this lesson.

Tiling documents

By default, Dreamweaver organizes open documents with a series of tabs in the upper-left corner of the document window. If you'd like to compare documents, or you simply prefer to use separate windows for each document, the tiling option provides an alternative for viewing open files. Next, you'll use this feature to simultaneously view the index page and the about page of the Sounds of Nature website.

1 Both **index.html** and **about.html** should still be open. If they are not, open them now.

2 Choose Window > Tile Vertically (Windows) or Window > Tile (Mac OS). This will send the two pages into two windows side-by-side. This feature can be useful for dragging and dropping objects from one page to another or to work on both pages if you have a big enough monitor.

The fastest way to group these two pages back together is different depending which platform you are on, Windows or MacOS.

3   On the Mac, click the **index.html** tab, drag it to the **about.html** tab, and then release it. They will now be grouped as tabs again. On Windows, the best way to group the two document windows again is to click the maximize button in the top right corner of one of the documents.

Self study

In this lesson, you followed a predetermined workflow that was tailored toward producing two pages in the Sounds of Nature website. The key to creating a streamlined workflow is planning ahead. Imagine you were creating a website for a local bakery. Make some sketches of what the pages would look like. In Dreamweaver, spend some time setting up a workspace that would make building the bakery website easier. Think about which elements you might use the most. Then, use the guides and the grid to help create a layout that reflects the sketches you made earlier.

Review

Questions

1   Is it possible to resize the document window to preview how a web page will appear on different users' monitors?

2   How can you position guides on the page without dragging them?

3   Are tabs the only way to organize open documents?

Answers

1   Yes. The Window Size drop-down menu at the bottom of the document window contains a number of preset sizes that correspond to common monitor sizes.

2   To more exactly position guides, simply double-click any guide to open the Move Guide dialog box.

3   No. If you prefer to use tiling, you can choose Window > Tile Vertically or Tile Horizontally to place two documents side by side. (On a Mac OS, you can choose Window > Tile.)

What you'll learn in this lesson:

- Inserting HTML5 video

- Inserting Flash video

- Adding QuickTime and Windows Media content

- Inserting animations with Flash and Edge Animate

- Adding audio content to your web pages

Adding Video, Audio and Interactivity

To meet the expectations of users with increased bandwidth, designers are increasingly turning to animation, sound, and video to help make web content more compelling and visually engaging. Dreamweaver CC adds support for HTML5 audio and video and integration with Adobe Edge Animate for plug-in free multimedia.

Starting up

Before starting, make sure that your tools and panels are consistent by resetting your workspace. See "Resetting the Dreamweaver workspace" in the Starting up section of this book.

You will work with several files from the dw11lessons folder in this lesson. Make sure that you have loaded the dwlessons folder onto your hard drive from the supplied DVD. See "Loading lesson files" in the Starting up section of this book.

Before you begin, you need to create a site definition that points to the dw11lessons folder. Go to Site > New Site, or, for details on creating a site definition, refer to Lesson 2, "Setting Up a New Site."

See Lesson 11 in action!

Use the accompanying video to gain a better understanding of how to use some of the features shown in this lesson. The video tutorial for this lesson can be found on the included DVD.

Making web content interesting

Adding video, sound, and animation to a web page is one way to make your pages more interesting and engaging. Video, for example, plays a key role in supplying interesting and varied web content. The barrier to creating original video has been virtually eliminated in recent years as has the barrier to distributing these videos online. Videos allow individuals and companies to post commercials, speeches, and other content that otherwise would be difficult or cost-prohibitive to reach a large audience.

Sound allows you to enhance web pages by supplementing visual content with music or sound effects. Sound also inspires user interaction (as you'll see later in this lesson), thereby giving the user a more interesting online experience.

Animation gives web pages a whole new life by adding movement and effects to images that still pictures just can't match. Something moving on a web page automatically draws a visitor's eye. Movement is especially effective for banner ads, buttons, and whatever else you'd like your visitors to pay attention to.

Adding video

Adding video to a web page is relatively easy, assuming the video has already been optimized for the Web. A full discussion about the various file formats and how to convert digital video to a web-optimized format is beyond the scope of this book. However, the decision to include web video should be based on an evaluation of your audience. The large file sizes associated with video can affect the experience of users who don't have high-speed Internet connections. In this section, you will learn how to integrate video into your web pages using four of the most popular formats: HTML5 video, Flash Video, QuickTime and Windows Media.

If you have just finished Lesson 10, you might still have your grids and rulers turned on. They are not necessary for this lesson and you can turn them off by choosing View > Rulers and unchecking Show and choosing View > Grid > and unchecking Show Grid.

HTML5 video

Before the advent of HTML5, you needed third party plug-ins such as Flash Player, QuickTime, or Silverlight to show video. HTML5 is quickly replacing this need by specifying an HTML video element that runs natively in the browser and integrates with JavaScript. Additionally, the HTML5 video element allows you to specify alternative source files to support various browsers and supply a poster image to be displayed before the video is played.

In this section, you will learn how to add video to your web page such that the video displays natively using the installed browser player controls.

1   In the Files panel, navigate to the dw11lessons folder, and double-click **html5video.html** to open it.

2   If the page opens in Split view, click the Design view button. In the Design view, click below the heading, *A look at our vegetables.*

3   Click the Insert tab to bring up the Insert panel and choose Media from the drop-down menu, then click HTML5 Video.

Dreamweaver inserts the HTML5 video element in your page and the Property Inspector displays the available settings and attributes.

The HTML5 video element settings in the Property Inspector.

4   Locate the source field in the Property Inspector and click the Browse button on the right to bring up the Select Video dialog box. The Select Video dialog box will display HTML5 compatible video files including .OGG, .MP4 and WebM video and others. Browse to the assets folder and select the **ou_veggies.ogg** file and then click OK (Windows) or Open (Mac OS).

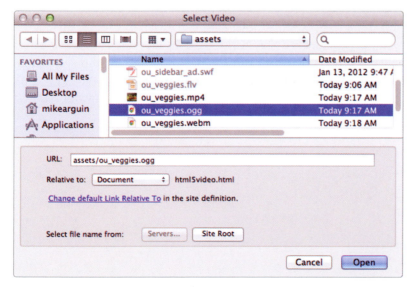

The Select Video dialog box.

You will notice that Dreamweaver added values in the Alt Source 1 and Alt Source 2 fields in the Property Inspector. Dreamweaver automatically detected these two web video files as having the same file name and alternative web video formats and associated them with the .ogg file.

Specifying alternate video formats in the Property Inspector.

5   When you insert an HTML5 video file you need to manually enter the size of the file: Dreamweaver will not automatically detect it for you. In the Property Inspector, type **400** in the W (width) field and **300** in the H (height) field. Setting the height and width of the video element will ensure other content on the page can load and flow around the video element as the page loads.

Dreamweaver enables the browser's native player controls by default, by placing a checkmark in the Controls check box in the Property Inspector. You would clear this check box if you did not want the player controls to appear.

6   Choose File > Save, then File > Preview in Browser to preview the video in a web browser. The video will display in the browser using the browser's own playback controls. Close the browser and return to Dreamweaver.

Currently the first frame of the video is being displayed before the user clicks play. You can also specify a poster image, which could include a title or other graphic identifying the topic of the clip.

7   Make sure your video element is selected and click the Browse button to the right of the Poster field in the Property Inspector to display the Select Image dialog box. Browse to the images folder and select **ou_poster400.png** and then click OK (Windows) or Open (Mac OS).

8   Press Ctrl+S (Windows) or Command+S (Mac OS) and then choose File > Preview in browser to see the poster image displayed. Close the browser window and the **html5video.html** file when you are finished previewing.

Previewing the HTML5 video element poster image.

Flash video

Flash video has been widely used for web video for a number of years and is still widely in use for a large number of sites. This is changing somewhat due to the rise of mobile devices (and specifically the lack of support for Flash video on these devices). Nevertheless, one of the primary advantages of Flash video is that playback is enabled for any browser with the Flash Player plug-in. Because more than 95% of all desktop web browsers have some version of the plug-in installed, this means your video will find the widest possible audience. Again, this is not always true on mobile. Additionally, Flash video can be compressed to a reasonable size while maintaining image quality.

Different programs create Flash video including the Adobe Media Encoder, Premiere Pro, and even Photoshop. Creating a video is a separate process, so you'll want to do your homework and learn as much as you can about how it works in order to get the best results. There are essentially two file formats that are used in Flashvideo: .flv and .f4v. The .flv format is the traditional Flash video format and .f4v is a newer format. In this exercise, you'll add a pre-existing .flv video file into your page and add simple player controls to allow users to control the playback of the movie.

1   Click the Files panel if necessary and then double-click **flashvideo.html**. In the Design view, click below the heading, *A look at our vegetables.*

2   Choose Insert > Media > Flash Video to open the Insert FLV dialog box. Make sure the video type is set to Progressive Download Video and then, to the right of the URL field, click Browse. The Insert FLV window opens. Browse to your assets folder and select **ou_veggies.flv** and then click OK (Windows) or Open (Mac OS).

The Insert FLV dialog box.

In this example, Progressive Download Video was chosen instead of Streaming Video because the former is the more common method among web developers. Progressive Download Video works by downloading the video to the user's hard-drive; however, the video will start to play as soon as it is able. In other words, the user doesn't have to wait for the entire video to download in order to see it. Streaming Video streams video content and plays it on a web page after a short buffer period. The buffer period ensures smooth playback. The catch is that to enable Streaming Video, your videos must be accessible through a web streaming service such as Adobe Flash Media Server. If you want to learn more about the process, click the Help button on the Insert FLV dialog box.

Next, you'll want to select a skin. A skin is a control panel that shows up on the bottom of the video, and allows the user to control video playback. In other words, this is where users can play, rewind, and fast-forward their videos.

3 Click the Skin drop-down menu to examine the choices. You see a preview of the skin just below the menu. In our case, we used Corona Skin 3.

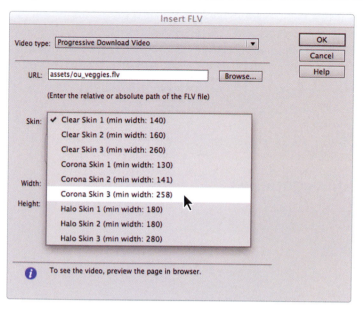

A number of skins are available in the Skin drop-down menu.

If your video is ten seconds or longer, choose a skin that includes a slider control so that users can scroll through the video at their convenience.

When you select a skin, such as Corona Skin 3, Dreamweaver will add several files to your site that are required to properly display and activate the player controls. In this case, Corona_Skin_3.swf provides the player controls and FLVPlayer_Progressive.swf provides the functionality to control video playback. These files should be uploaded to your web server along with your HTML and asset files in order for the FLV player to load properly.

4 Click the Detect Size button so that Dreamweaver can establish the physical space the video will occupy on the page. The size is based on the size of the actual video.

You can manually type in a size, too, although be sure you are aware of the dangers here. Entering a size that's bigger than the original video will either blur or pixelate your video. Additionally, the ratio of the width to height of a video is called the aspect ratio, and if you enter a width and height that do not match the original aspect ratio, then your viewers will see distorted video. In general, you should let Dreamweaver detect the video size.

5   Click OK to insert the video.

You can't see the video in Dreamweaver, so choose File > Save, then File > Preview in Browser to preview it in a web browser. This particular skin will allow you to scrub through your playback as well as mute and change the volume. Close the browser and return to Dreamweaver when you are finished previewing. At this point you can also close flashvideo.html.

The Flash video and player controls on your page.

QuickTime and Windows Media

QuickTime and Windows Media are also common video formats used on the Web. In many ways they are similar; both offer compressed video with various levels of image and sound quality. When adding either file format to a page, the key thing to keep in mind is that viewers must have the necessary plug-in to view the video. Unlike Flash video, this is not necessarily a sure thing. QuickTime is traditionally Mac OS-based and Windows Media Video is traditionally Windows-based.

You can download QuickTime from *Apple.com/quicktime/download*. To view Windows Media files, you need Windows Media Player, which you can download at *Microsoft.com/en-us/windows/download-windows-media-player/*. (At the time of this writing, there was no plug-in support from either Apple or Microsoft that allowed Windows Media Video to play on a Mac. However, there are third-party plug-ins that provide this functionality.)

The difference between the video formats is that users create QuickTime and Windows Media video using different software applications, for example Adobe Premiere Pro and Apple Final Cut Pro.

The process for inserting either QuickTime or Windows Media Video is the same. In this example, you can choose either format depending on your platform.

1   In the Files panel, open **insertvideo.html**. If necessary, click below the heading, *A look at our vegetables*.

2   Choose Window > Assets to bring up the Assets panel. Select the Movies button (▦) to show the videos available in your site.

3   Right-click (Windows) or Ctrl+click (Mac OS) on the veggies.mov file (or the veggies.wmv if in Windows) and choose Insert from the context menu to insert it into the page. You'll see a plug-in icon on the page, indicating that a plug-in is required to see the file.

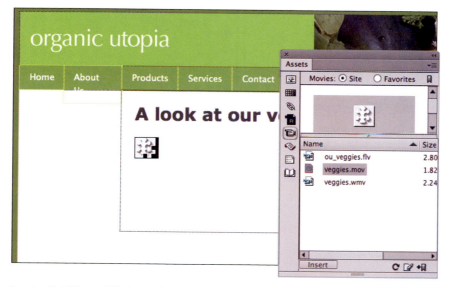

Inserting QuickTime or Windows Media video files creates a generic plug-in icon.

4   When you insert a plug-in file, you need to manually enter the size of the file; Dreamweaver will not automatically detect it for you. You will also need to add 20 pixels to the height to make room for built-in player controls. The source video here is 320 by 240 so in the Property Inspector, type **320** in the W (width) window and **260** in the H (height) window.

Again, you are using 260 for the height to allow space for the controller. QuickTime and Windows Media files already have a controller built in with the plug-in. You need to allow a little extra space for the video controls when you're entering a size manually.

5   To preview the file within Dreamweaver, click the Live button to enter Live View.

If you see a message that Dreamweaver was unable to find the plug-in that handles this media type, it does not necessarily mean your system cannot play the video (although this is still possible). It only means that Dreamweaver can't find the correct plug-in. If this should happen, try to preview the video in your browser; you might find it works there. Save your file if prompted and your video should now appear on your web page.

The problem of playing video on your system might also have to do with the lack of a codec. Web video can get a little tricky because there are file formats (such as .mov or .wmv) and there are codecs. The codec does the job of actually compressing the frames of your video and there could be any number of codecs used for a particular file format. Both QuickTime and Windows Media Player are generally good at identifying which codec you or your users might be missing and then providing links to download and install the necessary codec.

An Apple browser playing the MOV file.

6   Close the **insertvideo.html** file when you are finished previewing the video.

Other web video considerations

In addition to size, consider the following when you're preparing video for the Web:

Length: Unless you'll be offering video through a streaming video service, keep the video length down to keep the file size manageable and the progressive playback smooth.

Audio: Although stereo is nice, using stereo files on the Web is a little iffy, as many home users don't have stereo speakers hooked up to their computers. Stereo creates a larger file size and doesn't add that much to the quality of the sound unless you're doing some tricks with the balance between the speakers, which people without speakers won't hear anyway. Keep your video sound set to mono to help manage the file size a bit more effectively.

Movement, animated graphics, and effects: These things make a video look nice, but adding them can increase the file size and potentially interrupt playback.

Copywritten material: Be careful when choosing material for your video, especially when it comes to music. Pirating is a big issue today. Unless you have the rights to the music or you have permission from the music publisher and are paying royalties, you can't use music for promotional or commercial purposes when it comes to publishing material on the Web.

Inserting Flash animations

Adobe's Flash Professional CC application is used primarily to create animation and interactive projects. In terms of animation, you can use Flash to create animated web banners, buttons, splash pages, slide shows, and more. Inserting Flash animations into your web page is a great way to bring life to an otherwise static environment.

Web banners are a significant component of online advertising, and if a web banner includes moving elements, that movement automatically draws the user to the banner. In this exercise, you will add a flash banner to place on a website.

1   In the Files panel, navigate to the dw11lessons folder, and double-click the **banner.html** page to open it.

2   If the page opens in Split view, click the Design view button.

3   Click in the empty div element at the top of the sidebar on the right. A div element of 220 by 250 has been created for you.

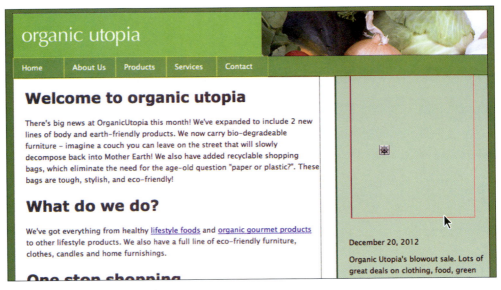

Click in the empty div element named `#sidebar _ ad`.

4   Choose Window > Assets to open the Assets panel if not already opened and locate the fourth button down, the Flash button, labeled SWF. Click this button to see the list of .swf files in this site.

Click the Flash button in the Assets panel.

Flash movies are labeled with the .swf extension. However, other programs, including After Effects and Dreamweaver, can create .swf files as well.

5 Select the **ou_sidebar_ad.swf** file and drag it to the sidebar_ad div to insert it.

6 Type **Organic Utopia sidebar ad** in the Title text field when the Object Tag Accessibility Attributes dialog box appears, then click OK.

As you can see, inserting a Flash .swf into a web page is much like inserting an image. The width and height of the .swf are automatically established based on the file's physical size, just as they are for images such as .jpeg and .gif files.

The .swf file appears with a generic Flash icon on a gray image.

You must have Flash Player, which is available free from Adobe, installed to view an .swf file. If you don't have the application installed, visit adobe.com/products/flashplayer to download and install it. Note that visitors to your website also must have Flash Player installed to view your Flash content. A good rule of thumb when including Flash content on a website is to let visitors know as soon as they get to your site that they'll need to have Flash Player. Be sure to include the link to the Flash Player web page (the URL provided at the beginning of this paragraph) so that visitors can download the Flash Player, if necessary.

7 To see the page in the browser choose File > Save, then File > Preview in Browser. If the Copy Dependent Files window appears, click OK. These are files that Dreamweaver automatically adds to the site. Included here is code to help users who might not have the Flash plug-in installed.

Your Flash web banner as seen in the browser.

8 After previewing, close the browser and the **banner.html** file. There are other options in the Properties Inspector available for Flash files. If you have the Flash authoring program installed you could click the Edit button, for example, and locate the .FLA authoring file connected with the .swf file. This would allow an easy link if you needed to update or modify your sidebar ad.

When designing web pages, be sure to include space in your design for .swf files, if you're going to incorporate them into the page. The files can vary in size, depending on what you're using them for. To learn more about Flash, visit adobe.com/products/flash.

Inserting Edge Animate animations

Dreamweaver CC adds support for inserting assets from Adobe Edge Animate, part of the Adobe Edge Suite. Like Flash, Edge Animate is used to create animation and interactive projects for the Web. However, Edge Animate creates assets that use HTML5 and JavaScript and do not require plug-ins to display. In this exercise, you will insert an Edge Animate banner similar to the Flash banner inserted in the last exercise.

1 In the Files panel, navigate to the dw11lessons folder, and double-click the **edgebanner.html** page to open it.

2 If the page opens in Split view, click the Design view button.

3 Click in the empty div element at the top of the sidebar on the right. Choose Insert > Media > Edge Animate Composition; the Select Edge Animate Package dialog box opens.

4   Browse to the assets folder and select **ou_sidebar_ad.oam**. Click OK (Windows) or
     Open (Mac OS).

Select the **ou_sidebar_ad.oam** *file from the Select Edge Animate Package dialog box.*

*Adobe Edge Animate projects can be exported as .OAM files, which include the necessary scripts
and assets required to properly display the object. For more information on Adobe Edge Animate
and the Edge Suite, visit* http://html.adobe.com/edge/.

5 Inserting an Edge Animate object into a web page is much like inserting a Flash video. The width and height of the .oam are automatically established based on the information in the package. In Design view, Edge Animate objects appear with a generic Animate icon on a gray image. Unlike Flash objects, Dreamweaver can render the Edge Animate object in Live view without the need for a plug-in.

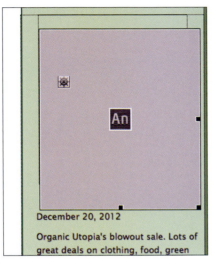

Adobe Edge Animate object inserted in Dreamweaver.

6 To see the page in the browser choose File > Save, then File > Preview in Browser. After previewing, close the browser and the **edgebanner.html** file.

Inserting sound with the HTML5 audio element

Sound is another element you can use to enhance your website. Prior to HTML5, adding sound was only accomplished through the use of a plug-in such as QuickTime or Windows Media Player. The HTML5 audio element allows you to embed audio in your web page and allow it to be played using the browser's native audio controls.

You can incorporate different types of sound files into a web page. Select a format that will run on any computer, whether the user is on the Windows or Mac OS platform. Three formats are common: .aif, .wav, and .mp3.

Files in the .aif or .wav format are similar; the main difference is where they originate. Windows is generally linked to the .wav format, and Mac OS is associated with the .aif format. The Windows and Mac OS platforms can read both formats. In addition, these files sound similar to one another: both are dynamic and depending on the settings can result in high-quality files.

You can also play .mp3 format files on both the Windows and Mac OS platforms. The big advantage to using an .mp3 file is that it's typically smaller in size than an .aif or .wav file. Depending on the compression settings, the .mp3 format might not reproduce full CD-quality sound, but it downloads faster and takes up less hard drive space. In this exercise, you'll add an mp3 file to your page.

1   In the Files panel, double-click the **sound.html** file. Click in the empty paragraph just below the *What fruit is being eaten in this clip?* paragraph.

2   Choose Insert > Media > HTML5 Audio.

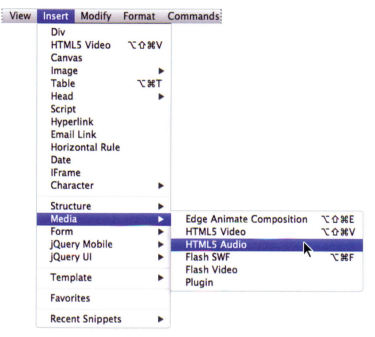

Choose the HTML5 Audio option to insert sound.

Dreamweaver will insert the HTML5 audio element using a speaker icon as a placeholder. The Property Inspector will display the various settings that can be applied to the audio element.

3 In the Property Inspector, locate the Source field and click the Browse button to bring up the Select Audio dialog box. Browse to the assets folder located in the dw11lessons root folder. Choose the **crunch.mp3** file and click OK (Windows) or Open (Mac OS).

HTML5 audio elements display in Design view as a speaker icon.

4 Choose File > Save, then preview the page in a browser by clicking the File > Preview in browser button. Visitors to the web page can control playback of the audio using their browser's built in audio playback controls.

To remove the users' ability to control the playback of the sound file, you will need to change a parameter back in Dreamweaver.

5 Close the browser. With the audio ell selected, locate the Controls check box in the Property Inspector. Clear this check box to remove the plays.

6 To make the audio play automatically, click the Autoplay check box.

The Property Inspector settings for HTML5 audio elements.

7 Choose File > Save, then preview the page in a browser again, and note that the sound will play automatically.

8   Close your browser and the **sound.html** file.

Preparing audio for the Web

Audio has the same considerations as any other digital file type. You need to pay attention to file size while trying to maintain quality.

Various programs offer audio-editing and format capabilities. This includes programs such as Adobe Audition CC, Apple Logic Pro, and Audacity (which is available as a free download on the Web).

Once you've edited a sound to your liking, you need to set up certain technical specifications for the final file. This includes the type of file you'll output (.mp3, .aif, and so on), whether the sound is in stereo or mono, and a sample rate. For the Web, a good sample rate is in the 22kHz–32kHz range; 22kHz is at the low end of acceptable quality, and anything higher than 32kHz starts to weigh down the file size.

Stereo is nice, but unnecessary, unless you're moving sound from the left speaker to the right speaker and vice versa. You can save a significant amount of file space by keeping the sound file set to mono.

There are a number of compression choices when it comes to audio. Your best bet is to experiment and see what gives you the results you want. Creating audio files is very much like creating video for the Web: there are no definite answers, and you need to experiment to find the best balance between file size and quality.

To learn more about digital audio go to http://help.adobe.com/en_US/audition/cs/using/ *and select the Digital Audio Fundamentals link.*

For a more detailed look at delivering multimedia and interactive content on the Web see the HTML5 Digital Classroom *book available in electronic and print formats.*

Self study

Try inserting and compressing videos using different codecs and file types. You'll find that the results will vary, depending on the file type and codec you choose.

Review

Questions

1   What are the benefits of using the HTML video and audio elements?

2   When inserting a Flash animation, what type of file is inserted into the web page?

3   What plug-in is needed to view an .flv file?

4   What is a *skin* when referring to a Flash Video file?

Answers

1   Both the HTML5 video and audio elements do not require plug-ins and play media through the browser's built-in playback controls.

2   When a Flash animation is inserted into a page in Dreamweaver, an .swf file is used.

3   In order to view an .flv file, a user must have the Flash Player plug-in installed on their computer.

4   A set of controls on the bottom of the video that control video playback.

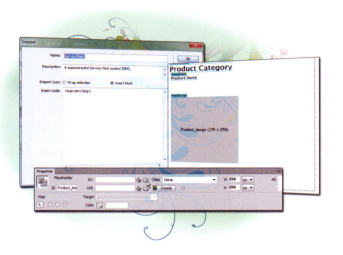

What you'll learn in this lesson:

- Using snippets

- Working with library items

- Creating and modifying templates

- Creating a repeating region in a template

Maximizing Site Design

Dreamweaver site definitions allow you to take advantage of extensive management and maintenance tools, including the ability to reuse, repeat, and maintain common items such as menus, logos, code, and even entire page layouts. Dreamweaver's unique snippets, library items, and page templates are indispensable for maintaining a consistent appearance and making sitewide updates a snap.

Starting up

Before starting, make sure that your tools and panels are consistent by resetting your workspace. See "Resetting the Dreamweaver workspace" in the Starting up section of this book.

You will work with several files from the dw12lessons folder in this lesson. Make sure that you have loaded the dwlessons folder onto your hard drive from the supplied DVD. See "Loading lesson files" in the Starting up section of this book.

Before you begin, you need to create a site definition that points to the dw12lessons folder from the included DVD that contains resources you need for these lessons. Go to Site > New Site, or, for details on creating a site definition, refer to Lesson 2, "Setting Up a New Site."

See Lesson 12 in action!

Use the accompanying video to gain a better understanding of how to use some of the features shown in this lesson. The video tutorial for this lesson can be found on the included DVD.

Creating modular page elements

You might have heard the term *modular* before; whether referring to a prebuilt house that you can cart away and place on your property, or a well–built, scalable website. Modular refers to anything you can break down into standardized, reusable components.

Most websites contain common elements such as headers, footers, and menus that appear consistently across each page. The ability to convert these elements into reusable items is essential for maintaining a consistent look and feel across your pages. Add the ability to make components manageable from a single place and to make sitewide updates, and editing becomes a breeze.

Dreamweaver provides three modular features: snippets, library items, and templates. Each feature offers a different level of reusability, from simple code tidbits to entire pages, complete with navigation, content, and styling.

Introducing snippets

As you build pages and websites, you'll find yourself creating many similar items several times over. Whether you're creating a two-column layout table or a contact form, snippets make it possible to add any piece of code to a common library, where you can reuse it by simply dragging and dropping it into the page. You can store virtually any item on a page as a snippet.

The Snippets panel is like a super clipboard, and using a snippet is similar to copying and pasting an element onto your page. Changes to a snippet in the Snippets panel do not update snippets you've already used in your pages. For this reason, snippets are a great way to store and place any common page elements that you don't need to manage globally.

Examples of snippets might include common navigation bars, form elements, and even JavaScripts. Snippets are stored as part of the Dreamweaver application, and they are not specific to any Dreamweaver site. You can add your own snippets directly within Dreamweaver, and they will be available for you to use at any time on any site.

The Snippets panel

The Snippets panel displays all available Dreamweaver snippets, broken down by category. You can add and edit snippets and categories directly from the Snippets panel. Using a snippet from the Snippets panel is as simple as locating it and dragging it from the panel to the page.

Dreamweaver provides many ready-to-use snippets that serve as great starting points for forms, lists, and navigation bars (to name a few); many of these require little more than text changes and some basic styling. In the following lesson, you will use some of these snippets to quickly build existing pages for the product display component of the Organic Utopia site.

1 Double-click the **home.html** file in the Files panel to open it. Choose Window > Snippets to launch the Snippets panel. In the category list, locate the Text folder and click the plus sign (+) (Windows) or arrow (Mac OS) to the left to expand it. You'll use the Service Mark snippet to add a service mark to this page.

The Snippets panel contains many categories
of pre-built snippets for your use.

2 Click to the right of the heading, *Welcome to organic utopia*. Inside the Text folder, double-click the service mark snippet, and a superscripted *sm* appears in the heading.

3   At the top of the Snippets panel is a preview of the code that was inserted. In the Snippets panel, click the panel menu (•≡) in the upper-right corner and choose Edit. The Snippets dialog box appears with a name, a description, the snippet type, and then the actual code. This snippet is using the `<sup>`, or superscript, HTML element.

Snippet		✕
Name: Service Mark		OK
Description: A superscripted Service Mark symbol ('SM').		Cancel
		Help
Snippet type: ◯ Wrap selection ⦿ Insert block		
Insert code: `<sup>sm</sup>`		
Preview type: ◯ Design ⦿ Code		

The Snippet dialog box.

4   Click Cancel, as you won't be making any changes at this time.

5   Choose File > Save.

Creating new snippets

Whenever you have something on a page that you'd like to reuse, creating a new snippet is a good option. You can create new snippets directly from the Snippets panel, and from any selected element(s) on a page.

In this section, you'll convert a pre-existing table to a snippet.

1   Choose File > Open, and open the **gardentips.html** page. This page has a pre-styled table. Converting this table to a snippet will allow you to place it anywhere you like.

2   Click anywhere inside the table, and then choose Modify > Table > Select Table. You could also click the edge of the table to select it.

3   At the bottom of the Snippets panel, click on the New Snippet icon (⬦). The Snippet dialog box opens, and all the code within the table is automatically copied into the *Insert before* window.

4   In the Name field, type **Vege_table**. In the Description field, type **A three column styled table listing the Latin and family names of common vegetables**. For the Snippet type, select the *Insert block* option. For Preview type, select the *Design* option and click OK.

Choosing the *Insert Block* option ensures that the table is inserted as a stand–alone element. Setting the Preview type to *Design* allows you to see a preview of the table in the Snippets panel, rather than the code.

Setting options in the Snippet dialog box.

In the Snippets panel, you see the new snippet listed. However, it may not have been placed in an ideal location. If the Service Mark snippet in the Text snippet folder was still selected, the new snippet may appear in the Text folder. Before you do anything else, you'll organize your Snippets panel.

5   In the bottom of the Snippets panel, click the New Snippet Folder icon (▣). A new folder appears; rename this folder **ou snippets**, then press Enter (Windows) or Return (Mac OS). Click the Vege_table snippet and drag it on top of this new folder. Additionally, you can drag and drop the ou_snippets folder below the ~Legacy folder to move it to the top level of folders.

Snippets are actually external files with the extension .csn and are stored deep within your operating system. If someone else has used your current computer to do this lesson, you might see this snippet already present. You can remove it by clicking the snippet and then clicking the Remove icon (🗑) at the bottom of the Snippets panel.

6 Click once on the *Vege_table* snippet, if necessary. In the top half of the panel, there is a design preview of the table. It is most likely cropped. Depending on how much space you have, it might not be possible to view the entire table; however, you can expand this window by clicking the dividing line of the panel, and dragging up or down.

Click and drag the dividing line in the Snippets panel to expand or contract the view.

7 Choose File > Open, and open the **latin_names.html** file. Click once below the heading, Latin and Family names for common vegetables. In the Snippets panel, double-click the *Vege_table* snippet, and it is inserted into the new page.

In many ways, a snippet is just a faster way to copy and paste. However, there are a few things to be aware of. Snippets only copy the HTML code and none of the associated CSS. If you look at the preview of the table snippet in the Snippets panel, you will see that it is unstyled. However, when you inserted it into the latin_names page, it appeared styled. This is because the Snippets panel only previews the raw HTML in the design view. The CSS rules for the table are being saved in an external stylesheet and all the pages in this site are already linked to this stylesheet. If you inserted this table into a blank page, it would appear unstyled until you attached the style sheet to the page.

8   In the Snippets panel, click the panel menu in the upper-right corner and choose Edit. The Snippet dialog box appears. In the first line of code, change the table width value to **350** and click OK. This has no effect on the current table because there is no link between the code in the Snippets panel and the code on your page. However, all future tables will use the new value.

Changing the table width when editing a snippet.

9   Choose File > Save All. Keep this document open for the next exercise.

The Snippets panel lets you modify a snippet only through its HTML code. Here's a shortcut: if you make a change in the Design view, you can recreate the snippet by selecting it and then choosing New Snippet from the Snippets panel. If you select the folder containing the original snippet and save it under the same name, you will be prompted to replace it.

Introducing library items

While snippets are useful, they are perhaps most useful for items that will never change, like a person's name or a logo. However, a more powerful concept is an item that you can add to multiple pages and have linked to an original master item. This is where Dreamweaver library items come in.

With Dreamweaver library items, you can save any common element and manage it from a master copy in your site folder. When you place a library item on a page, the item remains attached to its master; any changes you make to the master automatically update any instances of the item placed throughout your site. Dreamweaver makes sure that any instances of a library item are synchronized.

Library items (unlike snippets) are specific to each Dreamweaver site, and they are stored as separate .lbi files in your site's Library folder.

1   Library items are located in the Assets panel. Choose Window > Assets and then click the Library icon (📖) at the very bottom. The panel is empty because there are no library items in your site yet.

The Library Items category of the Assets panel.

You can add, edit, and manage all library items in your site directly from this panel. You will now convert the Global Navigation menu in your header to a library item.

2   Click the **home.html** tab in the top of your document window to open this page. Scrolling as needed, click the border of the GlobalNav <div> element in the upper-right corner to select it. (This is the small box that contains the Site Map | Login text.)

3 In the Assets panel, click the New Library Item button (⊕). You will see a dialog box appear, warning you that this style sheet information will not be copied with this item. Click OK. The selected menu is added as a new library item; name it **GlobalNav** and press Enter (Windows) or Return (Mac OS). If you're prompted to update links, choose Update. This ensures that any hyperlinks or references to image files are preserved. The GlobalNav div is now linked to the new library item you created. Note that your GlobaNav div is now highlighted in yellow; this is the visual indicator Dreamweaver uses for library items. Now you're ready to add this library item to other pages.

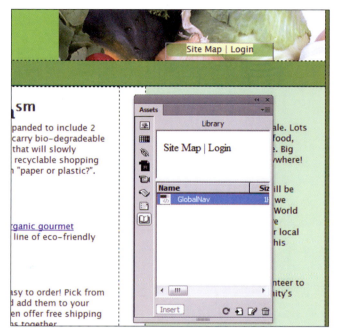

The GlobalNav <div> element is highlighted yellow because it is now a library item.

4 Click the **gardentips.html** tab at the top of your document window to view this page (or open the file it if it is closed). Locate the GlobalNav library item in the Assets panel, and drag it onto the header of the page. An instance of the GlobalNav <div> elemement is placed.

5 Click the **latin_names.html** tab at the top of your document window to view this page. If the file is closed, open it now. As you did in step 4, drag a copy of the GlobalNav library item from the Assets panel to the header section. Just as before, an instance of the GlobalNav <div> element is placed.

The GlobalNav is now set in the exact location across three pages of your site. You will now modify your library item and all three pages will change.

Modifying and updating library items

The convenience and power of library items are apparent when you need to update a common item across several pages. Because all instances of a library item remain attached to a master copy, when the master item is edited from the library item list, every instance mirrors these changes.

You can edit library items from the Assets panel or by choosing the Open button from the Property Inspector when a library item instance is selected on the page.

1   From the Library Items list in the Assets panel, double-click the GlobalNav library item to open it for editing. A new tab opens because the library item is actually a new file: GlobalNav.lbi.

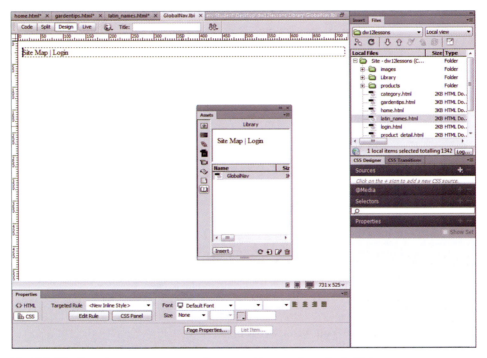

The GlobalNav library item opens as a separate document and has no style associated with it.

It's important to realize that there is no style information associated with this file, as Dreamweaver warned you when you created the item. However, this is actually a good thing; it simply takes getting used to the idea that you are modifying the HTML content—all the style information resides in the style sheet.

2   Where it currently reads *Login*, select the text, then type **Your Account**. You will now link the text within the GlobalNav menu to the appropriate HTML pages. Select the text *Your Account*, then in the Property Inspector, click the HTML button, if necessary. Next, click the Browse for File folder icon (📁) to the right of the Link box. In the Select File window, choose **login.html**. Click OK (Windows) or Open (Mac OS).

3 Select the Site Map text. In the Property Inspector, click the HTML tab if necessary, and click the Browse for File icon (📁) to the right of the Link field. In the Select File dialog box, choose **sitemap.html**, then click OK (Windows) or Open (Mac OS).

4 Choose File > Save. The Update Library Items dialog box appears with a list of the three files. Whenever you modify a library item and save it, a list of all files using the item appears, and you are given the choice to update or not.

When saving library items, any pages affected will appear in the Update Library Items dialog box.

5 Click Update. The files update and the Update Pages dialog box appears.

6 Click the *Show Log* option in the Update Pages dialog box. A list of the files that were updated appears; this is where you can check to see if there were any problems and how many files were updated. Click Close.

7 Open **home.html**, **gardentips.html**, and **latin_names.html** if they were not already open, and you see that all instances of the menu have been updated in all three pages. Library items are tremendously powerful; the larger the site, the more useful they become. They are tremendously useful with hyperlinked navigation, where they can help prevent broken hyperlinks.

For example, currently you have three documents all using a library item that is linked to the login.html and sitemap.html pages. But what happens if you move those two pages into a new folder? You will do this now so you can see how Dreamweaver keeps track of the move and prompts you to update the links.

8   Click the Files tab, if necessary, to view the list of files in your site. Click the root folder at the top of the panel (Site – dw12lessons), and then right-click (Windows) or Ctrl+click (Mac OS) to open a context menu. Choose New Folder. Rename the new folder **GlobalNav** and press Enter (Windows) or Return (Mac OS).

Right-clicking the root folder allows you to create a new folder.

9   In the Files panel, click and drag the **login.html** file into this new GlobalNav folder. As soon as you do, the Update Files dialog box appears with the list of all the files that need to be updated. This is a huge time-saver if you need to restructure your site. Traditionally, you would have to go to each page and relink everything that pointed to this page. Now click Update, and the links on each page are all updated behind the scenes.

10   Click and drag the **sitemap.html** file to the GlobalNav folder; click Update, and all the files are updated.

11   Choose File > Save All, update your pages if prompted, and then close all your open files.

Introducing templates

If you are creating several pages that need to share the same look and layout, Dreamweaver templates are for you. A Dreamweaver template is a master document from which other pages can be created; these pages inherit all the elements from the original template, but you can modify each page to include unique content and elements. As with library items, when you edit a template all pages based on that template update to reflect your changes.

When you create a template, you specify editable regions, or areas of the page that you can modify. By default, all elements of a page created from a template are locked to prevent editing. You can make changes only from the original master template. You can set sections of a page as editable so that you can add or modify content without accidentally (or intentionally) disturbing the original layout.

Templates are also a great mechanism for controlling access to pages on a site. If you need to provide editing ability to others, you can lock out important page elements and give users access to only certain sections of the page.

Templates are site-specific and are stored in a Templates folder under your site's root folder. You open, edit, or create templates from the Templates list in the Assets panel.

Dreamweaver templates work with Contribute, a basic but powerful web content management tool. You can design and manage templates that can be modified and published by Contribute users.

Creating a new template

For the Organic Utopia site, imagine that you need to create many different category and product detail pages for the products in the store. To do this, you'll set up templates for each page so that new pages can be easily created but will remain visually consistent with the master layout.

1   In the Files panel (Window > Files), locate and double-click the **product_detail.html** page to open it for editing. This page has generic text and a placeholder image that will serve as your template.

2   Click your Assets panel, and then click the library category. As you did with the other pages, click and drag the GlobalNav item onto the header. This page will shortly serve as a template, and by including a library item, you are maximizing automation.

3   Save the **product_detail.html** page as a template by choosing File > Save as Template. The Save As Template dialog box appears.

Naming a new template.

4   Choose Save to save the template. If prompted, allow Dreamweaver to update any links by choosing Yes from the dialog box.

Working with editable regions

Next, you will need to define editable regions that you can modify on any pages created from this template. When new HTML pages are generated from templates, there might be certain sections you would like to be editable and other areas that should remain uneditable.

1   Select the placeholder text in the product_detail template that reads *Product Category*. Choose Insert > Template > Editable Region. The New Editable Region dialog box appears.

2   Name the new editable region **ProductCategory** and click OK. The placeholder text now appears inside a black box with a blue tab at the top. This portion of the page and the content within it will now be editable in any pages created from this template.

Each editable region should have a unique name on your template files. Also, avoid using spaces or special characters when naming your editable regions.

3   Select the placeholder text in the product_detail template that reads *Product Name*. Choose Insert > Template > Editable Region. The New Editable Region dialog box appears. Name this **ProductName** and click OK.

4   Select the image placeholder, then choose Insert > Template > Editable Region. The New Editable Region window appears. Name this **ProductImage** and click OK.

Naming the Editable Region of the image placeholder.

5   Finally, select all the text in the sidebar. Choose Insert > Template > Editable Region. The New Editable Region dialog box appears. Name this **ProductDescription** and click OK.

6   Choose File > Save to save the template. You might see a warning about putting the editable region within a block tag; click OK.

At this point, you can create any number of pages and manage them from this template. The editable regions you created will allow you to add content to any new pages based on this template, but will protect the main layout and page elements from unintended changes.

Creating new pages from templates

Now you're ready to create multiple product pages that will be based on the new template you have built. You'll create two pages, enough to give you a sense of how templates work.

1   Choose File > New. In the New Document dialog box, click the Site Templates option. The Site column lists all the sites you have defined; click the dw12lessons site. In the second column, the product_detail template should be selected. Click Create. This opens a new, untitled document based on the template. Choose File > Save. When prompted, navigate to the products folder in the dw12lessons folder. Name this file **eggplants.html** and click Save.

2   Click inside the header of your page and notice that you are unable to select or move anything. This section is uneditable. Notice, in the upper-right corner, the yellow highlighted box that reads Template:product_detail. In a similar fashion to library items, this yellow highlight indicates that the page is based on a template.

Dividing a page into editable and non-editable regions can be useful for any situation where the designer of the site would like some control over how the site is modified. Someone not familiar with Dreamweaver could easily learn to update the editable regions, and at the same time, there would be little risk that they click something by accident and modify it.

3   Select the text inside the ProductCategory editable area and type **Vegetables**. Select the text in the ProductName area and type **Eggplants**. Select the Product_image placeholder, and in the Property Inspector, click the Browse for File button (📁) to the right of the Src text field.

Click the Folder icon to locate the eggplant image.

Navigate through your dw12lessons folder and locate the images folder. Select the **eggplant.jpg** image and click OK (Windows) or Open (Mac OS).

4   Double-click the products folder in the Files panel to open it, and then double-click the **eggplants.txt** file to open it in Dreamweaver. Select all the text, choose Edit > Copy, and then close the text file.

5   Select the text in the Product Description area of the sidebar, then choose Edit > Paste. Place your cursor after the word *Eggplant* in the first line, and then press Enter/Return to add a new line and separate the heading from the paragraph. Choose File > Save.

Now you'll base another new page on your template using the File > New command.

6 Choose File > New. In the New Document dialog box, click the *Site Templates* option. The Site column lists all the sites you have defined; click the Lesson 12 site. In the second column, the product_detail template should be selected. Click Create; the new page is created.

Choose File > New, and then click the Page from Template option.

7 Choose File > Save, and save this file as **beets.html** in your Products folder. Select the text inside the ProductCategory editable area and type **Vegetables**. Select the text in the ProductName area and type **Beets**. Select the Product_image placeholder, and in the Property Inspector, click the Browse for File button (📁) to the right of the Src text field.

Navigate through your dw12lessons folder and locate the images folder. Select the **beets.jpg** image and click OK (Windows) or Choose (Mac OS).

8 In the Files panel, double-click the Products folder to open it, if it is not already open, and double-click the **beets.txt** file to open it in Dreamweaver. Select all the text, choose Edit > Copy, and then close the text file.

9 Select the text in the Product Description area of the sidebar, and choose Edit > Paste. Place your cursor after the word *Beets* in the first line, and then press Enter/Return to add a new line and separate the description from the heading. Choose File > Save.

Modifying templates

In a similar fashion to library items, when you make changes to the original template, all linked pages are updated.

1   In the Assets panel, click the Templates button (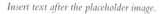) and then double-click the product_detail template to open it for editing. If you do not see your template in the Templates section of the Assets panel, click on the Refresh Site List button at the bottom of the panel.

2   Place your cursor after the image placeholder, and press Enter (Windows) or Return (Mac OS) twice; then type **This vegetable is in season** and press Enter or Return again.

Product Category
Product Name

Product_image (250 x 250)

This vegetable is in season.

Insert text after the placeholder image.

3   If you were to save right now, your text would be updated on your two linked pages; however, you need to convert it to an editable item unless you want the text to be locked on those pages.

4   Select the text and choose Insert > Template > Editable Region. Name this region **inseason** and click OK. Choose File > Save. (If you see the block tag warning, click OK.) The Update Files dialog box appears; any files linked to this template will now be changed. Click Update, then close the Update Pages dialog box.

5   Click the **beets.html** file; notice that it has automatically been updated. In the inseason editable region, update the text to read **This vegetable is not in season**.

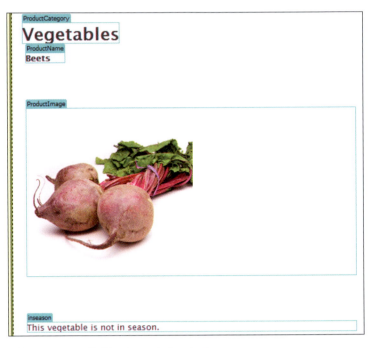

Updating your new editable region on the beets.html page.

6   Choose File > Save All, and then choose File > Close All to close all your open documents.

Repeating regions

A single region might not be the best way to display the content you add to a template-based page. You might require a template that can handle a number of items, such as a table that displays products in a category. If you need to build a flexible template that can hold any number of uniform items, you can add a repeating region to it.

Repeating regions allow you to define an element on a template as repeatable. When you create a page based on that template, you can increase, or repeat, the number of regions to accommodate the information. You'll also be able to reorder these repeated regions at any time without having to move the content. For example, you could set elements such as a table row, paragraph, or small display table as a repeating region, and then duplicate as many as you need to fit the content at hand.

A repeating region is not automatically editable. You need to set editable regions inside any repeating element in order to add to or edit its content.

In the following steps, you'll add a repeating region to your category.html page and convert it to a template so that you can use it to display any number of products in a specific category.

1 Open the **category.html** page from the Files panel.

2 The table in the center contains one row with two columns, each containing a placeholder image and product title placeholder. Click anywhere in the table and then click the `<table.styledtable>` tag in the tag selector at the bottom of the document window to select it.

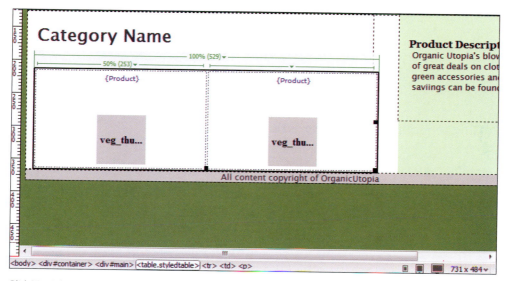

Click Tag Selector to choose `<table.styledtable>`.

3 Choose Insert > Template > Repeating Region. Because you haven't saved this page as a template yet, a dialog box appears, letting you know that you need to convert the page to a template before you add regions. Click OK.

4 When the Repeating Region dialog box appears, assign the new region the name **Products**, and click OK.

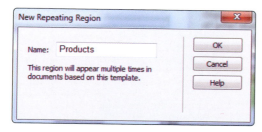

The row is now a repeating region, which you can duplicate in any page created from this template.

5 Choose File > Save As Template, and save the new template as **category_display**. Click Save and Update Links if asked.

6   In the left cell, highlight the Product text. Choose Insert > Template > Editable Region. Name the new region **ProductName**, and click OK.

7   Select the placeholder image below the new editable region, and choose Insert > Template > Editable Region. Name the new region **ProductImage**, and click OK.

8   In the right cell, highlight the Product text. Choose Insert >Template > Editable Region. Name the new region **ProductName2**, and click OK.

9   Select the placeholder image below the new editable region, and choose Insert > Template > Editable Region. Name the new region **ProductImage2**, and click OK.

10   Choose File > Save to save this template. If you see the block tag warning, click OK.

Templates can't contain duplicate region names. If you try to set two editable regions with the same name, Dreamweaver gives you an error message.

Putting repeating regions into action

You're now ready to create a page from the new category_display template and see how repeating regions work.

1   Open the Assets panel if necessary, then select the category_display template, and choose New from Template from the Assets panel menu. You might need to click the Refresh Site List button in the Assets panel to see your templates.

2   Save the new document as **chocolate.html** in your site's root folder. Notice the new repeating region in the middle of the page—its tab features four buttons that allow you to add, remove, and shift repeating regions up or down in the stacking order.

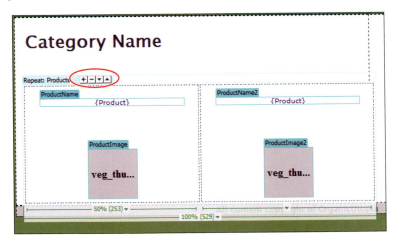

A repeating region has four buttons you can use.

3   Click the plus sign button (**+**) on the top of the repeating region; a new table row with two more product display tables appears. Click the plus sign button two more times to see how it will automatically add new rows. Click the minus sign button to see how to remove a row. In the next step, you'll fill in the first four products with information to complete your page.

4   In the first row, type **Belgian Chocolate** in the ProductName text field and **French Chocolate** in the ProductName2 text field. In the second row, type **German Chocolate** in the ProductName text field and **Swiss Chocolate** in the ProductName2 text field.

The four products now appear in the category page, and as an added benefit, if you wanted to reorder the rows you could do so using the repeating region toolbar.

5   Click the up arrow in the repeating region toolbar to push the second row to the top. This feature is especially useful for repeating regions with many rows.

A repeating region has four buttons you can use.

6   Choose File > Save All.

Detach from Template command

If you want to modify a template-based page beyond what the editable regions allow, you can use the Modify > Templates > Detach from Template command, which breaks the current page away from the master template, allowing you to edit it freely. Keep in mind that a page detached from a template will no longer be updated if you make any changes to the original template.

Self study

Create a new template based on **home.html** and then create new pages based on the the template for the following pages: **about_us.html**, **products.html**, **services.html**, and **contact.html**. Then return to the template and create links to these pages from the navigation bar. Which sections need to be editable and which do not?

Open the **eggplants.html** page you created, and use Detach from Template to break it away from the template. You'll then be able to freely edit other elements on the page that you did not include in the original editable regions. Create some variations on the newly detached page by trying a new layout, modifying product and picture positioning, or applying a new style to the product title, price, or description. Use the Templates section of the Assets panel to create a new template from the page.

Review

Questions

1 What are two key differences between snippets and library items?

2 How do you add a new snippet to a page in Dreamweaver?

3 Where are library items and page templates stored? Which panel do you use to manage them?

4 What happens to pages based on a template when you modify the original template?

5 True or False: Repeating regions are automatically editable in pages that use them.

Answers

1 Snippets are stored as part of the Dreamweaver application, and are available, regardless of which site or document you're working on; library items are specific to a site definition. Copies of a snippet never update when the original snippet is edited; a library item updates all instances of itself throughout a local site when a change is applied to it.

2 You can drag a snippet from the Snippets panel onto the page, or position your cursor in the page and double-click the snippet in the Snippets panel.

3 Library items and page templates are stored in the Library and Templates folders (respectively) under your local site. You can manage both, using their specific categories on the Assets panel.

4 Dreamweaver updates all pages based on that template to reflect any changes made to the original template.

5 False. You must first set editable regions within a repeating region to add content.

Lesson 13

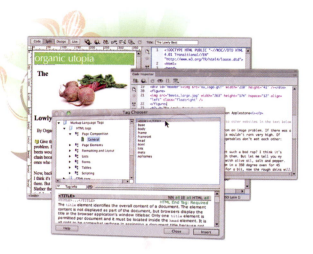

What you'll learn in this lesson:

- Using the Code and Design views
- Working with the Coding toolbar
- Validating your code
- Formatting and reformatting your code

Working with Code-editing Features

Dreamweaver provides exceptional code-editing support to complement its powerful visual layout tools and application development features. You can adapt the coding environment so that it fits the way you work. Learn how to change the way you view code, reformat your markup, or use your favorite tag library.

Starting up

Before starting, make sure that your tools and panels are consistent by resetting your workspace. See "Resetting the Dreamweaver workspace" in the Starting up section of this book.

You will work with several files from the dw13lessons folder in this lesson. Make sure that you have loaded the dwlessons folder onto your hard drive from the supplied DVD. See "Loading lesson files" in the Starting up section of this book.

Before you begin, you need to create site settings that point to the dw13lessons folder. Go to Site > New Site, or, for details on creating a site, refer to Lesson 2, "Setting Up a New Site."

See Lesson 13 in action!

Use the accompanying video to gain a better understanding of how to use some of the features shown in this lesson. The video tutorial for this lesson can be found on the included DVD.

Working with code

Although Dreamweaver's traditional audience has been for those who prefer to work in the Design view and not with code, there are many good reasons to dive into the code editing view. In this lesson, you will look at some of the unique functions available in the Code view by taking a look at an older web page.

Accessing code with the Quick Tag editor

In this exercise, you will use a feature called the Quick Tag editor. This feature is generally for users who are more familiar with their code. The Quick Tag editor offers an easy way to add CSS class or ID names as well as attributes to your code without having to leave the Design view. The Quick Tag editor works in conjunction with the tag selector. In this exercise, you'll apply a CSS class to an image to float it to the right.

1   In the Files panel, navigate to the dw13lessons folder and double-click the **oldcode.html** file to open it. Click the image of the beets. In the bottom-left of the document window is the tag selector which now has the `<img>` tag selected.

2   Right-click (Windows) or Ctrl+click (Mac OS) the `<img>` tag in the tag selector. A context menu appears with all the code for the selected image. Choose Quick Tag Editor from the menu. The Quick Tag Editor appears, displaying the code for this tag.

Viewing the attributes and properties of a tag in the Quick Tag Editor.

Instead of switching to the Code view to make changes to this code, you can make changes within the editor.

3   Click once after the `align="left"` code and press the spacebar. A code-hinting menu is triggered, allowing you to choose from a list of possible choices. Double-click the class option; the code will be written for you. Notice that the only option, `floatright`, is listed; press the Return (or Enter) key to apply this class. Your image now has the class applied and is floating to the right.

You can also use the Quick Tag Editor to remove unnecessary code. For example, this page uses the older `<font>` tag to style text.

4   Click anywhere inside the main paragraph of your document. In the tag selector, click the `<font>` tag and then right+click (Windows) or Ctrl-click (Mac OS) and from the context menu choose the Remove Tag option.

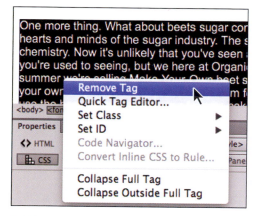

Quickly remove a tag by choosing Remove Tag.

This removes both the opening and closing font tags and the text now reverts to its default unstyled appearance.

Using HTML5 code-hinting

The internal library of code that is available to Dreamweaver CC evolves as the language of the Web evolves. If you are working with the next generation of web pages, Dreamweaver has access to the latest HTML5 elements.

1   In the Code view, locate the `<img>` element on or around line 19. Place your cursor immediately before the opening `<img>` tag and press Return (Mac OS) or Enter (PC) to move this code to the next line.

Click once in the empty line you just created above the `<img>` element. You will now be adding a new HTML5 element.

2   Type a left bracket (<); Dreamweaver's code-hinting panel appears. This is a complete list of every element that is a part of Dreamweaver's library of HTML tags.

Type the letters **fi**; notice that as you type, the list automatically narrows down to the available choices. Using the arrow keys on your keyboard, select the `<figure>` tag and press Return (Mac OS) or Enter (PC).

```
18   <body>
19   <div id="header"><img src="ou_logo.gif" width="210"
20   <fi
21   <im <> fieldset              h="263" height="174"
22   <h2 <> figcaption
23   <p> <> figure                r Jonathon Appleston
24   <p>
25     <!--We need to add two or three links to other web
26     Give the beet a break. Beets suffer from an image
       very high. Of course there is no food chain because
27   </p>
```

Use code-hinting to select the HTML5 figure tag.

3   Type the closing bracket. Dreamweaver will not automatically do it for you.

The HTML5 `<figure>` element is designed to help structure your web pages by giving you a more specific way to define images on your pages. For example, you could add a common style for all figures on your page.

4   You need to add the closing tag for the figure element, so click once at the end of the line of the `<img>` code and press Enter (Windows) or Return (Mac OS).

5   On this new line, type a left bracket and a forward slash: **</**. Dreamweaver will automatically complete (auto-complete) the rest of the tag.

```
18   <body>
19   <div id="header"><img src="ou_logo.gif" width="210" height="41" /></div>
20   <figure>
21   <img src="beets_large.jpg" width="263" height="174" hspace="12" align="left" class="floatright" />
22   </figure>
23   <h2> b The Lowly Beet<b></h2>
24   <p><i>By Organic Utopia's founder Jonathon Applestone<i></p>
```

Dreamweaver will auto-complete your closing tags.

You can choose to turn off the code-hinting and auto-complete options within your preferences. Choose Edit > Preferences (Windows) or Dreamweaver > Preferences (Mac OS). Select the Code Hints category. To turn off code-hinting, click to clear the Enable Code Hints check box. To prevent Dreamweaver from auto-completing your tags, select Never from the Close tags section.

Working in the Code view

As you've seen, the Code view is a hand-coding environment for writing and editing HTML and CSS. More experienced users who work in scripting languages such as JavaScript and PHP can modify their workspace to suit the way they prefer to work with code.

View options

You can set word wrapping, display line numbers for the code, highlight invalid code, set syntax coloring for code elements, set indenting, and show hidden characters from the View > Code View Options menu. The Code view options are not available when you are in the Design view, only when in Code or Split view.

Word Wrap: wraps the code so that you can view it without scrolling horizontally. This option doesn't insert line breaks; it just makes the code easier to view.

Line Numbers: displays line numbers along the side of the code.

Hidden Characters: displays special characters in place of white space. For example, a dot replaces each space, a double chevron replaces each tab, and a paragraph marker replaces each line break.

Highlight Invalid Code: causes Dreamweaver to highlight all HTML code that isn't valid in yellow. When you select an invalid tag, the Property Inspector displays information on how to correct the error.

Syntax Coloring: enables or disables code coloring.

Auto Indent: makes your code indent automatically when you press Enter or Return while writing code. The new line of code indents to the same level as the previous line.

Syntax Error Alerts: in Info Bar conveniently displays mistakes in your code.

Modifying the Code view workspace

You can view the source code for Dreamweaver documents in several ways. You can display it in the document window by switching to the Code view, you can split the document window to display both the visual page and its related code in Split view, or you can work in the Code Inspector, a separate coding window. The Code Inspector works like a detachable version of the Code view for the current page.

1   Choose View > Code and Design, to view the code and visually edit the page in the document window at the same time. By default the Code view is split with the Code on the left and Design view on the right.

2 From the View menu choose Design View on Left to swap the views.

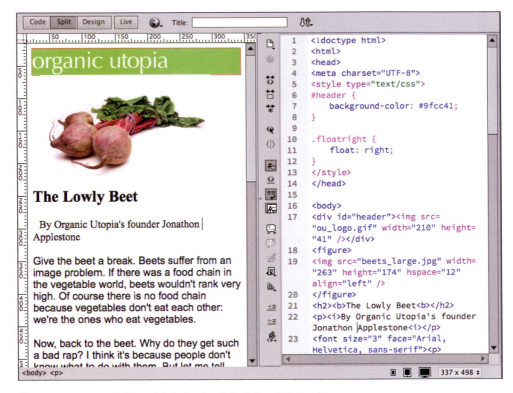

Choose Design View on Left to switch the location of the Code and Design views.

3 Place your cursor over the splitter bar between the Design view and the Code view. Click and drag the bar to the right and the Design view will expand as the Code view contracts.

4 Choose Window > Code Inspector. Working in the Code Inspector is just like working in the Code view, except that it is in a separate window. This might be useful, depending on how you choose to manage your workspace (for example, users who have two monitors could put this window in a separate window).

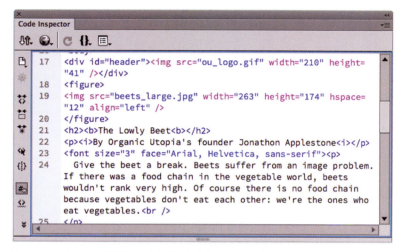

You can also view your HTML code in the Code Inspector window.

Click the Close button to close the Code Inspector for now. From the View menu, choose Design View on Left to return the split screen to its original orientation.

5 Choose View > Code. You will now look at some of the coding features available in the coding toolbar in Dreamweaver.

The Coding toolbar

The Coding toolbar contains buttons that let you perform many standard coding operations, such as collapsing and expanding code selections, highlighting invalid code, applying and removing comments, indenting code, and inserting recently used code snippets. The Coding toolbar is visible only in the Code view and appears vertically on the left side of the document window. To see what each button does, position the cursor over it until a tooltip appears.

ICON	TOOL NAME	USE
	Open Documents	Lists the documents that are open. When you select a document, it is displayed in the document window.
	Show Code Navigator	Displays a list of code sources related to a particular selection on your page. Use it to navigate to related code sources, such as internal and external CSS rules, server-side includes, external JavaScript files, parent template files, library files, and iframe source files. You can access the Code Navigator from Design, Code, and Split views, as well as from the Code Inspector.
	Collapse Full Tag	Collapses the content between a set of opening and closing tags (for example, the content between `<body>` and `</body>`). You must place the insertion point in the opening or closing tag and then click to collapse it.
	Collapse Selection	Collapses the selected code.
	Expand All	Restores all collapsed code.
	Select Parent Tag	Selects the content and surrounding opening and closing tags of the line in which you've placed the insertion point. If you repeatedly click this button, and your tags are balanced, Dreamweaver will eventually select the outermost `<html>` and `</html>` tags.
	Balance Braces	Selects the content and surrounding parentheses, braces, or square brackets of the line in which you've placed the insertion point. If you repeatedly click this button, and your surrounding symbols are balanced, Dreamweaver will eventually select the outermost braces, parentheses, or brackets in the document.
	Line Numbers	Hides or shows numbers at the beginning of each line of code.
	Highlight Invalid Code	Highlights invalid code in yellow.

ICON	TOOL NAME	USE
	Word Wrap	Changes the Word Wrap from Soft Wrap to Hard Wrap (or vice-versa)
	Syntax Error Alerts in Info Bar	Enables or disables an information bar at the top of the page that alerts you to syntax errors. When Dreamweaver detects a syntax error, the Syntax Error Information bar specifies the line in the code where the error occurs. Additionally, Dreamweaver highlights the error's line number on the left side of the document in Code view. The info bar is enabled by default, but only appears when Dreamweaver detects syntax errors in the page.
	Apply Comment	Wraps comment tags around selected code, or opens new comment tags.
	Remove Comment	Removes comment tags from the selected code. If a selection includes nested comments, only the outer comment tags are removed.
	Wrap Tag	Wraps selected code with the selected tag from the Quick Tag Editor.
	Recent Snippets	Inserts a recently used code snippet from the Snippets panel.
	Move or Convert CSS	Lets you move CSS to another location, or convert inline CSS to CSS rules.
	Indent Code	Shifts the selection to the right.
	Outdent Code	Shifts the selection to the left.
	Format Source Code	Applies previously specified code formats to selected code or to the entire page if no code is selected. You can also quickly set code formatting preferences by selecting Code Formatting Settings from the Format Source Code button, or edit tag libraries by selecting Edit Tag Libraries.

The number of buttons available in the Coding toolbar varies depending on the size of the Code view in the document window. To see all the available buttons, resize the Code view window or click the Show More arrow at the bottom of the Coding toolbar.

Collapsing and expanding tags and code blocks

Dreamweaver lets you collapse and expand code fragments so that you can hide and show various sections of your code. This can help reduce the amount of screen space that is taken up and also prevent mistakes since code that is collapsed cannot be edited. When you select code, Dreamweaver adds a set of collapse buttons next to the selection (minus symbols in Windows; vertical triangles in Mac OS). You can collapse code only in the Code view.

1   Make sure you are in the Code view by clicking the Code view button on the Document toolbar. Scroll to the top of the screen if necessary and click anywhere between lines 6 and 14, which is the `<style>`, tag that contains all your CSS.

2   Click the Collapse Full Tag button in the coding toolbar. You can also choose Edit > Code Collapse > Collapse Full Tag. The `<style>` tag is now collapsed. This feature is useful for reducing the amount of screen space that your code occupies on the screen.

The Collapse Full Tag button collapses the relevant tag.

Click the plus sign (Windows) or arrow (Mac OS) on the left to expand the code again.

3   In the Coding toolbar click the Select Parent Tag button. This will select the code that is nesting your existing selection. In this case, the parent is the `<head>` tag, which is now selected.

The Select Parent Tag button is a great alternative to selecting code by hand. Selecting by hand can often introduce mistakes; the Select Parent Tag will always be more reliable and faster.

4   In the Coding toolbar click the Collapse Selection button to collapse the `<head>` tag and all its content. You could have also chosen Edit > Code Collapse > Collapse Selection.

5   Click anywhere within your document and note that you could begin to work in your HTML and the `<head>` tag will always remain collapsed until you need to access it.

6   Double-click the head tag to expand it again.

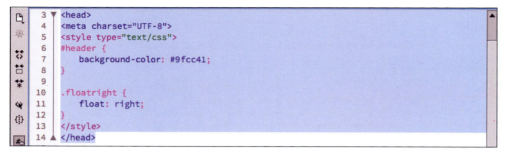

Double-clicking collapsed code will expand it.

To expand all code at once, you can also choose Edit > Code Collapse > Expand All. All your code fragments are now restored to their original view.

Validating your code

In addition to the many options available for formatting your code, you can also use Dreamweaver to find out if your code has tag or syntax errors. Dreamweaver can validate documents in many languages, including HTML, XHTML, PHP, ColdFusion Markup Language (CFML), Java Server Pages (JSP), Wireless Markup Language (WML), and XML. You can validate the current document or a selected tag.

Highlighting and correcting invalid code

You can set Dreamweaver to highlight invalid code (in yellow) in the Code view. When you select a highlighted section, the Property Inspector offers information on how to correct the error. Invalid code is not highlighted by default in Code view. In order to view the invalid code, you must enable this option in the View menu.

1   Select View > Code View Options and turn on the Highlight Invalid Code option by selecting it from the menu.

2   Two tags become highlighted in yellow the <b> and the <i> tags.

```
18   <body>
19   <div id="header"><img src="ou_logo.gif" width="210" height="41" /></div>
20   <figure>
21   <img src="beets_large.jpg" width="263" height="174" hspace="12" align="left" />
22   </figure>
23   <h2><b>The Lowly Beet<b></h2>
24   <p><i>By Organic Utopia's founder Jonathon Applestone<i></p>
25   <font size="3" face="Arial, Helvetica, sans-serif"><p>
26     Give the beet a break. Beets suffer from an image problem. If there was a food
     chain in the vegetable world, beets wouldn't rank very high. Of course there is no
     food chain because vegetables don't eat each other: we're the ones who eat
     vegetables.<br />
27   </p>
```

Invalid code is highlighted in yellow in the Code view.

3   Click once on the first highlighted (invalid) code for the <b> tag. In the Property Inspector, this has been identified as invalid markup because there is an unclosed or overlapping tag. (In this case, the author used two opening tags and no closing tags.)

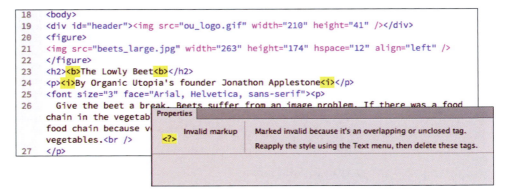

The Property Inspector identifies the invalid code and suggests how to correct it.

4   Correct the error by removing the incorrect markup. Individually select each of the four highlighted tags and then delete them. You can now style them correctly either in the Design view or the Code view; for now, you will leave them as is.

Running a report

Site reports allow you to scan your code using a set of criteria. Code which doesn't fit the criteria is identified, allowing you to fix it. In this exercise, you'll run all the reports for HTML.

1   Choose File > Save. Then choose Site > Reports and in the site Report window that appears, check all five boxes for HTML reports. Be sure that the Report on menu is set to Current Document. You can also run reports sitewide, for certain files only or an entire folder.

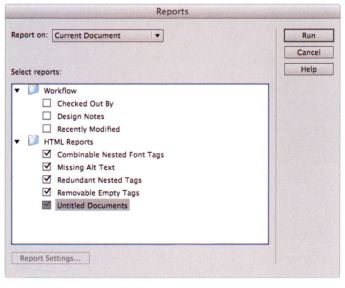

Check the HTML Reports you would like to run.

2   Click Run; the results of the Report appear in a new Site Reports panel below the Properties panel. In this case, there are three warnings; two warnings that the `alt` attribute is missing from your images and a third warning the file has no title tag. The alt attribute improves accessibility for images on your page for assistive devices, such as screenreaders. This is not technically required, but you should add them. The title tag is required for properly-formed HTML files and provides important information to the user in the title bar of their browser.

3   In the Site Reports panel, double-click the first warning. You will be sent directly to the code and the image will be selected. In the Properties panel, locate the Alt text field and type **Logo** and then click anywhere in the code window to commit the change.

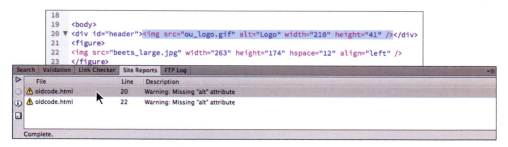

Clicking a warning in the Site Reports panel sends you to this code.

4   Repeat this step and double-click the second warning. This will select your other image. You could also click the `<img>` element on line 19 in the Code view to select this image. Type **Beets** in the Alt text field, then click anywhere in the code window to commit the change.

5   Choose File > Save to save your file. You should also close the entire group of the report tabs. You can do this by clicking the context menu at the top-right of the panel and choosing Close Tab Group.

Formatting code

Once you've validated your code, you can further change its look by specifying formatting preferences, such as indentation, line length, and the case of tag and attribute names. Many developers who code by hand have certain conventions or preferences for the way their code appears on the page or for the formatting used. Dreamweaver helps automate certain code formatting tasks that would otherwise be time-consuming and tedious.

1   Select Edit > Preferences (Windows) or Dreamweaver > Preferences (Mac OS).

2 When the Preferences dialog box appears, select Code Format from the Category list on the left. The Code Format preferences appear on the right.

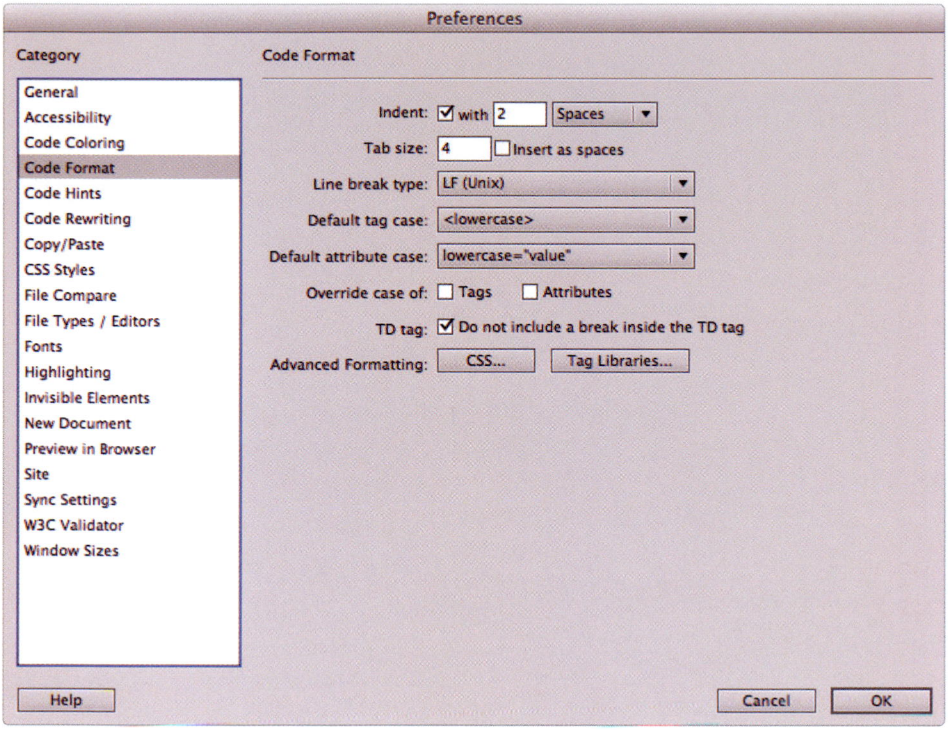

Choose from the Code Format preferences to further change the look of your code.

The Code Format preferences allow you to change the way code is written in Dreamweaver. For example, when you press the Tab key, your cursor indents four spaces. Using this preference window, you could increase or decrease the amount of the indent.

3 In the Advanced Formatting section, click the CSS button; the CSS Source Format Options window appears. This window allows you to specify the way your CSS code is written.

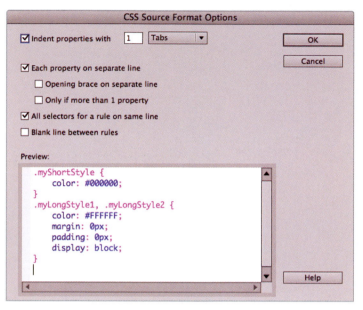

The CSS Source Format Options window allows you to change the way CSS syntax is written.

Click the Cancel button to close this window, and then click the Cancel button to close the Preferences window.

Applying source formatting

If you make changes in the Code Format preferences, those options are automatically applied only to new files created in Dreamweaver. To apply new formatting preferences to an existing file, you would need to then select Commands > Apply Source Formatting.

Indenting

Dreamweaver also offers indentation options for you as you write and edit code in the Code view or the Code Inspector. You can change the indentation level of a selected block or line of code, shifting it to the right or left by one tab.

1 In the Code view, click in front of the div element for the header on line 19, and press the Tab key twice. Alternatively, you could select Edit > Indent Code or use the indent button on the Coding Toolbar.

2 To outdent the selected block of code, press Shift+Tab, or you can select Edit > Outdent Code.

You can also select multiple elements and Indent and Outdent them.

3 Choose File > Save to save your work, then close the file by choosing File > Close.

Self study

Choose File > Save As and make a copy of the **oldcode.html** page. In the design view, experiment with the Quick Tag Editor and try some of the following: Convert the H2 tag of The Lowly Beet heading to an H3 tag. Use the Quick Tag editor to open the <img> tag for the beets and remove the align attribute as it is no longer needed.

In Code view make sure you understand the tools covered in the chapter by clicking elements and collapsing them. Try clicking within a paragraph and then clicking the Select Parent Tag button. Click it again to see what happens. Before you click a third time can you predict what will be selected?

Try formatting the readability of your code by indenting the nested elements in the file. Selecting multiple elements at once and then clicking the indent (or outdent) buttons will allow you to shift entire blocks of code to the left or right.

Review

Questions

1   What is the purpose of working in the Code view in Dreamweaver?

2   When are the code formatting options that you specify in Code Format preferences applied?

3   What advantages are there in using the tag selector to select, edit, and remove HTML code?

4   How do you know where invalid code exists in your document and how to fix it?

Answers

1   The Code view is a hand-coding environment for writing and editing HTML, JavaScript, server-language code such as PHP, and any other kind of code.

2   The code formatting options that you specify in Code Format preferences are automatically applied only to new documents that you subsequently create with Dreamweaver. However, you can apply new formatting preferences to existing documents using the Apply Source Formatting command.

3   You can use the tag selector to select, edit, and remove tags without exiting the Design view. The tag selector, situated in the status bar at the bottom of the document window, displays a series of tags that correspond to elements on your page.

4   With the Highlight Invalid Code option selected, Dreamweaver highlights invalid code in yellow in both the Design and Code views. When you select a highlighted section, the Property Inspector offers information on how to correct the error.

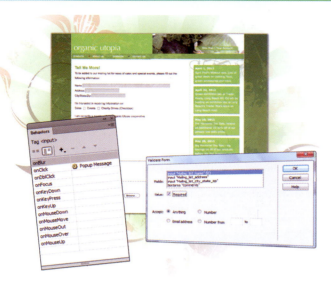

What you'll learn in this lesson:

- The basics of creating forms
- Working with the `<form>` tag
- Adding form elements
- Styling forms with CSS
- Choosing form processing options
- Validating forms
- Working with Behaviors

Building HTML5 Web Forms

Dreamweaver CC adds support for the new HTML5 form elements and attributes, allowing you to gather information from visitors to your website. In this lesson, you'll learn how to add form elements to make your site more interactive and use the new required, validation and placeholder input attributes.

Starting up

Before starting, make sure that your tools and panels are consistent by resetting your workspace. See "Resetting the Dreamweaver workspace" in the Starting up section of this book.

You will work with several files from the dw14lessons folder in this lesson. Make sure that you have loaded the dwlessons folder onto your hard drive from the supplied DVD. See "Loading lesson files" in the Starting up section of this book.

Before you begin, you need to create a site definition that points to the dw14lessons folder. Go to Site > New Site, or, for details on creating a site definition, refer to Lesson 2, "Setting Up a New Site."

See Lesson 14 in action!

Use the accompanying video to gain a better understanding of how to use some of the features shown in this lesson. The video tutorial for this lesson can be found on the included DVD.

The basics of HTML5 forms

HTML5 forms are commonly used for questionnaires, hotel reservations, order forms, data entry, and a variety of other applications. Users provide information by entering text, selecting menu items, and so on, and then submit that information to you through a server.

Here's the simple form you will be creating that includes labels, radio buttons, and push buttons (used to reset the form or submit it):

Forms are a great choice when you want to gather information from your audience.

How forms work

An HTML5 form is a section of a document that often contains content such as text or images, markup, special elements called controls check boxes, radio buttons, and menus, among others), and labels on those controls. A form is completed when a user modifies its controls (by entering text and selecting menu items), and submits the form to an agent for processing.

When you add form controls in Dreamweaver, you are essentially creating the front-end of the form. A user can add all the data required on the page, but this data needs to saved and processed at a specific location when the user clicks the Submit button. It's important to understand that Dreamweaver does not provide this location for you. You will need to work with your hosting provider or another service in order to have a system for accepting user data and then processing it in some way. You will learn more about this process a bit later in the lesson.

Building a contact form

In this lesson, you'll build a contact form for OrganicUtopia. This form allows users to be added to a mailing list for news of sales and special events, and it provides the site owners with relevant data, such as name, e-mail, and which information they would like to receive.

Inserting the <form> tag

The first step in building a form in Dreamweaver is to add a form element, which serves as a container for the form fields you'll be adding to it. In hand-coded HTML, you do this by inserting the `<form>` tag into your code. In the Design view, you can add a form element using the Form button.

1   Choose File > Open. When the Open dialog box appears, navigate to the dw14lessons folder. Select the **formbase.html** file and click Open. We have added most of the form content for you, but you will have to remove the placeholder text and add the proper form controls.

2   In the Design view, place an insertion cursor where you want your form to appear. Because this is an existing page, click with your mouse in the white area immediately to the left of the word *Name*.

Insert your cursor before the Name text field label.

3   In the Insert panel on the right side of your screen, choose the Form category from the drop-down menu to display options for adding form elements to a page.

4   From the Form category of the Insert panel, select the Form element (▤).

Options for adding form elements to a page are found in the Form category of the Insert panel.

5   You should now see a red outline on your page. This is how a form is displayed in the Design view. If you don't see this outline, choose View > Visual Aids > Invisible Elements to turn on the form element's visibility.

A dotted red outline on your page indicates a placed form element.

Now you'll take a look at the code generated by the steps you just completed in the Design view. This is for educational purposes to help you understand the foundations of how forms work.

6   In the Document toolbar just above your document window, click the Code view button to switch to your page's HTML code view.

7   In line 214 of your code, you should see the newly added `<form>` element. Take note of the default attributes and values (`ID="form1"` `name="form1"` `method="post"`). You'll learn more about these attributes shortly. For now, simply note that these were created.

```
<form id="form1" name="form1" method="post" action="">
</form>
<p>Name<br />
Address<br />
City/State/Zip</p>
<p>I'm interested in receiving information on:<br />
Sales (Checkbox) Events (Checkbox) Charity Drives (Checkbox)</p>
<p>I am currently a member of the Organic Utopia cooperative<br />
   (Radio Button) Yes<br />
(Radio Button) No<br />
(Radio Button) Can't Remember</p>
```

In HTML code, a form element is added using the `<form>` tag.

Since this form element is currently empty, you'll need to move the existing content (Name, Address, and so on) from the current location on the page to the form element you just created.

8   In the Document toolbar just above your document window, click the Design view button to switch to your page's visual layout view.

9   Starting with the text labeled Name, click and drag downward to select all the text below your form element.

10   Choose Edit > Cut to cut the text to your clipboard and remove it from its current location on the page.

11   Click inside the red outline that represents your form element to place an insertion cursor there.

12   Choose Edit > Paste to place the text from the clipboard into your form element.

All the text for your element label is now located inside the form element.

```
Name
Address
City/State/Zip

I'm interested in receiving information on:
Sales (Checkbox) Events (Checkbox) Charity Drives (Checkbox)

I am currently a member of the Organic Utopia cooperative
(Radio Button) Yes
(Radio Button) No
(Radio Button) Can't Remember

I'm interested in volunteering for:

(List) Store Events, Planting Season, Anything

(Comments)

Send us a picture of your garden! (Upload)
```

Cut and paste existing content from your page into the form element.

Setting form properties

As indicated previously, the `<form>` tag includes three different attributes and values by default. These attributes are listed as ID, name, and method, and they represent the HTML form element's properties. The default values for these attributes are not necessarily ideal, so you'll modify them.

1   Make sure the form element you added in the previous exercise is selected by clicking the edge of its red outline. A form field element must be selected before you modify its properties.

2   In the Property Inspector at the bottom of your document window, you now have access to some of the properties associated with the `<form>` tag.

The fields in the Property Inspector reflect properties found inside the `<form>` tag in HTML code.

The Form ID makes it possible to identify and control the form with a script, as well as to style the form with CSS. It is also very important for form validation, which is discussed later in this lesson.

A form ID is the same ID attribute you have been using to style divs. This form, for example, would have the ID `#form1` by default, which is not a useful name.

3 In the Form ID text field, type the name **contact**. Press Enter (Windows) or Return (Mac OS).

The Action field allows you to specify the script, for example, a Common Gateway Interface (CGI) script or a PHP page, that processes the user's form data. You can type the path to this file, or use the Browse button to navigate to the desired file. In most cases, you'll need to get this information from your system Administrator or hosting provider.

4 Because you have not yet defined the processing method for this form, leave the Action text field blank.

5 For method, make sure the POST method for this exercise is selected, which it likely is by default.

The Method menu

The Method drop-down menu is where you choose the method used to transmit the data to a server. The Method drop-down menu includes the following choices:

Default uses the browser's default setting to submit the form data to a server. Most browsers use the GET method by default.

GET includes the form data as part of the URL of the request to the server. GET has a length limitation of 8,192 characters in the URL and is less commonly used to send long forms than the POST method.

POST is similar to GET, but it embeds the form data in the header of the server request instead of in the URL. Although the POST method is the most commonly used, be aware that pages sent by this method cannot be bookmarked and are not encrypted for security purposes.

6 Choose *application/x-www-form-urlencoded* from the Enctype drop-down menu. The Enctype field defines the encoding type of the data being submitted to a server. Application/x-www-form-urlencoded is used in most situations, unless you're asking the user to upload a file, in which case you would choose multipart/form-data.

 The optional Target property specifies the window or frame in which to display the data that is returned. The target value is included in the <form> tag only when you choose to specify it.

Form properties are set in the Property Inspector.

Now that you've defined the properties of the form, you'll use options in the Insert panel's Forms section to add elements to the form.

Adding form elements

A Dreamweaver form is not a working form until you add the elements, or fields, that allow the user to provide information to you. Thankfully, the Form category in the Insert panel contains everything you need to insert any kind of form field into your page.

The Form category in the Insert panel contains everything you need to add interactive fields to your form.

Common form elements

Of the many form elements you can add using the Insert toolbar, these are the most commonly used ones:

Text fields accept alphanumeric text entries, in single- or multiple-line formats, or in a password (bulleted) format.

Check boxes: allow users to make as many choices as they want from a list of options.

Radio buttons allow only mutually exclusive choices in that selecting one radio button deselects all others in the group.

List menus permit the selection of single or multiple items from a scrolling list, whereas Jump menus allow you to set each option from a scrolling list to link to a document or file.

Buttons perform actions when clicked. You can assign the default Submit or Reset action to buttons, or define other processing tasks in a script.

A good way to understand all the options available in Dreamweaver for adding elements to a form is to add them to the form you created earlier.

Adding text fields

The simplest and most common type of form field is the text field. Users can enter anything, from their name, to their credit card number, to their dog's name, into a text field. You control the formatting of their responses using the Property Inspector.

1   Within your form, select the word Name and press Ctrl+X (Windows) or Command+X (Mac OS) to cut the text and place it on the clipboard.

2   Click the Text Field button (▭) in the Insert panel. Dreamweaver will insert a text input element and a matching label element with the default text Text Field. Select Text Field and press Ctrl+V (Windows) or Command+V (Mac OS) to paste the word Name you cut earlier. The label element in a form provides additional usability for the user.

Tell Me More!

To be added to our mailing list for news of sales and special events, please fill out the following information:

Name:

Address

City/State/Zip

I'm interested in receiving information on:

Sales (Checkbox) Events (Checkbox) Charity Drives (Checkbox)

I am currently a member of the Organic Utopia cooperative

(Radio Button) Yes

(Radio Button) No

(Radio Button) Can't Remember

I'm interested in volunteering for:

(List) Store Events, Planting Season, Anything

The label element provides additional usability for the user.

3   Select the text field by clicking it and notice the options that are available in the Property Inspector.

The Property Inspector displays the new HTML5 properties for the text element.

4   In the Name section, type **Mailing_list_name** and press Enter (Windows) or Return (Mac OS). Dreamweaver will use the value of this Name field to set both the Name and ID of the form element. The importance of this distinction will be covered in a moment.

5   Type **55** in the Size text field in the Property Inspector to set the text input area to a width of 55 characters.

6   Type **30** in the Max Length text field to set the maximum number of characters that can be entered. For example, if this were a telephone number field, you probably would have limited it to ten characters.

7   Choose contact from the Form drop-down menu. Associating the text field with a specific form will be helpful in the event there are multiple forms on a page.

8   Repeat steps 1 to 7 to add Address and City/State/Zip text fields beneath the Name field. When creating the Address text field, give it the ID **Mailing_list_address** and give the last text field the ID **Mailing_list_city_state_zip**. When naming form elements, you should stay away from using spaces between words. It is better to use underscores or hyphens instead.

9   Choose File > Save As. In the Save As dialog box, navigate to the dw14lessons folder and type **organicform.html** into the Name text field. Click Save.

Now preview the open page in a browser by clicking the Preview/Debug in browser button on the Document toolbar. Your form should look like this:

Tell Me More!

To be added to our mailing list for news of sales and special events, please fill out the following information:

Name

Address

City/State/Zip

This is what your form should look like in the browser with text fields added.

10   Close the browser and return to Dreamweaver.

Adding a new HTML5 text field

HTML5 has added new text fields to make it easier to handle specific types of information such as e-mail addresses, web addresses and telephone numbers. You will use the e-mail text field to request the user's email address and later validate that a properly-formed e-mail address was entered.

1   Within your form, select the word Email and delete the text.

2   Click the Email button (@) in the Insert panel. Dreamweaver inserts an Email field that will accept a properly-formed email address as input.

3   Select the Email field by clicking it and notice the options that are available in the Property Inspector.

The Property Inspector displays the properties for the new HTML5 email element.

4   In the Name section, type **Mailing_list_email** and press Enter (Windows) or Return (Mac OS).

5   Type **55** in the Size text field in the Property Inspector to set the text input area to a width of 55 characters.

6   Type **128** in the Max Length text field to set the maximum number of characters that can be entered.

7   Choose contact from the Form drop-down menu, associating the text field with your contact form.

8   Choose File > Save and preview the open page in a browser by clicking the Preview/Debug in browser button on the Document toolbar. Your form should look like this:

This is what your form should look like with the email field added.

9   Close the browser and return to Dreamweaver.

HTML5 form elements

Dreamweaver CC adds support for the new HTML5 form elements, including new attributes such as required, validation and pattern. The most common HTML5 form elements are listed below:

Email fields accept alphanumeric text entries entered as e-mail addresses which can be validated prior to submitting the form.

URL allows users to enter alphanumeric text representing a fully-qualified domain name and validate the field prior to form submission.

Telephone allows users to enter text representing a telephone number.

Search allows users to enter text to be used to submit a search.

Date elements allow users to submit date/time information using a popup calendar or other format without the need for additional JavaScript.

Color inputs allow users to choose a color from a color palette.

For a more in-depth look at all of the HTML5 form elements and how to use them with their various attributes, see the *HTML5 Digital Classroom* book available in electronic and print formats.

Adding check boxes

Check boxes are another valuable tool in your form control toolkit. They're valuable when you want to get specific responses from your users and you don't want to give them the opportunity to enter incorrect information into text fields. Again, you control the formatting of their responses using the Property Inspector. In this exercise, you will take a look at the use of form labels as well as the importance of setting the names of your form elements.

1   Click and drag to select both the word Sales and the (Checkbox) placeholder text and delete them.

2   Click the Checkbox element (☑) in the Insert panel. Dreamweaver inserts a check box in your page along with a label element with default text, Checkbox. Select the word Checkbox and type **Sales**. The label tag is an optional element that adds an extra level of usability to your check boxes. Users will now be able to click the text (in addition to the check box) in order to make their selection.

3 Click the check box to select it, and notice the options that become available in the Property Inspector. In the Name field, type **Sales**, then press Enter (Windows) or Return (Mac OS).

Settings that are specific to the check box you've just added to your form appear in the Property Inspector.

4 As mentioned earlier, when you set the Name of the check box, Dreamweaver also sets the ID to the same value and associates the label to that field ID. It is important to understand the distinction between the Name and the ID. An ID is used to style an element and each ID must be unique, while the Name is what gets passed for scripting and validation when the user clicks Submit. In the case of check boxes, you want all of them to have the same Name, but they must each have a unique ID. To do this you will need to override Dreamweaver's default settings. To make sure Dreamweaver only changes the Name, right-click (Windows) or Ctrl+click (Mac OS) the check box, select Name… from the popup menu, then type **Receive_Info** and press Enter (Windows) or Return (Mac OS).

5 With the check box still selected, type **Sales** in the Value text field in the Property Inspector to define the data that's passed to the server when the user checks this check box.

6 Choose contact from the Form drop-down menu to associate this field with the contact form.

7 The Checked field defines how the check box should appear when the page is first loaded. It should not be selected; if it is, uncheck it now.

8 Next, select the word Events and the placeholder (Checkbox) text and delete them. Click the Checkbox element in the Insert panel. Dreamweaver inserts a check box in your page along with a label element with default text, Checkbox. Select the word Checkbox and type **Events**.

9 Click the check box and change the Name to **Events** in the Property Inspector. Remember, you will want the name to be same as the first check box, so that users will be able to check both and have the values passed. However, because Dreamweaver also sets the ID to this value, you need to manually intervene. To set only the Name, right-click (Windows) or Ctrl+click (Mac OS) the check box and select Name… from the popup menu, then type **Receive_Info** and press Enter (Windows) or Return (Mac OS). This will leave the ID set to Events while changing the Name so that the user can select both check boxes and have both values passed.

10 With the check box still selected, type **Events** in the Value text field in the Property Inspector to define the data that's passed to the server when the user checks this check box. Choose contact from the Form drop-down menu to associate this field with the contact form and make sure Checked field is not checked.

11 Repeat steps 8, 9 and 10 with different values for the ID and Label to add a third check box for Charity Drive. Again, be sure to rename the check box **Receive_Info** by using the right-click (Windows) or Option+click (Mac OS) method to link the Name and ID values.

Now, preview the open page in a browser. Your form should look like this:

Your form, with check boxes inserted, should look like this.

12 With the page open in the browser, click the text next to the check boxes; notice that this action selects the box. This is a function of the label tag. Try clicking the text of your Name and Address text fields. They have the same behavior because they also have labels.

Labels improve accessibility for all users, in particular for those who might be using screen readers or other devices.

13 Close your browser and return to Dreamweaver.

Adding radio buttons

When you add radio buttons to your form, you encounter the same settings in the Property inspector as you do when you add check boxes. The only difference between check boxes and radio buttons is that from a group of radio buttons, only a single option can be selected. Check boxes allow the selection of multiple options.

To make two or more individual radio buttons mutually exclusive, you select two or more radio buttons and give them the same name in the Property Inspector.

Creating a group of radio buttons by adding buttons one by one is often more time-consuming than it's worth. Thankfully, Dreamweaver offers a more efficient method for creating a list of mutually exclusive options: the radio group.

Adding radio groups

The Radio Group element in the Insert toolbar provides a quick and easy way to add a list of radio buttons to your form. The same rules regarding naming and values apply, but the Radio Group dialog box allows you to include several entries in a group at once.

1   Click and drag to select the three (Radio Button) placeholders and their labels (Yes, No, and Can't Remember). Press Delete to remove them from your form. You'll create your own labels for this group.

2   Click the Radio Group button in the Insert panel. The Radio Group dialog box opens, and offers several property options.

Set properties for your radio group in the Radio Group dialog box.

3   In the Name text field of the Radio Group dialog box, type **Membership Status** to give the group a name that associates all the radio buttons together.

You will now create a unique label for each button.

4   Click the first entry in the Label column and type **Member**.

5   In the Value column of the Radio buttons section, you assign a value to each button to be passed back to the server. Click the first entry in this column and type **member**. This returns a value of member when the user clicks on the Member radio button.

6   Make sure Line breaks (
 tags) is selected in the *Layout using* section at the bottom of the dialog box. This will place a hard return after each radio button.

7   Repeat steps 4 to 6, but this time create a label called **Non-Member** and a value of **nonmember**.

8   Click OK. Choose File > Save, and then preview the open page in a browser. Click each of the two radio buttons and note that only one radio button can ever be selected. This is a function of a radio button group: for cases where you want more than one option to be selected and returned, you could use check boxes.

Tell Me More!

To be added to our mailing list for news of sales and special events, please fill out the following information:

Name:

Address:

City/State/Zip:

I'm interested in receiving information on:

☐ Sales

☐ Events

☐ Charity Drive

I am currently a member of the Organic Utopia cooperative

◯ Member

◯ Non-Member

After adding the radio group, your form should look like this.

9   Close your browser and return to Dreamweaver.

Check boxes can also be added as groups using the Checkbox Group option in the Insert panel.

Adding lists and menus

Lists and menus show choices within a list that permit users to choose single or multiple options. The List option displays as a scrolling list, and the Menu option displays as a drop-down menu. Both items are inserted using the Select element, but the behavior is determined by the properties you set in the Property Inspector.

1   Click and drag to select the placeholder text—(List) Store Events, Planting Season, Anything—that follows your radio group. Press Delete to remove it from your form. You'll create your own labels for this list.

2   Click the Select button (▤) in the Insert panel and a new list or menu appears within the form outline on your page.

3   Select the text *Select:* in the label in front of the newly created form element and press Delete.

4 Click the Select form element to select it, and notice the options that are now available in the Property Inspector. Type **Volunteer** in the Name text field, then press Enter (Windows) or Return (Mac OS).

Enter the settings for your newly added list or menu in the Property Inspector.

5 Choose contact from the Form drop-down menu.

6 Click the check box labeled Multiple to the left of the Form drop-down menu to allow multiple selections. With this feature activated, the Select element will appear as a multi-select form field and allow users to choose more than one option from your list at a time.

7 Click the List Values button to enter items for your scrolling list. The structure of the List Values dialog box is identical to that of the Radio Group dialog box. Type **Store Events** as your first Item Label and **store_events** for the first value to be returned.

Now you will add two more items to the list.

8 Click the Plus button (+) in the left corner of the List Values window, and type **Planting Season** as the second Item Label. Then click under the Events value and type **planting_season**. Click the Plus button (+) again. Type **Anything** as the third Item Label, and, finally, click under the Planting value and type **any_event**. Click OK.

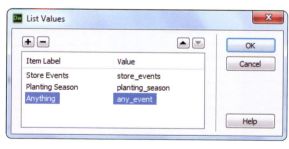

Adding the labels and values for a list control.

9 Choose File > Save to save your work. Preview your page in the browser and click one of the labels to see how it is selected. Close your browser and return to Dreamweaver.

Adding a Text Area

Sometimes within a Dreamweaver form, you want to have a field that simply provides an open area into which users can enter text. For this form, you'll add a Text Area element to provide a region for users to type in their comments about the site.

1   Click and drag to select the placeholder text, (Comments), and delete it.

2   Click the Text Area button (▣) in the Insert panel and Dreamweaver inserts a new Text Area element in your page.

3   Select the words *Text Area* in the label to the left of the field, and replace them by typing **Comments** then press Shift+Enter (Windows) or Shift+Return (Mac OS) to move the Text Area down one line.

4   Click the Text Area, and notice the options that are now available in the Property Inspector.

5   Type **Comments** in the Name text field and press Enter (Windows) or Return (Mac OS).

6   Choose contact from the Form drop-down menu.

7   Type **5** in the Rows text field.

8   Type **40** in the Cols text field to set the text input area to a width of 40 characters.

9   Leave the other settings at their defaults and choose File > Save; then preview the open page in a browser. The Text Area will allow users to type inside of the box, and if the amount of text goes below the bottom of the text area, then a scrollbar will automatically appear.

The form at this point, rendered by Internet Explorer.

Adding a File Upload field

If you want users to be able to upload a file to your server—for example, a photo for ID purposes—you'll want to add a File Upload field.

1 Close the browser and return to **organicform.html** in Dreamweaver. Click and drag to select (Upload), and delete it to place an insertion cursor next to your label.

2 Click the File button (▣) in the Insert panel and a new File element, with the Browse button included, appears within the form outline on your page. Select the text *Send us a picture of your garden!* and press Ctrl+X (Windows) or Command+X (Mac OS) to cut the text and place it in the clipboard. Next, select the word File in the label to the left of the File control and press Ctrl+V (Windows) or Command+V (Mac OS) to paste text in the clipboard as the new label.

3 Click to select the File field, and notice the options that become available in the Property Inspector.

4 Choose contact from the Form drop-down menu.

Set the properties for your File field in the Property Inspector.

The Class drop-down menu allows you to apply CSS to style this form field. Using CSS to style form fields is discussed in more detail later in this lesson.

You are now finished with the file field section of your form. Users can now either enter the desired file name or click Browse to navigate to it.

For the file field element to actually upload a user's file to your server, you'll need to ask your server Administrator how the server is configured to accept files.

5   Choose File > Save, then preview the open page in a browser. Your form should look like this:

Tell Me More!
To be added to our mailing list for news of sales and special events, please fill out the following information:

Name: [   ]
Address: [   ]
City/State/Zip: [   ]

I'm interested in receiving information on:
☐ Sales
☐ Events
☐ Charity Drive

I am currently a member of the Organic Utopia cooperative

○ Member
○ Non-Member

I'm interested in volunteering for:

Store Events
Planting Season
Anything

Comments:
[   ]

Send us a picture of your garden!: (Browse)

You're almost finished adding form fields to your form.

6   Close the browser and return to Dreamweaver.

Creating Submit and Reset buttons

As you might expect, none of the field elements you've been adding to your form do any good if the user doesn't have a way to send the information to you. Buttons provide the means for the user to either submit form data, or reset the fields and start over.

1   Place your cursor after the Browse button, then press Enter (Windows) or Return (Mac OS) to specify where you want your button(s) to appear.

2   Click the Submit Button element (▣) in the Forms category of the Insert panel. A new button, labeled *Submit* by default, appears within the form outline on your page.

3 If it's not already selected, click to select the Submit button, and notice the options that are now available in the Property Inspector.

Button properties are set in the Property Inspector.

4 The word *Submit* is displayed in the Value field as well. You could change this value to a more user-friendly name such as Send, however, for now leave it as is.

5 Choose contact from the Form drop-down menu to associate this button with your contact form.

6 Place your cursor after the Submit button, then click the Reset Button element (⟳) in the Insert panel. A new button, labeled *Reset* by default, appears within the form outline on your page.

7 Choose contact from the Form drop-down menu to associate this button with your contact form.

8 Finally, you will use the Button element to create a Validate button. Place your cursor to the right of the Reset button, then click the Button element (▣) in the Insert panel. A new button, labeled Button by default, appears next to your Reset button.

9 Click the Button element and type **Validate** in the Name text field within the Property Inspector. Additionally, you will need to type Validate in the Value field to change the default value.

10 Choose contact from the Form drop-down menu to associate this button with your contact form.

Send us a picture of your garden!: [   ] [Browse...]

[Submit] [Reset] [Validate]

The Submit, Reset, and Validate button are now placed in the form.

11 Choose File > Save All to save your work.

Now that you've finished adding the necessary form fields to your Contact Form page, you'll add style to the form and its elements, using CSS.

Styling forms with CSS

In Lesson 4, "Styling Your Pages with CSS," you explored the many ways you can use CSS to format text and position content on an HTML page in Dreamweaver. However, the usefulness of CSS is not limited to static page content. Dynamic content, such as form fields, can also be successfully and creatively styled using CSS.

Attaching external styles

This exercise assumes you have already learned some of the basics of working with styles covered in previous lessons. You will now focus on applying some existing styles to the form elements that you've added in this lesson. The styles you apply have been created for you, but you must attach them to your form page in order to access them.

1 If your CSS Designer panel is not currently open, open it now by choosing Window > CSS Designer.

2 In the CSS Styles panel, click the Add CSS Source button (⊞) in the Sources menu bar and choose Attach Existing CSS File. The Attach External CSS File dialog box opens.

Select the CSS file you want to attach using the Attach External CSS File dialog box.

3 Next to the File/URL field, click the Browse button and select **formstyles.css** from the dw14lessons folder. Press OK (Windows) or Open (Mac OS) to exit the Select Style Sheet File dialog box.

4 In the Attach External CSS File dialog box, click the Link radio button to create a link <href> tag in the code for this page, and reference the location of the published style sheet. Most major web browsers support the link method.

5 In the Conditional Usage section of the Media drop-down menu, you can define the target medium for your style sheet. For this exercise, leave this setting at its default, which is blank.

For more information on media-dependent style sheets, see the World Wide Web Consortium (W3C) website at W3.org/TR/CSS21/media.html.

6 Click OK to attach the style sheet to this document.

Setting a background color

Once the formstyles.css style sheet is attached, the backgrounds of your form fields change to a light blue color. This happens because formstyles.css contains a tag selector rule, which instructs the `<form>` tag you added earlier in the lesson to include a background color. The rule redefines the `<form>` tag, so the color is applied only to the background of the form fields themselves, and not to the entire body of the page.

Tell Me More!

To be added to our mailing list for news of sales and special events, please fill out the following information:

Name:

Address:

City/State/Zip:

Email:

I'm interested in receiving information on:

☐ Sales

☐ Events

☐ Charity Drive

I am currently a member of the Organic Utopia cooperative

○ Member

○ Non-Member

The formstyles CSS contains a rule that specifies a background color.

A major benefit of using CSS is that once you complete the initial styling, you can revisit the CSS file and change the included style rules. Because the blue background doesn't fit in with the color scheme of your site, you'll edit the form rule to change the background to a light gray.

1   In the CSS Designer panel, click the Sources menu bar to show all styles attached to this document. Locate formstyles.css in the list of Sources and click the filename. (You can expand and collapse the Sources pane by clicking the Sources menu bar.)

2 From the list of Selectors included within formstyles.css, click the input rule in the Selectors pane to select it for editing. Click the Show Set check box in the Properties Navigation bar to limit the list to only those properties that are set.

Selecting the input selector in your formstyles.css style sheet reveals the style being used.

3 Click the Background color text field in the Properties pane and type the hexadecimal code **#d7d7d7** to replace the current color.

4 Press Enter (Windows) or Return (Mac OS) to preview the change to the background color.

You've successfully changed the background color of your form fields by editing an attached CSS.

You've just used a tag selector CSS rule to change the background color of your form. Next, you'll use a class style to change the appearance of the labels on your form fields.

Styling form elements

You might have noticed another CSS rule included in formstyles.css along with the `<form>` definition. It's a class style called `.labels`, and it contains properties that change the font, color, and weight of your form field labels.

1 In the CSS Designer panel, click the .labels selector to select it; in the Properties pane, you can see the properties currently set for the class.

The font-family has been changed to Arial, Helvetica, sans-serif.

The font-weight is set to bolder.

The color has been set to a hexadecimal notation of #9FCC41, or green.

The `.labels` selector can also be edited in the CSS Designer panel.

You'll now apply this style.

2 In the document window, click anywhere within the Name label, which precedes the first text field in your form.

3 In the Property Inspector, click the HTML button if necessary; click the Class menu and choose labels from the list. Because the Name, Address, City/State/Zip, and Email are all within the same paragraph, the style will be applied, making them all green.

The `.labels` *class applied to your form.*

These are just a few of the ways you can use CSS to style form elements. Experiment further with different properties to make your form more visually pleasing.

Form processing and validation

As attractive as CSS styling can make your form in Dreamweaver, you can't collect form data without using a server-side script or application (for example, CGI, PHP, ASP) to process the data.

CGI scripts are perhaps the oldest method of server-side scripting used to process form data. Several websites offer free CGI scripts that you can use. The hosting company for your website could also provide CGI scripts that perform many common tasks, such as collecting e-mail addresses or allowing visitors to send you comments through a web form. Other methods include the use of other scripting languages, such as PHP, ASP, and others. It is beyond the scope of this book to cover all the various ways to process form data.

Prior to HTML5, form validation, a method for ensuring that the user has entered the correct type of data in the form's fields, also required scripting to work correctly. HTML5 adds built-in form validation that checks the contents of specified text fields directly within the browser. This functionality is automatically applied to forms in HTML5 and can be overridden using the `novalidate` form attribute. However, older browsers might still require the use of JavaScript so you will need to supply some level of scripting. Fortunately, Dreamweaver is capable of adding JavaScript to code that checks the contents of specified text fields. This code is added through the Validate Form behavior. You will be shown both methods of validation so that you can build your pages to work across various browsers.

HTML5 validation

HTML5 validation uses built-in browser support for the new HTML5 input elements and attributes. In order to take advantage of this validation you will mark certain fields as required to make sure the user has entered a value. You will also add new HTML5 input elements to collect the user's e-mail address and check to make sure the user has entered a properly formed e-mail address.

1   Return to **organicform.html** in Dreamweaver. Before you make any form fields required, it is common practice to provide visual clues to user. Click to place an Insert cursor after the Name label in your form template and type an asterisk (★). Repeat this step and add asterisks after the Address, City, State, Zip, and Email labels.

2   Next, you will add a message informing users that fields marked with an asterisk are required. Place your Insert cursor after the colon (:) in the first paragraph of text. Type **(Required fields are marked with an asterisk ★)** and be sure to include the parenthesis.

Tell Me More!

To be added to our mailing list for news of sales and special events, please fill out the following information: (Required fields are marked with an asterisk *)

Name*:
Address*:
City/State/Zip*:
Email*:

Visual cues inform users of required fields.

3   You are now ready to add the required attribute to the form fields. Click the Name text field to select it. The Property Inspector lists the attributes for this input element. Click the Required check box to place a checkmark in the box, marking this item as required. Browsers that support the HTML5 form elements will enforce that the user has typed a value in this field when the form is submitted.

Properties					
Text	Name Mailing_list_name	Class labels	Size 55	Value	Title
			Max Length 30		Place Holder
☐ Disabled ☑ Required ☐ Auto Complete	Form contact	Pattern	Tab Index	List
☐ Auto Focus ☐ Read Only				

The Property Inspector displays the new HTML5 input attributes.

4   Since the Name field is the first input element in the form, you can use the Auto Focus attribute to automatically place the user's Insert cursor in the text box when the form loads. Click the Auto Focus check box to instruct the user's Browser to set this field to the active field when the page loads.

5   Another attribute that can improve usability for a user is the Placeholder attribute. The Placeholder can include a text description or example to assist the user in entering the requested information. With the Name field still selected, type **Please enter your full name** in the Placeholder field in the Property Inspector.

The attributes Required, Auto Focus and Placeholder set for the Name input field.

6   Press Ctrl+S (Windows) or Command+S (Mac OS) to save your progress and choose File > Preview in Browser to test your browser's support for these HTML5 attributes. At the time of this writing, all current browsers, including Internet Explorer 10, support these attributes.

7   Click the Submit button without entering any data in the first field. If you are using the current version of any modern browser, you should see a popup window pointing to the Name field with a message asking the user to enter a value.

Firefox handles the required field by placing the input cursor in the field, showing a popup window, and outlining the field in a red border.

Older browsers will require JavaScript to process form validation. You will use Dreamweaver's Validate Form Behavior to ensure backwards compatibility with older browsers in the next activity.

Another way to ensure backwards compatibility for HTML5 form elements and attributes is to use polyfills. Polyfills use JavaScript to detect browser support of HTML5 and CSS3 features and provide scripted workarounds in browsers that do not support the features. Two commonly used polyfill techniques are the WebShims Lib (http://afarkas.github.io/webshim/demos/) and H5F (https://github.com/ryanseddon/H5F)

The Validate Form behavior

The Validate Form behavior provides checks and balances for users when they complete forms on your site. You can make certain fields required, make sure a user has entered a value in a required field, or make sure a user has entered the correct type of information in a field. You can run validation on all fields in a form, or on individual fields contained in that form.

The first step, however, is to get to know the Behaviors panel.

A look at the Behaviors panel

Generally speaking, the Behaviors panel provides a means for you to add JavaScript code to your page without actually having to type in the code. The code it inserts adds interactivity to your site, and is usually triggered by some user action. For example, when the user clicks on or hovers over a link, the behavior performs a task. Behaviors are hardly limited to use with forms, as they're commonly used to add rollovers, open new windows, check for plug-ins, and add navigation elements, among other functions.

Specifically, you use the Behaviors panel to add, modify, and remove behaviors. Because you can apply multiple behaviors to the same object, you can also reorder them in the Behaviors panel.

1   Access the Behaviors panel by choosing Window > Behaviors. If necessary, expand the panel grouping.

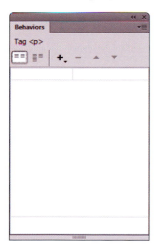

The Behaviors panel.

2   In the document window, click the Validate button you created earlier. You need to attach a behavior to objects on your page. For this exercise, you need to attach a behavior to the Validate button.

3   Click the Plus button (+) at the top of the Behaviors panel to see the list of available options for the selected object. In this case, the menu displays options associated with a button element. If an option is grayed out, that action is not available for the selected object.

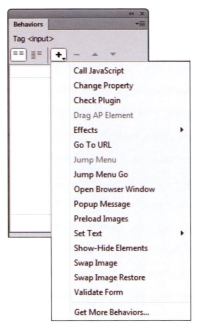

The list of available behaviors for your selected button element.

4   Select the Popup Message action. The Popup Message dialog box appears.

5   Type **Validate this form!** into the Message text field, and click OK.

Enter text into the Popup Message dialog box to have it appear on the screen.

The behavior is set, but it needs an event, or trigger.

Setting an event or trigger

An event (or trigger) is generally a specific user action needed for the Popup Window (or other behaviors) to work. In this case, you'll set the window to appear when the user clicks the Validate button.

1 In the top-left corner of the Behaviors panel, click the Show All Events button (▮▪). The Show All Events button provides a complete list of all possible triggers for this behavior.

There are a number of choices for the event that triggers your specific behavior.

In this case, the default option `onClick` is the correct choice.

2 Choose File > Save All and preview your page in a browser.

3 Click the Validate button at the bottom of your form. The popup message you set earlier appears.

Use this feature to warn your viewers, or to guide them in a certain direction.

Depending on the security configurations of your browser, you might be prompted to allow blocked content. If you'd like to change your preferences to avoid conflicts with scripts created in the Behaviors panel, refer to your browser's documentation for instructions on changing the default settings.

4   Click OK to close the message, and close your browser window and return to Dreamweaver.

To further explore the Behaviors panel and its features, you'll add a Form Validation behavior to the same button.

Validating form fields

The Validate Form action allows you to prevent the submission of a form unless a certain field (or fields) is filled in by the user. You'll apply this action to the Validate button you created.

1   In the document window, select the Validate button at the bottom of your form. The Behaviors panel should display the Popup Message action you added in the last exercise.

2   At the top of the Behaviors panel, click the Plus button (**+**), and select Validate Form from the drop-down menu that appears. The Validate Form dialog box opens. Dreamweaver automatically identifies the fields you have used on the page and lists them in the fields section.

3   Choose *Mailing_list_name* the first entry in the Fields list. Click the Required check box to require data entry into this field before the user can submit the form.

4   Click the Anything radio button so the field accepts any alphanumeric entry. If you want to require that only numerical data be entered, you would select the Number radio button. If you want to check for an @ symbol within the entered data, you would click the Email address radio button. Finally, if you want to check for a number within a specific range, you could enter that range in the Number from and to fields.

Specify which form elements get validated, and what is accepted.

5   Click OK to close the Validate Form dialog box.

6   Choose File > Save, then preview the form page in your browser. Leave the Name field blank, and click the Validate button at the bottom of your form.

Unfortunately, the Popup Message behavior you added earlier runs before the Validate Form behavior, requiring you to close the Popup Message window to see the results of your validation. After you dismiss the Popup Message you will see the error message stating that the Mailing list name is required.

This means you have just a little more work to do; you'll now adjust the Validate Form behavior to correct these errors.

Changing a form field's behavior order

To keep the popup message from appearing before the results of your validation, you'll need to change the Validate Form behavior's position in the behavior order, delete it, and reapply it to the correct button.

1   In the Dreamweaver document window, click the Validate button to select it.

2   Click the Show Set Events button in the Behaviors panel to toggle over to this view (if necessary). You will now see your two actions, Popup Message and Validate Form, which share the same event, or trigger.

*Use the Behaviors panel to reorder behaviors
and make them behave differently for the viewer.*

3   Click the Validate Form behavior to select it, and click the up arrow at the top of the panel to move it to a position above the Popup Message behavior. Although this makes the Validate Form action run first, the popup message still appears after the validation window is closed. It actually makes more sense not to have the Validate Form behavior attached to the Validate button at all. You will now remove this behavior and attach it to the Submit button instead.

4 Click the Minus button (–) to delete it from the behaviors associated with the Validate button.

5 Click the Submit button at the bottom of your form to select it. Repeat steps 2-4 in the preceding exercise to add the validation action to the Submit button.

Now it's time to see the fruits of your labor.

Verifying field contents

Now that you've adjusted the Validate Form behavior, you'll need to make sure the form function as you expect it to.

1 Preview the open page in your browser, and click the Validate button. This should now display only the popup message. Close it.

2 Click the Submit button. Even though the data is not actually submitted (for lack of a CGI script), the Validate Form warns you that required fields have not been filled.

Live View Alert

The following error(s) occurred:
- Mailing_list_name is required.

OK

The Validate Form behavior functions as you originally intended, thanks to some editing in the Behaviors panel.

You've successfully added validation to your form.

For a more detailed look at adding modern forms to a website, see the HTML5 Digital Classroom *book available in electronic and print formats.*

Self study

Using your new knowledge of building and editing web forms in Dreamweaver, try some of the following tasks using **organicform.html** to build on your experience:

Add the HTML5 url or telephone input types to ask the user for their website address or telephone number. Test HTML5 validation of these input fields by viewing the page in a browser and entering both valid and invalid values for web addresses and telephone numbers.

Edit the Validate Form behavior you applied to the Submit button in the last exercise. Apply validation to the other text fields in your form, providing checks for the specific content to be filled out in each field. Preview the page in your browser to ensure that the validation works.

Create an internal CSS that redefines the `<input>` tag. Set the background color of each form field to light green to match your page's color scheme. Experiment with the other styling options available to you in the CSS Rule Definition dialog box to further style your form elements.

Explore the other form field elements in the Forms category of the Insert panel. Add a hidden field to return the creation date of the form when it is submitted, while keeping this information hidden from the user. Add an Image field to turn a placed image into a button with a behavior attached. Group your form fields into labeled sections, using the Fieldset button.

Review

Questions

1   Why is it important to add a form element when building a web form in Dreamweaver?

2   When should you use a radio button group, as opposed to a set of check boxes, in a form?

3   How does CSS add creativity and efficiency to the form creation process?

4   What do you need in order to collect the form data that a user enters into your form?

5   Where would you access the different JavaScript actions that can be applied to a button in Dreamweaver?

6   How do the new HTML5 form features make it possible to handle and validate form data without JavaScript?

Answers

1 The form element serves as a container for the fields you'll be adding to the form. If you simply add form fields to a page in Dreamweaver, the user's browser won't know what to do with the user's information when they click the Submit button. To identify this information as part of a package, and to specify the route that information should take when submitted, you need to create a Dreamweaver form.

2 The difference between adding check boxes and radio buttons in a form is that from a group of radio buttons, only a single option can be selected. Check boxes allow the selection of multiple options.

3 Because CSS allows you to apply several formatting attributes with a single mouse click, both static and dynamic content (such as form fields) can be successfully and creatively styled using CSS. CSS also streamlines your workflow by allowing you to revisit CSS files and change the included style rules once you've completed the initial styling.

4 You can't collect form data without using a server-side script or application such as CGI, JSP, or ASP to process the data. CGI scripts are the most popular form of server-side scripting mechanism to process form data. Several websites offer free CGI scripts that you can use. Your site's ISP could also provide CGI scripts for you.

5 The Behaviors panel provides a means for you to add JavaScript code to your page without actually having to type in the code. The code it inserts adds interactivity to your site, and is usually triggered by some user action. For example, when the user clicks on or hovers over a link, the behavior performs a task. Behaviors are commonly used to add rollovers, open new windows, check for plug-ins, and add navigation elements. You use the Behaviors panel to add, modify, remove, or reorder behaviors.

6 The new HTML5 form features, such as the Required attribute, and the new input types for e-mail, web address and telephone number, make it possible to process and validate forms using functionality built into modern web browsers instead of relying on JavaScript.

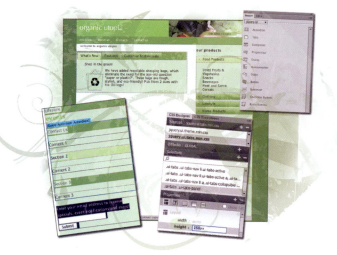

Adding Interactivity with the jQuery UI Library

The average user's expectations of how a website looks and feels has changed significantly over the years. Highly interactive websites that function more like traditional desktop applications are becoming more the norm. Dreamweaver CC includes jQuery UI Widgets: a library of interactive menus, panels, and animated user interfaces, that can be added to your projects and customized to take your pages to the next level.

Starting up

Before starting, make sure that your tools and panels are consistent by resetting your workspace. See "Resetting the Dreamweaver workspace" in the Starting up section of this book.

You will work with several files from the dw15lessons folder in this lesson. Make sure that you have loaded the dwlessons folder onto your hard drive from the supplied DVD. See "Loading lesson files" in the Starting up section of this book.

Before you begin, you need to create site settings that point to the dw15lessons folder. Go to Site > New Site, or, for details on creating a site, refer to Lesson 2, "Setting Up a New Site."

See Lesson 15 in action!

Use the accompanying video to gain a better understanding of how to use some of the features shown in this lesson. The video tutorial for this lesson can be found on the included DVD.

Introducing the jQuery UI Widgets

Dreamweaver CC introduces jQuery UI Widgets, giving you the ability to create powerful, interactive navigation and user interface elements with easy-to-use insert bar objects. The jQuery UI Widgets replace the Spry Widgets and include accordion menus, interactive controls, and tabbed containers, all of which harness the power of CSS for easy customization and styling to match any project. They are a great way to enhance navigation, organize content, and add dynamic style to your web pages.

The jQuery UI Library

Developed by the jQuery Foundation, jQuery UI is a curated set of user interface interactions, effects, widgets, and themes built on top of the jQuery JavaScript Library. Whether you're building highly interactive web applications or you just need to add a date picker to a form control, jQuery UI makes the task possible.

The jQuery UI Widgets included in Dreamweaver allow you to easily add the most frequently used features and functionality of this library.

A look at the project

In this lesson, you'll be completing the OrganicUtopia home page by using and customizing different jQuery UI Widgets. Before you get started, take a look at the completed version of the page to get an idea of what you'll be working toward.

1   In the Files panel, locate the **index_done.html** page in the done folder, and double-click it to open it.

2 To view the jQuery UI Widgets in action, choose File > Preview in Browser, and select a browser to preview the page. Depending on which browser you are using, you might see a message indicating that scripts are being blocked. Click the Allow Blocked Content button to allow the scripts to run.

The completed jQuery UI page contains numerous interactive elements.

3 Click the accordion-style menu found on the right to expand and contract different categories of products.

4 In the center of the page, locate the three tabs labeled *What's New*, *Featured*, and *Customer Testimonials*. Click each one to reveal a different content area—notice that the page doesn't refresh when you do this.

5 In the lower-right corner, click the Contact Us bar to show or hide a sign-up box.

6 Close the browser and return to Dreamweaver. Then, choose File > Close to close the current file.

The jQuery Tabbed panel

The jQuery Tabbed panel widget organizes content into several panels that you can toggle between by clicking tabs. This is a great way to organize items on a page: it saves space and can improve usability when used correctly.

Editing the content of the tabbed panels is easy; you can type directly within the tabs or containers in the document window. Tabbed panels can contain almost any type of content, including text, images, video, and animation.

You'll now add a jQuery Tabbed panel to your page to display three pieces of featured content.

1   From the Files menu, locate and open the **index_start.html** file for editing.

2   Choose File > Save As and save the page as **index_work.html** into your site's root folder.

3   Near the top of your page, select the placeholder text that reads {tabbed panels here}, and delete it. Leave your cursor at this position.

4   Click the Insert panel (if necessary) to expand it and choose the jQuery UI category. Locate and click the Tabs button (⊡) and click it to add a new tabs panel set.

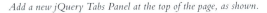

Add a new jQuery Tabs Panel at the top of the page, as shown.

5   Click inside the Tabs widget and then click <div#Tabs1> in the tag selector. Locate the Panels column in the center of the Property Inspector below. This shows you the current panels (and tabs) in your panel set, and lets you add new ones.

6   In the Property Inspector, click Tab 1 to activate it. On the page and within the tab, select the text *Tab 1* and type **What's New** in its place.

Select the text inside Tab 1 and rename it to What's New.

7   Select the text within Tab 2 and type **Featured**. Select the text within Tab 3 and type **Customer Testimonials**. Be careful as you move from one tab to the next: if the eye icon appears and you click it, the tab will open up. For now, you just want to rename the tab headings.

Next, you will add content into the areas inside each tab.

8   Below the tabbed panel, you'll see three paragraphs of content that you'll move and organize into the new panel group. Highlight the entire first paragraph, beginning with the headline Shop In the Green and be sure to include the recycle bag image. Choose Edit > Cut.

9   Select the placeholder text within the first tab (*Content 1*), then choose Edit > Paste to paste the content directly into the *What's New* panel. You will now place content into the Featured panel.

10 Place your cursor over the Featured tab but don't click yet.

Clicking the eye icon will bring that tab to the front.

11 Wait for the eye icon to appear and then click once to bring the tab to the front.

12 Select the *Featured Stuff!* heading, paragraph and the image of the couch and choose Edit > Cut. Select the placeholder text Content 2 and then choose Edit > Paste.

13 Repeat steps 7, 8, and 9; cut the remaining content (Our loyal customers) from the page and paste it into the third panel (Customer Testimonials).

14 Click the Live view button on the Document toolbar to preview the tabbed panel so far. Click each of the three tabs in order to view the contents of each. Click the Live view button again to return to Design view.

Your new jQuery UI Tabbed panels set after moving the page contents to each of the three tabs (shown in Live view).

15 Choose File > Save All and preview your page in the browser to see your tabs in action. The copy dependent files dialog box will appear. Click OK to accept.

jQuery UI support files

The first time you save a page that includes a jQuery UI Widget, you are prompted to save new and necessary files to your site. If you look at your Files panel, you will notice that a new jQuery Assets folder has been added to your site files. This folder contains essential JavaScript, CSS, and image files that style your new widget and make it work. *Be sure to copy this folder to your web server when publishing your site—your widgets will not work without it.*

16 Close the browser and return to Dreamweaver. Now we will style this panel to match the page theme.

Styling jQuery UI widgets with CSS

One of the many benefits of using the jQuery UI widgets is that they share a common set of style sheets that you can customize to match to the color scheme of your website. In this exercise, you will change the color of the panel headings and tabs so that they match the OrganicUtopia color scheme. Once applied, these styles will apply to other jQuery UI widgets that you will add to your page.

1 In the Sources pane of the CSS Designer panel, locate and select the style sheet named `jquery.ui.theme.min.css`, which was attached when you added the tabbed panel group. This is the primary style sheet on which all of the jQuery UI widget styles are based. The jQuery UI tabbed panel also has a specific style sheet that you can modify to change its appearance, as you will see later in this exercise.

2 Click the Selector named `.ui-widget-header` to display its properties. Click the Show set check box in the Properties Navigation bar to show all of the properties and then click the Background button to display the background properties. Click the `background-color` value, type **#88B036** (dark green), and then press Enter (Windows) or Return (Mac OS). This changes the color of the entire panel.

The jQuery UI Widgets also use an image to create a glossy appearance, which you will now disable to allow the green color to show through,

3   Locate the background-image property and click the Disable CSS Property button () to disable the background-image.

Modify the `.ui-widget-header` *rule to change the appearance of the tab background.*

4   Click the Selector beginning with `.ui-state-active,.ui-widget-content`. Click the `background-color` value, type **#CF9** (light green), and then press Enter (Windows) or Return (Mac OS). Disable the background-image as you did with the previous selector. This changes the color of the currently selected tab.

5   Click the Selector beginning with `.ui-state-hover,.ui-widget-content`. Click the background-color value, type **#88B036,** press Enter (Windows) or Return (Mac OS), and then disable the `background-image`. This sets the background color of the non-active tabs to the same shade of green as the active tab when you hover your mouse over them.

The panel's height is currently being defined by the amount of content. If you wanted to override this, you could set an explicit height for the panels.

6   Locate the file jquery.ui.tabs.min.css in the Sources pane of the CSS Designer panel. This style sheet specifies the style rules for the tabs control. Scroll to the bottom of the Selectors list and click the `.ui-tabs .ui-tabs-panel` selector.

7   Click the Layout button in the Properties Navigation bar and locate the `height` property. Click the drop-down menu to the right and choose `px` from the pop-up menu. In the new field that appears, type **250** (make sure px is specified) and then press Enter (Windows) or Return (Mac OS). This increases the overall height of the content panels.

You can override the height of the panels by modifying the `.ui-tabs` `.ui-tabs-pabel` *style.*

8   Choose File > Save All. Then preview your page in the browser to see your tabs in action. The copy dependent files dialog box will appear. Click OK to accept. There are a few other styles that you could modify here, but for now, you'll move on to the next jQuery UI Widget: the Accordion Panel.

jQuery Themeroller

Styling your jQuery UI Widgets can be a daunting task for a beginner web designer. Fortunately, the jQuery Foundation has provided an easy to use tool for creating custom themes that can be applied to your web pages.

The jQuery Themeroller allows you to change every aspect of the jQuery UI Widget styles and then export those changes as a custom theme. For more information on the jQuery Themeroller, visit *http://jqueryui.com/themeroller/*

The jQuery UI Accordion panel

At first glance, the jQuery Accordion panel resembles a standard vertical menu bar. As the name suggests, however, each item contracts and expands to reveal a content panel where you can add text and images. The accordion panel allows you to have only one panel open at a time.

Accordion panels are great for navigation, tree-style navigation or lists, or organizing related content (such as a Frequently Asked Questions list) into a clean, panel-style format. As with the other jQuery UI Widgets, the jQuery UI Accordion uses its own style sheet, which you can easily modify to make it match your current theme.

1   In the right column, locate the placeholder text that reads {accordion here}. Select and delete the placeholder text, and leave your cursor in place.

2   From the Insert panel, click and add a new Accordion at the cursor position. Click inside the Accordion widget and then click `<div#Accordion1>` in the tag selector.

The jQuery UI Accordion added to the sidebar.

The Property Inspector below now displays the properties for the new widget.

3   In the Property Inspector, you see a list of the panels currently in your accordion (Section 1, Section 2 and Section 3). Click the plus sign (+) above the list to add a new panel, for a total of four. A label displays above each new panel.

4   Click Section 4 in the Panels menu, and then press the down arrow twice to push Section 4 to the bottom of the list. This step is not mandatory, but it helps to keep your label order straight.

5 On your page, highlight the Section 1 text. Delete it and type **Food Products** in its place. Do *not* press Enter (Windows) or Return (Mac OS) after typing.

Type directly within the accordion labels to rename them.

6 Repeat step 5 for the Sections 2, 3, and 4, renaming them **Clothing**, **Home Products**, and **Lifestyle**, respectively. Next, you'll add content to each panel that corresponds to its label.

7 In your Files panel, locate the text folder and expand it. Double-click and open the file named **accordiontext.html**. This contains the text you'll add to the accordion panel.

8 Select the text below the Food Products heading (don't include the heading itself), and choose Edit > Cut. Return back to your **index_work.html** page.

9 Click inside the Accordion widget and then click <div#Accordion1> in the tag selector to ensure it is selected; then, in the Properties panel, click the Food Products panel to open it.

Open the Food Products panel by clicking it in the Properties panel.

Highlight the placeholder text on your page, and then choose Edit > Paste to paste it in the text from your content file.

10 Repeat steps 8 and 9 for the remaining paragraphs in the accordiontext.html file, pasting them into the *Clothing*, *Home Products*, and *Lifestyle* panels, respectively.

One of the benefits of using the jQuery UI widgets is that they share CSS files for common features. Since we changed the background, active and default states for these styles when inserting the Tabs panel, the Accordion has automatically received the same styles.

11 Choose File > Save All to save your page. If the Copy Dependent Files dialog box appears, click OK to allow Dreamweaver to copy any necessary files for your new widget to the site folder.

12 Choose File > Preview in Browser to see your new tabbed panel group in action. When you are done, close the browser and return to Dreamweaver.

Create a single collapsible panel

A collapsible panel displays or reveals its contents when clicked, and is a great way to hide information that doesn't need to be visible at all times. You can create a collapsible panel using a jQuery UI Accordion that displays a single panel and label.

You'll add a jQuery UI Accordion panel to create a collapsible e-mail sign-up form at the bottom of your page.

1 In the bottom half of the right column, locate the placeholder text that reads {Email signup box here}. Select and delete the placeholder text and leave your cursor positioned in its place.

2 On the Insert panel, locate and click the Accordion button to add a panel at your cursor position.

3 Select the text that reads Section 1 at the top of the panel, and type **Contact Us** in its place.

4 Below the panel, select the paragraph that reads Enter your e-mail address to receive specials, event notifications and more! and also select the form elements.

Select all the content immediately below the jQuery UI Accordion panel.

5 Choose Edit > Cut.

6 Select the text that reads Content 1 shown in the panel area of your accordion panel, and paste the content you cut in its place. The text and form field now appear inside the panel.

7 Click the blue tab above the Accordion panel: Accordion 2 to select it. In the Property Inspector, click *Section 2* in the Panels window to select it, and then click the minus sign (–) to delete the panel. Repeat these steps to delete Section 3 as well.

You can also define the default appearance of the accordion panel; in this case, you would like it to be able to be fully collapsed.

8 In the Property Inspector, click the Collapsible check box to set it so that the panel can be fully collapsed.

Use the Property Inspector to set the new panel's Collapsible state.

9 Choose File > Save All to save your page. When the Copy Dependent Files dialog box appears, click OK to allow Dreamweaver to copy any necessary files to your site folder.

10 Choose File > Preview in Browser, and select a browser to test your page and see your new Collapsible panel in action. When you click the Contact Us label, the sign-up text and form appears—click it again to close it.

11 Close the browser and return to Dreamweaver.

Self study

As you can see, creating highly interactive web pages is made easy with jQuery UI Widgets. Whether it's a fancy tabbed panel, or an accordion, the addition of a few widgets can make the difference between a good page and a great one. Further explore the different jQuery UI Widgets, and experiment with adding a DatePicker to your sidebar to display a calendar of events.

Practice working with the jQuery UI Tab Widget by adding a new tab to your existing panel or add another panel to the Accordion widget.

Review

Questions

1   What are the two primary jQuery UI Widgets that you can use for navigation and content presentation?

2   What is the significance of the jQueryAssets folder that is copied to your site when using a jQuery UI Widget?

3   What is the CSS file that contains the primary styles for all jQuery UI Widgets?

Answers

1   The jQuery UI Accordion panel and the jQuery UI Tabs panel.

2   It contains necessary support files such as CSS, JavaScript, and image files that your widgets need in order to function.

3   The `jquery.ui.theme.min.css` file contains the base CSS styles used by all of the jQuery UI Widgets.

What you'll learn in this lesson:

- Previewing your web page using window sizes
- Working with Media Queries
- Creating styles for a mobile device
- Working with Fluid Grids

Responsive Design and Layout for Mobile Devices

The Web is no longer only about desktop screens. Users of the Web are looking for their sites to function on many different size screens and devices. Dreamweaver has a few features designed to help you make your site compatible for mobile devices.

Starting up

Before starting, make sure that your tools and panels are consistent by resetting your workspace. See "Resetting the Dreamweaver workspace" in the Starting up section of this book.

You will work with several files from the dw16lessons folder in this lesson. Make sure that you have loaded the dwlessons folder onto your hard-drive from the supplied DVD. See "Loading lesson files" in the Starting up section of this book.

Before you begin, you need to create site settings that point to the dw16essons folder. Go to Site > New Site, or for details on creating a site, refer to Lesson 2, "Setting Up a New Site."

See Lesson 16 in action!

Use the accompanying video to gain a better understanding of how to use some of the features shown in this lesson. The video tutorial for this lesson can be found on the included DVD.

The rise of the mobile web

Creating websites has always presented certain challenges. Among these challenges is the fact that the people who visit your site might have different size monitors; therefore, the page layout that works well on one screen might not work so well on another screen. Another challenge is the different versions of web browsers that users might have. A page that looks one way in Internet Explorer 10 might not look the same way on Internet Explorer 6. Despite these challenges, the Web has thrived and grown tremendously because the benefits it offers far outweigh the downsides. Instant access to information, the ability to easily share information through hyperlinks and e-mail, the convenience of online shopping and payment: these are all major benefits.

The mobile web has all these benefits and more. The Web is now portable. It is no longer tethered to a desktop and is accessible wherever a user has a connection. In many cases, external peripherals, such as the keyboard and mouse, have dropped in favor of touchscreens' miniature keyboards. Built-in features such as GPS and cameras can also come into play, allowing the user to interact with the Web in new and different ways.

However, with all these benefits come new challenges. Portable screens also mean smaller screens. Consequently, your great desktop design suffers as it scales. Navigation that works well on the desktop could become difficult to click at ¼ the size. Other challenges include the still-limited bandwidth that currently exists when using a cellular network, the inability to play certain media such as Flash or web video, and web browser incompatibility, which is an issue that has not been resolved.

Dreamweaver tools for mobile layout

Dreamweaver CC has a few different tools for designers and developers who want to optimize their content for mobile devices. Before proceeding, you should learn about the different categories of the mobile web, which are explained next.

• **Native applications**

Smartphones, such as those on iOS, Android, and Windows Mobile platforms, have achieved a tremendous amount of growth and popularity since 2007 and the introduction of Apple's iPhone. Native applications, or apps, live on a user's device. Apps are tightly integrated with the Web and display content from the Web, but they are not exclusively dependent on the Web. Dreamweaver CC is capable of creating native applications for iOS, Android, and Blackberry; however, it does so with the help of the Phonegap framework. With PhoneGap and Dreamweaver CC, you start with an HTML and JavaScript document and are able to then build multiple apps for the different platforms. We do not cover PhoneGap functionality in this lesson or in this book. For more information go to *phonegap.com*. You can also launch the PhoneGap service in Dreamweaver CC by choosing Site > PhoneGap Build Service.

The PhoneGap service integrated with Dreamweaver CC allows you to build native applications for mobile devices.

- **Websites**

    All websites that can be accessed on a desktop browser can also be accessed on a mobile browser; therefore, every web page is part of the mobile web. However, as you will soon see, when a mobile web browser visits a website, the appearance of that site might be different from the desktop version. There are a few different explanations for this:

    — The appearance of a web page on a mobile device might be different than the desktop version due to the scaling effect that the device's web browser applies. Apple's popular mobile Safari browser, for example, scales a web page to fit the screen and also allows for touch gestures such as pinch, zoom, or swiping in order to navigate through a page. Websites that were never intended for mobile viewing will still have these features because they are built-in to the browser itself.

    — The appearance of a web page on a mobile device might be different than the desktop version because the designer or developer has created a separate version designed for mobile. All web browsers, whether they are mobile or desktop, advertise themselves with something called a user agent. The creator of a website can let in all desktop user agents to their standard site and redirect all mobile users to a separate mobile site.

Mobile website features in Dreamweaver

This lesson focuses on two methods for creating websites optimized for mobile. The first method focuses on using CSS3 Media Queries. In the exercise for this method, you will take the existing layout created in Lesson 6 and create a layout optimized for a mobile device, such as a smartphone. The second method focuses on the Fluid Grid Layout feature in Dreamweaver CC. This method also uses CSS3 Media Queries, but in a slightly different and more advanced way than the first exercise.

Dreamweaver does its best to simplify the process used to create mobile optimized sites, but you should note that this is the most advanced and difficult lesson in this book. You should also realize that at the time of this writing, there is no application on the market that makes designing a website for multiple screens easy. We firmly believe that a thorough understanding of the fundamentals of HTML, particularly CSS, is important when working with your sites. Therefore, once you have learned some of these fundamentals, you will find the tools in Dreamweaver to be extremely helpful and efficient.

Previewing your web page using window sizes

Dreamweaver CC allows you to preview your web page as it would appear on different screen sizes. Specifically, this preview shows you your design in three different views by default: one for the desktop, and the other two for the smaller screens found in smartphone and tablet devices. Given that mobile device screens come in different sizes, you can also customize these views to any resolution you want. Additionally, Dreamweaver takes advantage of CSS3 Media Queries to let you build individual style sheets customized for each view. If you have not worked with Media Queries before, this exercise is designed to introduce you to the concept and also to help you learn how to use them in Dreamweaver.

1   In the Files panel, double-click the media_queries folder and then double-click **16_index.html** to open it. The basic design here is based on the one you created in Lesson 6 and uses floats and clears to create columns.

2   Choose File > Preview in Browser and select a browser. This page has a fixed-width size of 960 pixels and works well on most desktop monitor resolutions.

To preview this page as it would appear on a mobile device such as a Smartphone or tablet device, you can use Dreamweaver CC's Window Size option.

3   Return to Dreamweaver and locate the three small buttons at the bottom–right corner of the document window.

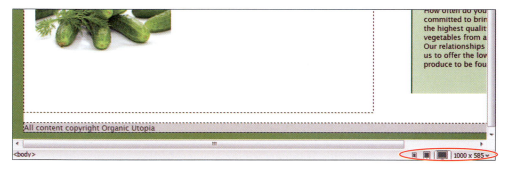

You can find the Window Sizes buttons just above the Property Inspector.

Each icon represents one of three common window sizes; Mobile (480 × 800), Tablet (768 × 1024) and Desktop (1000w). Note that the height of the Desktop view might be different on your screen but the width will always default to 1000 pixels wide.

Dreamweaver's window size previews provide three views by default: Phone, Tablet, and Desktop.

As you can see from the previews, the Mobile view and the Tablet view are not wide enough to fit your fixed-width page. You should note that the window sizes are not an emulator. (An emulator is software that attempts to imitate a hardware phone or other computer device.) Most modern smartphones would actually scale your entire page to fit in the browser window. The window sizes are showing you the page based on a strict interpretation of the viewport.

A viewport, as it relates to mobile devices, is best described as a viewing area on the screen through which a user views a web page.

4 Click the Mobile Size button in the lower-right corner of the document window. Select View > Window Size; the default window sizes appear in a pop-up menu. The default value for the Mobile viewport is *480 × 800 SmartPhone*. Click the Tablet size button to the right of the Mobile size button. Select View > Window Sizes again; the default values for the Tablet viewport is *768w by 1024h*.

These numbers are not arbitrary; the Mobile viewport width is 480 and the Tablet viewport width is 768 because these are typical screen resolutions for devices such as the iPhone, iPad, and others.

Screen resolutions actually do vary among devices, but Dreamweaver has chosen these as standards.

5 You can change the viewport sizes by clicking Edit Sizes… to bring up the Window Sizes category in the Dreamweaver Preferences panel; however, we recommend you use the default sizes until you become more familiar with the reasons for modifying the sizes.

These viewport sizes are important because you can create unique style sheets that will only apply to viewports of a certain size. For example, for the smallest viewport you might want a layout that is only a single column, instead of the current three-column layout design used for the desktop layout. You can do this in Dreamweaver using window sizes and a related feature called Media Queries.

Media Queries defined

Media Queries in Dreamweaver take advantage of a feature in CSS3, which is the latest version of CSS. This feature is part of the CSS3 specification called CSS3 Media Queries. Media Queries are a way of delivering different page layouts to users based on the capabilities of their screen or screens.

You can think of a CSS3 media query as a combination of HTML and CSS syntax that examines the capability of a user agent, typically a web browser, and lets you send it styles based on certain values. The most common capability queried is the width of a screen or a mobile device; other capabilities, such as the device orientation (landscape or portrait), can also be detected. Since media queries detect the capabilities of a user's screen and serve styles that fit that screen, they are well-suited for today's web environment with its different monitor resolutions. The following diagram shows a simplified version of how media queries work: each device gets a specific style sheet based on the size of its screen.

Unique style sheets are delivered to users depending on their screen capabilities.

Here is a different example: suppose a user has a smartphone with a screen resolution of 480 pixels wide by 800 pixels high, and the phone is in portrait mode (vertical). This user visits a website that uses media queries. When the user visits the site, the media queries built into the page detect the capabilities of the phone and serve it a specific style sheet with a single column layout. When the user rotates the phone into landscape position, the change is detected and the media queries send a style sheet designed for a 800 pixel-wide screen (the layout might have two columns instead of one).

From the perspective of users, they are simply getting the ideal layout for the screen size they are using. Users might notice this change in layout momentarily as they rotate their screen or visit the site on different devices, but the overall goal is to improve their experience on the site by improving aspects such as readability, navigation, and presentation of content.

For more details on the technical aspects of CSS Media Queries, visit http://www.w3.org/TR/css3-mediaqueries/.

Creating media queries

As noted earlier, media queries are a relatively new advance in web design and are part of the CSS3 specification. (Most of the CSS you have been working on throughout this book has been part of the CSS2.0 specification.) There are many benefits to using media queries, but their use is a tradeoff because they are not fully supported by all browsers (particularly older browsers).

Dreamweaver CC adds Media Query support through the new CSS Designer panel. You create the Media Queries in the @Query pane and the code is added to either an internal or external style sheet. In this exercise, you'll learn how to create new Media Queries for a Mobile layout and a Tablet layout.

1   Click the CSS Designer tab to open the CSS Designer panel.

2   Click the Add CSS Source button in the Sources menu bar (⊞) and choose Create a New CSS File from the pop-up menu. The Create a New CSS File dialog box opens.

3   Click the Browse button to bring up the Save Style Sheet File As window. Navigate to your site root folder then type **mobile.css** as the File name and click Save to return to the Create New CSS File window.

4   Click OK to create the new CSS File.

5   Repeat steps 2–4 to create another new style sheet. Save the second sheet as **tablet.css**.

6   The two new style sheets now show up in the Sources pane of the CSS Designer panel. You will now attach Media Queries to each style sheet so that they are utilized for specific screen resolutions.

7   Click **mobile.css** in the Sources pane and then click the Add Media Query button in the @Media menu bar. The Define Media Query window is displayed.

The Conditions section of this window allows you to specify the parameters that must be met for a browser to use this style sheet. The first condition listed will apply the Media Query if the media field is set to screen when the browser reports its user-agent information.

8   Place your cursor over the blank area to the right of the screen drop-down menu and Dreamweaver will display the Add condition button (➕) and Remove condition button (➖).

The Conditional Usage section of the Define Media Query dialog box.

9   Click the Add condition button (➕) to add another condition. The next condition will appear as orientation landscape. Click the down arrow to the right of landscape and choose portrait. Most mobile devices are used in the portrait mode, facing up and down, and when not used facing up and down, referred to as landscape mode, their width in pixels is about as wide as a tablet.

10   Hover your cursor to the right of the second condition and click the Add condition button again. This time the condition will appear as min-width. Usually a condition might have a `min-width` but in this case we only care to show the styles in mobile.css if the screen width is reported as 480px or less. Click the down arrow to the right of min-width and choose max-width from the menu.

11 Type **480** in the width text box and click anywhere outside the field. Notice that the code: window lists the Media Query using the `@media` keyword and the conditions that you selected.

Define Media Query

Please define the media query you would like to use below:

Conditions

media	▼	screen	▼	AND **+ −**
orientation	▼	portrait	▼	AND
max-width	▼	480	px ▼	

Code

```
@media screen and (orientation:portrait) and
(max-width:480px){
}
```

Help   Cancel   OK

The three conditions for the Media Query for mobile.css have been set.

Click OK. You have now specified the conditions which will be used to apply the styles in the mobile.css style sheet. You will now create the Media Query for **tablet.css** to define the conditions for tablet devices.

12 Click tablet.css in the Sources pane of the CSS Designer panel then click the Add New Media Query button in the @Media menu bar.

13 Click the Add condition button (**+**) to the right of the media screen condition.

14 Click the down arrow to the right of landscape and choose portrait. Most tablet devices are also used in the portrait mode and when not used facing up and down, they are about as many pixels wide as a desktop or laptop computer screen.

15 Hover your cursor to the right of the second condition and click the Add condition button again. This time the condition will appear as `min-width`.

16 Type **481** in the min-width text box and click the Add condition button once again. The final condition is max-width.

17 Type **768** in the max-width text box and click OK.

*The three conditions for Media Query for **tablet.css** have been set.*

Specifying the min and max width creates a Media Query suitable for tablets, which typically have widths of over the 480px of a mobile phone and narrower than the 768px of a desktop or laptop computer.

The preceding steps might seem long, but you only need to do them the first time you set up media queries. Once you have them set up, you have a framework for creating unique styles for screens of different sizes.

Creating a layout optimized for mobile

Now that you have prepared your site with Media Queries and associated style sheets, you can begin using them. The general principle of CSS3 Media Queries is that you use the exact same names for the style rules in your mobile and tablet style sheets as the style rules in your main style sheet. By using the same names, you override the main style wherever needed. For example, you will first apply this rule with the ID style called #container. In your main style sheet, this ID style defines the width of the entire page as 960 pixels. In your mobile style sheet, you will create another rule with the name #container, but you will set the width to 100% for this style.

In the following exercise, you will only work with the mobile style sheet; use the tablet style sheet for practice.

1 Click the Mobile window size button in the bottom right corner of the document window. From all appearances, the preview looks exactly the same as it did at the beginning of the lesson, and yet all the work you did in the last few exercises will now begin to pay off.

2 In the Sources pane of the CSS Designer, click the **mobile.css** file and then click the Media Query in the @Media pane. The Selectors list for this style sheet is blank as there are currently no styles in this sheet. Your first task is to change the width of your container.

3 In the CSS Designer panel, click the Add Selector button, and then in the Selector pane, type **#container**. Press Enter (Windows) or Return (Mac OS).

4 Click the Add CSS Property button (⊞) in the Properties menu bar, then click the Layout button (▦) in the Properties Navigation bar. Locate the width property and double-click the placeholder in the width box, then type **100%** and press Enter (Windows) or Return (Mac OS) to change the width.

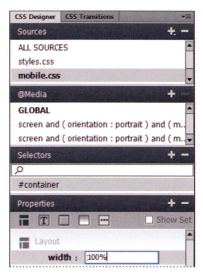

Creating a new rule for the container ID in your mobile.css style sheet.

5 When viewing your page in Design view using the Mobile window size, you will see your page has dramatically changed in the Mobile viewport. By setting the width of the container to 100%, it will only be as wide as the viewport and most of the content within will have shifted or is overlapping. For example, the background image of the vegetables is now under the logo. Scroll down the page and note that your side columns have shifted.

The Mobile view shows the effect of changing the container width to 100%.

As you can see, creating a page optimized for mobile is not as simple as setting the container width to 100%. The page has changed, and you will need to modify it. The layout elements inside the container need to be addressed as well, since most of them have height or width values set as pixels. Also, some of the elements are floating. To fix the rest of the page, you will add rules that remove floats and override any explicit pixel width or height value. The goal is to create a single column layout.

Tips and strategies for optimizing pages for mobile

The following is a list of tips and strategies to consider when designing pages for mobile. Navigating and using websites on smaller screens or screens that are touch-enabled is very different from the desktop, and you should take it into consideration.

- Navigation should be at or near the top of the screen to be easily accessible. Repeat navigation at the bottom of all your pages so the user does not have to scroll up after reading a page.

- For touchscreen devices, use a large target size for navigation links to prevent accidental clicking.

- Touchscreen devices do not always have a hover capability as triggered by the mouse cursor on desktops. Plan your styles accordingly and avoid rollover styles.

- Avoid image-based navigation; use list-based navigation styled with CSS.

- Single-column layout is much easier to navigate and read on a smaller screen. A general strategy for accomplishing this with media queries is by removing floated elements and most layout containers with fixed width and height pixel values.

6 You will now add more styles to your mobile.css style sheet and create a single-column layout.

7 Click the **mobile.css** file in the Sources pane of the CSS Designer panel. You'll now add styles for the header section.

8 In the Selector pane, click the Add Selector button, and then in the Selector text box, type **header**. Press Enter (Windows) or Return (Mac OS).

9 Click the Add CSS Property button in the Properties menu bar and then click the Background button. Click the text label *url* under the background-image category and choose none from the drop-down menu. This will remove the image of the vegetables, which works well in the desktop version, but not in the mobile version.

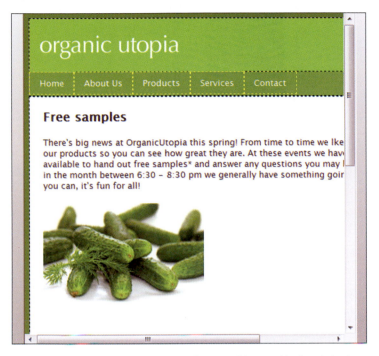

Setting the background-image to none removes the image of the vegetables from the header.

10 Choose File > Save all.

Your next step is to address the styles of the navigation bar. Typically, CSS navigation bars have a few different rules that you need to modify.

Creating styles for navigation and a single-column layout

Creating easy-to-use mobile navigation is very important because you want users to read your content and not be frustrated by content that's difficult to access. The hit target for mobile navigation should be large enough for touchscreens and easy to read. You'll add these styles now.

1 Click the mobile.css file in the Sources pane of the CSS Designer panel and then click the Media Query in the @Media pane. In the Selectors pane, click the Add Selector button, and then in the Selector name box, type **nav** and press Enter (Windows) or Return (Mac OS).

2 In the Properties pane, click the Text button and choose the keyword medium in the font-size property drop-down menu. This action prevents issues when there are differences between device screen resolutions.

3 Click the Layout button, and set the height property to auto to override the fixed height of 36 pixels from the original style sheet.

You will need to do more work to make the navigation look better. There are often different rules for CSS navigation menus, so you also need to modify these.

4 In the Selector pane of the CSS Designer panel, click the Add Selector button, and then in the Selector name box, type **nav ul li**. This targets the style of the list items in the nav bar.

Create a compound selector to make a style for the navigation list items.

Press Enter (Windows) or Return (Mac OS).

5 Click the Layout button in the Properties Navigation bar, locate the float property, and choose none. This overrides the float:left rule set in your original style sheet.

6 Notice that by setting the float property of the list items to none, the list reverts to its default positioning, which is vertical.

Changing the float value of list items to none creates a vertical navigation instead of a horizontal one.

Your page is starting to improve: the navigation is now a single column. Place your cursor over the links and notice that the original hover styles are still present. One of the benefits of CSS3 Media Queries is that the original styles that have no overrides are still used.

Scroll down and notice that you still need to improve other areas: the main content and the sidebar still appear broken, but this is relatively easy to fix.

7 Click the mobile.css file in the Sources pane of the CSS Designer panel and then click the Media Query in the @Query pane.

8 In the Selectors menu bar click the Add Selector button, and then in the Selector name box type **#main**. Press Enter (Windows) or Return (Mac OS).

9 In the Properties Navigation bar, click the Layout button, scroll down to the float property, and choose none. This overrides the `float:left` property and value set in your original style sheet.

10 Scroll to the width property menu and choose auto.

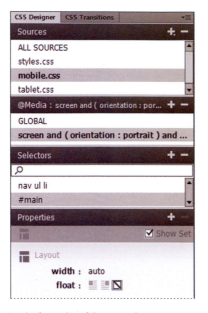

Set the float value of the main column to none and the width to auto.

11 Repeat Steps 8, 9, and 10, but use the Selector name **sidebar** instead of #main.

12 Click the Background button ( ) and set the background-color to white (#ffffff).

13 Choose File > Save All Related Files. Scroll down your page and notice that your content section and sidebar now fill the screen from edge to edge. Also, notice that by removing the floats, your sidebar is now located below the main content.

14 Click the Design button to switch to this view. Then click the Live view button. Live view uses the WebKit rendering engine, which is the same as Apple Safari and Google Chrome browser.

15 Click the Mobile window size button located on the bottom right of your document window; your window will automatically adjust to this size and your media query file will be applied. This will also work in the Design view; however, you should place your cursor over the navigation. Note that in Live view the rollovers are active.

You can also preview your page in the browser and reduce the width of the window. Note that some browsers will not let you make the window that small. The phone.css is designed for phone browsers, not desktop browsers.

Preview in Browser. When the width is less than 480, the layout switches to the mobile.css styles.

You can create and add other styles to the mobile style sheet. You now have the foundations of how to create different layouts using media queries in Dreamweaver CC, and apply them to the tablet style sheet. You can close the currently open files; you will not need them.

The basics of Fluid Grid Layout

Dreamweaver's Fluid Grid Layout expands on the concept of media queries. To understand fluid grids, think about page layout. Remember that the layout you began working with at the beginning of this lesson was a fixed-width layout set to a width of 960 pixels wide. Fixed-width layouts are very common on the Web because they are reliable to work with and control. However, one of the downsides of fixed-width layouts is that they do not respond well to different size screens. Many designers feel that fixed-width layouts do not reflect the nature of the Web and that flexible or fluid layouts are better suited for content. Flexible layouts generally use percentages or em units to define the various sections on the page. For example, the width of a sidebar might be defined as 33% of the page rather than 450 pixels.

If you would like to see the results of this exercise before you begin, navigate to the done folder within the fluidgrid folder, open the **index.html** *file within a browser that supports media queries and resize the browser window.*

1   Chose File > New …; the New Document window appears. Click the Fluid Grid Layout category on the left side of the window to display the Fluid Grid Layout settings.

The first major change you will see is that Fluid Grids actually create three layouts at a time: Mobile, Tablet, and Desktop. Each of these layouts is defined as media queries; in this way, the settings are very similar to the ones you saw in the last exercise. However, notice that fluid grids use media queries, and they add grid structure to help you align content on the page.

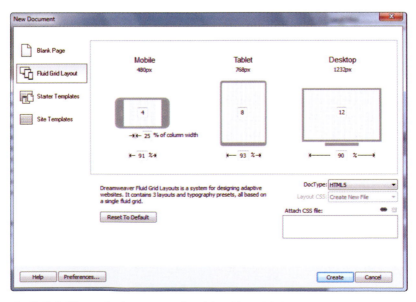

The Fluid Grid Layout has layout settings for mobile, tablet, and desktop.

Each of the three layouts has a number of columns that will be created by default. The Mobile layout has four columns, the Tablet layout has 8 columns, and the Desktop layout has 12 columns. You can type any number of columns you want for each type of layout, but for now, you will use the defaults. Notice that the mobile layout has a unique setting, 25% of column width. This represents the space between each of the columns, otherwise known as the *gutter width*. Additionally, each of the three layouts has a default page width listed at the bottom. For mobile, this is 91%; for tablet, this is 93%; and for the desktop, this is 90%. This means all the layouts will have a small amount of padding on the left and right sides.

If you do not see these values, click the Reset to Default button.

2   Click Create; you will be prompted to generate a new external style sheet. Navigate to your dw16lessons folder, locate the fluidgrid folder, save this style sheet as **base.css**, and then click OK. A new document opens; you are in the unique fluid grid mode with a five column layout and a default grid layout div element with placeholder text. You'll learn more about both of these features shortly. For now, we'll discuss the structure of this page and the related files created for Fluid Grid Layouts.

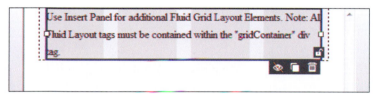

The default grid layout with a fluid grid layout div and placeholder content.

3   Choose File > Save and navigate to the fluidgrids folder if necessary. Save this document as **index.html** and click OK. You will be prompted to copy two dependent files: boilerplate.css and respond.min.js. You'll learn more about the role of these files shortly; for now, click OK. The two files will be saved into your fluidgrids folder.

Working with Fluid Grids is different from what you might be used to. This initial view of five columns is the Mobile view for your web page. There are two other views as well: Tablet and Desktop. These views can be accessed by clicking any of the three icons.

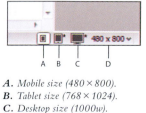

A. Mobile size (480 × 800).
B. Tablet size (768 × 1024).
C. Desktop size (1000w).
D. Window Size.

4   Click the Tablet Size icon; the size of the window changes to 768 by 1024 and displays 8 columns.

5   Click the Desktop Size icon; the size of the window changes to 1000 wide; the height is set to the vertical space on your screen.

Regardless of the view you are in, you should note that the columns are visual aids only and are designed to help you align the Fluid Grid Layout Divs.

6   In the document toolbar, click the Switch to Fluid Grid View button to turn off the guides. The reason for turning off the guides is to see your page design better; however, these guides are key to working with the Fluid Grid feature, click the Switch to Fluid Grid View button again to turn them back on.

7   Click the Mobile Size icon to return to the default five-column view. Dreamweaver opens this view initially because one of the foundations of Fluid Grid Layout is a concept called "mobile first." The basic idea is that when designing a website from scratch, you start with the mobile design and layout first, and then move upward to the larger tablet and desktop sizes.

The foundations of "mobile first" design

Mobile first is a concept in web design that has been gaining popularity among designers in recent years. The basic idea is that when you are creating a new website design, you begin working with the mobile design first, and then move on to your larger screen designs. The rationale is that technique forces you to identify your most important or core features first, thus ensuring that they are folded into the mobile experience for your users.

The traditional technique of starting with your complex desktop layout and removing or restyling parts until you arrive at your mobile layout can lead to design compromises and inefficient styles. By incorporating mobile first concepts into Fluid Grid Layouts, Dreamweaver is helping to promote the adoption and importance of designing for different size screens.

Creating your mobile layout

In the first half of this lesson, you covered the basics of using media query files. Note that you are still using media queries with Fluid Grid Layouts. However in this case, rather than dividing your media queries into separate style sheets, the rules for your three layouts are gathered in one style sheet (in this case, base.css). Specifically, as you begin to create the styles for the single column layout in this exercise, keep in mind that all these styles will automatically be applied to your larger tablet and desktop layouts.

1   Click in the default div that was created by Dreamweaver. In the Properties panel, locate the Div ID field, select the default value, and type **header.**

Change the name of the default fluid grid layout div to **header**.

2   Select the placeholder text inside the header and delete it. Choose Insert > Image. Navigate to the images folder inside the fluidgrid folder and locate the ou_logo.png file. Click Open (Mac OS) or OK (Windows). Click OK and then type **logo** in the Alt text field in the Property Inspector.

You just added the image to a Fluid Grid Layout Div Tag. Dreamweaver always adds a Fluid Grid Layout Div Tag to your page when you start a new Fluid Grid Layout. You can add new ones to your page as needed.

3   Click the Insert tab to bring up the Insert Panel and choose Structure from the drop-down menu. Then, in the Insert panel, click the Div button; the Insert Div dialog box appears. Make sure the Insert as Fluid Element check box is checked then click the ID radio button and type **introcontent** in the ID field, then click OK.

A new fluid grid layout div appears below the header. Select the placeholder text and then press delete to remove it.

4 In your files panel, double-click the intro_content.html document. Select everything on the page by pressing Ctrl+A (Windows) or Command+A (Mac OS) and then copy it. Toggle back to your index page, click inside the introcontent div, and press Ctrl+V (Windows) or Command+V (Mac OS) to paste it.

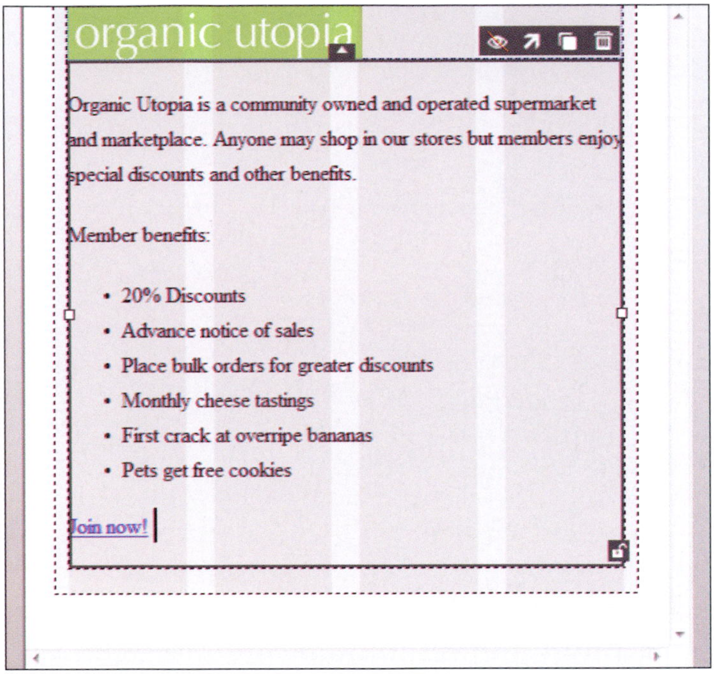

The introcontent fluid grid div with content.

5 Click the edge of your introcontent div to select it. Then, in the Insert panel, click Div button and the Insert Div dialog box appears. Make sure that the Insert as Fluid Element check box is checked, then choose the ID radio button and type **secondarycontent** for the ID and then click OK.

A new fluid grid layout div appears below the header. Select the placeholder text that appears and delete it.

6 In your files panel, double-click the secondary_content.html document. Select everything on the page by pressing Ctrl+A (Windows) or Command+A (Mac OS) and then copy it. Toggle back to your index page, click inside the secondarycontent div, and press Ctrl+V (Windows) or Command+V (Mac OS) to paste it.

7 Click the edge of your secondarycontent div to select it. Then, in the Insert panel, click the Div button. In the Insert Div dialog box, make sure that the Insert as Fluid Element check box is checked, choose the ID radio button and type **events** for the ID, and then click OK.

8 In your files panel, double-click the events.html document. Select everything on the page by pressing Ctrl+A (Windows) or Command+A (Mac OS) and then copy it. Toggle back to your index page, click inside the events div, and press Ctrl+V (Windows) or Command+V (Mac OS) to paste it.

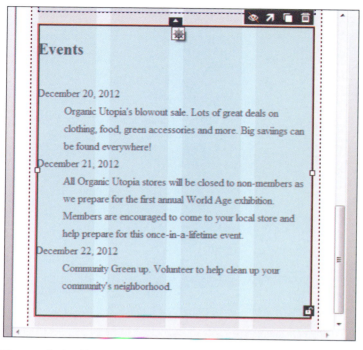

The events fluid grid layout div is located below secondarycontent.

9 Click the edge of your events div to select it. Then, in the Insert panel, click the Div object; a dialog box appears. Type **footer** in the ID field, then make sure the Insert as Fluid Element check box is checked and click OK. You'll leave the placeholder content in here for now.

10 Within the secondarycontent div, click below the heading *Celebrate Vegetables*. Choose Insert > Image. Navigate to your images folder, select **beets_fluid.jpg**, and click Open (Mac OS) or OK (Windows) and click OK. Type **beets** in the Alternate Text field in the Property Inspector. The image is inserted below the heading.

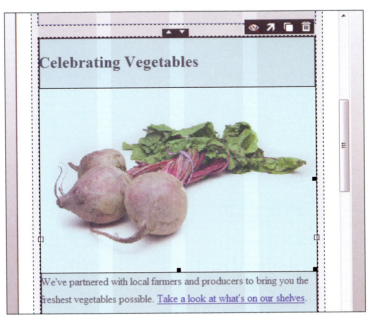

An image added below your heading.

11 Choose File > Save All.

This is the foundation of a mobile layout. There is much more you could do in regards to styling, but now that you have a basic layout with content, you'll take a look at the way Fluid Grid Layouts work with additional layouts.

Creating a tablet layout

You have seen the three views that are part of Fluid Grid layouts, and you just created a simple single-column layout for a mobile device. Note that Dreamweaver created styles for the mobile view, the tablet view, and the desktop view. In fact, it has placed these styles in three separate media queries (one for mobile, one for tablet, one for desktop). You'll now modify your mobile layout so that it is better suited for a tablet device.

1 Click the Tablet Size icon to switch to this view. As you begin adjusting the layout to two columns, keep in mind that *the new styles will only apply to the tablet layout.*

2   Click the edge of the introcontent div to select it and place your cursor on the anchor point located on the right of the div. Click and drag to the left to begin resizing the container.

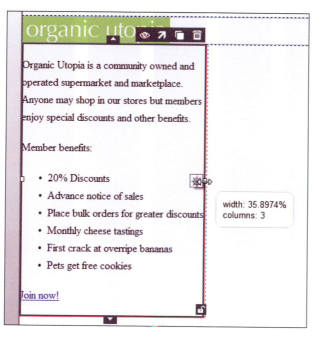

Resize a fluid grid div by clicking and dragging the right edge.

Note as you drag that the indicator shows you the width and how many columns you have. Drag until you reach three columns and approximately 35% width.

3   Click the edge of the secondarycontent div to select it and notice on the top-right corner there is an arrow. Hover over this for a moment, and the tool tip indicates the arrow will move the div up a row. Click the arrow; notice that the div doesn't shift position. This is because the div is currently too wide, so you will need to resize the div in order to fit in the space above.

4   Place your cursor on the resize anchor point (on the right edge of the div) and drag to the left. When the div width reaches five columns, click the arrow button in the top-right corner and it will jump up into the space above. If necessary, resize the div until it is four columns wide.

5 Now place your cursor on the anchor point on the left edge of this div and wait for the tooltip. This indicates that it will shift the div. Click and drag to the right until the right edge of the div snaps to the furthest column.

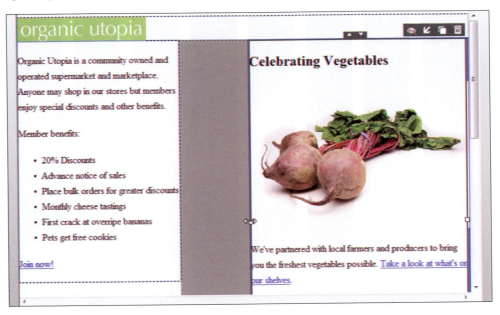

Reposition or shift a fluid grid div by clicking and dragging the left edge.

At this point, you have the basics of a two-column layout, but for the tablet view only.

6 Click the Mobile Size icon to switch back to this view; note that the mobile layout has remained in its single column view. Click the Tablet Size icon to see the two-column view you just created, and then click the Desktop view. This view is still using the single column layout; it has not been affected by the changes made in the Tablet view.

7 Choose File > Save All to save your work, but keep this document open. In the next exercise, you will build a three-column layout for the desktop.

Creating a three-column fluid layout for the desktop

In keeping with the mobile first philosophy, the desktop is the last design you will work on.

1 Click the Desktop view icon if you are not currently in this view.

2 Click the edge of the introcontent div to select it, and place your cursor on the anchor point located on the right of the div. Click and drag to the left to begin resizing the container. Resize this div until you reach four columns.

3 Click the edge of the secondarycontent div to select it and click the arrow on the top right. This will attempt to move the div up a row, but as before, the div is too wide and you have to resize it in order to fit in the space above.

4   Place your cursor on the anchor point located on the right of the div and drag it to the left. When the div is narrow enough, it will jump up into the space above. Continue resizing the div until it snaps to four columns, which is a width of approximately 32.3%.

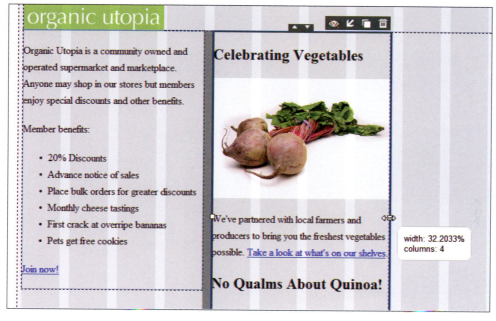

Resize a fluid grid div by clicking and dragging the right edge.

Now click the arrow in the top navigation box on the div to reposition it next to the introcontent div.

5   Click the edge of the events div to select it. As with the other divs, you need to resize it in order to fit into the available space.

6   Place your cursor on the anchor point located on the right side of the div and drag to the left. When the div is narrow enough click the arrow icon in the tool bar at the top of the div and it will jump up into the space above. If necessary, resize the div until it snaps to four columns, which is a width of approximately 32.3%, then click the arrow button in the navigation bar at the top of the div to shift it up to the top row.

7   Choose File > Save All. At this point you have the foundations of a fluid and adaptive layout.

8   Click the Live button to see your layout in the Live View. When using Fluid Grid Layouts, the Live View behaves a bit differently. Typically, the Live View acts as a web browser and only allows you to view your content, not edit it. However, you can see that the Visual Aids are still visible. Additionally, if you click the edge of any of your divs, it will become active and you can then adjust their size or shift them as needed.

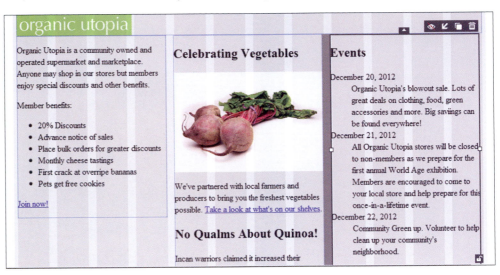

In the Live view, the Fluid Grid layout is still visible and the layout divs can be adjusted as well.

If you need to see your layout in action, the browser is still the best place.

9   Choose File > Preview in Browser; your page will load in the three column layout view (most likely). Slowly reduce the width of your web browser and note how the columns of text begin to resize. This is the fluid part of fluid layouts: because your columns are defined by percentages, not pixels, this is the expected behavior. At the same time, the amount of space between these columns also remains proportional.

10 Keep reducing the width of the browser; it will eventually switch to the two-column layout. Continue reducing the width of the browser until it switches to the single-column Mobile layout.

11 Continue resizing your browser window back and forth between the three views, and pay particular attention to the image in the middle column. This image is also fluid; in other words, it will resize according to how much space it has available. This is most obvious in the single-column mobile view.

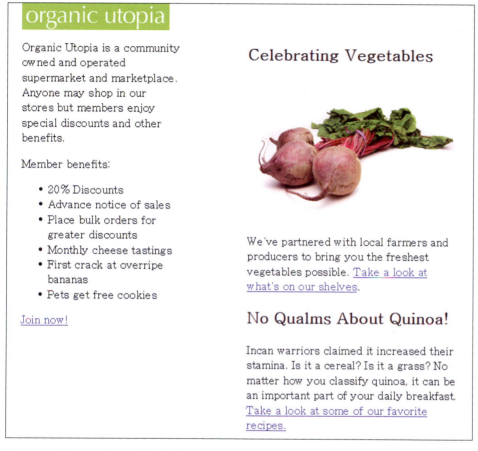

The images added to your layout will be fluid or responsive by default.

This fluid image behavior is actually made possible by the inclusion of the boilerplate. css support file that all Fluid Grid Layouts include by default. (You saw these dependent files created in step 1 of the first exercise.)

12 Close your browser and return to Dreamweaver. You will now take a look at how to style your pages.

Looking deeper into the dependent files

When you create a fluid grid layout, the two dependent files that are created are boilerplate.css and respond.min.js. For the most part, you will not touch any of these files. If you are familiar with what they do and need to modify them, you can.

boilerplate.css: This is a popular framework for modern websites that has been customized and modified for Dreamweaver's fluid grid layout documents. Essentially, you can think of this as a well-tested and documented CSS reset file that pays special attention to the formatting of page styles in older browsers and supports some of the newer media query features. For detailed information on this page, visit *http://html5boilerplate.com/docs/The-style/*.

respond.min.js: This external JavaScript file provides support for CSS3 media queries in web browsers that do not support them natively. For detailed information on what this code does, visit *https://github.com/scottjehl/Respond*.

Styling elements in your fluid grid layout

The layout you created is fairly minimal at the moment. The method of creating and applying styles is not new when working with Fluid Grids; however, there is added complexity you have to take into account. Remember that every time you create a style, it is not just created in one place, but three. To see how to manage this, you'll style the header of your page.

1 Click the Mobile size icon to view your single-column layout.

2   Look within your CSS Designer Panel and click **base.css** file in the Sources pane. If necessary expand the Selectors pane to see all the rules.

The list of rules within your base.css style.

3   Starting at the top of the list, scroll down until you find the first #header style. After you locate it, keep scrolling down the list to find a second #header rule. Continue scrolling down through the list to find the third #header style.

Although it is not immediately obvious, the first header rule sets the style for the mobile styles, the second header sets the style for the tablet, and the third header rule sets the style for the desktop.

4 Click the first `#header` rule. In the Properties Navigation bar, click the Background button. In the background-color field, type **#b1d564** and press Enter (Windows) or Return (Mac OS). This is the same shade of green as the background color of the organic utopia logo.

Applying a background color to the header.

5 In the Design view, note that your header is now the same color as the background. Click the Tablet and Desktop views, and note that they have inherited the same background color.

Generally, this is not a problem since you don't want to style the header three different times. However, there might be times when you do want the style of an element to be different in your tablet or desktop views.

6 In your CSS styles panel, double-click the second `#header` style (the one for the tablet). Click the background category, then click the Background-color swatch, and then choose a dark red (the exact shade is not important). Click OK.

This header style is now specific only to the Tablet view. Click the Tablet view to see it.

7   Choose File > Save All, and then preview your page in the browser. Resize your browser window until it switches to the tablet view layout. You will see the background color of the header change.

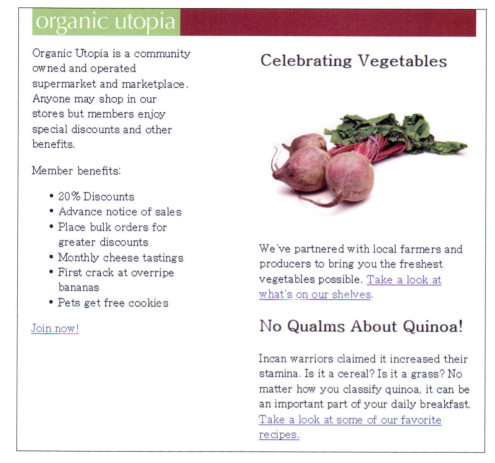

organic utopia

Organic Utopia is a community owned and operated supermarket and marketplace. Anyone may shop in our stores but members enjoy special discounts and other benefits.

Member benefits:

- 20% Discounts
- Advance notice of sales
- Place bulk orders for greater discounts
- Monthly cheese tastings
- First crack at overripe bananas
- Pets get free cookies

Join now!

Celebrating Vegetables

We've partnered with local farmers and producers to bring you the freshest vegetables possible. Take a look at what's on our shelves.

No Qualms About Quinoa!

Incan warriors claimed it increased their stamina. Is it a cereal? Is it a grass? No matter how you classify quinoa, it can be an important part of your daily breakfast. Take a look at some of our favorite recipes.

The header in your tablet view has a different background color style.

Typically, you wouldn't change the background color style of a header. This exercise was just a demonstration of how to apply styles for specific layouts.

8   Close your browser and return to Dreamweaver. Double-click the second #header rule in the CSS Styles panel, click the background color property, and remove the color you added in Step 5. Click OK.

9   Choose File > Save All to finish the lesson.

Self study

Using your new knowledge of media queries and fluid grid layouts in Dreamweaver, perform the following tasks to build your experience:

To practice with media queries, return to your exercise file within the media queries file, and start building styles for the **tablet.css** style sheet. Answer some of the following questions: should navigation in a tablet layout reflect the mobile or desktop model? What about the number of columns?

The navigation bar used for the **mobile.css** style sheet is only one option for creating layout. Come up with another model, such as separating the navigation into two columns. You will have to create new and unique styles for the unordered and list elements to do this.

For the Fluid Grid layout, continue styling your page elements. Think of styles that you can add to the mobile styles that will cascade down to the tablet and desktop styles.

Review

Questions

1 `Min-width` and `max-width` are two examples of media queries. Describe a scenario in which you would use the `min-width` media query and describe a scenario in which you would use the `max-width` media query.

2 When you create a new fluid grid layout, what defaults can you change in the very first step of the process?

3 What is the purpose of the two dependent files saved by Dreamweaver when you create a new Fluid Layout?

Answers

1 The `min-width` media query can be interpreted as greater than or equal to and the `max-width` media query can be interpreted as less than or equal to. For example, if you have a media query that uses a min-width value of 700 pixels, a style that applies only to screens 700 pixels wide or higher is set. A media query that uses a max-width value of 320 pixels means a style that applies only to screens 320 pixels wide or less is set.

2 When creating a new fluid grid layout, you are prompted to set up the number of columns for your mobile, tablet, and desktop layouts. Additionally, you can change the percentage width of each of these layouts, and within the mobile layout, you can change gutter space between columns.

3 The purpose of boilerplate.css and respond.min.js are to provide the necessary functionality to allow pages to be resized and apply the various Media Queries.

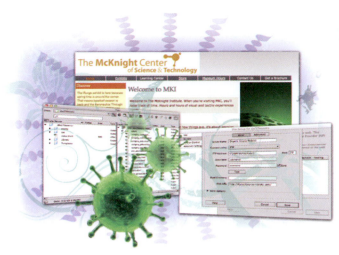

What you'll learn in this lesson:

- Uploading and managing files
- Optimizing pages for performance and search engines
- Checking site integrity
- Using site reports

Managing your Website: Reports, Optimization, and Maintenance

When it's time to release your website to the world, you'll want to take some final steps to make sure your site works and looks its best. Dreamweaver has a powerful set of reports, link checkers, and problem-solving tools to locate and fix any potential issues before final upload. When you're ready, the built-in FTP and synchronization features of the Files panel will get you up-and-running.

Starting up

Before starting, make sure that your tools and panels are consistent by resetting your workspace. See "Resetting the Dreamweaver workspace" in the Starting up section of this book.

You will work with several files from the dw17lessons folder in this lesson. Make sure that you have loaded the dwlessons folder onto your hard drive from the supplied DVD. See "Loading lesson files" in the Starting up section of this book.

Before you begin, you need to create a site definition that points to the dw17lessons folder. Go to Site > New Site, or, for details on creating a site definition, refer to Lesson 2, "Setting Up a New Site."

See Lesson 17 in action!

Use the accompanying video to gain a better understanding of how to use some of the features shown in this lesson. The video tutorial for this lesson can be found on the included DVD.

Working with the Files panel

You've already used the Files panel throughout this book to locate and open files within your site projects. In addition to serving as a useful file browser, the Files panel also serves as a full-featured file transfer application and synchronization tool. From the Files panel, you can upload your site to a web server, synchronize local and remote files, and manage files and notes between multiple designers.

Creating a remote connection

The Files panel uploads, retrieves, and synchronizes files between your local site and a web server. Typically, this is done using File Transfer Protocol (FTP), which connects to and allows interaction between your local machine and a web server (there are other options as well, including SFTP, WebDav, and more). Before you can transfer files, you'll first need to establish a remote connection to the web server that stores your website files.

You will not be able to proceed with this portion of the lesson if you do not have FTP information available for a web server. If you do not have this information or do not have a connection to the Internet, you can choose to read through the steps or skip to the Testing Site Integrity *exercise in this lesson.*

To get started, make sure you have the following:

- **The FTP address of the web server and specific directory.** This would be provided by your web-hosting provider as part of your account details, or from your company or organization's IT department. A typical FTP address looks like *ftp.mysite.com.*

- **A user login and password for access to the server.** Most web servers require a user login and password for access. This information should be available from your web-hosting provider as part of your account details, or from your organization's IT department.

- **The specific directory to which your files should be uploaded.** In many cases, this is the main directory or folder that appears when you connect to your web server. However, in certain cases, you'll need to upload files to a specific directory other than the main directory.

- **The web address (URL) or IP address where you can view your uploaded files on the server.** Sample addresses would be *www.mysite.com/*, *www.mysite.com/2013/*, or *http://100.0.0.1.*

1 To begin creating a remote connection, choose Site > Manage Sites. The Manage Sites dialog box appears.

2 Select the dw17lessons site from the list of Your Sites (you set this up at the beginning of the lesson) and click the pencil icon in the lower-left corner (Edit the currently selected site). If you haven't created a site definition for this lesson, make sure you do so now, as discussed in Lesson 2, "Setting Up a New Site."

3 The Site Setup window appears. Click the Servers button to access the server setup screen. Click the Plus button in the lower left.

	Site Setup for dw17lessons
Site	Here you'll select the server that will host your pages on the web. The
Servers	settings for this dialog box come from your Internet Service Provider (ISP)
Version Control	or your web administrator.
▶ Advanced Settings	*Note: You do not need to complete this step to begin working on your Dreamweaver site. You only need to define a remote server when you want to connect to the web and post your pages.*

Name	Address	Connection	Remote	Testing

➕ ➖ 🖉 🗇

| Help | | Cancel | Save |

Click the Add new Server button.

This opens up the Basic tab where you will need to add the required information to access your server.

4   Enter your specific FTP information in the text fields (not our sample information). The Server Name should be a common sense label that will help you identify which site you are modifying. The FTP Address, Username, and Password are the mandatory pieces of information.

Sample remote connection information. Your information should include an FTP address, login, and password, with a possible folder name.

Connection options

Clicking the Connect Using menu reveals additional options. FTP is still the default choice in Dreamweaver CC; however, FTP is an aging protocol. Many people are wary of security concerns related to FTP because data sent over FTP is not encrypted.

- SFTP stands for SSH File Transfer Protocol and represents a more secure version of FTP.

- FTP over SSL/TLS is another more secure version of FTP that relies on encryption. For this option, a server must have previously been specifically set up as trusted.

- Local/Network allows you to define a remote folder on a network drive you might be connected to. Depending on the setup, this network could or could not also be connected to the internet.

- WebDAV is a technology that allows file access to a remote server. It is often used collaboratively with multiple users allowed access to the same file system.

- RDS is a security component of ColdFusion Server that permits users to access files and databases through a remote HTTP connection.

5 Click the Test button to verify that Dreamweaver can connect to your server. If the information you've provided is valid and you have a live Internet connection, a dialog box appears, confirming that Dreamweaver has successfully connected to your web server.

> **Dreamweaver**
>
> Dreamweaver connected to your Web server successfully.
>
> **OK**

A dialog box lets you know if your connection was successful. If you receive an FTP error, double-check your FTP information, and make any necessary corrections.

6 Click the Save button and you will see your site listed in the Server window.

> **Site Setup for dw17lessons**
>
> Site
> **Servers**
> Version Control
> ▶ Advanced Settings
>
> Here you'll select the server that will host your pages on the web. The settings for this dialog box come from your Internet Service Provider (ISP) or your web administrator.
>
> *Note: You do not need to complete this step to begin working on your Dreamweaver site. You only need to define a remote server when you want to connect to the web and post your pages.*
>
> | Name | Address | Connection | Remote | Testing |
> |------|---------|------------|--------|---------|
> | Organic Utopia Website | digitalclassroom.com | FTP | ☑ | ☐ |
>
> ＋ － ✎ ⎘
>
> Help   Cancel   Save

Your site is now listed in the Server window.

7 Click the Save button in the Site Setup window. This might trigger an activity window that updates your site settings. Now that you're finished editing the site definition, click Done in the Manage Sites dialog box.

Viewing files on a remote web server

Once you've established a connection to your web server, you can expand the Files panel for a split view that displays both your remote and local files. You can easily drag and drop between both sides to upload or download files and update existing files.

1   If necessary, choose Window > Files to open the Files panel. Click the Expand button (⊡) at the top of the Files panel to ungroup and expand it to full view.

2   Locate and click the Connect button (✎) above the left column at the top of the panel. Dreamweaver attempts to connect to your remote server, and, if successful, displays all its files on the left side of the Files panel.

It's important to note that web servers can be configured in many different ways, and you might need to edit your site settings again once you have made a successful connection (in particular, the folder information). A discussion of the different ways that web servers might be configured is outside the scope of this book. If you have specific questions regarding your site, you should contact an IT professional or your web-hosting company.

Remote Server	Size	Type	Local Files	Size	Type
▼ 📁 /dw17lessons/			▼ 📁 Site – dw17lessons (...		Folder
▶ 📁 assets		Folder	▶ 📁 assets		Folder
▶ 📁 css		Folder	📄 category_books...	5KB	HTML File
📄 index.html	5KB	HTML Fil	📄 category_clothin...	5KB	HTML File
▶ 📁 Library		Folder	📄 category_dvds.h...	5KB	HTML File
▶ 📁 Templates		Folder	📄 category_giftcer...	5KB	HTML File
			📄 category_toys.ht...	7KB	HTML File
			▶ 📁 css		Folder
			📄 ex1_aeronautics...	3KB	HTML File
			📄 ex2_trains.html	3KB	HTML File
			📄 ex4_sticky.html	4KB	HTML File
			📄 ex5_water.html	4KB	HTML File
			📄 exhibits.html	4KB	HTML File
			📄 index.html	5KB	HTML File
			▶ 📁 Library		Folder
			📄 museumhours.h...	3KB	HTML File
			📄 store.html	4KB	HTML File
			▶ 📁 Templates		Folder
			📄 toys_gyroscope....	4KB	HTML File

1 local items selected totalling 4353 bytes.   Log...

Click the Connect button to view files on your remote server in the left column of the Files panel.

Transferring files to and from a remote server with Get and Put

The built-in FTP and file transfer functionality of the Files panel makes it a snap to place files on your remote server or download files onto your local machine. This can be accomplished using the Get and Put buttons, or by dragging and dropping files between the Remote and Local file listings in the Files panel. Please note again, this exercise involves publishing your sample documents to a remote server, and therefore publishing them to the Internet. Be very careful not to overwrite any pre-existing files that might be crucial to your website.

1　Make sure you've connected to the remote server as described in the previous exercise, and that you can see your remote files in the left column of the Files panel.

2　Select the **index.html** file from the local file listing on the right side of your Files panel, and click the Put button (⬆) at the top of the panel. Choose *No* when asked if you would like to include dependent files.

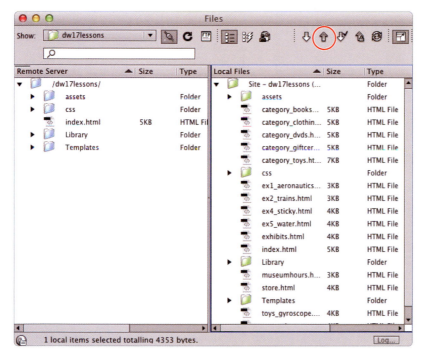

Select a file and click the Put button to upload it to the remote server.

When you transfer a document between a local and remote folder, a window could open, offering you the option of transferring the document's dependent files. Dependent files are images, external style sheets, and other files referenced in your document that a browser loads when it loads the document. This feature can be very useful: think of it as a way to make sure that any files which are linked to a particular document come along for the ride. For the purposes of this exercise, it will not be necessary to transfer dependent files.

Alternatively, you can click and drag a file from the right (local) column to the left (remote) column.

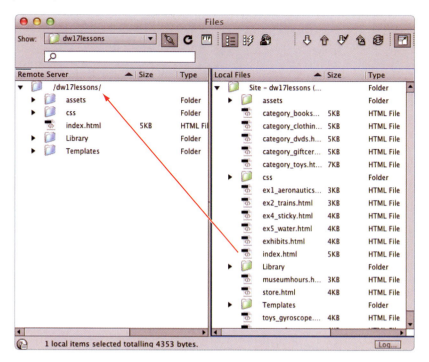

Drag a file from the right column to the left to upload it to the remote server.

To get (download) a file from the remote server:

1   Make sure you've connected to the remote server as described in the previous exercise, and that you can see your remote files in the left column of the Files panel.

2   Select the **index.html** file from the remote file listing on the left side of your Files panel, and click the Get button (⬇) at the top of the panel. Note that in your case this does not make a lot of sense since you just uploaded your index.html document.

You can update the local or remote file listing at any time by clicking the Refresh button (↻) at the top of the Files panel.

Using Check In/Check Out and Design Notes

If you're collaborating with others on a project, you'll want to set up an environment where everyone can edit files independently without overlapping or overwriting someone else's work. For these situations, the Check In/Out and Design Notes features can help you manage workflow and communicate with others on a Dreamweaver site project.

Check In and Check Out

Dreamweaver's Check In/Check Out feature is a way of letting others know that you are working on a file and don't want it disturbed. When Check In/Check Out is enabled, a document that you're editing becomes locked on the remote server to prevent others from modifying the same file at the same time. If you attempt to open a file that's been checked out by another user, you see a warning that lets you know that the file is in use and also who is currently working with it. Check In/Check Out doesn't require any additional software to run, and other Dreamweaver users can check out files if they also have Check In/Check Out enabled in their site definition.

The Check In/Check Out system does not work with a testing server. To transfer files to and from a testing server (if one is set up), use the standard Get and Put commands.

1   Choose Site > Manage Sites. Select the Dreamweaver site that you want to enable Check In/Check Out for and choose the pencil icon to edit the currently selected site.

2   In the Site Setup window, click the Servers button, then select your site and click the pencil icon at the bottom to edit the server settings.

3   Click the Advanced button and then click the Enable file check-out check box.

Type your name and e-mail. This information will appear to other users who attempt to retrieve a file that you have checked out (as long as they are using Dreamweaver). Click Save and then click Save again to exit.

Enable check in/check out in the Site Definition panel to manage workflow between several users.

How does Check In/Check Out work?

Dreamweaver creates a lock (LCK) file for every document that is checked out; this basic text file contains the name and e-mail address of the user who has checked out the file. LCK files are written to both the remote server and local folder using the same name as the active file. When files are checked back in, the LCK files are deleted from both the remote server and the local folder.

Although LCK files are not visible in the Files panel, they work behind-the-scenes to let Dreamweaver know what's checked out and what isn't. Checked-out files appear on both the local and remote file listings with a checkmark next to them. Note that a colleague not using Dreamweaver can potentially overwrite a file that's checked out; however, LCK files are visible in applications other than Dreamweaver, and their appearance alone can help avoid any overwriting issues.

A user will be allowed to override your lock and switch checkout status to themselves. Make sure you establish rules with others about how to share and manage locked files.

Checking files in and out

When you check a file out, you are downloading it from the remote server to your local root folder, and placing a lock on the remote copy. Both your local copy and the remote copy appear with check marks next to them, which indicate that the file is currently checked out for editing. When you check a file back in, you are uploading the modified version to the remote server, and removing any locks currently on it.

1   Launch the Files panel and click the Expand button to expand it so that you can see both your local and remote files listed.

2   Select the file in your local folder that you want to check out, and use the Check Out button ( ) at the top of the panel. Note that Dreamweaver overwrites your local copy of the file, as it needs to get the remote file from the server. The local and remote versions of the file appear with check marks next to them in the Files panel.

Check files out before modifying them so other users won't accidentally overwrite your work.

3   Open the checked file from your Local Files panel for editing. Make any necessary changes to the file, then save and close it.

4 From the Files panel, select the file again in the local Files panel and check it back in, using the Check In button (🔒) at the top of the panel. The file is uploaded to—and unlocked on—the remote server.

When you transfer a document between a local and remote folder, a window could open offering you the option of transferring the document's dependent files. Dependent files are images, external style sheets, and other files referenced in your document that a browser loads when it loads the document. For this exercise, it won't be necessary for you to transfer dependent files.

Your local copy becomes read-only, and appears with a padlock next to it. Next time you open the file for editing, Dreamweaver will automatically check out and get the latest copy from the server.

5 Collapse the Files panel to return it to the dock.

Using Design Notes

Design Notes store additional information about a file or media object in your Dreamweaver site. These notes can be for your own use, or they can be shared with others using the same root folder. Design Notes can be set to appear automatically when the file is opened, making it easy to display up-to-date information to others working on the same site. All Design Notes are stored as separate files in a *_notes* folder inside of your site's root directory.

What can be put in Design Notes?

Design Notes can contain any information that is important to the file or project; you can store design instructions, updates about the project, or contact information for project managers and supervisors. You can also store sensitive information that you ideally would not want in the file itself, such as the name of the last designer to work on the file or the location of important assets. You can even set the status of the file to indicate what stage of the revision the file is in.

1 To create a Design Note, under the Files panel, open the **store.html** file from the current site.

2 Choose File > Design Notes. The Design Notes dialog box appears.

3 Type a message in the Notes field. If you want to insert the current date stamp, you can click the Calendar button (📅) above the Notes field on the right side. If you want the note displayed when the file is next opened, check Show when file is opened.

The Status menu is used to set the document status; this can be useful in letting other collaborators know the revision stage of the current document.

4   Click OK to create the Design Note.

To view a Design Note, choose File > Design Notes when a file is open in the document window. As mentioned earlier, you can also choose to have Design Notes automatically appear when the file is first opened.

Design Notes can also be created or viewed directly from the Files panel. Simply right-click (Windows) or Ctrl+click (Mac OS) a document in the files list and choose Design Notes from the context menu.

Sharing Design Notes

By default, Design Notes are stored only in the local site folder, and are not automatically copied to the remote server. However, you can share Design Notes with other collaborators by having Dreamweaver automatically upload and update them on the remote server.

1   Choose Site > Manage Sites. Select your site and choose Edit (the pencil in the bottom-left corner of the Sites dialog box). The Site Setup window appears.

2   Click the Advanced Settings options and choose Design Notes from the left.

3   Under the Design Notes panel, check Enable Upload Design Notes for sharing. Design Notes are now copied and updated on the remote server so that other users can share them.

Set up Design Notes for sharing so other Dreamweaver users can see and modify Design Notes on the remote server.

4   Choose Save to update the site definition, then click Done to close the Manage Sites dialog box.

Displaying Design Notes in the Files panel

A convenient way to view and access Design Notes is by enabling the Design Notes column in the Files panel. An icon that can be used to open and edit Design Notes accompanies documents that have an associated Design Note. This feature also allows you to see all available Design Notes at a glance.

1   Choose Site > Manage Sites. Select your site from the Sites panel and choose Edit. In Advanced Setting options, choose File View Columns.

Site Setup for dw17lessons

Site	
Servers	
Version Control	
▼ Advanced Settings	
Local Info	
Cloaking	
Design Notes	
File View Columns	
Contribute	
Templates	
jQuery	
Web Fonts	
Edge Animate Assets	

When you view a Dreamweaver site in the Files panel, information about the files and folders is displayed in columns. For example, you can see the file type or the date a file was modified. You can also add custom columns to work with Design Notes.

Name	Type	Show
Name	Built In	Show
Notes	Built In	Hide
Size	Built In	Show
Type	Built In	Show
Modified	Built In	Show
Checked Out By	Built In	Show

☐ Enable Column Sharing

Help   Cancel   Save

Use the Site Definition panel's File View Columns category to show Design Notes in both the local and remote file listings.

2   Double-click the Notes item from the list and click the Show check box and then click Save.

3   Choose Save to update the site definition, then click Done to close the Manage Sites dialog box. You will likely see the Background File Activity window appear; wait for this to complete. A Notes column appears in the Files panel; a Notes icon (📝) is displayed next to each file that is currently associated with a Design Note.

Testing site integrity

Catching potential issues on a page before your visitors do is key to ensuring success from the start. Broken links, display issues, or unreadable pages can make the difference between a great first impression and a poor one. To help you identify and address problems before you publish your site, Dreamweaver provides useful tools that can point out potential hazards and, in some cases, help you find a solution.

Checking links sitewide

Dreamweaver can check links on a single document, on multiple documents (through the Files panel), or on an entire local site.

1   Choose Site > Check Links Sitewide.

2   The Link Checker panel appears; by default, all broken links are displayed. All the broken links here are referencing the same incorrect link to category_books_cds.html. This could have happened if you or a collaborator on the site changed the name of the file within the operating system or another web editor.

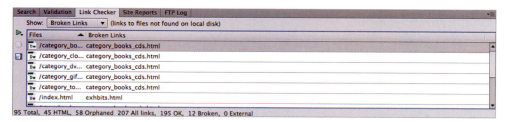

Choose Site > Check Links Sitewide to check for broken links throughout the current local site.
The Link Checker panel opens and displays any broken links found.

3   To view external links, choose External Links from the Show drop-down menu at the top of the panel. This site will have none, but any links to outside web pages that you have on your site would be listed here.

External links are displayed, but aren't validated by Dreamweaver. The Link Checker can only validate links between local documents and files.

4   To view orphaned files, choose Orphaned Files from the Show drop-down menu at the top of the panel. In this site, a number of files will appear. Orphaned files are files in your site that are not currently being linked to. This might include stray multimedia files that have not been added to a page yet. You will not be doing anything with these files at this time.

5   Choose Broken Links from the Show drop-down menu to return to the broken links report. Click the first of the broken links shown to edit it. Click the Folder icon and browse through your site folder to locate the **category_bookscds.html file**. Select this file, click Open and then press Enter (Windows) or Return (Mac OS).

6   A dialog box appears, asking if you'd like to make the same correction throughout the entire current local site.

Adjust a link directly from the Link Checker panel to correct it across the site.

7 Click Yes. Behind the scenes Dreamweaver will go through all the pages and automatically update to the correct link. This feature is a great timesaver since you don't need to open the files to make changes.

Viewing Link Checker results

If and when the Link Checker returns results, you can jump to any problem document to view and fix any issues. The Link Checker panel's Show menu (located at the top of the panel) toggles between three different Link Checker reports: Broken Links, Orphaned Files, and External Links.

Broken Links are lists links that point to files not found within the local site. To jump to a page that contains a broken link, double-click the filename shown in the left column of the Link Checker panel. To correct a link directly from the Link Checker panel, click the link shown under the Broken Links column of the panel to edit it. Type in the proper page name or use the folder to browse to the proper file. If you edit a broken link this way, Dreamweaver can apply the same correction throughout other pages on your site.

Orphaned Files are any pages, images, or media files not linked to, referenced, or used by any files in your site. This report can be useful in identifying unused files that can be cleaned up from the local site, or pages that should be linked to (like a site map) but were overlooked.

External Links list any links to outside websites, pages, or files; and like the Broken Links panel, allows you to directly edit them or jump to the page that contains them. It's important to note, however, that Dreamweaver does not validate external links—you will still be responsible for double-checking these links on your own. You'll also notice that e-mail (mailto:) links are included in this list.

Generating site reports

Dreamweaver's site reports feature is an indispensable asset for detecting potential design and accessibility issues before publishing your site to the Web. Reports can be generated in several categories to give you a virtual picture of health, and the opportunity to locate and fix minor or major issues across an entire Dreamweaver site. These issues can include missing alternate text or titles and recommendations for better accessibility practices, based on the W3C's Web Consortium Accessibility Guidelines (WCAG).

Reports can be generated for a single page, selected documents, or the entire current local site. Any results open and display in the Results panel, where you can see a list of issues and the pages on which they are located.

1 To run a site report, choose Site > Reports. The Reports dialog box opens, displaying two categories of reports: Workflow and HTML.

It is not necessary to have a document open in order to run sitewide reports.

Workflow reports display information about Design Notes, Check In and Check Out operations, and recently modified files. HTML reports display potential design, accessibility, and display issues based on best practices and W3C/WCAG accessibility guidelines.

2 In the Reports panel, check all the reports under the HTML category. At the top of the panel, select Entire Current Local Site from the Report on drop-down menu.

Choose Site > Reports, and select the reports you'd like to run in the Site Reports dialog box.

3 Click Run in the top-right corner of the Reports panel. The Results panel appears, displaying any potential issues. Note that depending on the size of your site and number of issues found, it might take a few moments for all results to display.

4 Leave the Results panel open; you'll learn how to read and address issues in the next exercise.

Search	Validation	Link Checker	Site Reports	FTP Log	

	File	Line	Description
	ex4_sticky.html	3	Warning: Document uses default title 'Untitled Document'
	ex5_water.html	28	Warning: Missing "alt" attribute
	ex5_water.html	5	Warning: Document uses default title 'Untitled Document'
	index.html	12	Warning: Missing "alt" attribute
	index.html	5	Warning: Document uses default title 'Untitled Document'
	store.html	66	Warning: Missing "alt" attribute
	toys_gyroscope.html	6	Warning: Document uses default title 'Untitled Document'
	toys_microscope.html	6	Warning: Document uses default title 'Untitled Document'

Complete.

The Results panel displays issues found across your entire current local site.

Understanding report results

At first glance, you might be overwhelmed at the amount of information returned by site reports. Keep in mind that many of the listings returned are recommendations or possible issues that should be looked into, not necessarily items that will prevent a site from working. Learning to read these site reports a little more closely will enable you to decide which items are crucial to your site's performance, requiring immediate action. Listings are displayed with three distinct icons.

ICON	NAME	USE
?	Question Mark	These listings suggest possible accessibility issues that should be investigated. Many of these issues have a reference to a specific W3C/WCAG guideline.
X	Red X	These listings indicate a failure to meet a certain guideline or requirement. Possible listings could include missing header information, deprecated HTML markup, or page titles that are not defined properly.
⚠	Warning Sign	Warnings indicate missing information that could be potentially detrimental to a site's performance, such as missing ALT text for images.

Addressing a listed item

After you've sifted through the report results, you'll want to use the Results panel to address items listed in the Site Reports tab.

1. Go to the Site Reports tab on the Results panel. Click the Description column header to sort the results. Scroll to the bottom of the page as needed, and locate the **store.html** listing.

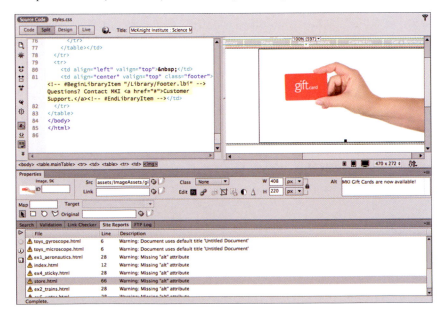

Select a listing and click the More Info button to display a detailed description about the issue found.

The Description column shows that an image on this page is missing the ALT attribute and alternate text. This attribute can potentially affect accessibility of your site; you don't need to fix it, but we highly recommend you do.

2. Double-click the **store.html** listing to open the page for editing. Your document window will divide into the Code view and Design view; the image appears selected in the Design view and highlighted in the Code view.

3. In the Property Inspector, type **MKI Gift Cards are now available!** in the Alt field and press Enter (Windows) or Return (Mac OS).

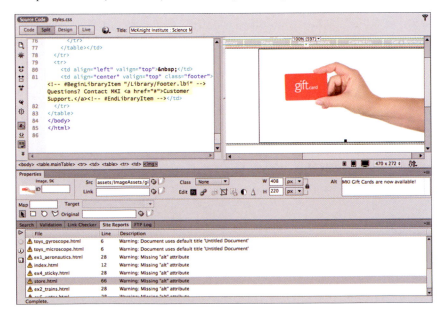

Select the problem image and enter text in the Alt field to rectify the problem.

Whenever you have multiple results as you do here, you might want to save them for future reference. Reports can be saved as XML for import into databases, existing template files, and archival files. You can sort report results using the Results panel before saving them.

4 Click the Save Report button (⊞) on the left edge of the Results panel. When the Save Report dialog box appears, assign the report a name, and choose a location for the file.

5 Save and close the page, and close the Results panel.

A full listing of accessibility guidelines, or WCAG, for web page designers and developers is available at the World Wide Web Consortium (W3C) website at W3.org.

Optimizing pages for launch

Although page optimization is discussed at this latter point in the book, it is by no means an afterthought. A big part of preparing a site for success involves making it accessible to users with special needs, such as those who are visually impaired, or preparing it for indexing by various search engines. In addition to clean design and well-written content, pages can be optimized through the use of keywords, descriptions, and often-overlooked tag attributes, such as alternate text (alt) for images and a page's Title area. Combined, these pieces of information facilitate site usability and visibility in several essential ways.

Search engine visibility and Search Engine Optimization

A big part of a website's success stems from its visibility. Visibility comes through good advertising, networking with other sites, and, above all, proper indexing and listings on the Web's major search engines. Search engines can be a key to generating business and visits to your site, but only if your website can be easily found. Major search engines such as Google (which powers AOL, MySpace, and Netscape searches), Yahoo! (which powers AltaVista and others), and Bing (formerly LiveSearch) use a variety of factors to index and generate listings for websites. Many of these factors start at home, or more appropriately, on your home page.

Titling your documents with the <title> tag

Each document's head area contains a `<title>` tag, which Dreamweaver automatically inserts with any new HTML/XHTML document. At its most basic, the `<title>` tag sets a display title for a page that appears at the top of the browser window. You can modify the `<title>` tag contents using the Title text field that sits at the top of your document window. By default, each new document is issued the default title of Untitled Document. The `<title>` tag and its contents, however, can be a powerful and effective way to assist search engines in indexing your page.

What makes a good title?

A good document title ideally should include keywords that describe your site's main service, locale, and category of business or information. In addition to the obvious—your company's name—think about the categories you would want your site to appear under on a web directory or as the result of a web search. For instance, the McKnight Institute would ideally want users looking for science museums or exhibits in the Philadelphia, Pennsylvania, area to find them first. A possible title could be: The McKnight Institute: Science Museum, Educational Exhibits and Attractions, Philadelphia, Pennsylvania.

This title contains several important keywords that describe the Institute's offerings, and features the Institute's name and location. In addition, reshuffling these phrases and words produces several other search terms that could be beneficial to the Institute, such as:

- Science Exhibits
- Philadelphia Museum
- Pennsylvania Attractions

Avoid the rookie mistake of including only your company name in the document title. Remember, web searchers who haven't used your business before will only search by terms that apply to the service they are seeking (for example, wedding photographers, Washington, D.C.). Even the most recognized names on the Web, such as eBay and Amazon, include generic search terms in their page titles.

To add a title to your web page:

1   From the Files panel, select and open the **index.html** document to open it for editing.

2   Locate the Title text field at the top of the document window. It currently displays the default title of Untitled Document. Select its contents and type **The McKnight Institute: Science Museum, Educational Exhibits and Attractions, Philadelphia, Pennsylvania** and press Enter (Windows) or Return (Mac OS).

Add a well-constructed title to the index.html page to make it more search-engine and bookmark friendly.

3   Choose File > Save to save the document, and then choose File > Preview in Browser > [Default browser] to open the document in your system's primary browser.

4   Note the title that now appears in the bar at the top of the browser window. Close the browser window and return to Dreamweaver.

The most basic purpose of the <title> tag is to display a title at the top of the browser window. If used properly, it can also be used as a powerful hook for search engines.

While there is technically no limit to title length, the W3C's Web Consortium Accessibility Guide recommends that page titles be a maximum of 64 characters to be considered 'well-defined.' Titles exceeding this length could generate warnings in the Site Reports Results panel. Longer titles could also appear truncated (cut off) when displayed in some browser windows.

Bookmark-ability: another benefit of the `<title>` tag

It's common for users to bookmark a site or specific page they've found so that they can easily return to it. Every browser has a bookmark feature, which allows users to mark and display favorite sites in an organized list; sometimes, favorite sites are listed in a Bookmarks bar in the browser window.

The document title determines the text that appears with a bookmark, so it's important to consider this when creating a good document title. Using a vague or nondescriptive title (or even worse, the default Untitled Document text) can make it impossible for a user to remember which bookmark is yours. A good title appears as a descriptive bookmark in a browser's Favorites list or Bookmarks bar.

Adding meta keywords and descriptions

While Search Engine Optimization (SEO) is a broad topic that's far beyond the scope of this book, good SEO methods begin at the design level. Search engines use a variety of factors to rank and list web pages. Keywords and descriptions can help specify the search terms that are associated with your site and how it's listed. The HTML <meta> tag enables you to associate any page with a specific list of search terms, as well as a brief description of the page or the website itself. Like the <title> tag, <meta> tags are placed in the <head> section of a page, and can be added from the Common Insert bar on the right side of your workspace.

1 If it's not already open, open the **index.html** document for editing.

2 From the Common Insert bar, choose the Keywords button from the Head tags group.

3 When the Keywords window appears, add a comma-separated list of search keywords that you'd like associated with this page, or the site in general. While there is no general consensus on the limit of how many keywords you can use, common sense says that you should be able to categorize your site in roughly 20 keywords or fewer. For example, type **museum, technology exhibits, attractions, family attractions, philadelphia, pennsylvania museums**. Click OK to add the keywords.

From the Common category of the Insert panel, choose the Keywords object from the Head tags group and enter a list of keywords in the resulting dialog box.

4 Now you'll add a description that a search engine can use to summarize your page when creating a listing for it. Choose the Description button from the Head tags group on the Common Insert bar.

5 When the Description dialog box appears, type in a brief descriptive paragraph (fewer than 250 characters, including spaces). For example, type **The McKnight Center is a family-oriented education center and museum that explores the history of technology and scientific discovery through hands-on exhibits and events**. Click OK.

Add a short description that search engines can use to display a caption for your site listing.

6 Choose File > Save, then choose File > Close to close the file.

Launching your site

Before launching your site for the public—and to ensure that your site looks and works at its best—take a moment to go over this pre-flight checklist.

Site launch checklist

- Enter FTP or upload information and test your FTP connection.

- Check links sitewide and repair missing or broken links and images.

- Run site reports and address crucial issues. Put special emphasis on:

  - Missing document titles

  - Missing alt text

  - Invalid markup that could cause display issues

- Open the homepage (index.html, and so on) and navigate through your site, using menus, links in copy, and linked images to check page flow. Do this in several browsers, and, if possible, on both Windows and Macintosh platforms.

- View your home page and major section pages in a web browser in the three most common screen resolutions: 640 × 480, 800 × 600, and 1024 × 768.

Uploading your site

From this point forward, the exercise assumes that you have access to a remote FTP server.

1   If you're ready to upload your site to the remote web server, make sure that the Files panel is open (Window > Files).

2   Click the Expand button (⊡) at the top of the Files panel to display it in two-column expanded view.

3   Click the Connect button (⚡) above the left (remote view) column to connect to your remote web server.

You need to have created a valid connection, as described earlier in the lesson.

Once a successful connection is made, the remote files (if any) display in the left column.

4   In the right column, click and select the Folder icon at the very top of the file listing. This should be the root folder, and displays the current site definition title (dw17lessons).

5   Click the Put button at the top of the Files panel to copy the entire current local site and all included files to the current directory on the remote server. A dialog box appears with the message, *Are you sure you wish to put the entire site?*

Select the root folder of your local site, and click the Put button to upload the entire site to the web server.

6 Click OK to begin copying the files to the remote server. The Background File Activity window appears with a progress bar and a list of the files being transferred.

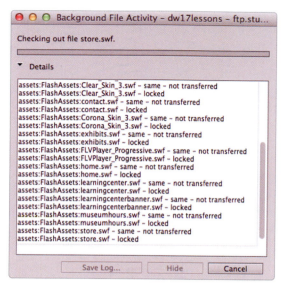

Files being transferred in the Background File Activity window.

7 Collapse the Files panel to return it to the dock. Your site is now live!

Getting help

Whether you are seeking a solution to a Dreamweaver-specific problem, or looking up the appropriate CSS rule to format a page item, you can use Dreamweaver's built-in Help system and integrated reference guides. In addition, the Help menu provides direct links to many online resources and Adobe support areas where you can seek help from Adobe professionals and the Dreamweaver user community.

1 To access the Help system, choose Help > Dreamweaver Help. The Adobe Help Viewer panel appears.

2 Enter a search term at the top of the panel, or browse by topic on the left side of the panel.

3 For more help options and a searchable knowledge base, choose Help > Dreamweaver Support Center. For the Dreamweaver support forums, choose Help > Adobe Online Forums.

Suggested next steps

You have now launched your first Dreamweaver site project. There's nothing more exciting than having your hard work on the Web and available for the world to see. The important thing to remember is that your website should not be static; part of maintaining a successful website requires continuously evolving it to meet the needs of your viewers, and keeping the content fresh and new.

Whether your site is for business, pleasure, or self-promotion, be sure to solicit feedback from friends, family, and colleagues after you've launched. Alert a small and trusted group about the launch by sending out an e-mail, mailing a postcard, or posting a notice on a blog (sometimes this is referred to as the 'beta' stage). Feedback and constructive criticism (a little praise is OK, too) are the best ways to objectively know what needs improvement. You'll probably receive more feedback and suggestions than you can handle, so focus on points that are common across multiple users, and address any major issues before making a more public launch (for instance, to your entire client base).

Focus on focus groups

Focus groups are an excellent way to get nonbiased feedback on a major new site or product launch, and they have been a regular practice in product marketing and research for years. A focus group is composed of a group of individuals who are brought together to analyze, try out, and comment on a specific product—in this case, your website—for the purpose of obtaining feedback and testing the product's effectiveness.

Groups can be guided through certain portions or processes on the site, or can be encouraged to navigate it on their own. Afterwards, they are polled with specific questions about their experience, and the results are put together to form a picture of the site's usability, effectiveness, and impact. This can include questions such as the following:

- Did you feel the website was easy to navigate? On a scale from 1 to 10, how would you rate the difficulty level in locating specific pages or topics?

- Did the design, including graphics and color themes, effectively help communicate the website's offerings?

- On a scale from 1 to 10, how would you rate the quality of the written content on the site?

Focus groups are often interactive, encouraging participants to talk with each other and share their opinions. In some cases, a moderator can be used to regulate group discussions and hand out questionnaires. Participants can be composed of a focused demographic group (for instance, 25- to 35-year-old technology professionals), or they can represent a diverse professional and demographic range.

Focus groups are reasonable for any size company to organize—even if it's just you and five friends—and are a highly effective way to find out what's currently working and what's not. Give it a try; you might find the results encouraging, surprising, or even slightly discouraging. The trick is to use this feedback wisely toward the main purpose of making a better website, and you'll be glad you did.

Website design resources

There is a vast amount of information, and many tutorial-based websites, covering topics from web page standards to advanced CSS design. Here is a small sampling of some useful sites that can help you take your skills and knowledge further. Use these in conjunction with Dreamweaver's built-in reference guides and Adobe's online support forums:

- W3C (World Wide Web Consortium)—*www.w3.org*
- Adobe's Dreamweaver Developer Center—*www.adobe.com/devnet/dreamweaver*
- DigitalClassroom—*www.DigitalClassroom.com*

Self study

Import a site from a previous lesson from this book or import your own site, and run a site report for broken links, orphaned files, and so on.

Review

Questions

1   What does FTP stand for, and what is it used for?

2   What three purposes do document titles serve, and why are they important?

3   What are three possible pre-flight checklist items you need to address before launching a website?

Answers

1   File Transfer Protocol. FTP is used to connect to and transfer files between your local machine and a web server.

2   Document titles display a title at the top of the browser window, in a user's bookmarks bar, and are an important hook for search engines.

3   **a**. Enter and test your FTP connection information in the Site Definition panel.

   b. Run site reports to rectify any potential design or accessibility issues, such as missing alternate text for images or empty document titles.

   c. Run the Link Checker site wide to check for broken links between pages or incorrect image references.

- CSS Designer panel
- CSS Gradients and styles
- jQuery UI Widgets
- Adobe Edge Web Fonts
- Native HTML5 Support
- Adobe Edge Animate Integration

Dreamweaver CC New Features

Dreamweaver's features evolve as the Web evolves. In this lesson, you'll take a tour of Dreamweaver's new features.

Starting up

There are no lesson files used in this lesson.

See Lesson 18 in action!

Use the accompanying video to gain a better understanding of how to use some of the features shown in this lesson. The video tutorial for this lesson can be found on the included DVD.

What's new in Dreamweaver CC?

Dreamweaver CC follows the release of Dreamweaver CS6 and offers a number of significant changes and improvements over the previous release. While many of the features are new, subscribers to Adobe's Creative Cloud service have been able to utilize some of them as part of Adobe's ongoing upgrade process. This is due to the fact that web technology continues to evolve at a rapid pace and a program such as Dreamweaver needs to keep pace with these changes. Features such as native HTML5 support, improved Fluid Grid Layouts, Adobe Edge Web Fonts integration, Adobe Animate support and improved FTP support have made their way into the Cloud Subscription version and are now available.

Dreamweaver CC boasts many new features on top of those made available to CS6 Creative Cloud subscribers, specifically, a new CSS Designer panel with a visual workflow and improved support of CSS3 including CSS3 Transitions, Gradients, rounded borders, and the addition of jQuery UI Widgets replace Adobe's proprietary Spry Frameworks. Whether the new features were first added in CS6 Creative Cloud or in CC, they have all been integrated into the exercises in this book for users who might have upgraded from the retail version of CS6 to CC without the benefit of the CS6 Creative Cloud updates.

Starting in Lesson 4, "Styling your pages with CSS" and throughout the exercises, HTML5 semantic elements replace many of the divs for structuring content. Lesson 6, "Advanced Page Layout" covers the semantic elements in-depth. Lesson 7, "CSS3 Transitions and Styles" introduces CSS3 gradients and transforms while coverage of Web Fonts has been expanded into a lesson of its own. Lesson 8, "Using Web Fonts" addresses the addition of Adobe Edge Web Fonts. Lesson 11, "Adding Video, Audio, and Interactivity" covers the addition of HTML5 audio and video, Adobe Edge Animate integration and Flash. Lesson 14, "Building HTML5 Web Forms" expands on Web Forms with the addition of new HTML5 input elements, attributes and form validation. Finally, Lesson 15, "Adding Interactivity with the jQuery UI Library" introduces the new jQuery UI Widgets such as the Tab and Accordion.

CSS Designer panel

Dreamweaver's new CSS Designer panel expands upon and replaces the New CSS Styles dialog box and panel, adding a visual workflow and methodology for CSS properties such as margins, padding, and borders. This new panel makes creating and editing styles as easy as pointing and clicking and provides a visual representation of the applied styles.

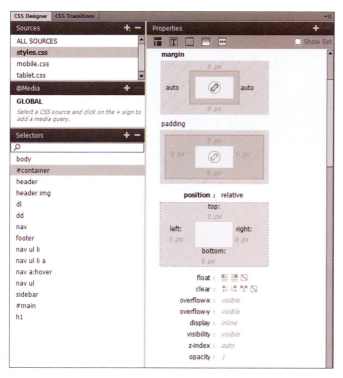

The margin, padding, and border controls in the Properties panel.

Extensive use of the CSS Designer panel is made throughout nearly every lesson of the book as it is a vital part of the workflow in designing web pages with Dreamweaver.

CSS3 transitions and styles

Dreamweaver CC has new CSS transitions and styles that provide the ability to add gradient backgrounds, rounded corners, and animation effects to objects on your page. CSS gradients replace the need to use a fixed image to create a gradient background. An example of a transition is a button that gradually changes color when the user hovers over it, known as a rollover effect. In previous versions of Dreamweaver, you had to use some form of JavaScript to create a rollover effect, perhaps even one of the Spry effects (which are JavaScript). CSS gradients and styles in Dreamweaver are built with CSS3 syntax that allows you to set the duration, delay, and easing of many CSS properties, including color stops in gradients, height, width, positioning, and much more.

The CSS Gradient control allows you to create linear or radial gradients with multiple color stops.

One of the benefits of CSS gradients and transforms is that you can create basic visual effects within Dreamweaver without JavaScript or Flash. A good use of transitions, for example, is to create a smooth resizing effect on the user interface, such as drop-down or slide-out menus.

jQuery UI widgets

Dreamweaver CC incorporates jQuery UI Widgets, part of the jQuery JavaScript Frameworks, to add open-source and industry-standard user interface controls. Use the Insert panel to add interactive features to your site and customize them using CSS3 to match your website theme. Dreamweaver includes jQuery UI Widgets to insert Accordion menus, Tabs panels, Date Pickers, Progress bars, Buttons and more.

The jQuery UI Tab widget can make efficient use of space.

Additional new features in Dreamweaver CC

The Adobe Edge Web Fonts, improved HTML5 and CSS3 functionality and Adobe Edge Animate composition support are perhaps the biggest changes that were made available to Dreamweaver CS6 Creative Cloud subscribers and are also included in Dreamweaver CC. These new features are designed to help streamline and support a more efficient and visual workflow within the product.

Adobe Edge Web Fonts

Dreamweaver CC takes major steps toward addressing the lack of choice in fonts to use on the Web with the new Adobe Edge Web Fonts feature. This feature takes advantage of the vast library of free web fonts, provided by companies like Adobe and Google, to give Dreamweaver users a much easier way to add new fonts to their page. When you choose Modify > Manage Fonts, the Manage Fonts dialog box appears, allowing you to link to any Adobe Edge Web Font or to add a local copy of any commercially-licensed web font you want to embed on your page.

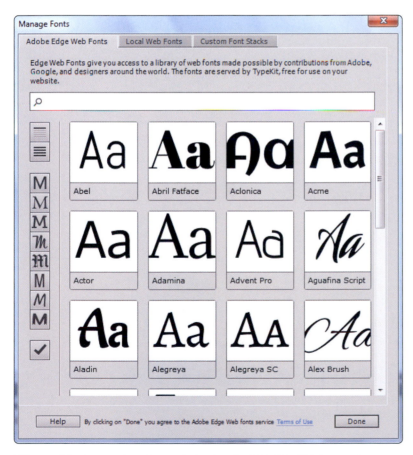

Adding a web font is as simple as choosing the font from the Adobe Edge Web Fonts service.

After you embed a specific web font on your page, you can easily apply the style of the font using the Property Inspector. The addition of Adobe Edge Web Fonts in Dreamweaver means it is quite easy to add unique styles to page elements such as headings and still maintain the benefits of CSS.

A heading with a Web Font style applied.

Faster HTML5 elements insertion

Dreamweaver CC has a newly reorganized Insert panel and improvements to the Property Inspector allowing you to work intuitively with the new HTML5 elements. Examples of HTML5 elements you can now insert include the semantic elements; `<header>`, `<nav>`, `<section>`, `<aside>`, and `<footer>` and all of the new HTML5 Form elements. In previous versions of Dreamweaver, there was no visual support for these elements. Users could add them in code view using Dreamweaver's code hinting interface, but they could not add them with the Insert panel or set their properties using the Property Inspector.

You can easily add HTML5 elements in Dreamweaver with the revised Insert Panel.

Similarly, the Insert panel has added the new HTML5 form elements allowing you to take advantage of the built-in support available in today's modern browsers. The HTML5 form elements allow you to mark fields as required, provide placeholder text, and validate form input without the need of JavaScript.

Insert	Files
Form ▼	
Form	
Text	
Email	
Password	
Url	
Tel	
Search	
Number	
Range	
Color	
Month	
Week	
Date	
Time	
Date Time	
Date Time Local	
Text Area	
Button	
Submit Button	
Reset Button	
File	
Image Button	
Hidden	
Select	

You can also use the Insert panel to add HTML5 Form elements in Dreamweaver.

Streamlined HTML5 audio and video

Dreamweaver CC's HTML5 improvements don't stop with semantic elements and forms. Add HTML5 Audio and Video to your site for plugin-free multimedia in today's modern browsers and mobile devices. The new Insert panel and Property Inspector improvements extend to HTML5 Audio and Video allowing you to insert multimedia into your site without plugins, extending your audience to a wider variety of devices.

*Add plugin-free audio and video with the
HTML5 elements in Dreamweaver.*

You can also style HTML5 Audio and Video elements using CSS to create unique user interfaces and playback controls that would be nearly impossible with plugin-based multimedia. Use a CSS3 transform to tilt the HTML5 Video element and play your video at an angle of 25 degrees or round the corners of the video to mimic a vintage picture tube television set.

Edge Animate composition support

Dreamweaver CC lets you bring your pages to life by adding standards-based compositions right from Adobe Edge Animate. Edge Animate compositions can be used where Flash animation and interactive media elements were previously used and work with the built-in HTML5, CSS3 and JavaScript support in today's modern browsers. Use the Media category of the Insert panel to insert compositions directly into your page and view them directly in Dreamweaver using Live view.

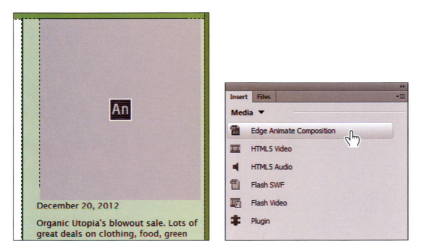

Add standards-based compositions directly from Adobe Edge Animate.

You can create interactive animations, animated web banners, and more with Adobe Edge Animate, part of the Adobe Edge suite available with a free Adobe Creative Cloud subscription. See http://creative.adobe.com *for more information.*

Additional features

Dreamweaver CC also added improved FTP performance using a robust multi-threaded FTP engine making the transfer of large projects easier and more efficient. Live Search on Mac OS makes it faster to find files with real-time search results that update as you type. HD video and images are increasingly in demand on today's high-end mobile devices. Dreamweaver CC is compatible with HiDPI to support today's devices with HD capability such as Apple's Retina display.

Index

setting margins and borders, 147–152
rule weight, 125
setting background color, 361–362
setting width and floating columns, 165–166
snippets and, 304
styling form elements, 363–364
syntax, 65
tables
    advanced styling, 248–252
    alternate row styling, 252–253
    controlling cell alignment, padding, and
      borders, 250–252
    formatting and styling, 245–247
    reusing for other tables, 254
CSS color property, 96
CSS Designer panel
    class style created with, 105–107
    creating CSS rules, 94–96
    description of, 15, 60
    expanded mode of, 108
    new features, 456–457
    Sources pane, 121
    Text-transform section, 113
.css file (external style sheet), 124–126
CSS Gradients
    adding, 199–202
    benefits of, 199, 457
    browser support for, 201
    description of, 457
    page background, applying to, 203–205
CSS rules
    Code Navigator
      creating, 98
      locating, 100
    Code view, 96
    CSS Designer panel, 94–96
    internal and external style sheets, 99
CSS Starter Pages, 20
CSS Styles panel
    creating and modifying styles, 108–110
    Disable/Enable CSS Property button, 153
CSS Transitions
    adding, 184–189
    browser support for, 189, 195
    easing, 192
    Internet Explorer support for, 189
    modifying, 190–195
    navigation menu, adding to, 196–199
    support for, 189
CSS Transitions panel, 260–261
CSS3
    border-radius property, 206
    description of, 20, 40, 180, 184
    @font-face, 212
    Media Queries
      definition of, 394–395

description of, 12, 40, 392
principles of, 399
resource for, 395
style sheets, 395
transitions. *See* CSS Transitions
CSS3 Gradient, 200
CSS3 Transitions window, 191
.csv (comma-separated values) file format, 230
Cubic-bezier(x1,y1,x2,y2) option, 192
customizable workspace layout, 14
Customize Favorite Objects dialog box, 263–264
customizing
    panel groups, 260–263
    panels, 260–263

D

Database, Bindings, and Server Behavior extensions,
    19
Default Images folder, 40
Default option, Method drop-down menu, 345
default split view, 325
default workspace, Dreamweaver, 53
dependent files, 420, 431, 436
Description dialog box, 449
descriptions, adding to page, 448–449
design
    layout tools and, 10
    mobile
      creating, 411–414
      description of, 12
      navigation, 404–407
      optimizing of, for mobile web, 399–403
      single-column, 404–407
      tools for, 390–391
    site
      library items, 306–310
      modular page elements, 300
      overview, 299–300
      repeating regions, 316–319
      snippets, 300–305
      templates, 310–316
    tables, 230
Design Notes
    displaying in Files panel, 438
    overview, 436
    sharing, 437
Design Notes category, Site Setup dialog box, 40
design tools, 10
Design view
    content management system file preview in, 19
    CSS Transitions, 185
    CSS-styled text, 92
    description of, 13, 52
    modifying snippets, 305
    resizing document window, 264–267
    setting form properties, 345

John Wiley & Sons, Inc.
End-User License Agreement

READ THIS. You should carefully read these terms and conditions before opening the software packet(s) included with this book "Book". This is a license agreement "Agreement" between you and John Wiley & Sons, Inc. "WILEY". By opening the accompanying software packet(s), you acknowledge that you have read and accept the following terms and conditions. If you do not agree and do not want to be bound by such terms and conditions, promptly return the Book and the unopened software packet(s) to the place you obtained them for a full refund.

1. **License Grant**. WILEY grants to you (either an individual or entity) a nonexclusive license to use one copy of the enclosed software program(s) (collectively, the "Software") solely for your own personal or business purposes on a single computer (whether a standard computer or a workstation component of a multi-user network). The Software is in use on a computer when it is loaded into temporary memory (RAM) or installed into permanent memory (hard disk, CD-ROM, or other storage device). WILEY reserves all rights not expressly granted herein.

2. **Ownership.** WILEY is the owner of all right, title, and interest, including copyright, in and to the compilation of the Software recorded on the physical packet included with this Book "Software Media". Copyright to the individual programs recorded on the Software Media is owned by the author or other authorized copyright owner of each program. Ownership of the Software and all proprietary rights relating thereto remain with WILEY and its licensers.

3. **Restrictions on Use and Transfer.**

   (a)   You may only (i) make one copy of the Software for backup or archival purposes, or (ii) transfer the Software to a single hard disk, provided that you keep the original for backup or archival purposes. You may not (i) rent or lease the Software, (ii) copy or reproduce the Software through a LAN or other network system or through any computer subscriber system or bulletin-board system, or (iii) modify, adapt, or create derivative works based on the Software.

   (b)   You may not reverse engineer, decompile, or disassemble the Software. You may transfer the Software and user documentation on a permanent basis, provided that the transferee agrees to accept the terms and conditions of this Agreement and you retain no copies. If the Software is an update or has been updated, any transfer must include the most recent update and all prior versions.

4. **Restrictions on Use of Individual Programs.** You must follow the individual requirements and restrictions detailed for each individual program in the "About the CD" appendix of this Book or on the Software Media. These limitations are also contained in the individual license agreements recorded on the Software Media. These limitations may include a requirement that after using the program for a specified period of time, the user must pay a registration fee or discontinue use. By opening the Software packet(s), you agree to abide by the licenses and restrictions for these individual programs that are detailed in the "About the CD" appendix and/or on the Software Media. None of the material on this Software Media or listed in this Book may ever be redistributed, in original or modified form, for commercial purposes.

5. Limited Warranty.

(a) WILEY warrants that the Software and Software Media are free from defects in materials and workmanship under normal use for a period of sixty (60) days from the date of purchase of this Book. If WILEY receives notification within the warranty period of defects in materials or workmanship, WILEY will replace the defective Software Media.

(b) WILEY AND THE AUTHOR(S) OF THE BOOK DISCLAIM ALL OTHER WARRANTIES, EXPRESS OR IMPLIED, INCLUDING WITHOUT LIMITATION IMPLIED WARRANTIES OF MERCHANTABILITY AND FITNESS FOR A PARTICULAR PURPOSE, WITH RESPECT TO THE SOFTWARE, THE PROGRAMS, THE SOURCE CODE CONTAINED THEREIN, AND/OR THE TECHNIQUES DESCRIBED IN THIS BOOK. WILEY DOES NOT WARRANT THAT THE FUNCTIONS CONTAINED IN THE SOFTWARE WILL MEET YOUR REQUIREMENTS OR THAT THE OPERATION OF THE SOFTWARE WILL BE ERROR FREE.

(c) This limited warranty gives you specific legal rights, and you may have other rights that vary from jurisdiction to jurisdiction.

6. Remedies.

(a) WILEY's entire liability and your exclusive remedy for defects in materials and workmanship shall be limited to replacement of the Software Media, which may be returned to WILEY with a copy of your receipt at the following address: Software Media Fulfillment Department, Attn.: *Adobe Dreamweaver CC Digital Classroom*, John Wiley & Sons, Inc., 10475 Crosspoint Blvd., Indianapolis, IN 46256, or call 1-800-762-2974. Please allow four to six weeks for delivery. This Limited Warranty is void if failure of the Software Media has resulted from accident, abuse, or misapplication. Any replacement Software Media will be warranted for the remainder of the original warranty period or thirty (30) days, whichever is longer.

(b) In no event shall WILEY or the author be liable for any damages whatsoever (including without limitation damages for loss of business profits, business interruption, loss of business information, or any other pecuniary loss) arising from the use of or inability to use the Book or the Software, even if WILEY has been advised of the possibility of such damages.

(c) Because some jurisdictions do not allow the exclusion or limitation of liability for consequential or incidental damages, the above limitation or exclusion may not apply to you.

7. U.S. Government Restricted Rights.
Use, duplication, or disclosure of the Software for or on behalf of the United States of America, its agencies and/or instrumentalities "U.S. Government" is subject to restrictions as stated in paragraph (c)(1)(ii) of the Rights in Technical Data and Computer Software clause of DFARS 252.227-7013, or subparagraphs (c) (1) and (2) of the Commercial Computer Software - Restricted Rights clause at FAR 52.227-19, and in similar clauses in the NASA FAR supplement, as applicable.

8. General.
This Agreement constitutes the entire understanding of the parties and revokes and supersedes all prior agreements, oral or written, between them and may not be modified or amended except in a writing signed by both parties hereto that specifically refers to this Agreement. This Agreement shall take precedence over any other documents that may be in conflict herewith. If any one or more provisions contained in this Agreement are held by any court or tribunal to be invalid, illegal, or otherwise unenforceable, each and every other provision shall remain in full force and effect.